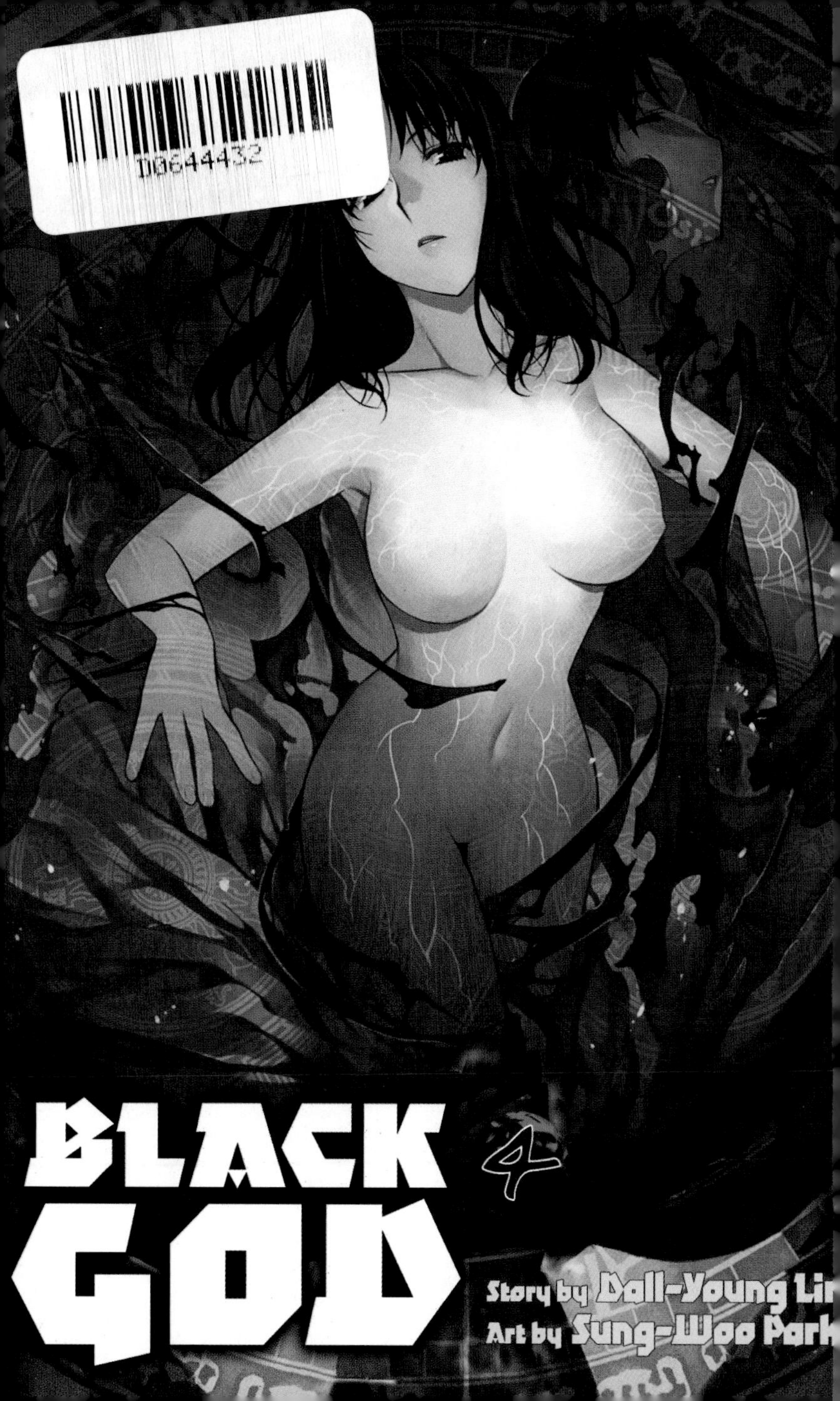

BLACK GOD 4

Story by Dall-Young Lim
Art by Sung-Woo Park

CONTENTS

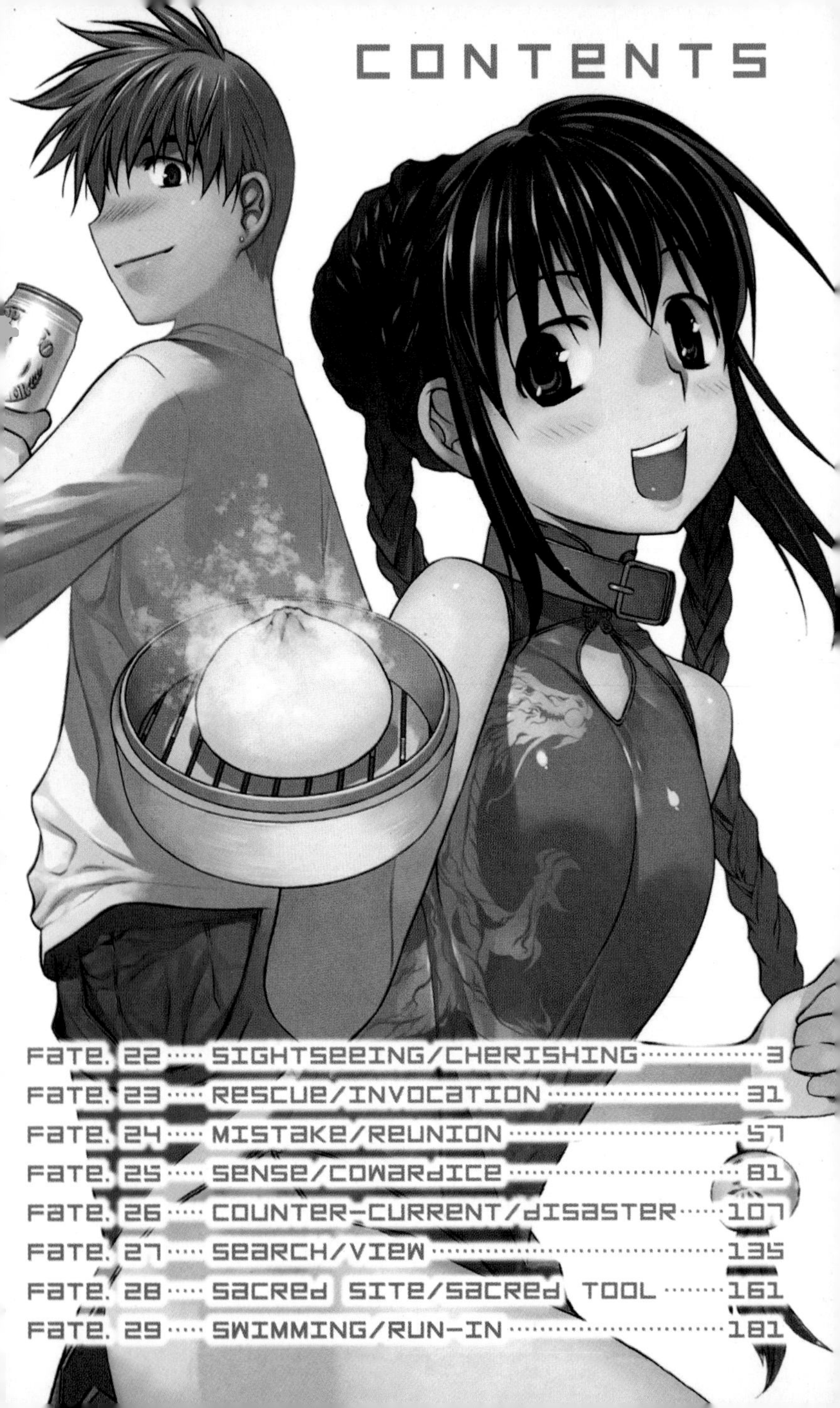

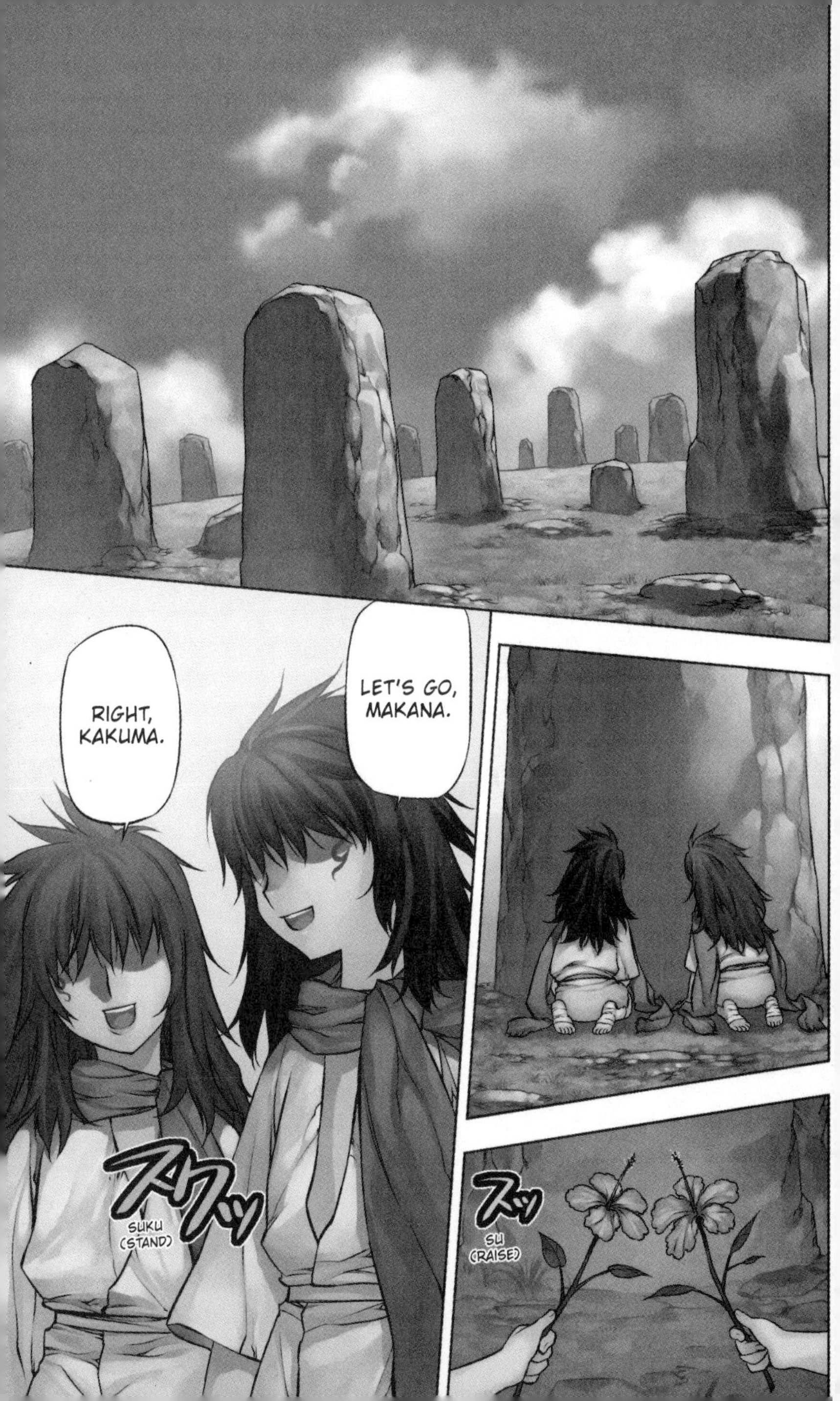
LET'S GO, MAKANA.
RIGHT, KAKUMA.
SU (RAISE)
SUKU (STAND)

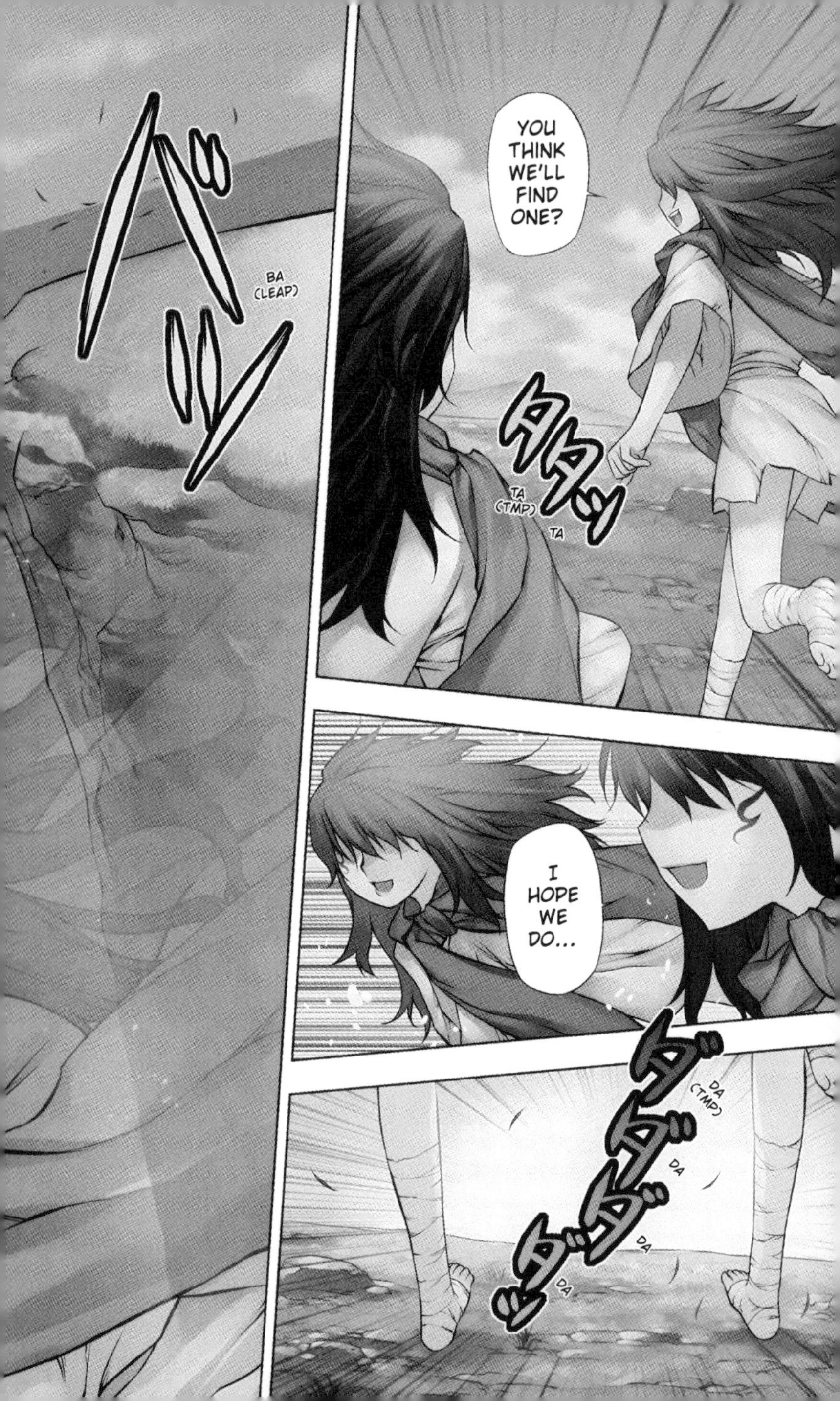
YOU THINK WE'LL FIND ONE?
TA (TMP)
TA
I HOPE WE DO...
DA (TMP)
DA
DA
DA
BA (LEAP)

FATE.22 SIGHTSEEING • CHERISHING

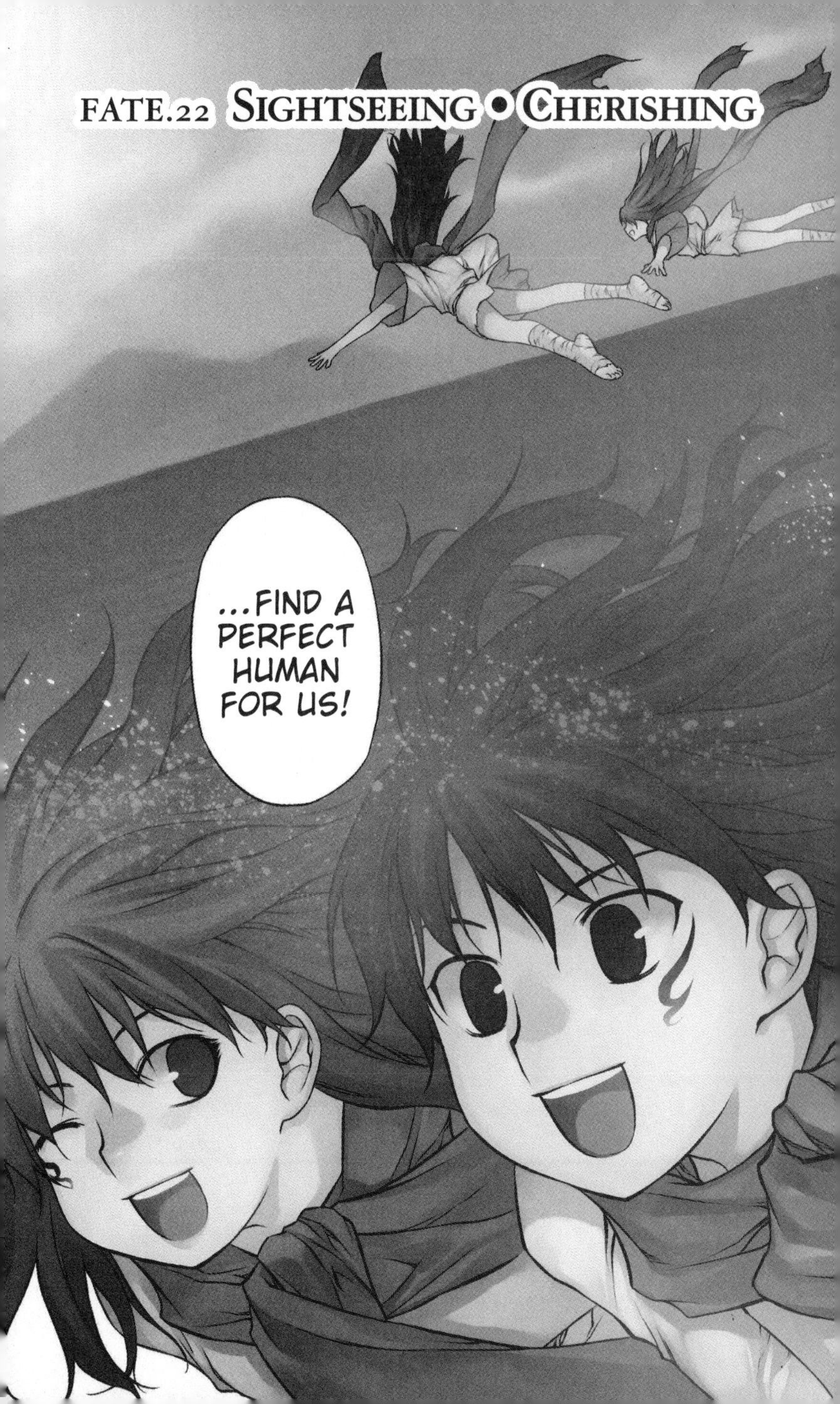
...FIND A PERFECT HUMAN FOR US!

PUNI PUNI

黒神 BLACK GOD which majibako balance in the world.

Nirai Kanai Arc

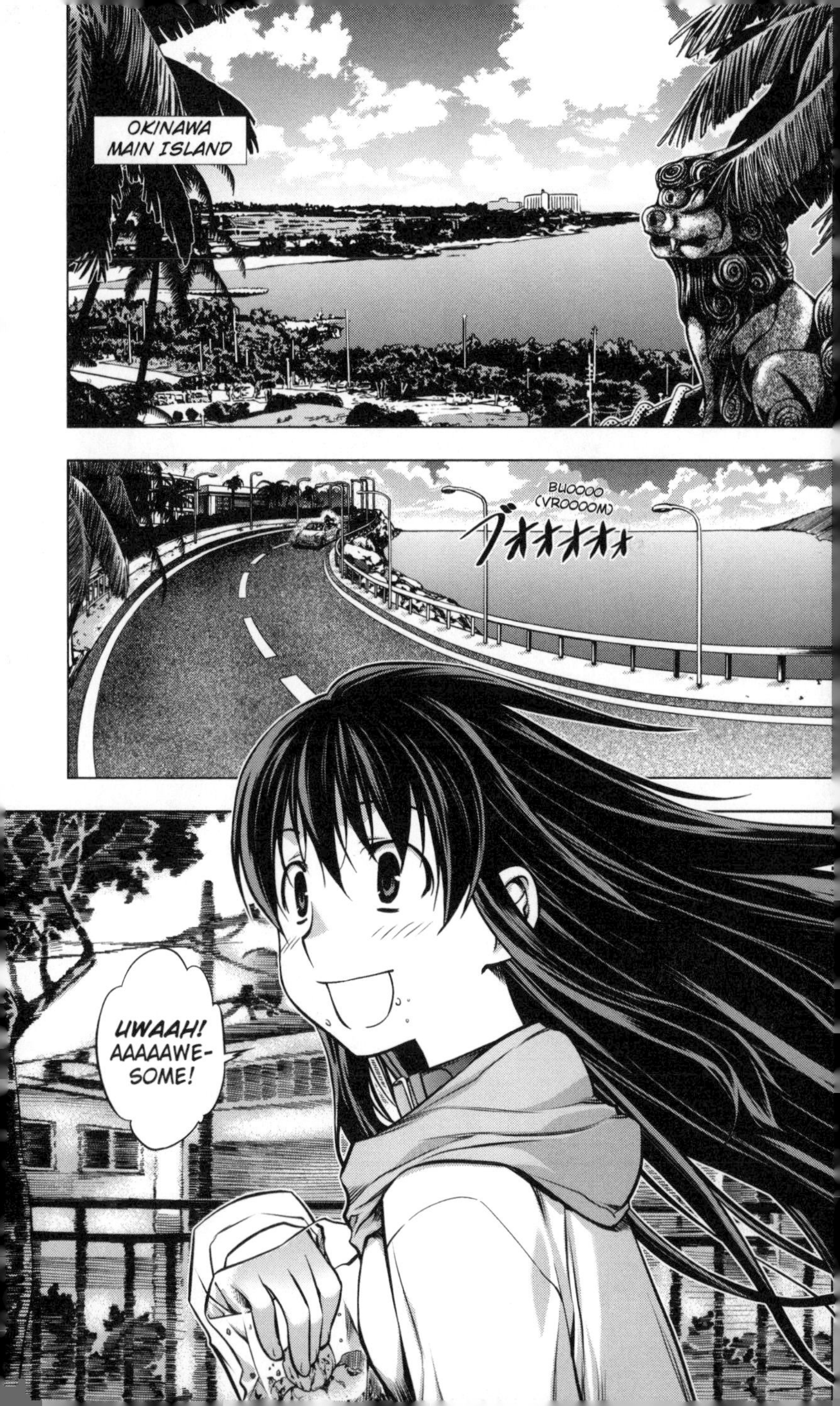
OKINAWA MAIN ISLAND
BUOOOO (VROOOOM)
ブォォォォォォ
UWAAH! AAAAAWE-SOME!

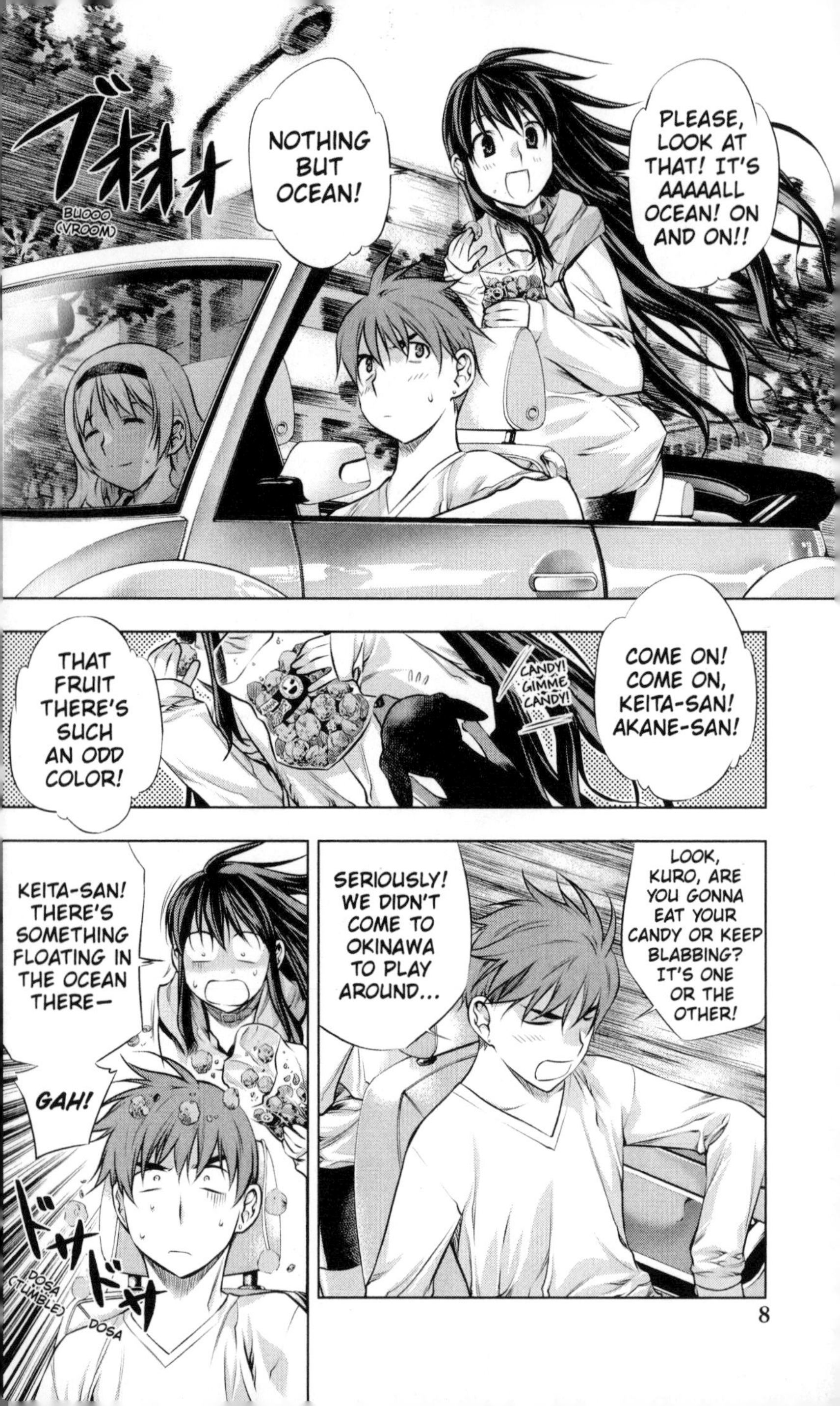
PLEASE, LOOK AT THAT! IT'S AAAAALL OCEAN! ON AND ON!!
NOTHING BUT OCEAN!
BUOOO (VROOM)
COME ON! COME ON, KEITA-SAN! AKANE-SAN!
CANDY! GIMME CANDY!
THAT FRUIT THERE'S SUCH AN ODD COLOR!
LOOK, KURO, ARE YOU GONNA EAT YOUR CANDY OR KEEP BLABBING? IT'S ONE OR THE OTHER!
SERIOUSLY! WE DIDN'T COME TO OKINAWA TO PLAY AROUND...
KEITA-SAN! THERE'S SOMETHING FLOATING IN THE OCEAN THERE—
GAH!
DOSA (TUMBLE)
DOSA

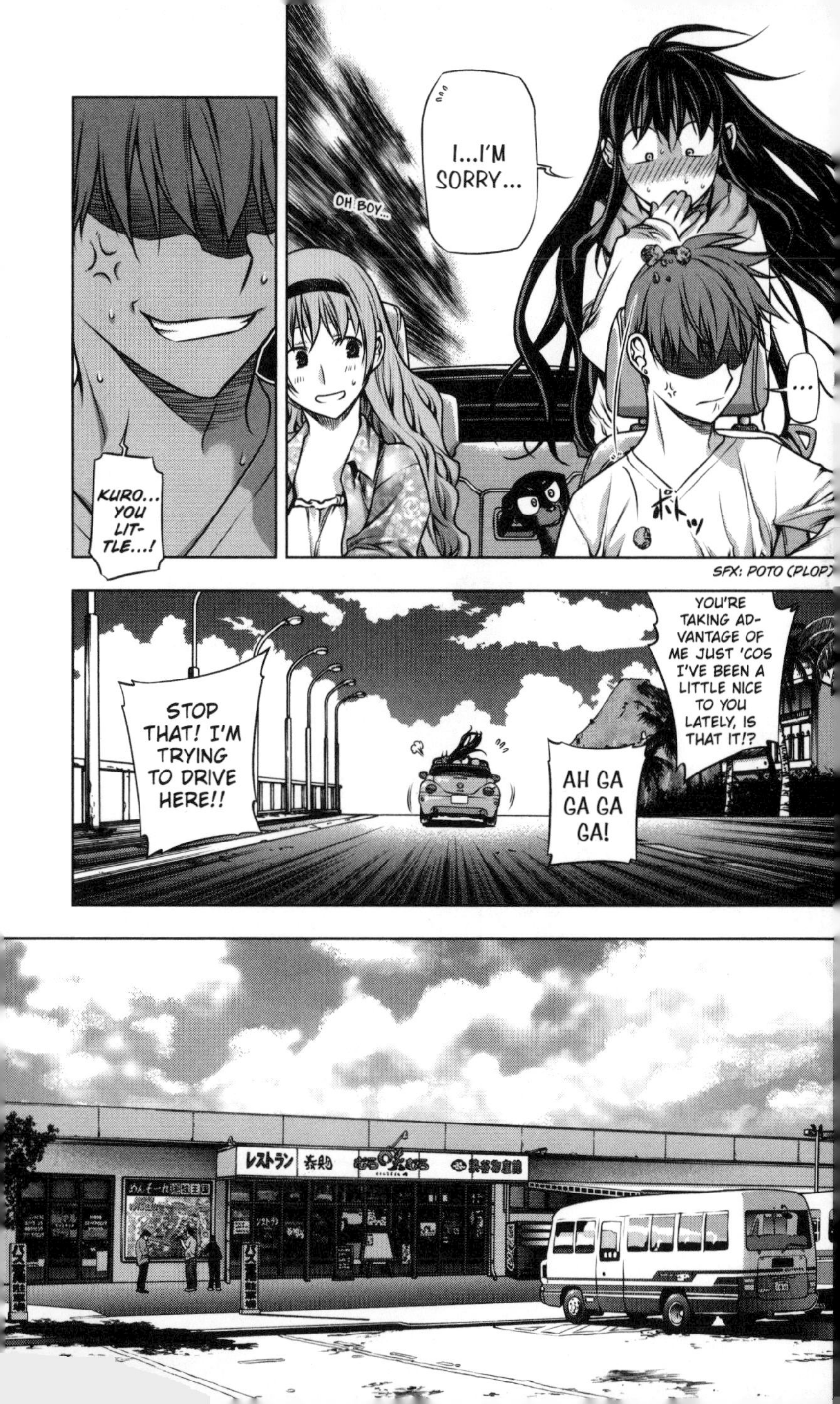
I...I'M SORRY...
OH BOY...
...
ポトッ
SFX: POTO (PLOP)
KURO... YOU LIT-TLE...!
YOU'RE TAKING AD-VANTAGE OF ME JUST 'COS I'VE BEEN A LITTLE NICE TO YOU LATELY, IS THAT IT!?
AH GA GA GA GA!
STOP THAT! I'M TRYING TO DRIVE HERE!!
レストラン

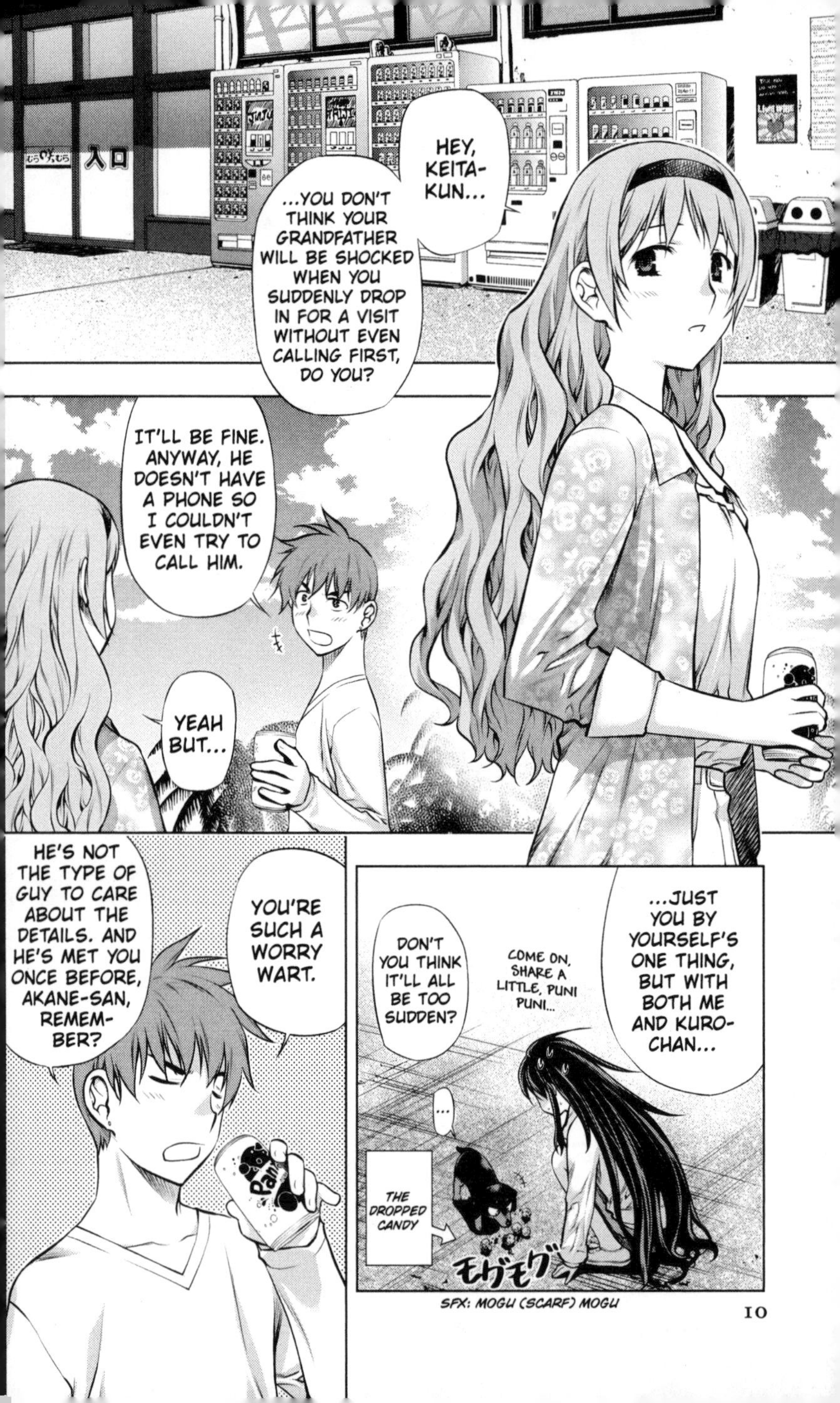
入口
HEY, KEITA-KUN...
...YOU DON'T THINK YOUR GRANDFATHER WILL BE SHOCKED WHEN YOU SUDDENLY DROP IN FOR A VISIT WITHOUT EVEN CALLING FIRST, DO YOU?
IT'LL BE FINE. ANYWAY, HE DOESN'T HAVE A PHONE SO I COULDN'T EVEN TRY TO CALL HIM.
YEAH BUT...
...JUST YOU BY YOURSELF'S ONE THING, BUT WITH BOTH ME AND KURO-CHAN...
DON'T YOU THINK IT'LL ALL BE TOO SUDDEN?
COME ON, SHARE A LITTLE, PUNI PUNI...
...
THE DROPPED CANDY
モグモグ
YOU'RE SUCH A WORRY WART.
HE'S NOT THE TYPE OF GUY TO CARE ABOUT THE DETAILS. AND HE'S MET YOU ONCE BEFORE, AKANE-SAN, REMEMBER?
SFX: MOGU (SCARF) MOGU

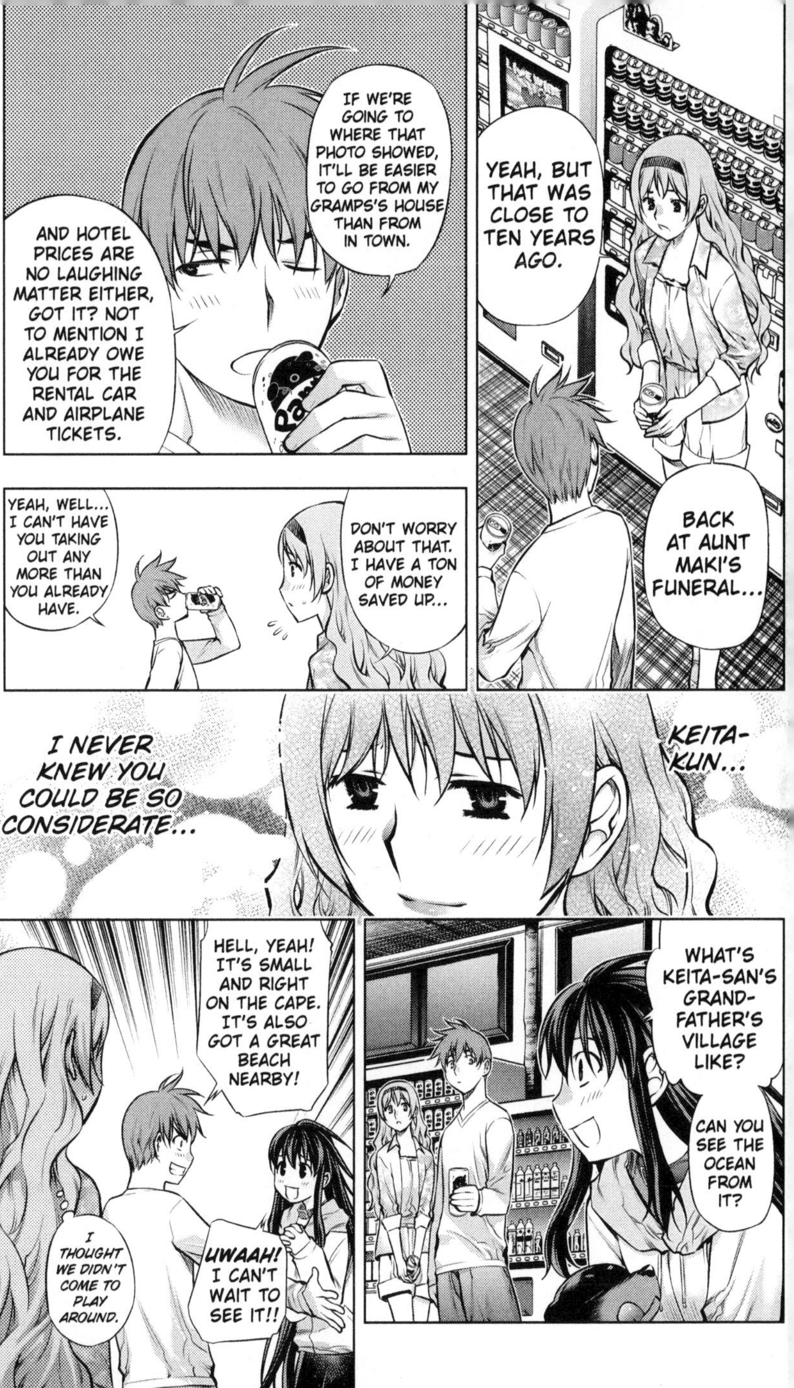
YEAH, BUT THAT WAS CLOSE TO TEN YEARS AGO.
BACK AT AUNT MAKI'S FUNERAL...
IF WE'RE GOING TO WHERE THAT PHOTO SHOWED, IT'LL BE EASIER TO GO FROM MY GRAMPS'S HOUSE THAN FROM IN TOWN.
AND HOTEL PRICES ARE NO LAUGHING MATTER EITHER, GOT IT? NOT TO MENTION I ALREADY OWE YOU FOR THE RENTAL CAR AND AIRPLANE TICKETS.
DON'T WORRY ABOUT THAT. I HAVE A TON OF MONEY SAVED UP...
YEAH, WELL... I CAN'T HAVE YOU TAKING OUT ANY MORE THAN YOU ALREADY HAVE.
KEITA-KUN...
I NEVER KNEW YOU COULD BE SO CONSIDERATE...
WHAT'S KEITA-SAN'S GRANDFATHER'S VILLAGE LIKE?
CAN YOU SEE THE OCEAN FROM IT?
HELL, YEAH! IT'S SMALL AND RIGHT ON THE CAPE. IT'S ALSO GOT A GREAT BEACH NEARBY!
UWAAH! I CAN'T WAIT TO SEE IT!!
I THOUGHT WE DIDN'T COME TO PLAY AROUND.

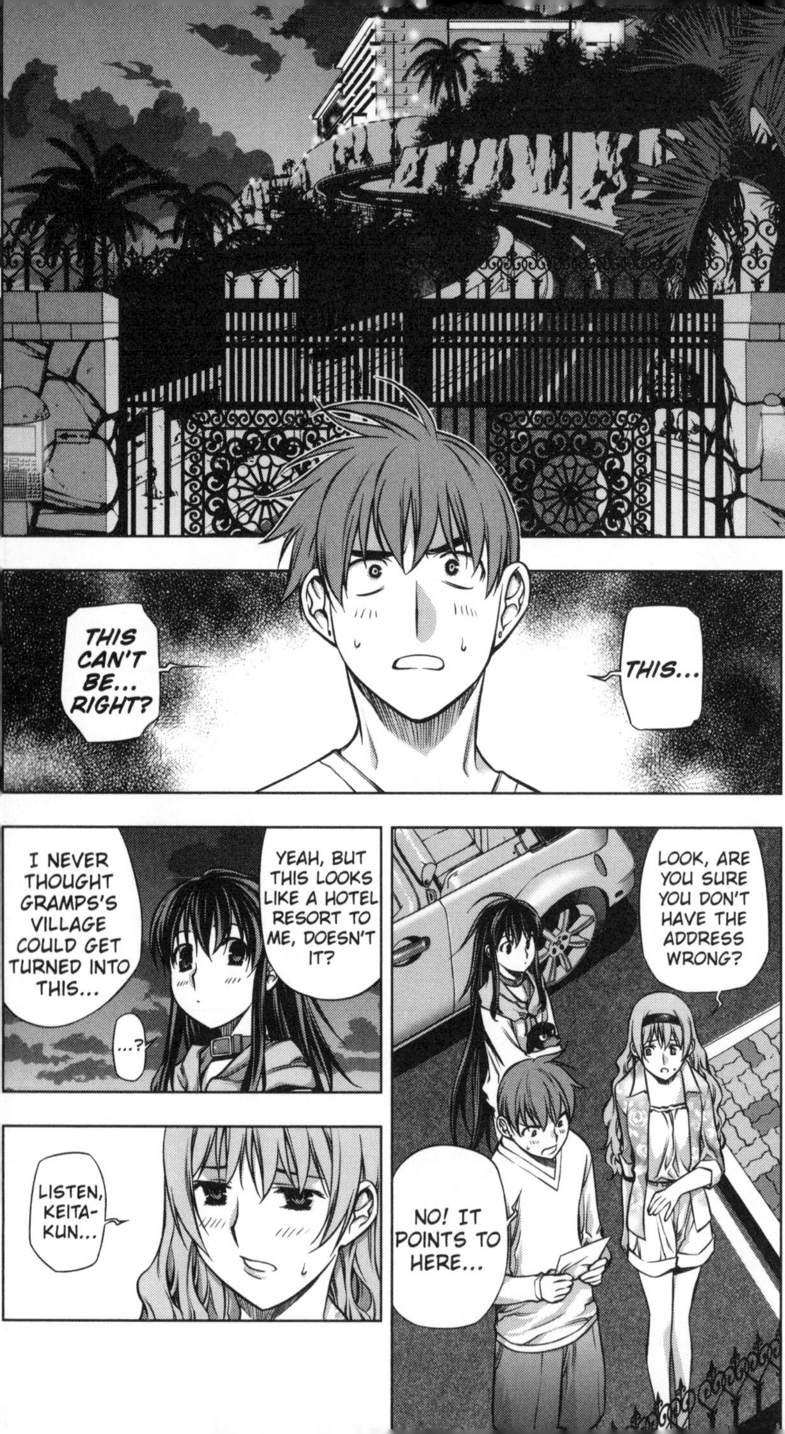
THIS...
THIS CAN'T BE... RIGHT?
LOOK, ARE YOU SURE YOU DON'T HAVE THE ADDRESS WRONG?
NO! IT POINTS TO HERE...
YEAH, BUT THIS LOOKS LIKE A HOTEL RESORT TO ME, DOESN'T IT?
I NEVER THOUGHT GRAMPS'S VILLAGE COULD GET TURNED INTO THIS...
...?
LISTEN, KEITA-KUN...

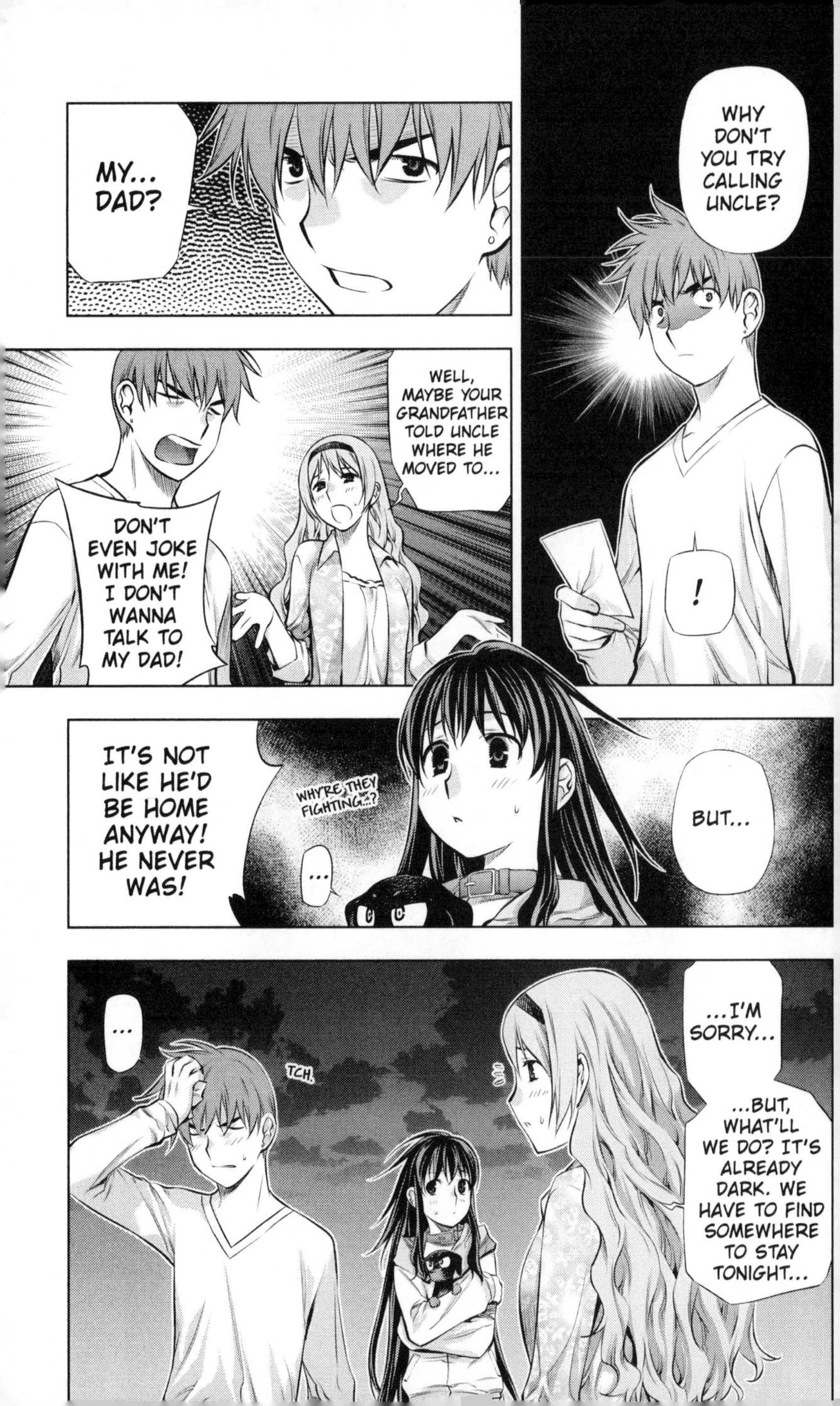
WHY DON'T YOU TRY CALLING UNCLE?
!
MY... DAD?
WELL, MAYBE YOUR GRANDFATHER TOLD UNCLE WHERE HE MOVED TO...
DON'T EVEN JOKE WITH ME! I DON'T WANNA TALK TO MY DAD!
BUT...
WHY'RE THEY FIGHTING...?
IT'S NOT LIKE HE'D BE HOME ANYWAY! HE NEVER WAS!
...
...I'M SORRY...
...BUT, WHAT'LL WE DO? IT'S ALREADY DARK. WE HAVE TO FIND SOMEWHERE TO STAY TONIGHT...
TCH.
...

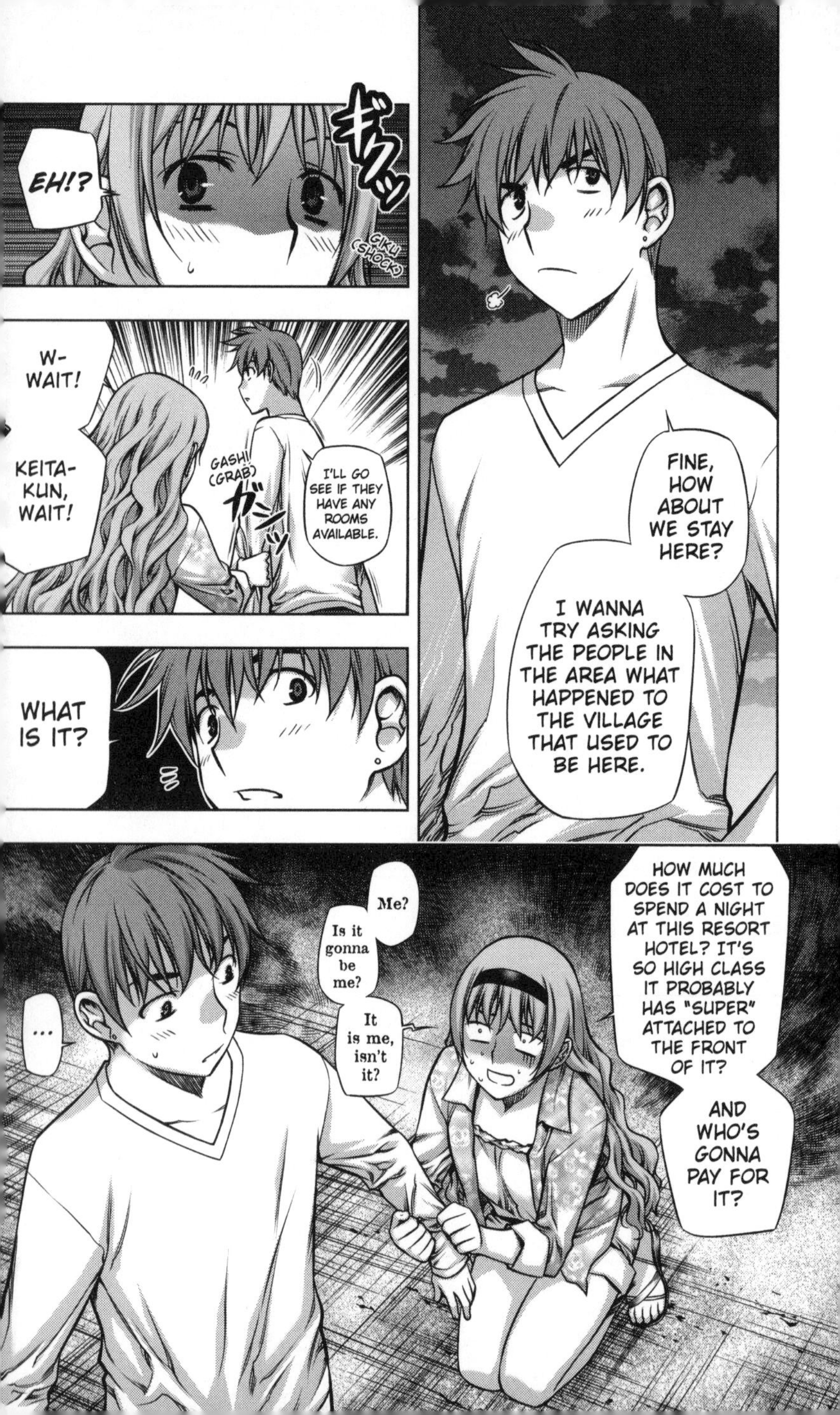
FINE, HOW ABOUT WE STAY HERE?
I WANNA TRY ASKING THE PEOPLE IN THE AREA WHAT HAPPENED TO THE VILLAGE THAT USED TO BE HERE.
GIKU (SHOCK)
EH!?
I'LL GO SEE IF THEY HAVE ANY ROOMS AVAILABLE.
GASH! (GRAB)
W-WAIT!
KEITA-KUN, WAIT!
WHAT IS IT?
HOW MUCH DOES IT COST TO SPEND A NIGHT AT THIS RESORT HOTEL? IT'S SO HIGH CLASS IT PROBABLY HAS "SUPER" ATTACHED TO THE FRONT OF IT?
AND WHO'S GONNA PAY FOR IT?
Me?
Is it gonna be me?
It is me, isn't it?
...

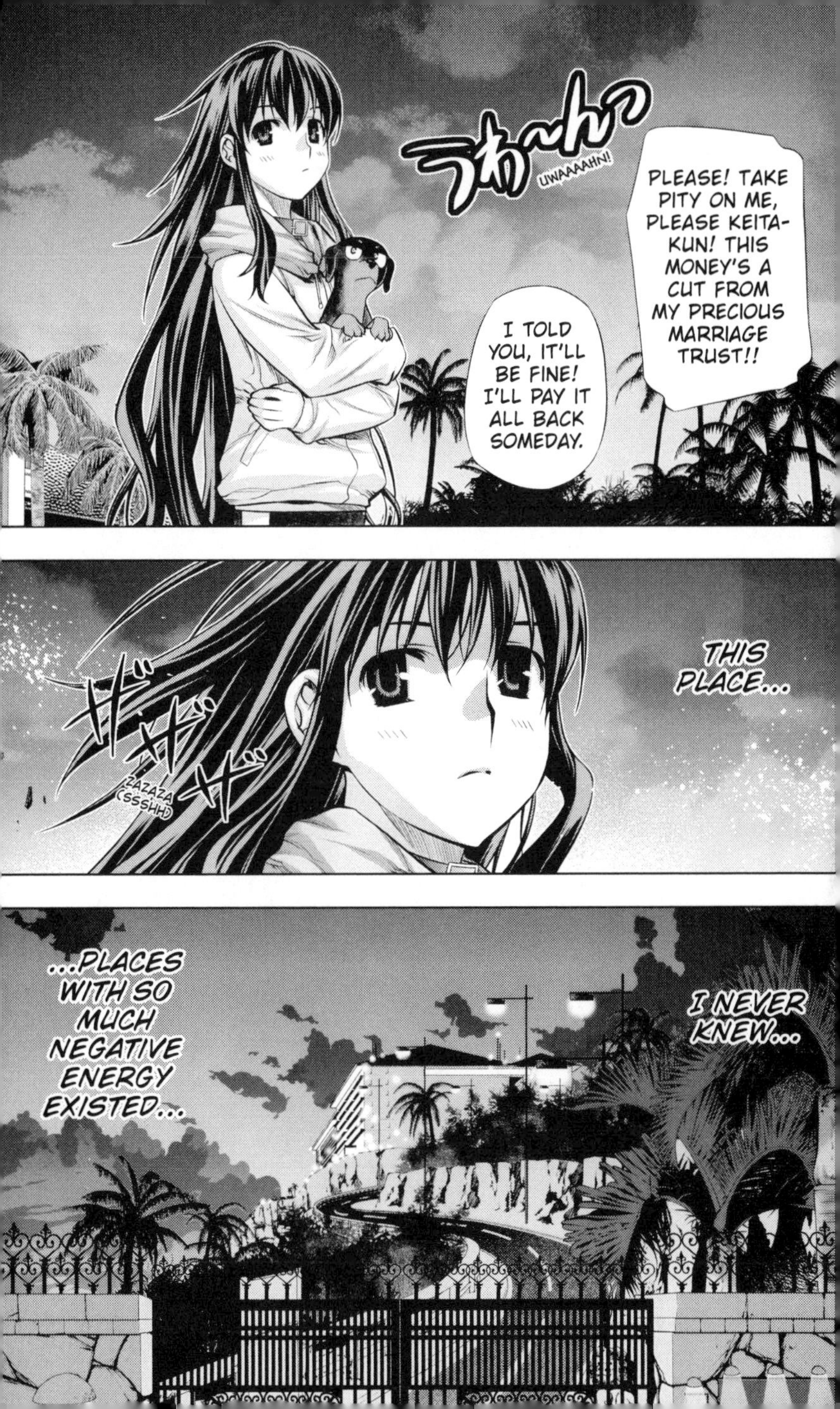
PLEASE! TAKE PITY ON ME, PLEASE KEITA-KUN! THIS MONEY'S A CUT FROM MY PRECIOUS MARRIAGE TRUST!!
うわ~んっ
UWAAAAHN!
I TOLD YOU, IT'LL BE FINE! I'LL PAY IT ALL BACK SOMEDAY.
THIS PLACE...
ザザザ
ZAZAZA (SSSHHD)
I NEVER KNEW...
...PLACES WITH SO MUCH NEGATIVE ENERGY EXISTED...

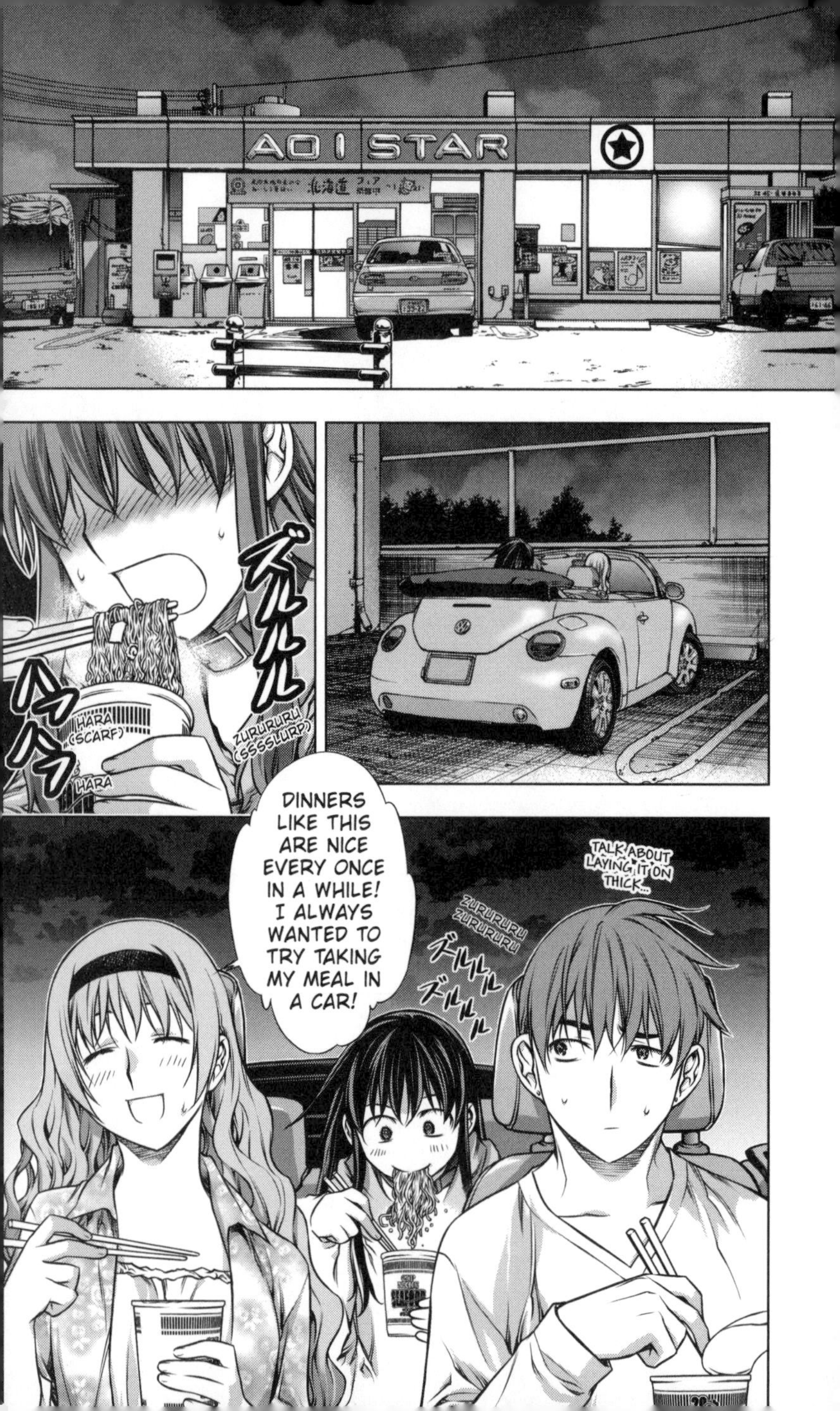

AOI STAR
北海道
ZURURURU (SSSSLURP)
HARA (SCARF)
HARA
TALK ABOUT LAYING IT ON THICK...
ZURURURU ZURURURU
DINNERS LIKE THIS ARE NICE EVERY ONCE IN A WHILE! I ALWAYS WANTED TO TRY TAKING MY MEAL IN A CAR!

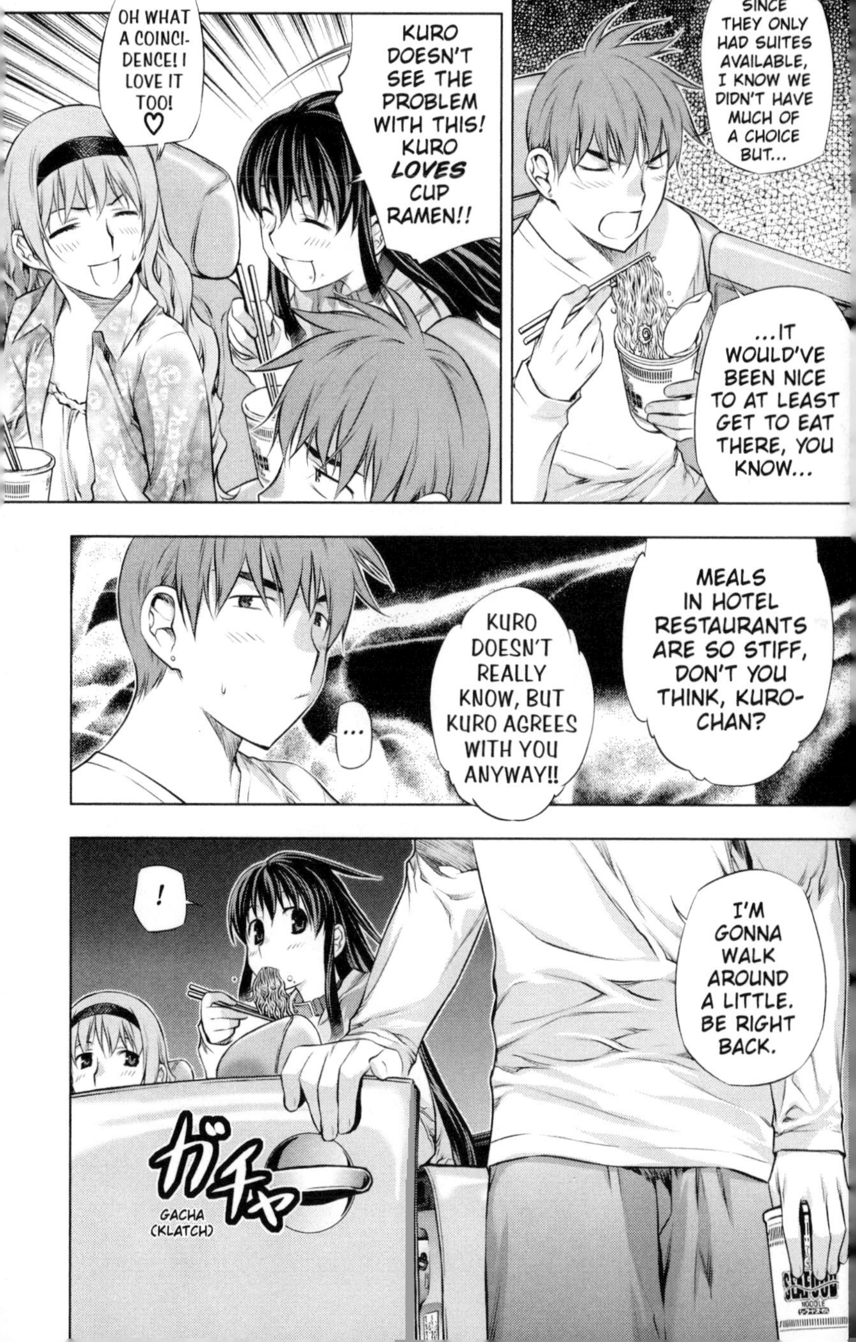
SINCE THEY ONLY HAD SUITES AVAILABLE, I KNOW WE DIDN'T HAVE MUCH OF A CHOICE BUT...
...IT WOULD'VE BEEN NICE TO AT LEAST GET TO EAT THERE, YOU KNOW...
KURO DOESN'T SEE THE PROBLEM WITH THIS! KURO ***LOVES*** CUP RAMEN!!
OH WHAT A COINCI-DENCE! I LOVE IT TOO! ♡
MEALS IN HOTEL RESTAURANTS ARE SO STIFF, DON'T YOU THINK, KURO-CHAN?
KURO DOESN'T REALLY KNOW, BUT KURO AGREES WITH YOU ANYWAY!!
...
I'M GONNA WALK AROUND A LITTLE. BE RIGHT BACK.
!
ガチャ
GACHA (KLATCH)

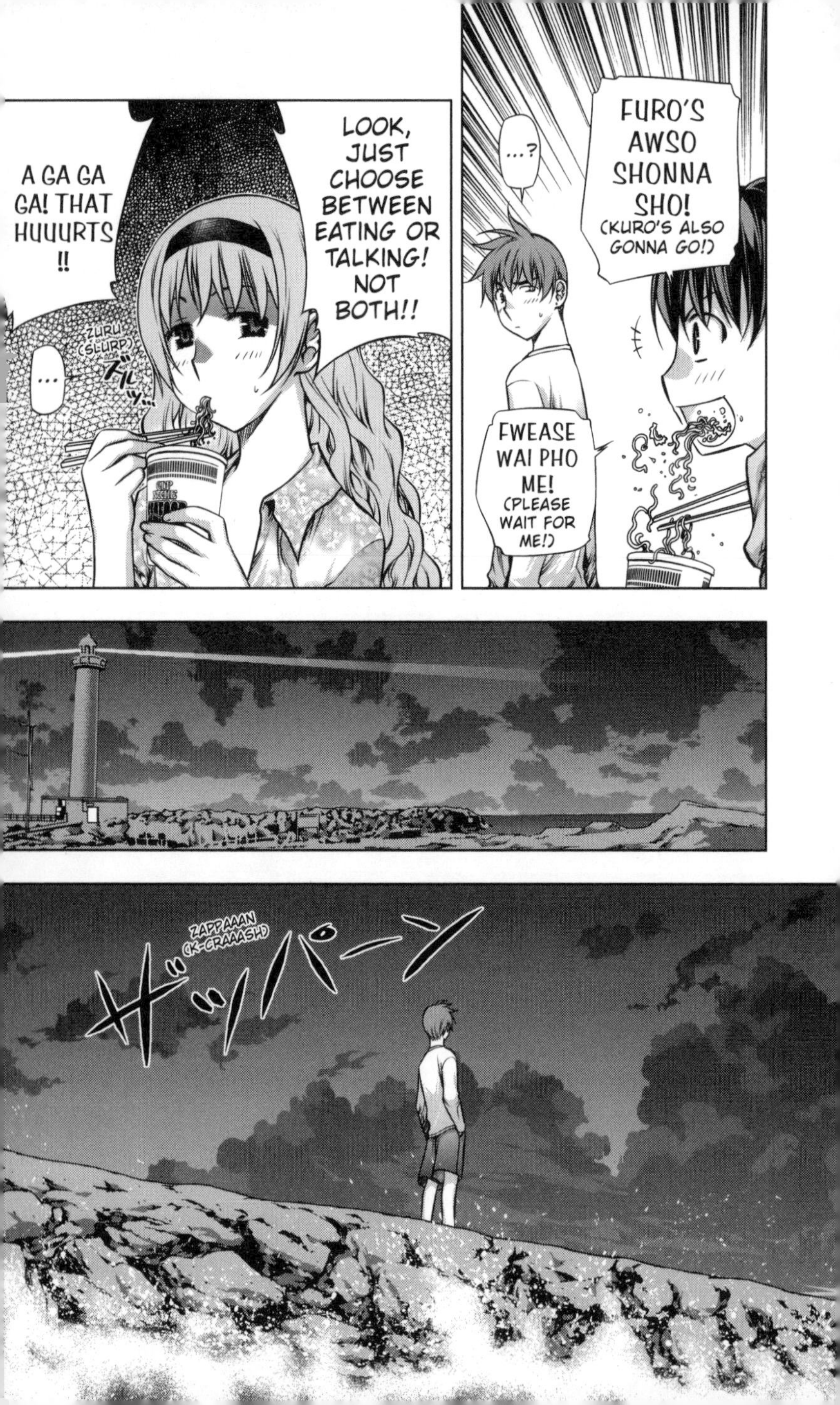
FURO'S AWSO SHONNA SHO!
(KURO'S ALSO GONNA GO!)
...?
FWEASE WAI PHO ME!
(PLEASE WAIT FOR ME!)
LOOK, JUST CHOOSE BETWEEN EATING OR TALKING! NOT BOTH!!
A GA GA GA! THAT HUUURTS!!
ZURU (SLURP)
ズルッ
...
ZAPPAAAN (K-CRAAASH)
ザッパーン

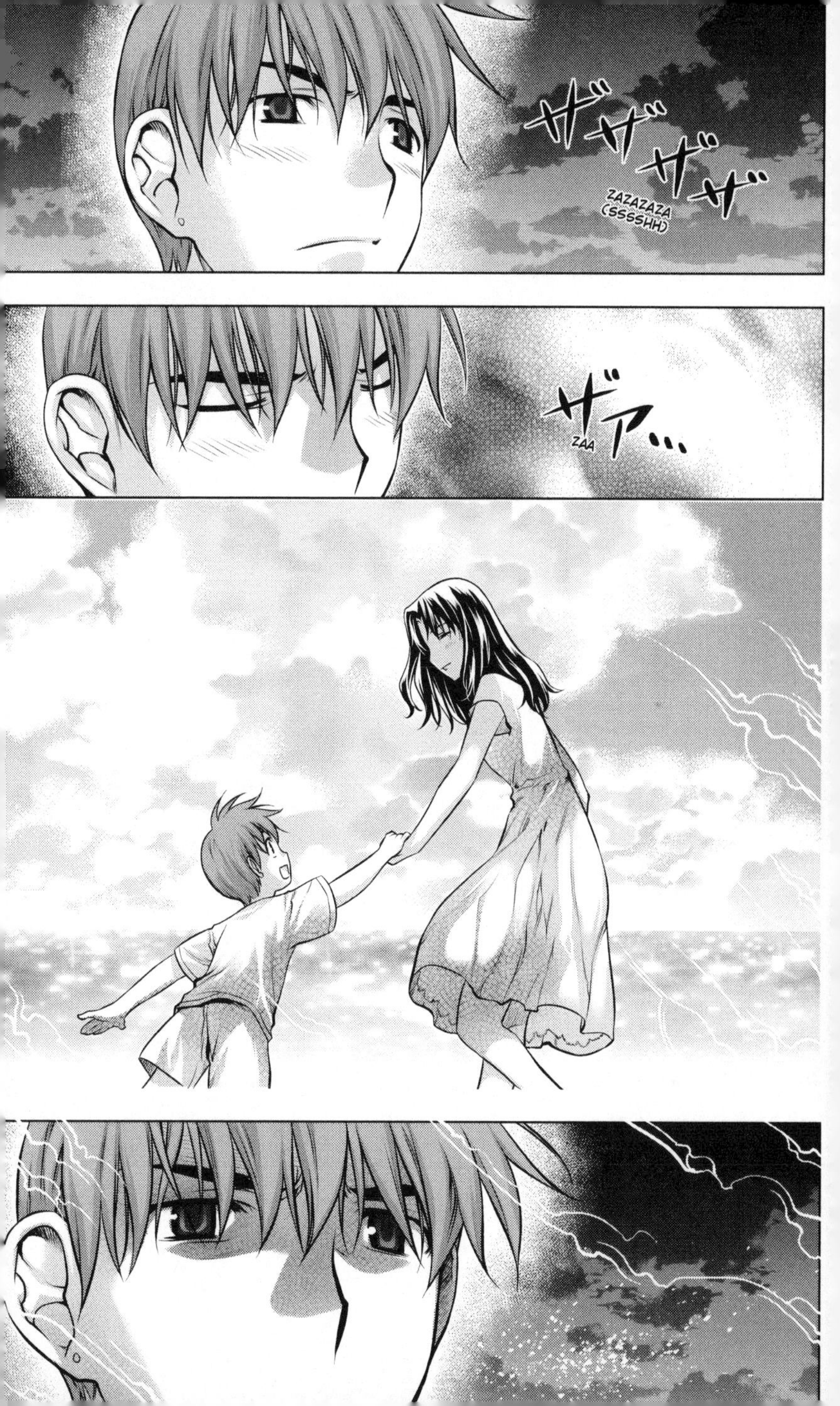
ザザザザ
ZAZAZAZA (SSSSHH)
ザア…
ZAA

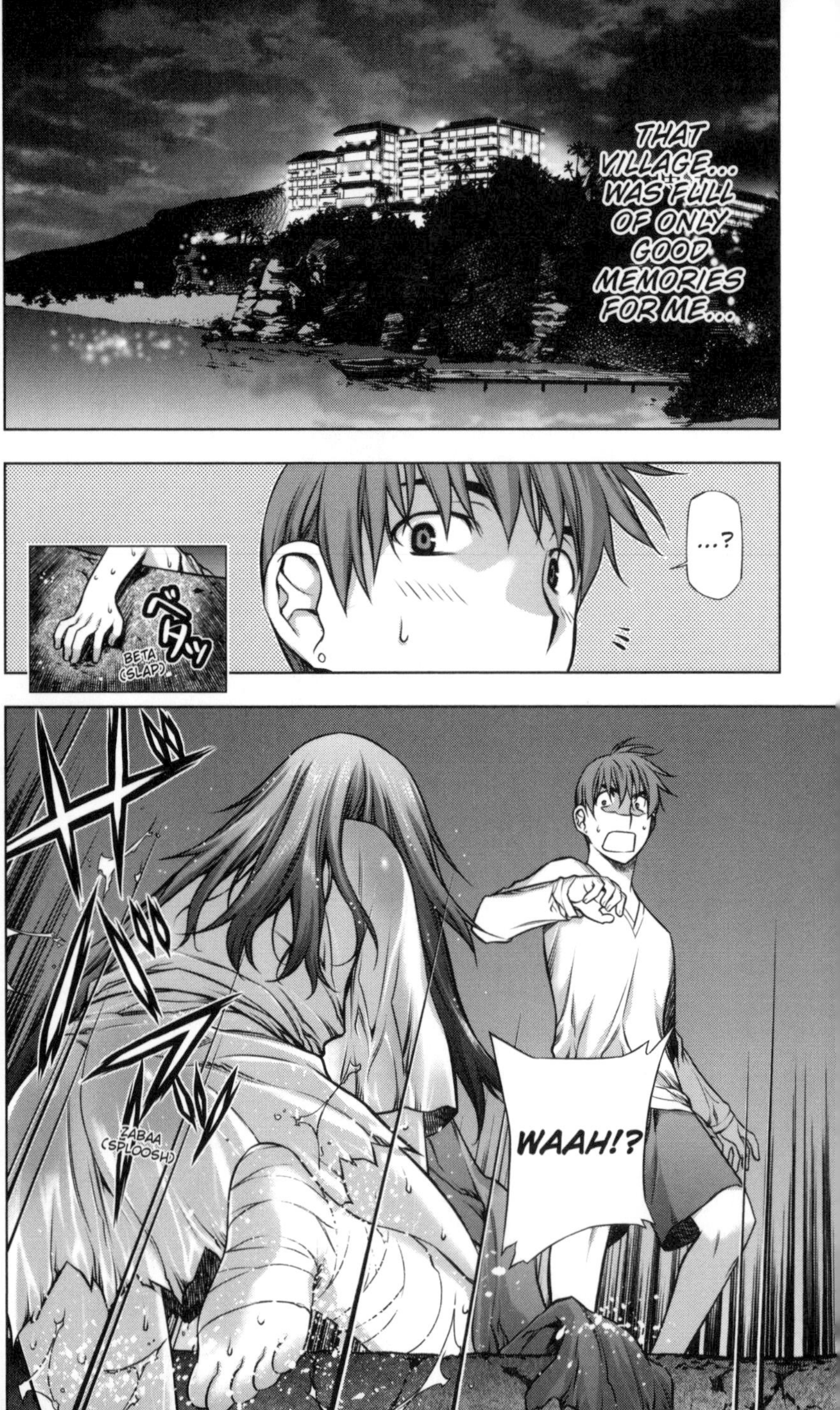
THAT VILLAGE... WAS FULL OF ONLY GOOD MEMORIES FOR ME...
...?
ベタッ
BETA (SLAP)
WAAH!?
ZABAA (SPLOOSH)

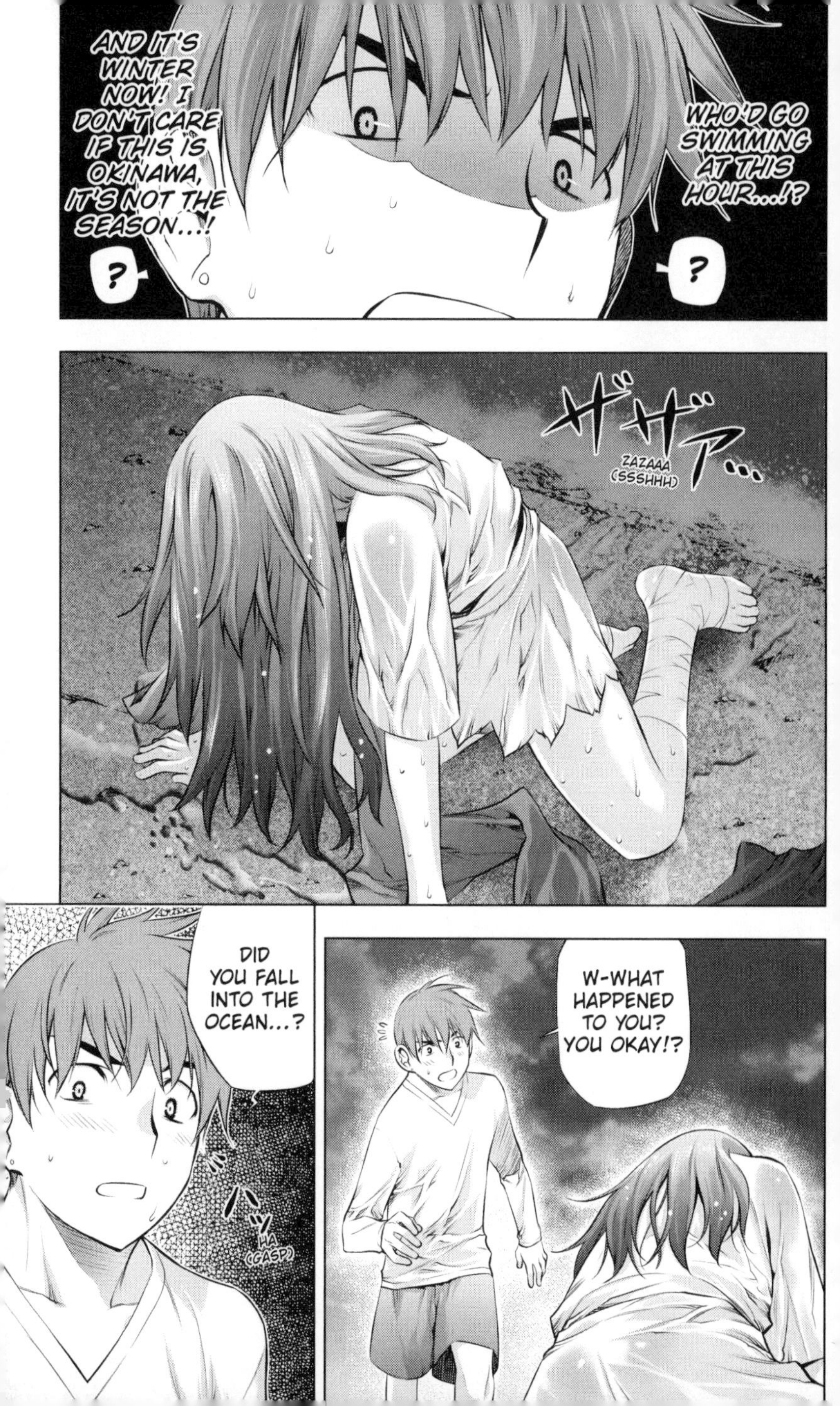
WHO'D GO SWIMMING AT THIS HOUR...!?
?
AND IT'S WINTER NOW! I DON'T CARE IF THIS IS OKINAWA, IT'S NOT THE SEASON...!
?
ザザァ...
ZAZAAA (SSSHHH)
W-WHAT HAPPENED TO YOU? YOU OKAY!?
DID YOU FALL INTO THE OCEAN...?
ハッ
HA (GASP)

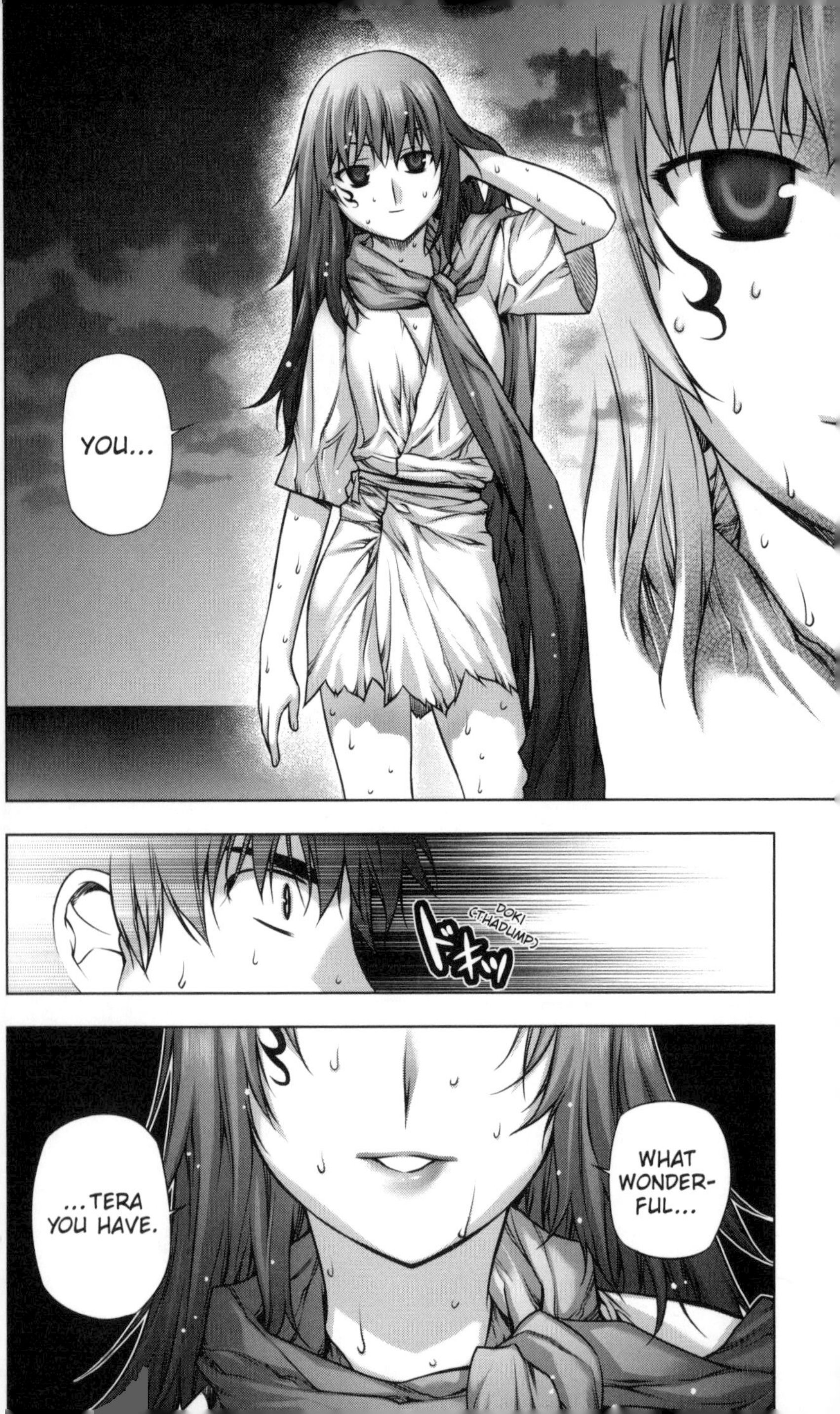
YOU...
DOKI (THADUMP)
ドキッ
WHAT WONDER-FUL...
...TERA YOU HAVE.

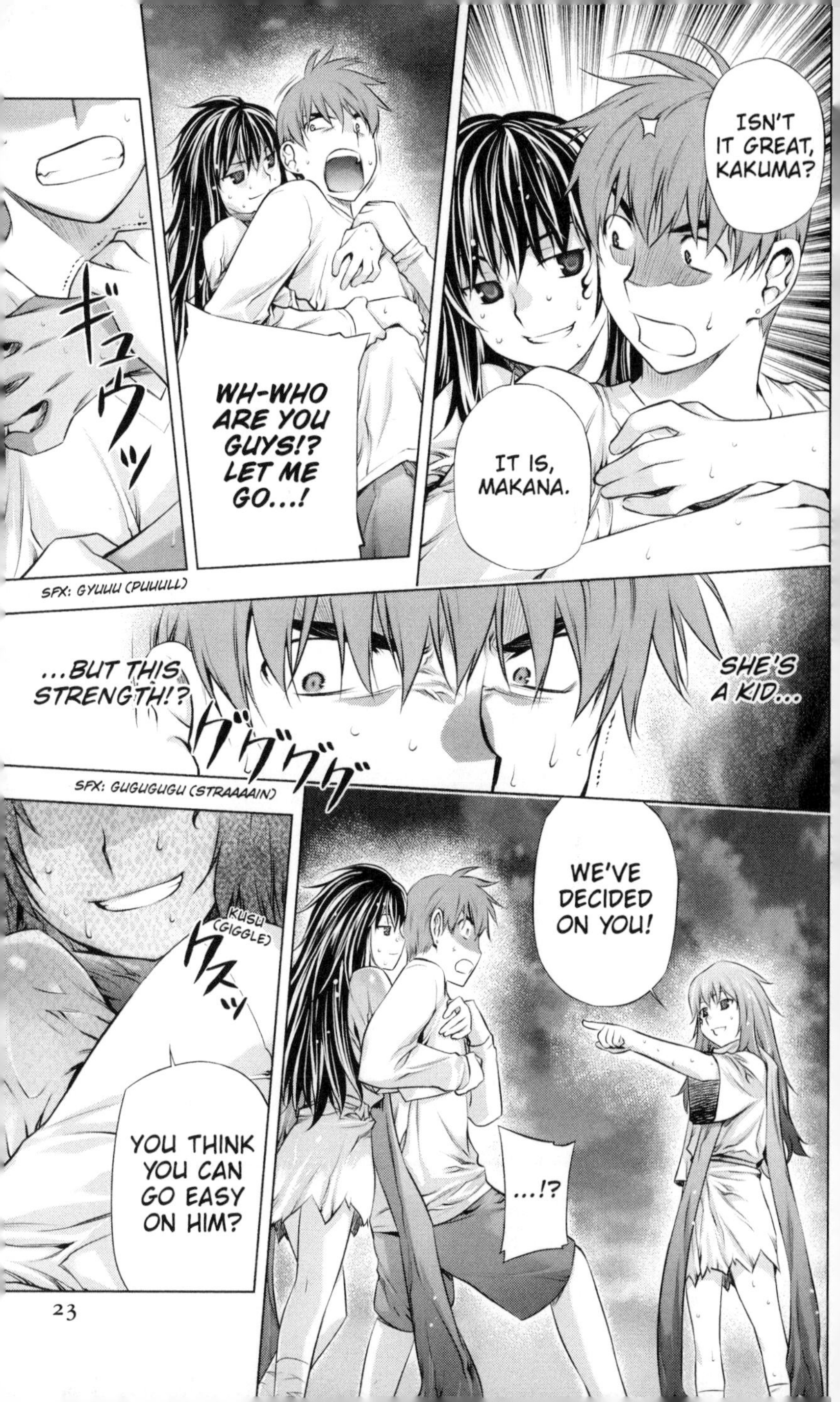
ISN'T IT GREAT, KAKUMA?
IT IS, MAKANA.
WH-WHO ARE YOU GUYS!? LET ME GO...!
ギュウッ
SFX: GYUUU (PUUULL)
SHE'S A KID...
...BUT THIS STRENGTH!?
ググググ
SFX: GUGUGUGU (STRAAAAIN)
WE'VE DECIDED ON YOU!
...!?
クスッ
KUSU (GIGGLE)
YOU THINK YOU CAN GO EASY ON HIM?

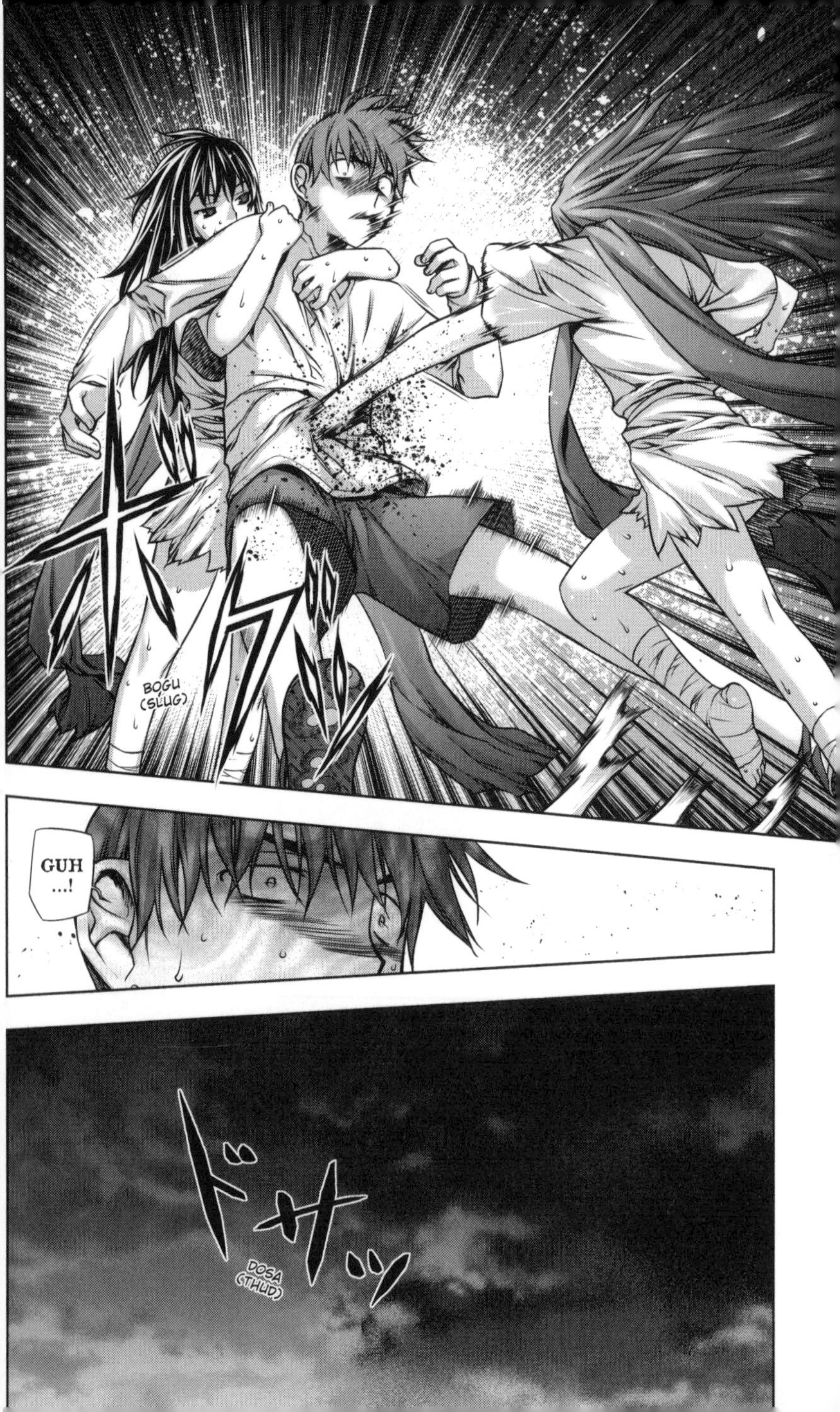
BOGU (SLUG)
GUH ...!
DOSA (THUD)

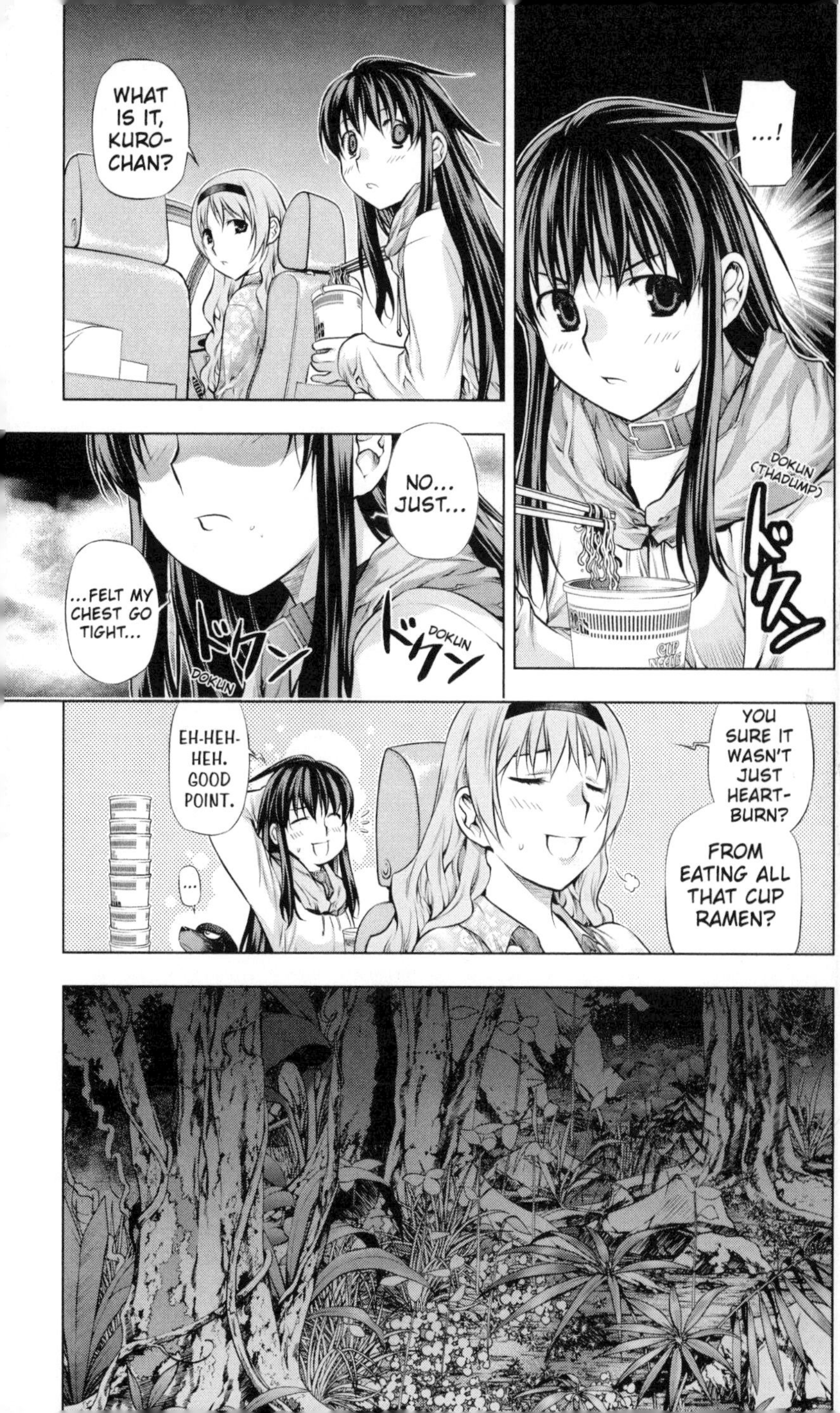
...!
DOKUN (THADUMP)
WHAT IS IT, KURO-CHAN?
NO... JUST...
...FELT MY CHEST GO TIGHT...
DOKUN
DOKUN
YOU SURE IT WASN'T JUST HEART-BURN?
FROM EATING ALL THAT CUP RAMEN?
EH-HEH-HEH. GOOD POINT.
...

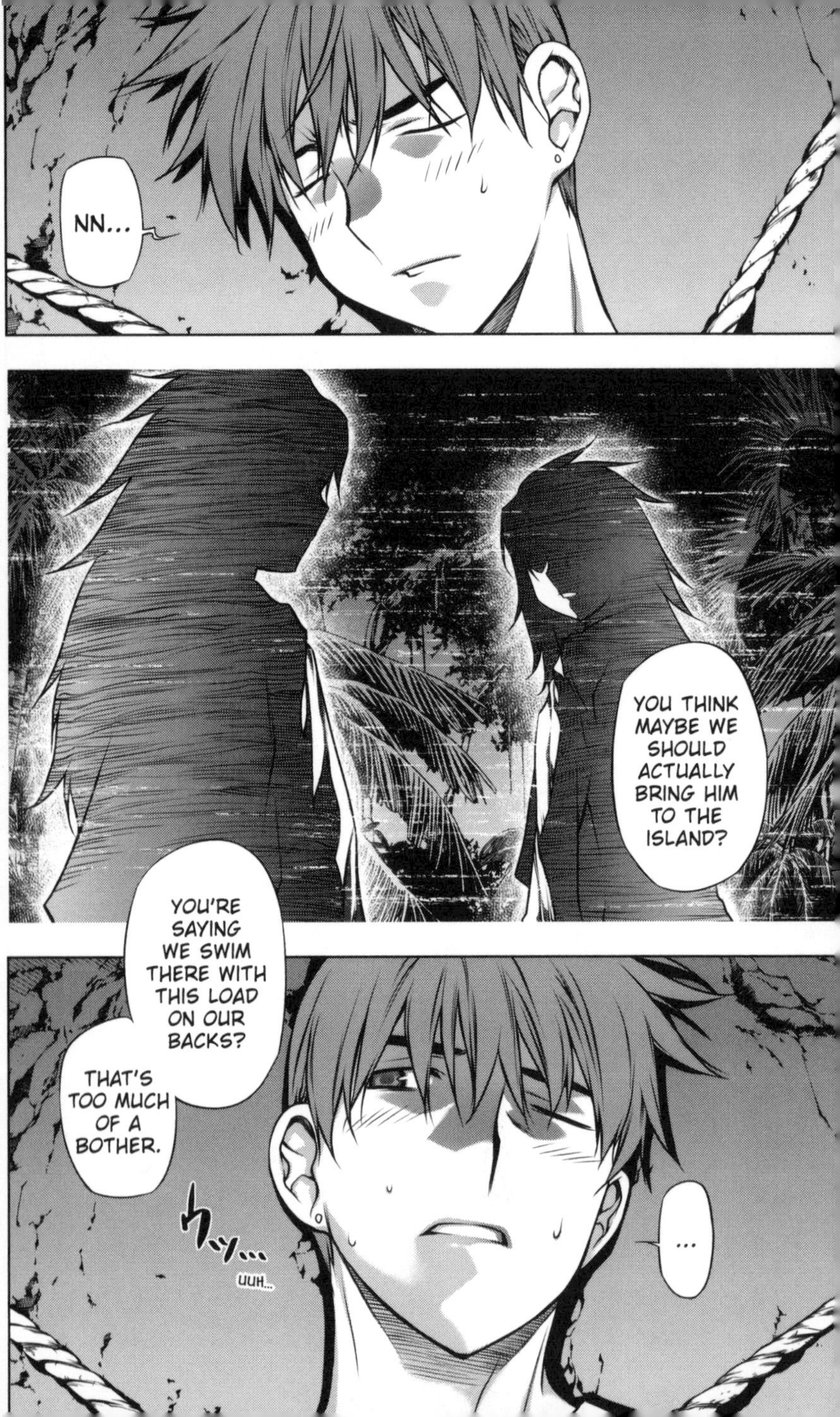
NN...
YOU THINK MAYBE WE SHOULD ACTUALLY BRING HIM TO THE ISLAND?
YOU'RE SAYING WE SWIM THERE WITH THIS LOAD ON OUR BACKS?
THAT'S TOO MUCH OF A BOTHER.
UUH...
...

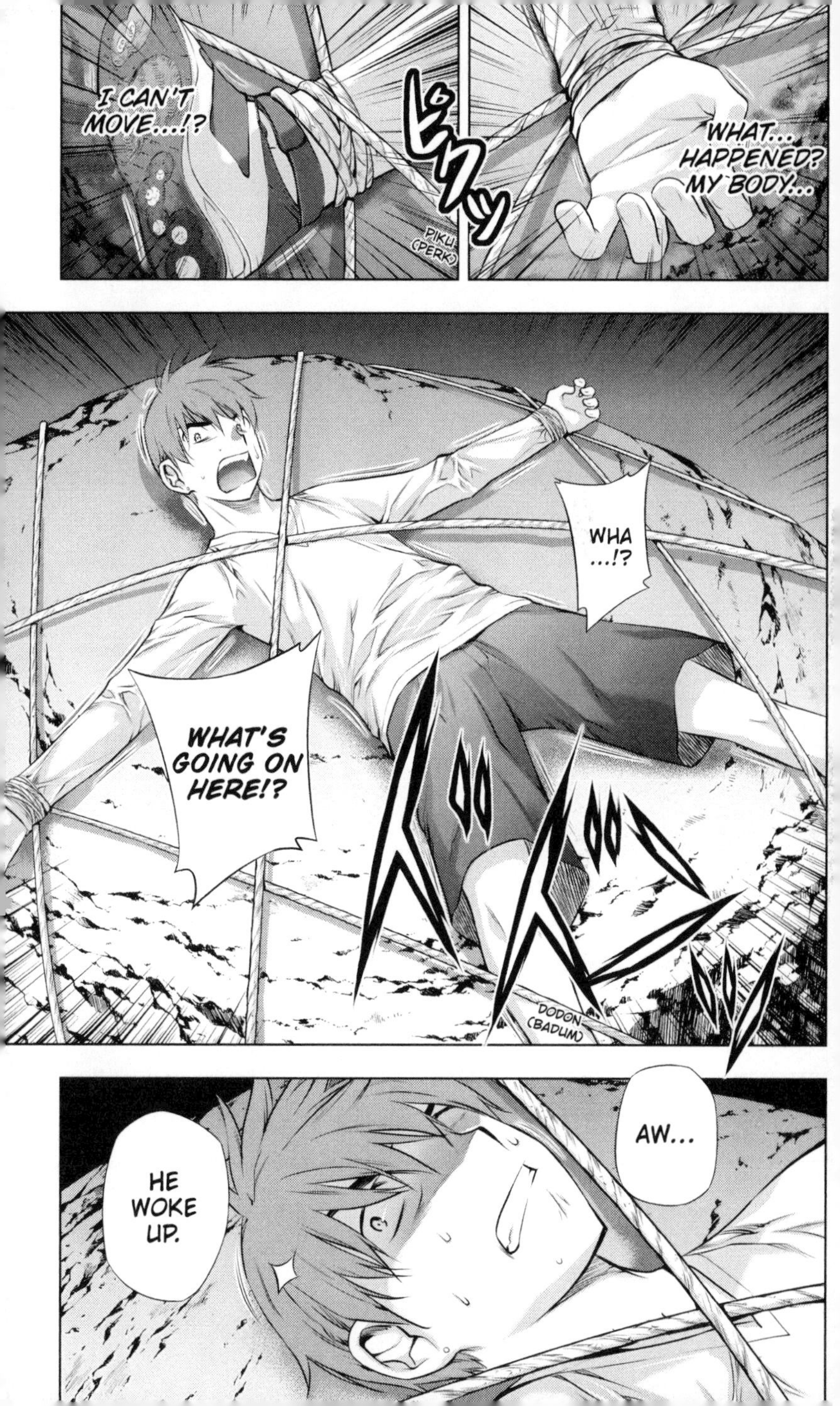

WHAT... HAPPENED? MY BODY...
ピクッ
PIKU (PERK)
I CAN'T MOVE...!?
WHA ...!?
WHAT'S GOING ON HERE!?
DODON (BADUM)
AW...
HE WOKE UP.

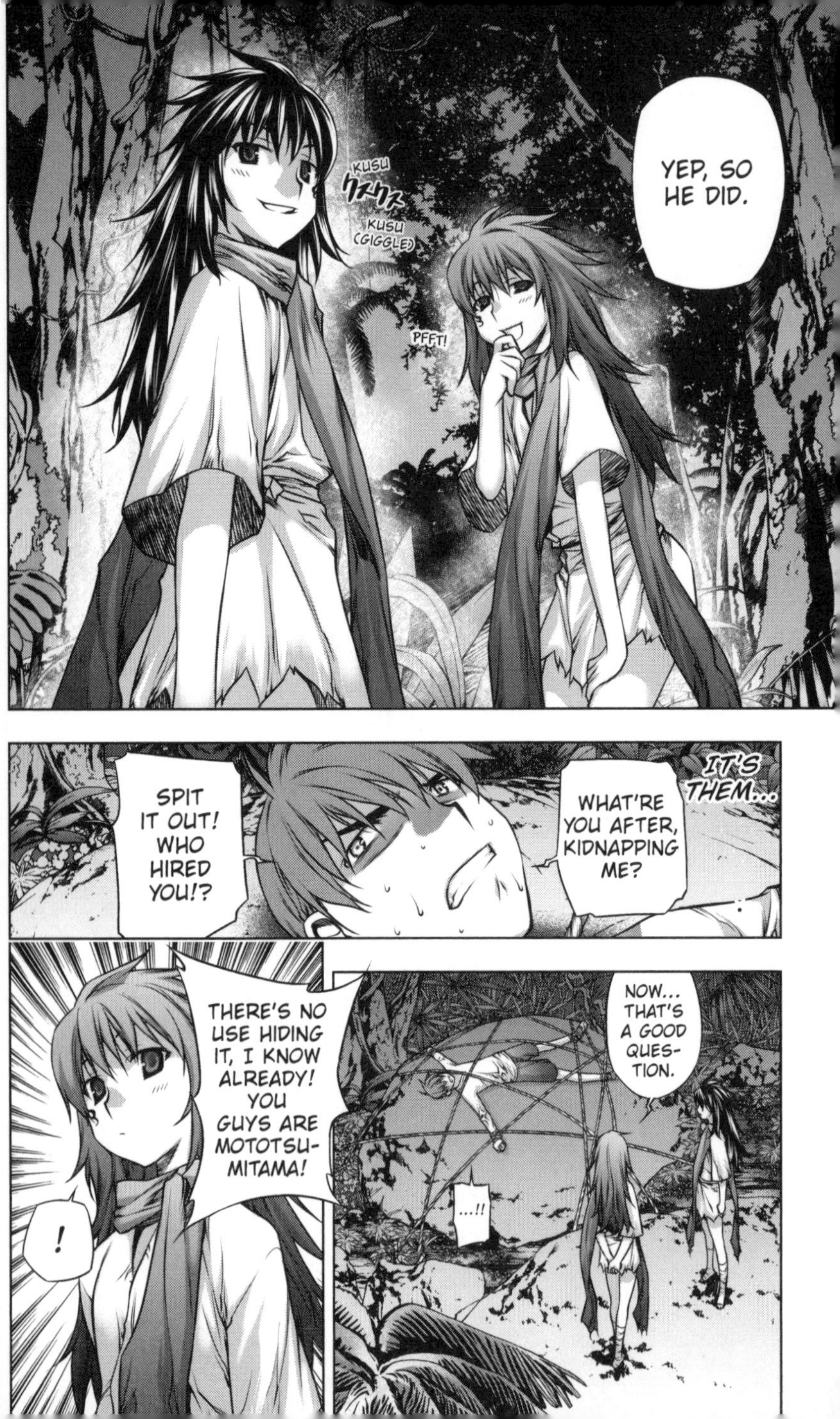
YEP, SO HE DID.
KUSU
クスクス
KUSU (GIGGLE)
PFFT!
IT'S THEM...
WHAT'RE YOU AFTER, KIDNAPPING ME?
SPIT IT OUT! WHO HIRED YOU!?
NOW... THAT'S A GOOD QUES-TION.
...!!
THERE'S NO USE HIDING IT, I KNOW ALREADY! YOU GUYS ARE MOTOTSU-MITAMA!
!

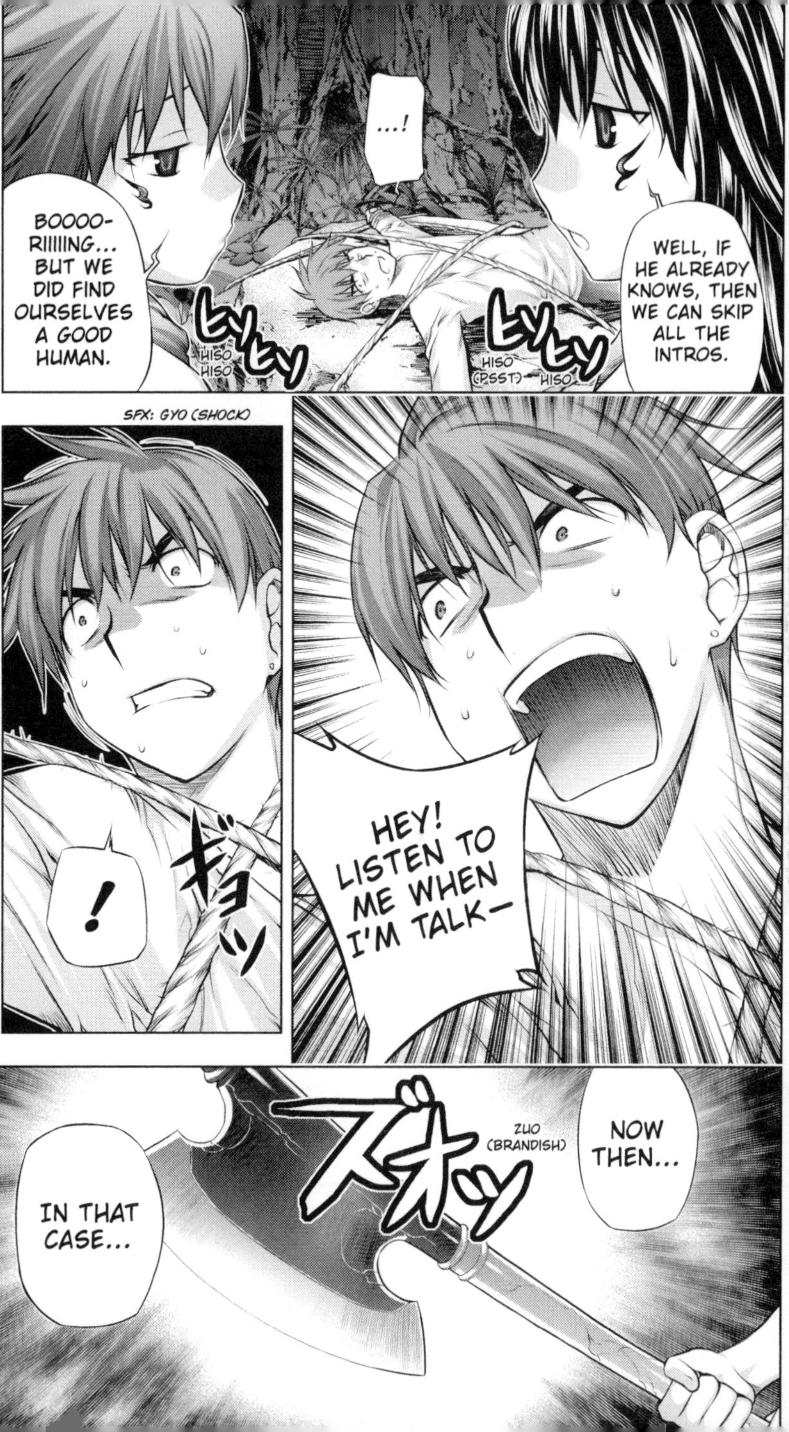
...!
WELL, IF HE ALREADY KNOWS, THEN WE CAN SKIP ALL THE INTROS.
ヒソヒソ
HISO (PSST) HISO
BOOOO-RIIIIING... BUT WE DID FIND OURSELVES A GOOD HUMAN.
ヒソヒソ
HISO HISO
HEY! LISTEN TO ME WHEN I'M TALK—
SFX: GYO (SHOCK)
ギョッ
!
NOW THEN...
ズオッ
ZUO (BRANDISH)
IN THAT CASE...

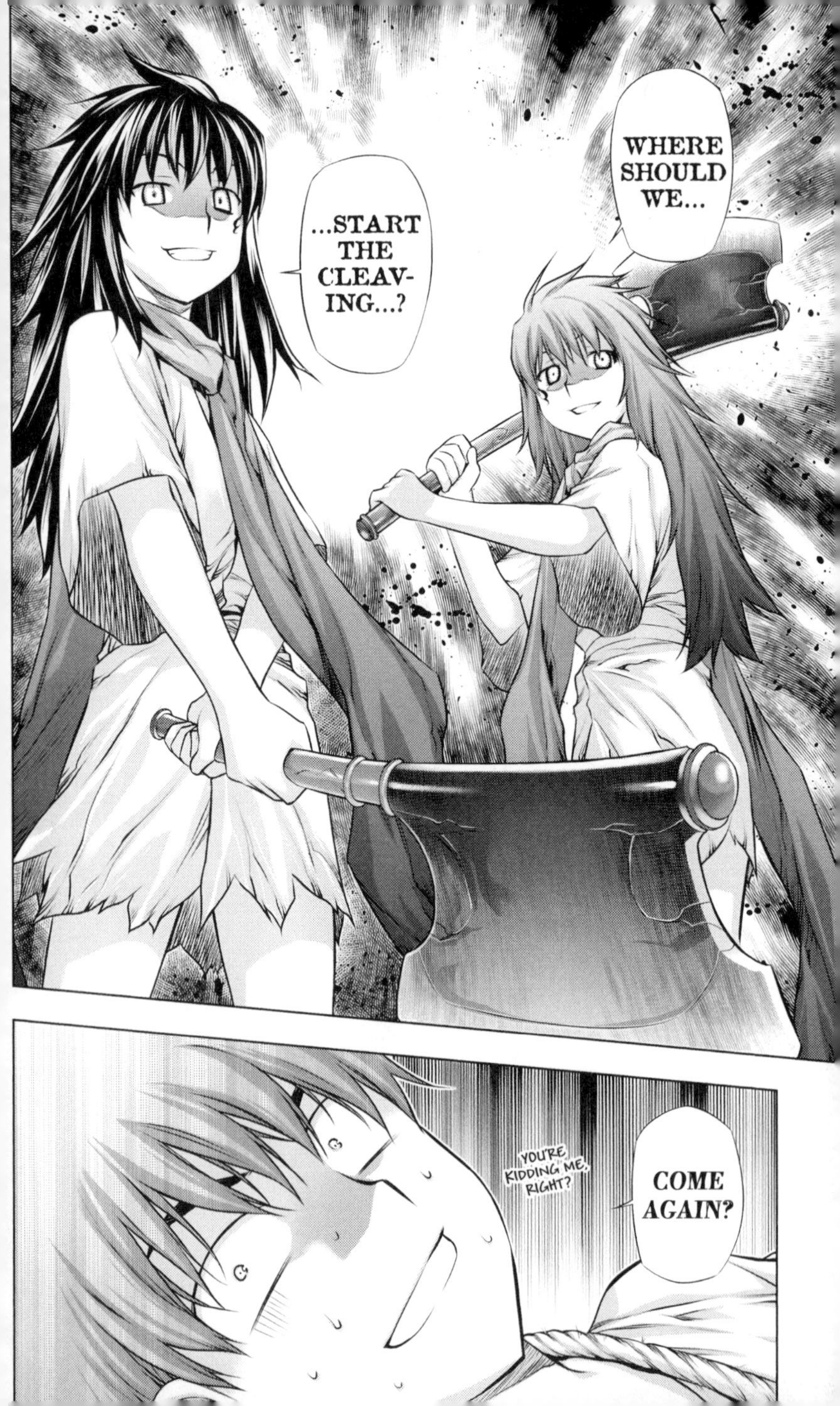
WHERE SHOULD WE...
...START THE CLEAV-ING...?
COME AGAIN?
YOU'RE KIDDING ME, RIGHT?

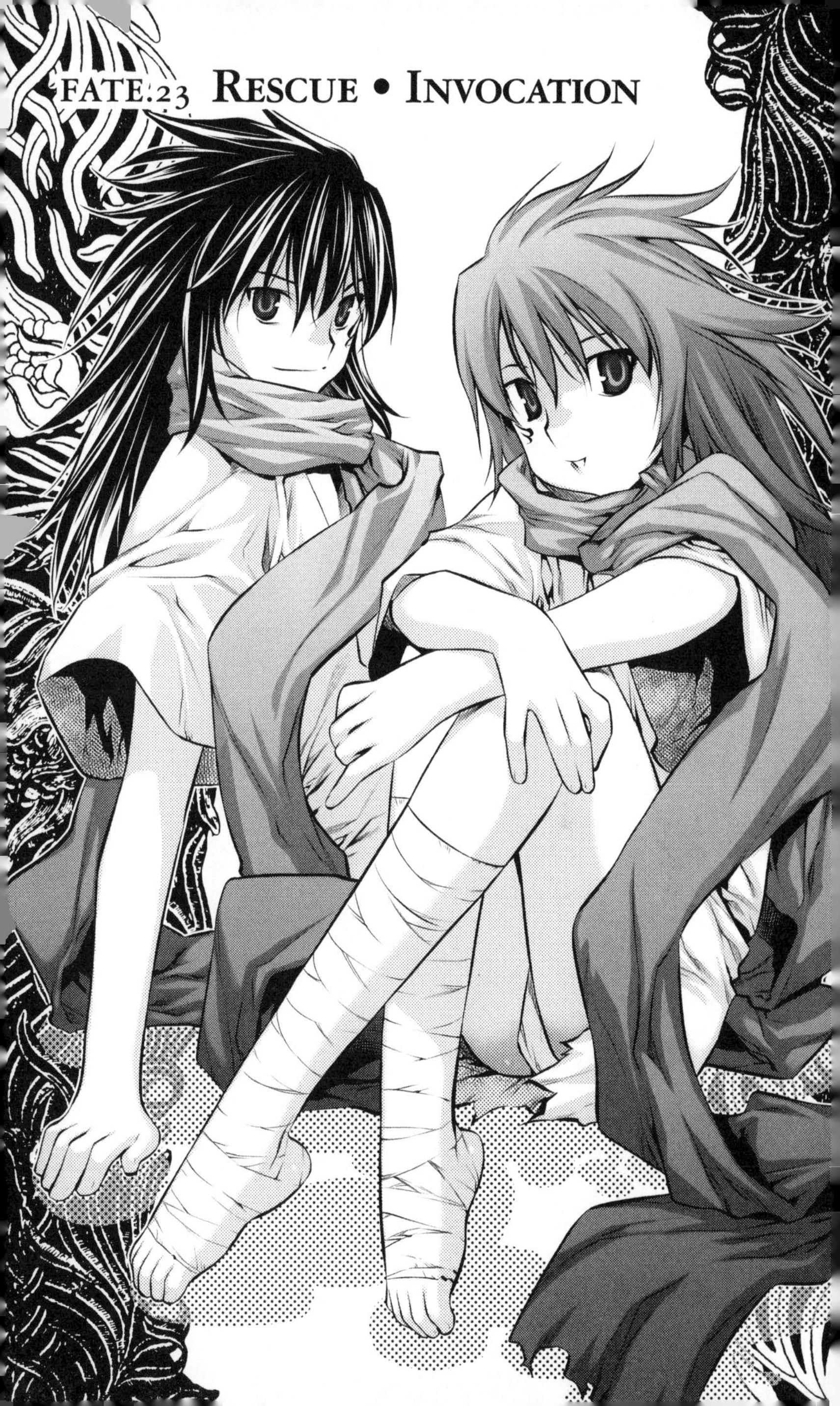
FATE.23 RESCUE • INVOCATION

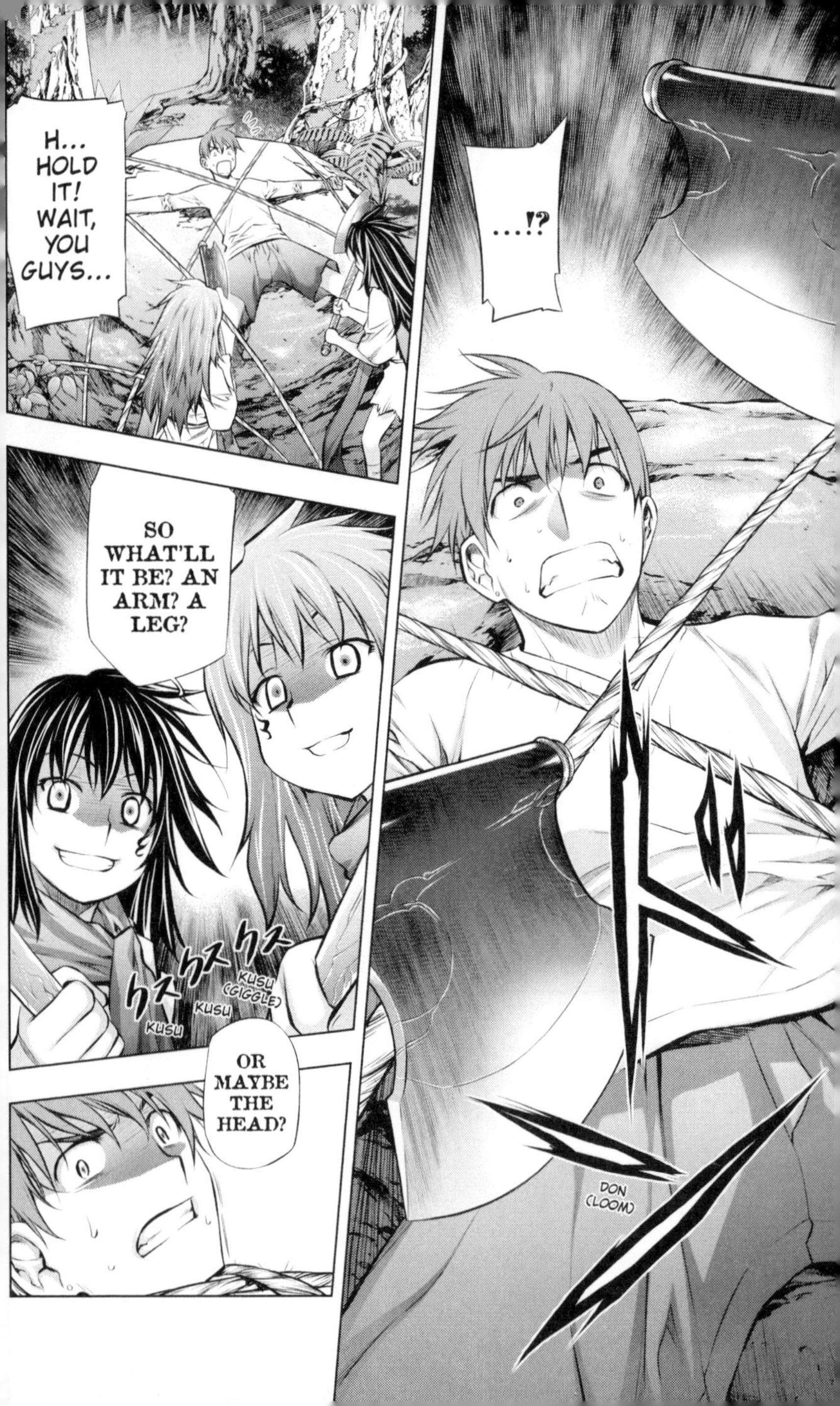
...!?
DON (LOOM)
H... HOLD IT! WAIT, YOU GUYS...
SO WHAT'LL IT BE? AN ARM? A LEG?
クスクスクス
KUSU (GIGGLE)
KUSU
KUSU
OR MAYBE THE HEAD?

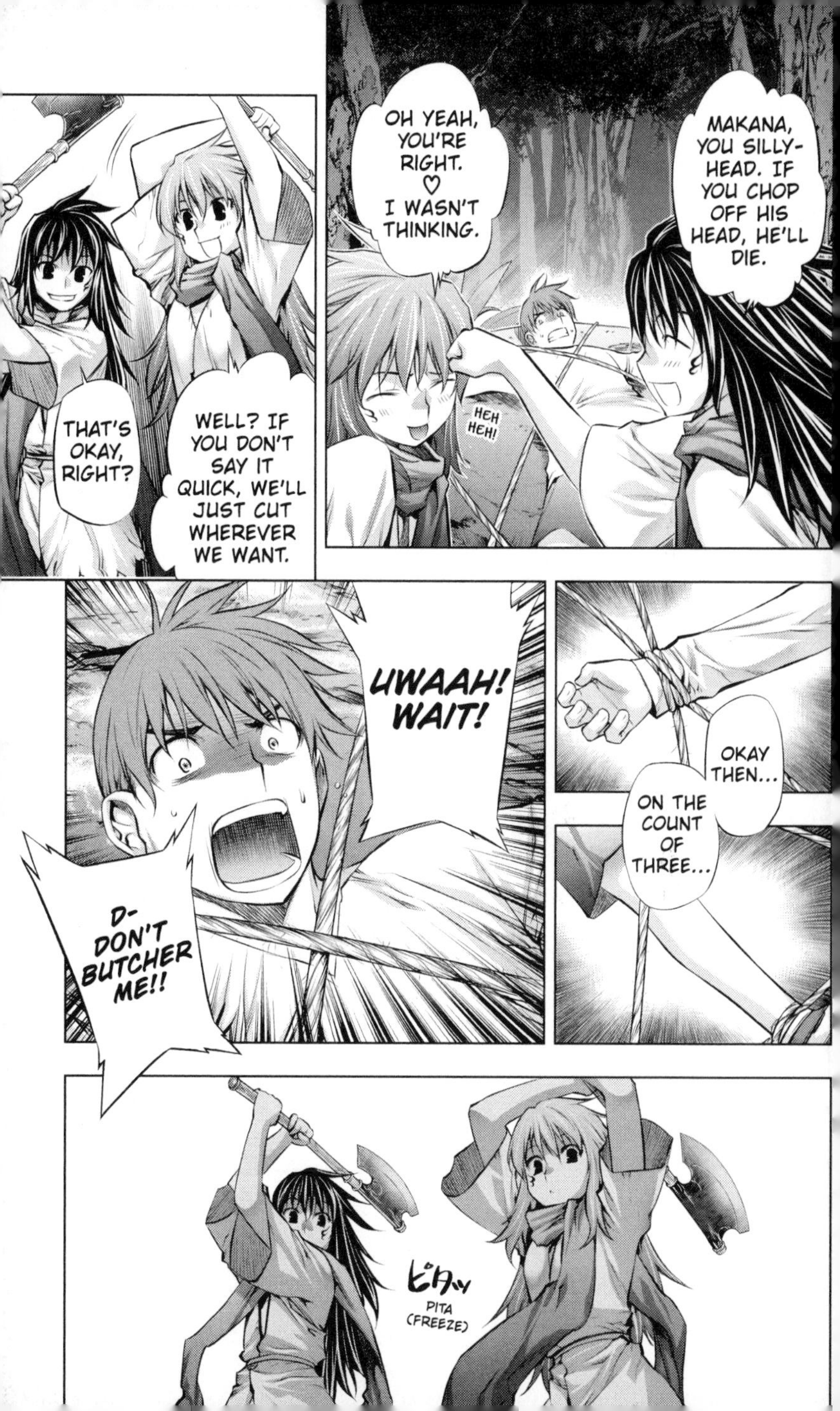
MAKANA, YOU SILLY-HEAD. IF YOU CHOP OFF HIS HEAD, HE'LL DIE.
OH YEAH, YOU'RE RIGHT. ♡ I WASN'T THINKING.
HEH HEH!
WELL? IF YOU DON'T SAY IT QUICK, WE'LL JUST CUT WHEREVER WE WANT.
THAT'S OKAY, RIGHT?
OKAY THEN...
ON THE COUNT OF THREE...
UWAAH! WAIT!
D-DON'T BUTCHER ME!!
ピタッ
PITA (FREEZE)

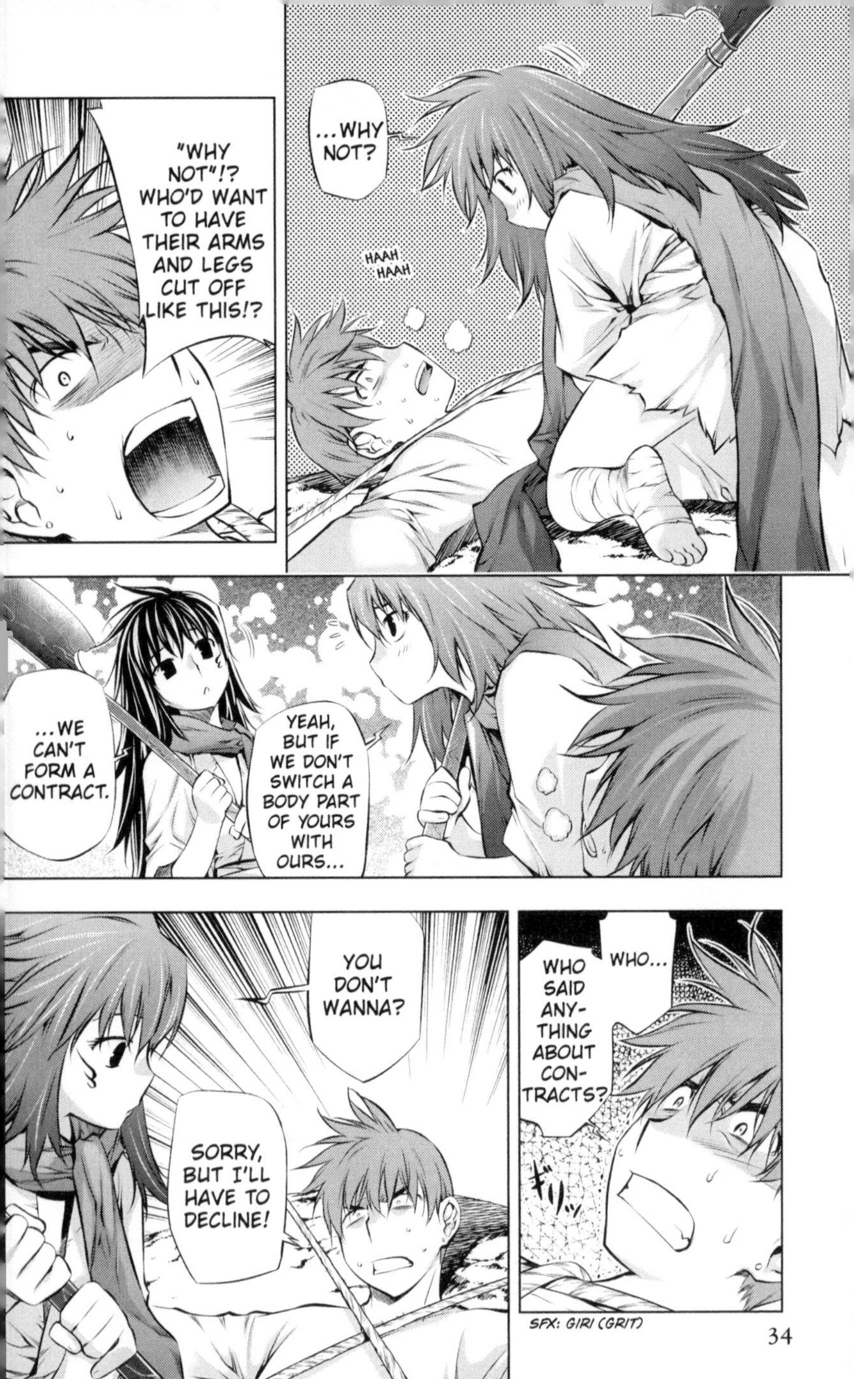
...WHY NOT?
HAAH HAAH
"WHY NOT"!? WHO'D WANT TO HAVE THEIR ARMS AND LEGS CUT OFF LIKE THIS!?
YEAH, BUT IF WE DON'T SWITCH A BODY PART OF YOURS WITH OURS...
...WE CAN'T FORM A CONTRACT.
WHO...
WHO SAID ANY-THING ABOUT CON-TRACTS?
ギリッ
YOU DON'T WANNA?
SORRY, BUT I'LL HAVE TO DECLINE!

SFX: GIRI (GRIT)

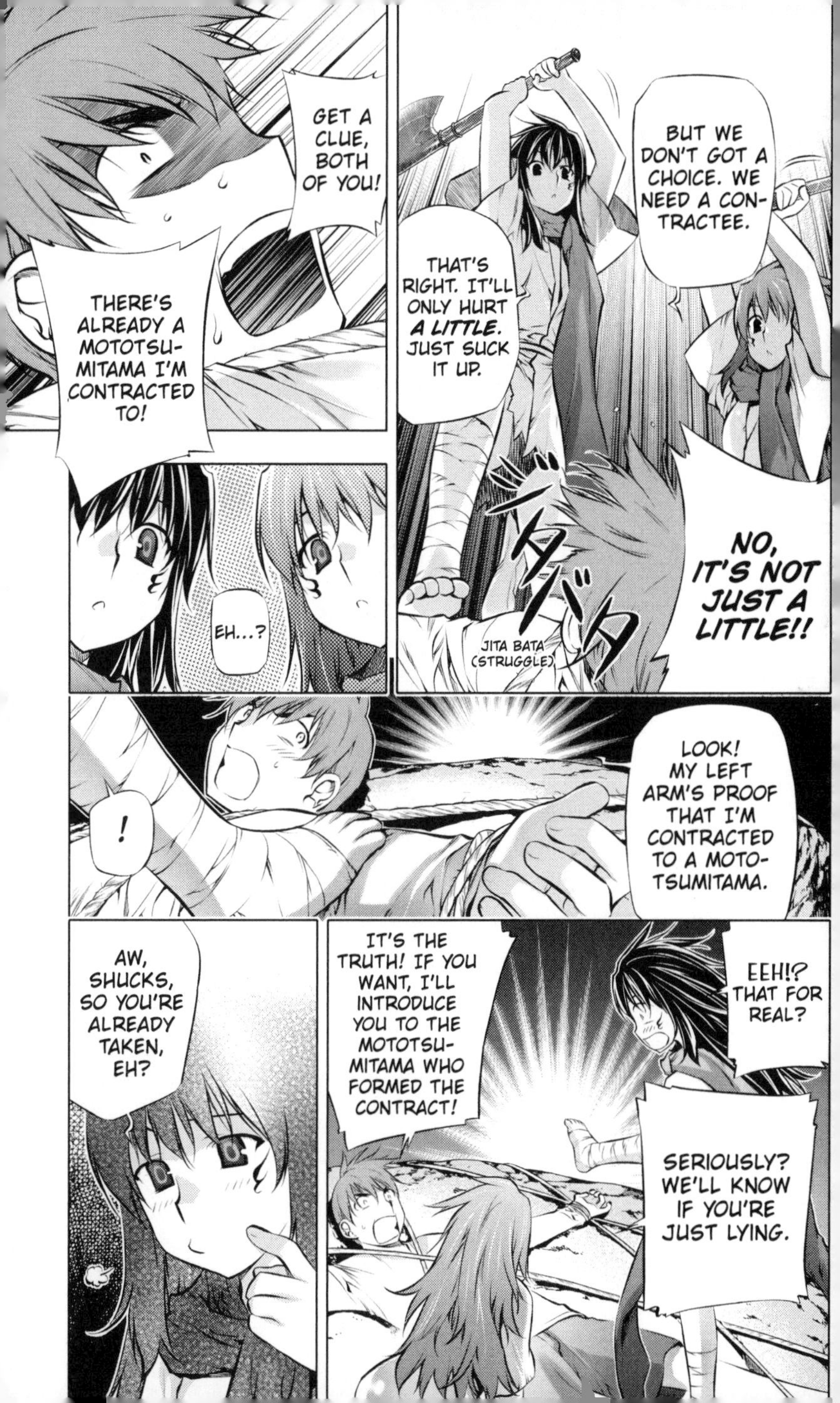
BUT WE DON'T GOT A CHOICE. WE NEED A CONTRACTEE.
THAT'S RIGHT. IT'LL ONLY HURT *A LITTLE*. JUST SUCK IT UP.
ジタバタ
JITA BATA (STRUGGLE)
NO, IT'S NOT JUST A LITTLE!!
GET A CLUE, BOTH OF YOU!
THERE'S ALREADY A MOTOTSUMITAMA I'M CONTRACTED TO!
EH...?
LOOK! MY LEFT ARM'S PROOF THAT I'M CONTRACTED TO A MOTOTSUMITAMA.
!
EEH!? THAT FOR REAL?
SERIOUSLY? WE'LL KNOW IF YOU'RE JUST LYING.
IT'S THE TRUTH! IF YOU WANT, I'LL INTRODUCE YOU TO THE MOTOTSUMITAMA WHO FORMED THE CONTRACT!
AW, SHUCKS, SO YOU'RE ALREADY TAKEN, EH?

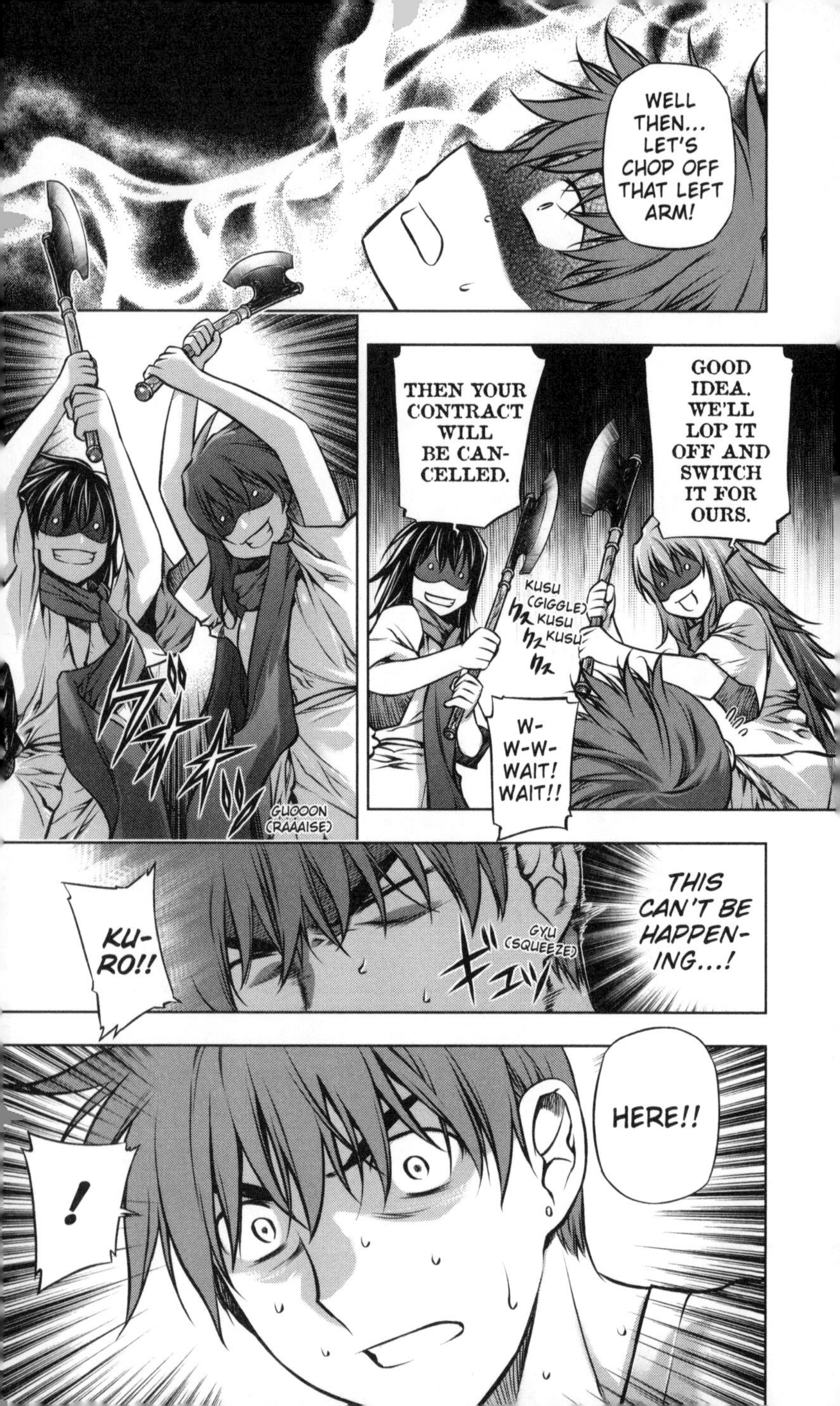
WELL THEN... LET'S CHOP OFF THAT LEFT ARM!
GOOD IDEA. WE'LL LOP IT OFF AND SWITCH IT FOR OURS.
THEN YOUR CONTRACT WILL BE CAN-CELLED.
KUSU (GIGGLE) KUSU KUSU
W-W-W-WAIT! WAIT!!
GUOOON (RAAAISE)
THIS CAN'T BE HAPPEN-ING...!
GYU (SQUEEZE)
KU-RO!!
HERE!!
!

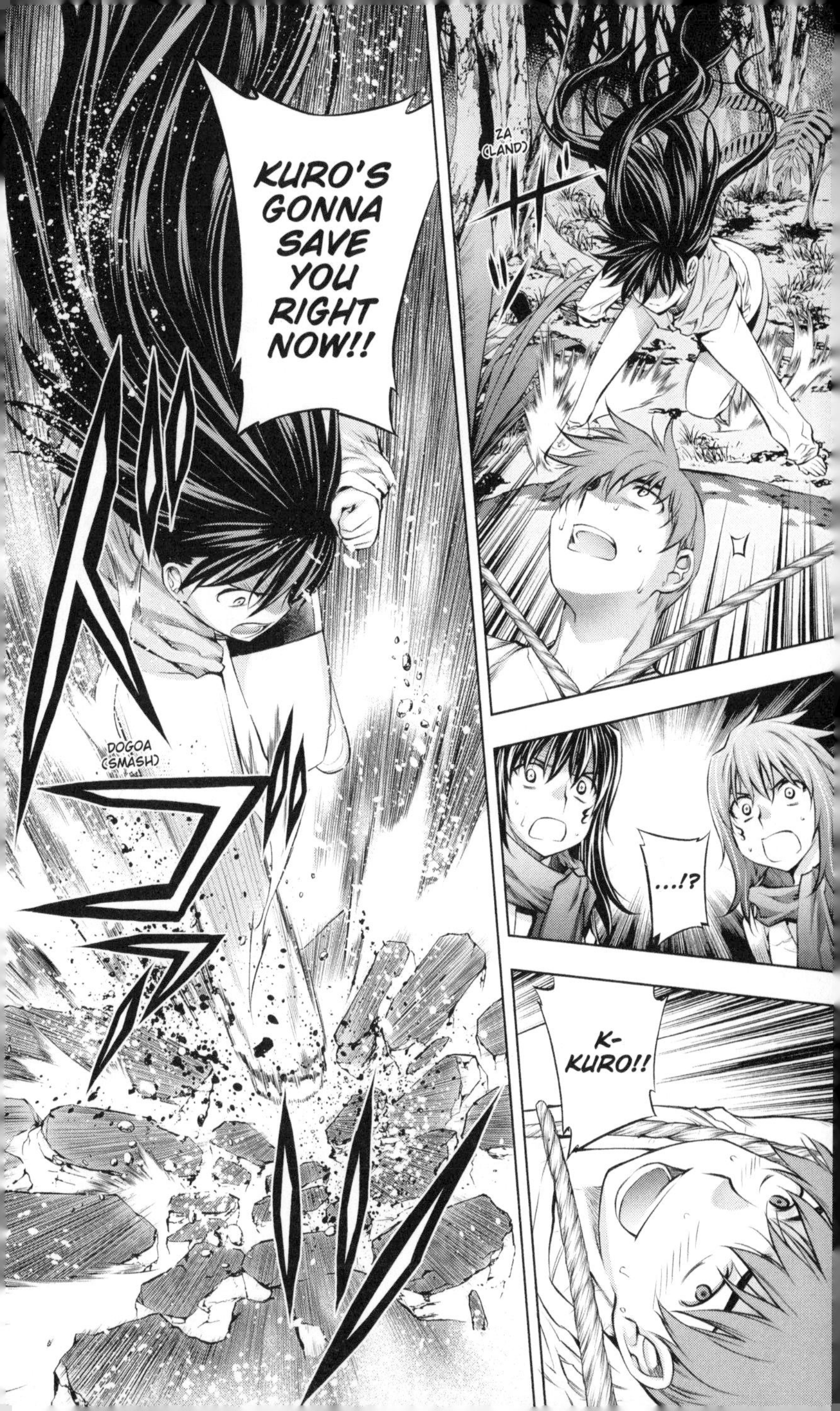
ZA (LAND)
...!?
K-KURO!!
KURO'S GONNA SAVE YOU RIGHT NOW!!
DOGOA (SMASH)

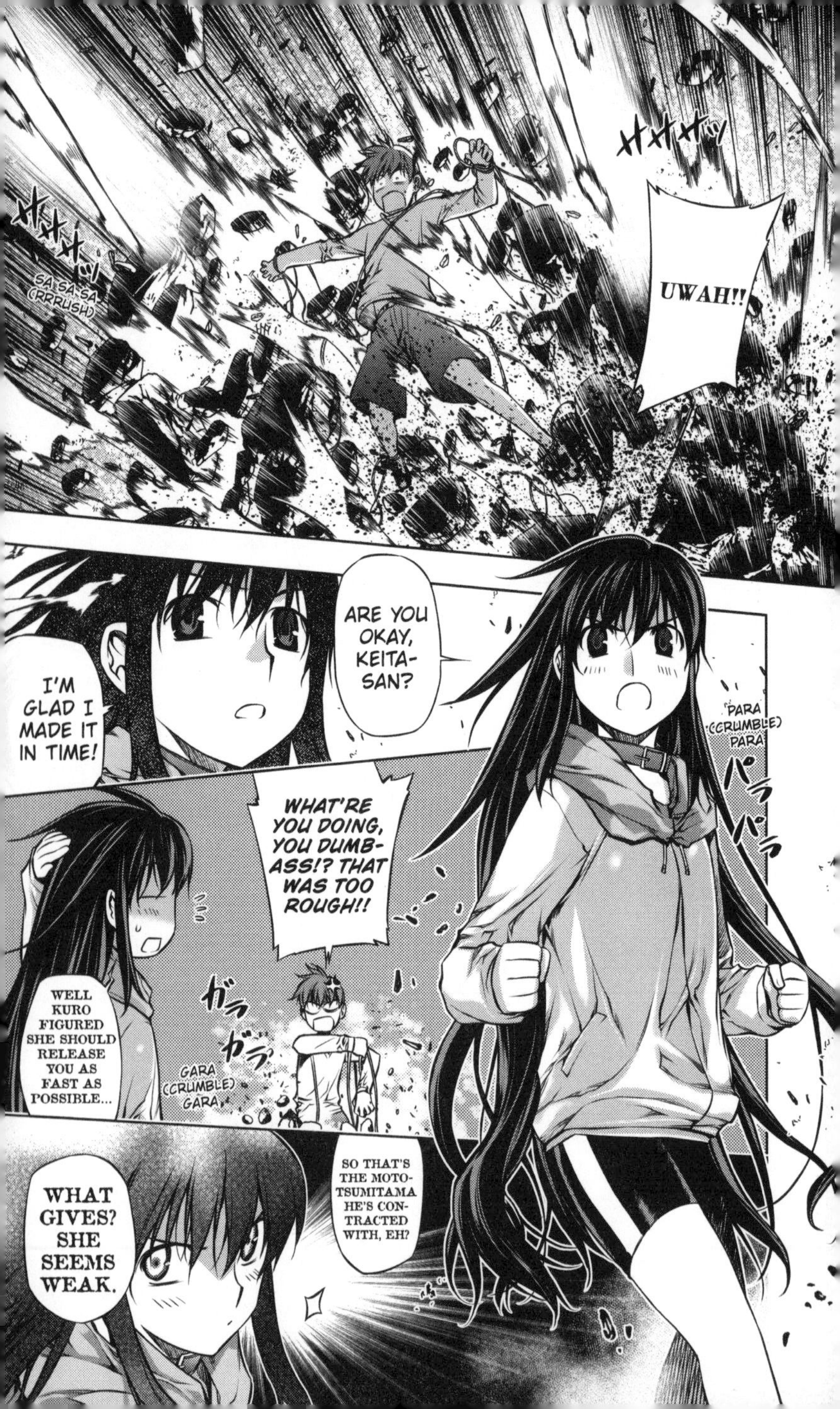

UWAH!!
SA SA SA (RRRUSH)
PARA (CRUMBLE) PARA
ARE YOU OKAY, KEITA-SAN?
I'M GLAD I MADE IT IN TIME!
WHAT'RE YOU DOING, YOU DUMB-ASS!? THAT WAS TOO ROUGH!!
WELL KURO FIGURED SHE SHOULD RELEASE YOU AS FAST AS POSSIBLE...
GARA (CRUMBLE) GARA
SO THAT'S THE MOTO-TSUMITAMA HE'S CON-TRACTED WITH, EH?
WHAT GIVES? SHE SEEMS WEAK.

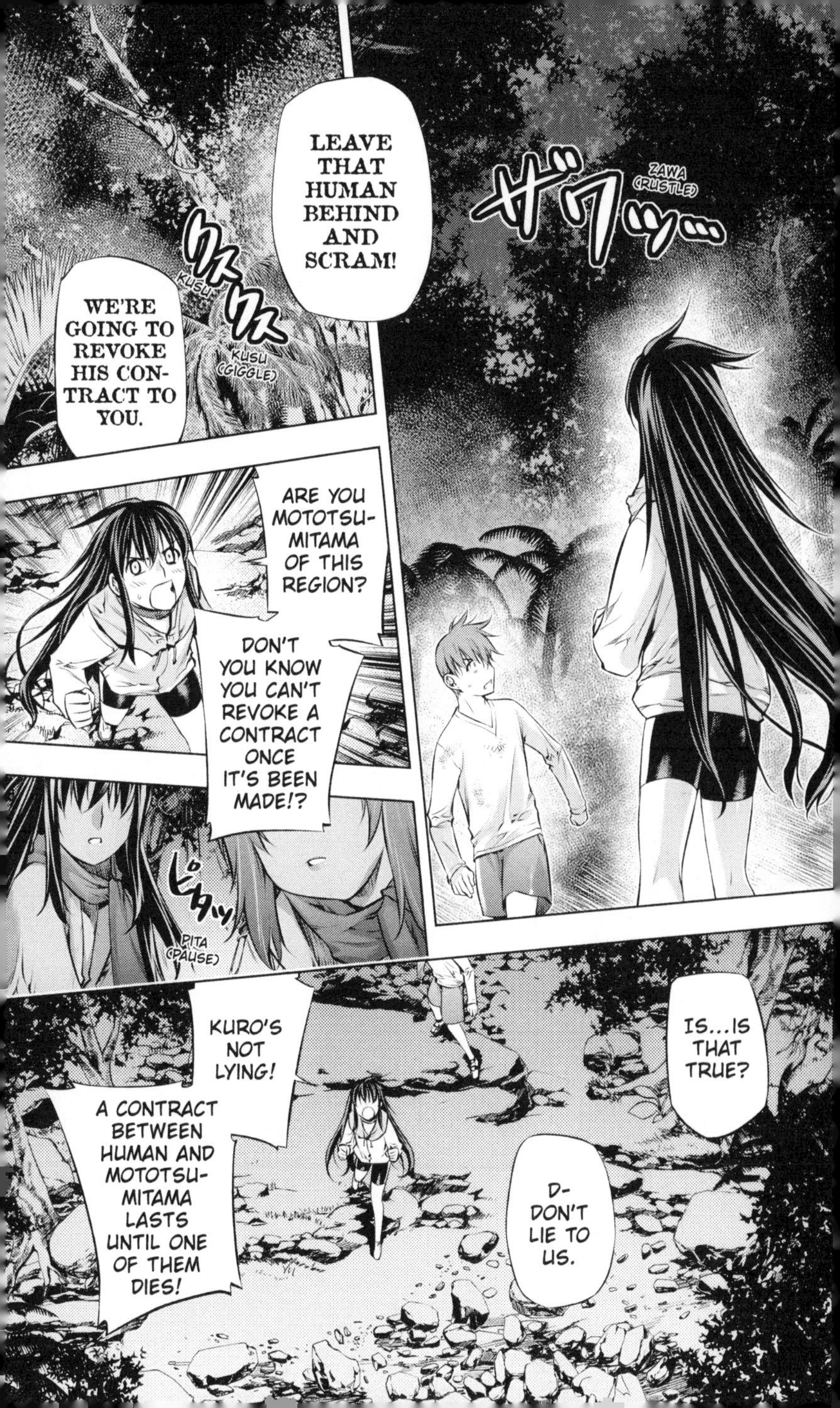
ZAWA (RUSTLE)
LEAVE THAT HUMAN BEHIND AND SCRAM!
KUSU KUSU (GIGGLE)
WE'RE GOING TO REVOKE HIS CONTRACT TO YOU.
ARE YOU MOTOTSUMITAMA OF THIS REGION?
DON'T YOU KNOW YOU CAN'T REVOKE A CONTRACT ONCE IT'S BEEN MADE!?
PITA (PAUSE)
IS...IS THAT TRUE?
D-DON'T LIE TO US.
KURO'S NOT LYING!
A CONTRACT BETWEEN HUMAN AND MOTOTSUMITAMA LASTS UNTIL ONE OF THEM DIES!

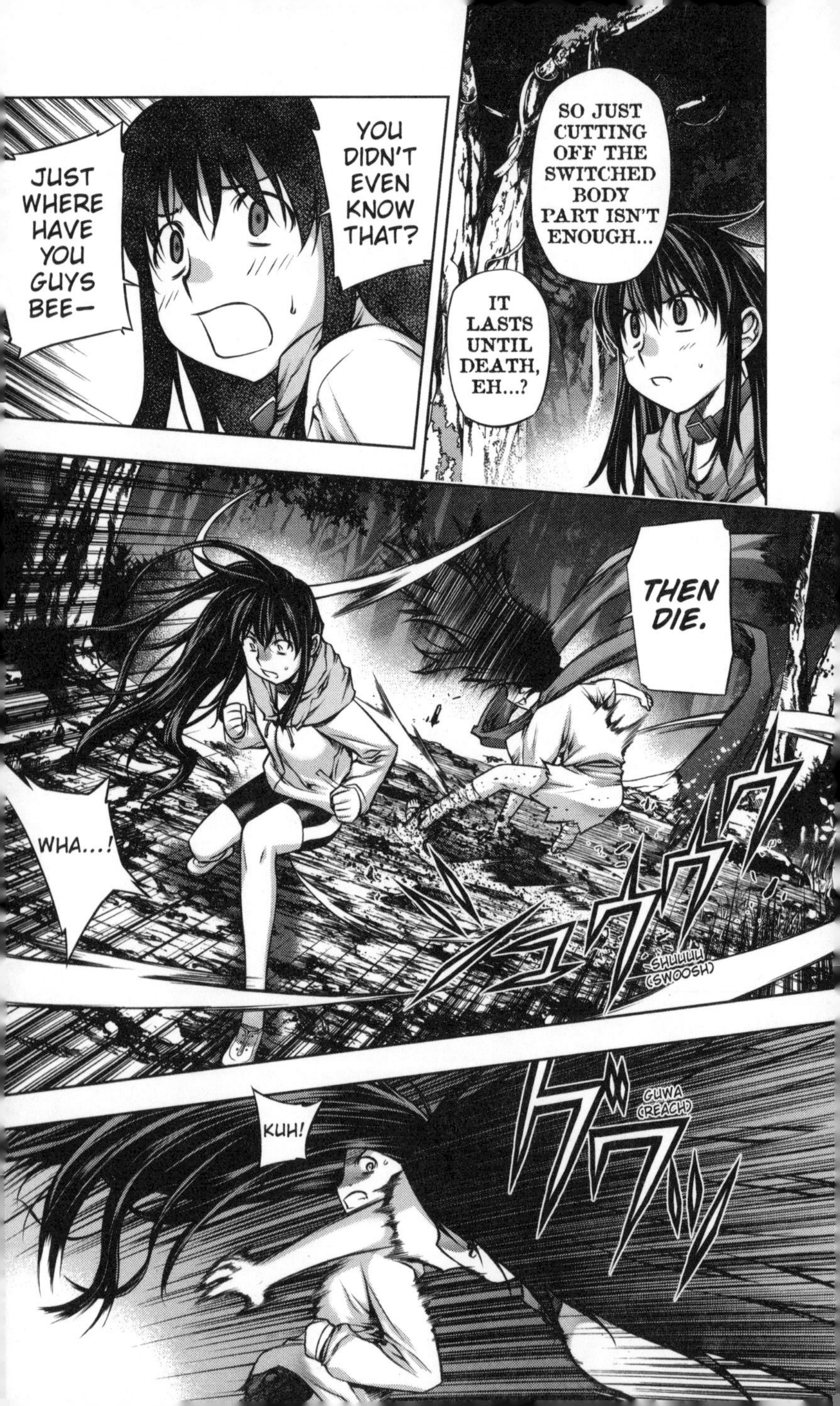
SO JUST CUTTING OFF THE SWITCHED BODY PART ISN'T ENOUGH...
IT LASTS UNTIL DEATH, EH...?
YOU DIDN'T EVEN KNOW THAT?
JUST WHERE HAVE YOU GUYS BEE—
THEN DIE.
WHA...!
SHUUUUU (SWOOSH)
GUWA (REACH)
KUH!

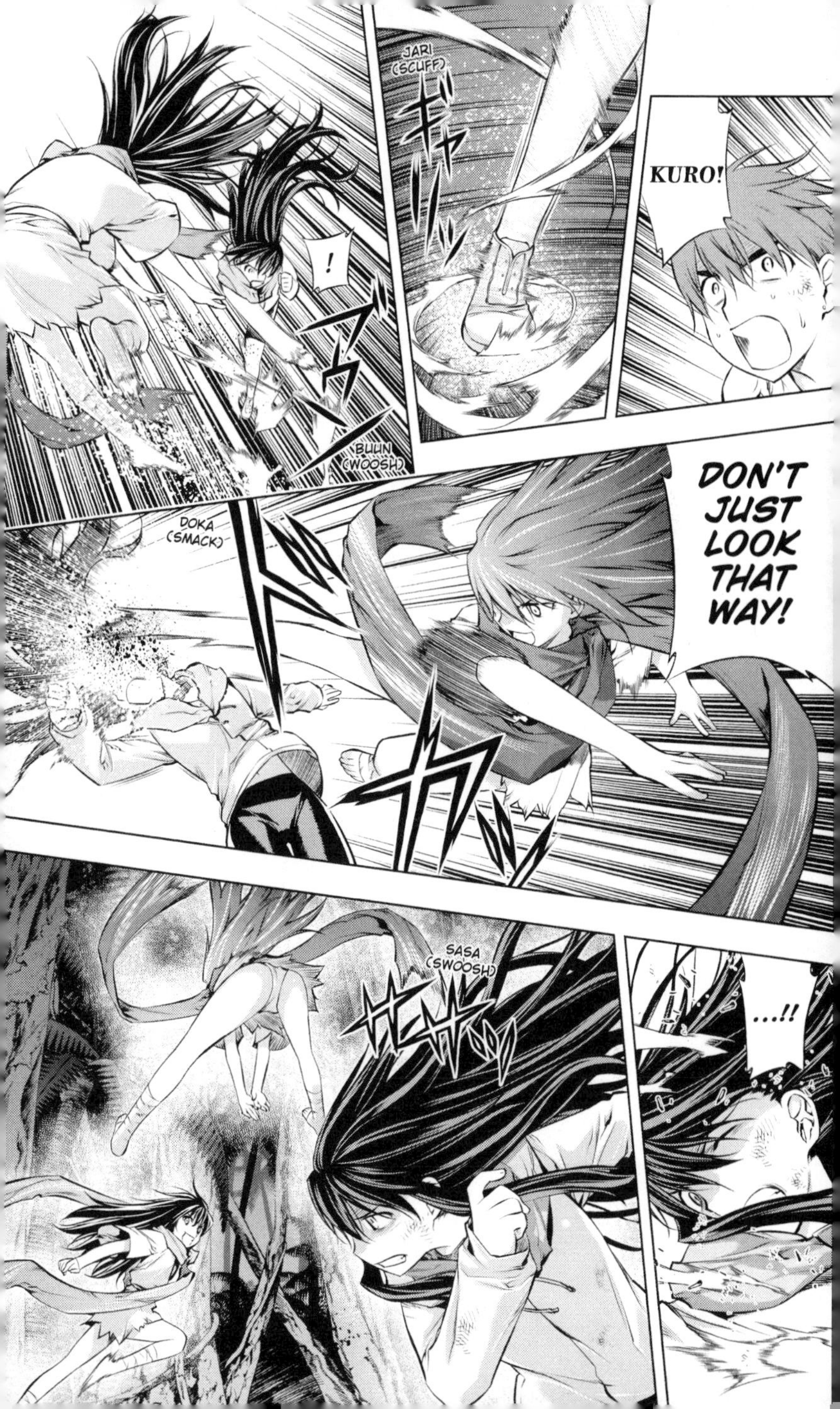
KURO!
JARI (SCUFF)
!
BULN (WOOSH)
DON'T JUST LOOK THAT WAY!
DOKA (SMACK)
...!!
SASA (SWOOSH)

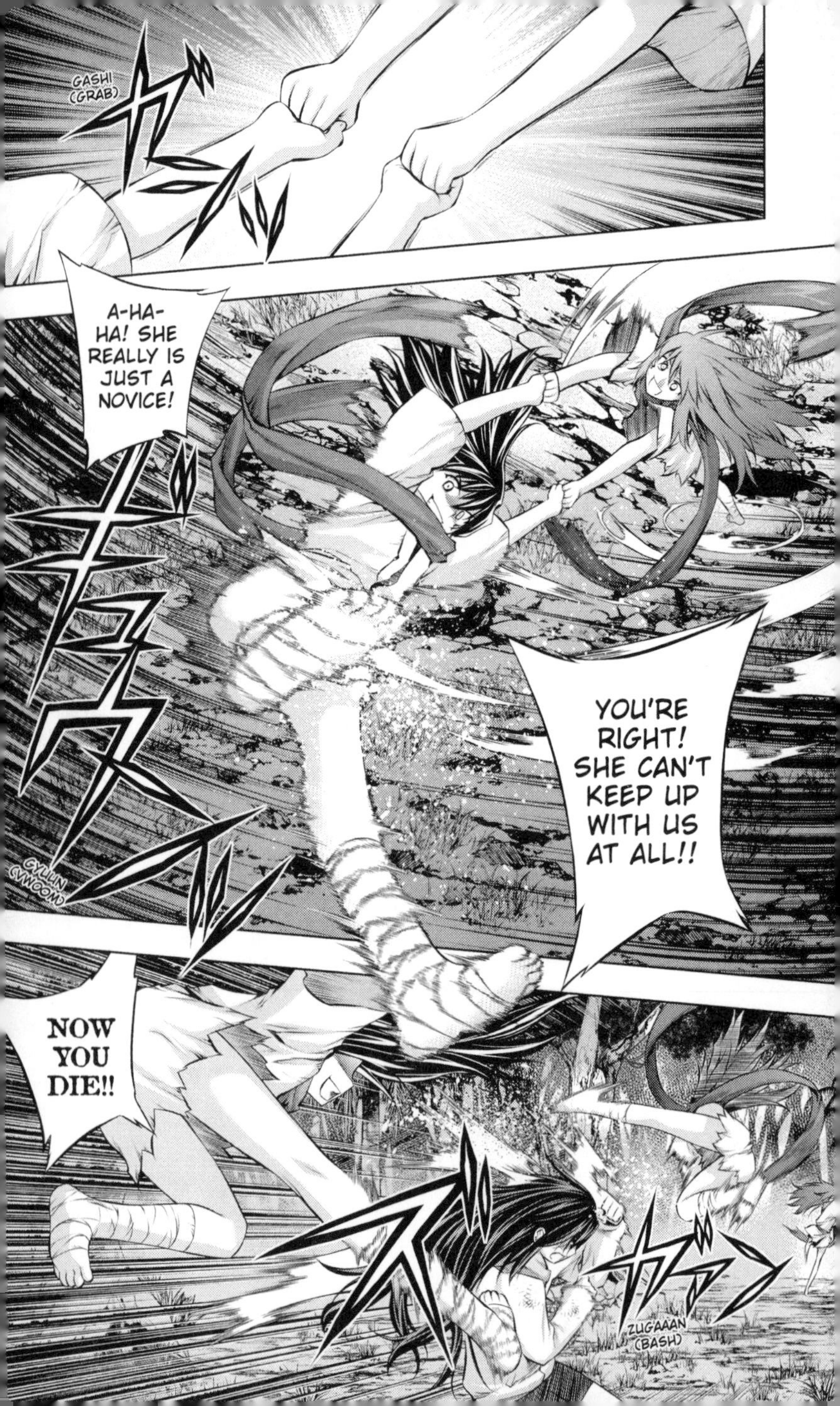
GASHI (GRAB)
A-HA-HA! SHE REALLY IS JUST A NOVICE!
YOU'RE RIGHT! SHE CAN'T KEEP UP WITH US AT ALL!!
GYUUN (VWOOM)
NOW YOU DIE!!
ZUGAAAN (BASH)

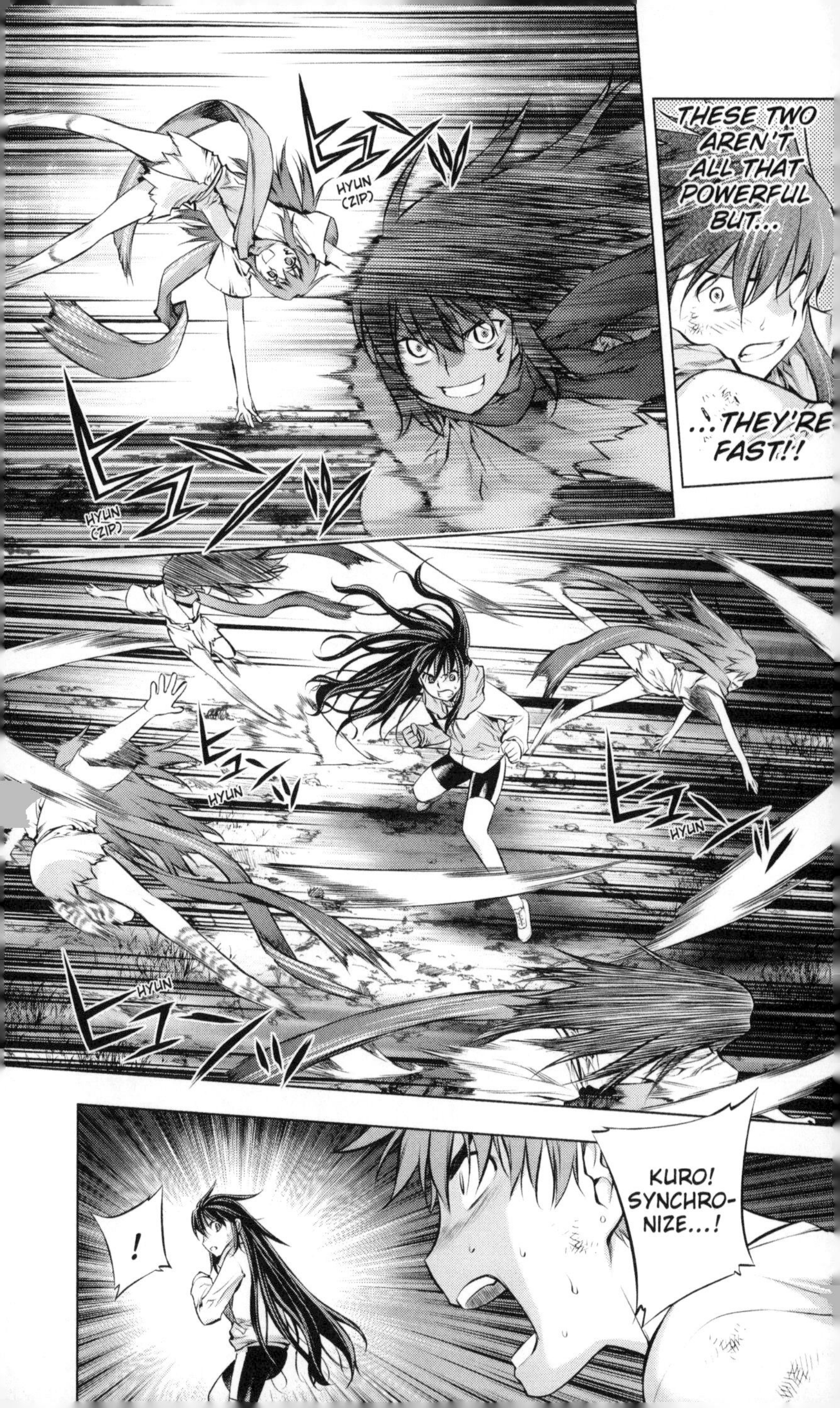
THESE TWO AREN'T ALL THAT POWERFUL BUT...
...THEY'RE FAST!!
HYUN (ZIP)
HYUN (ZIP)
HYUN
HYUN
HYUN
KURO! SYNCHRO-NIZE...!
!

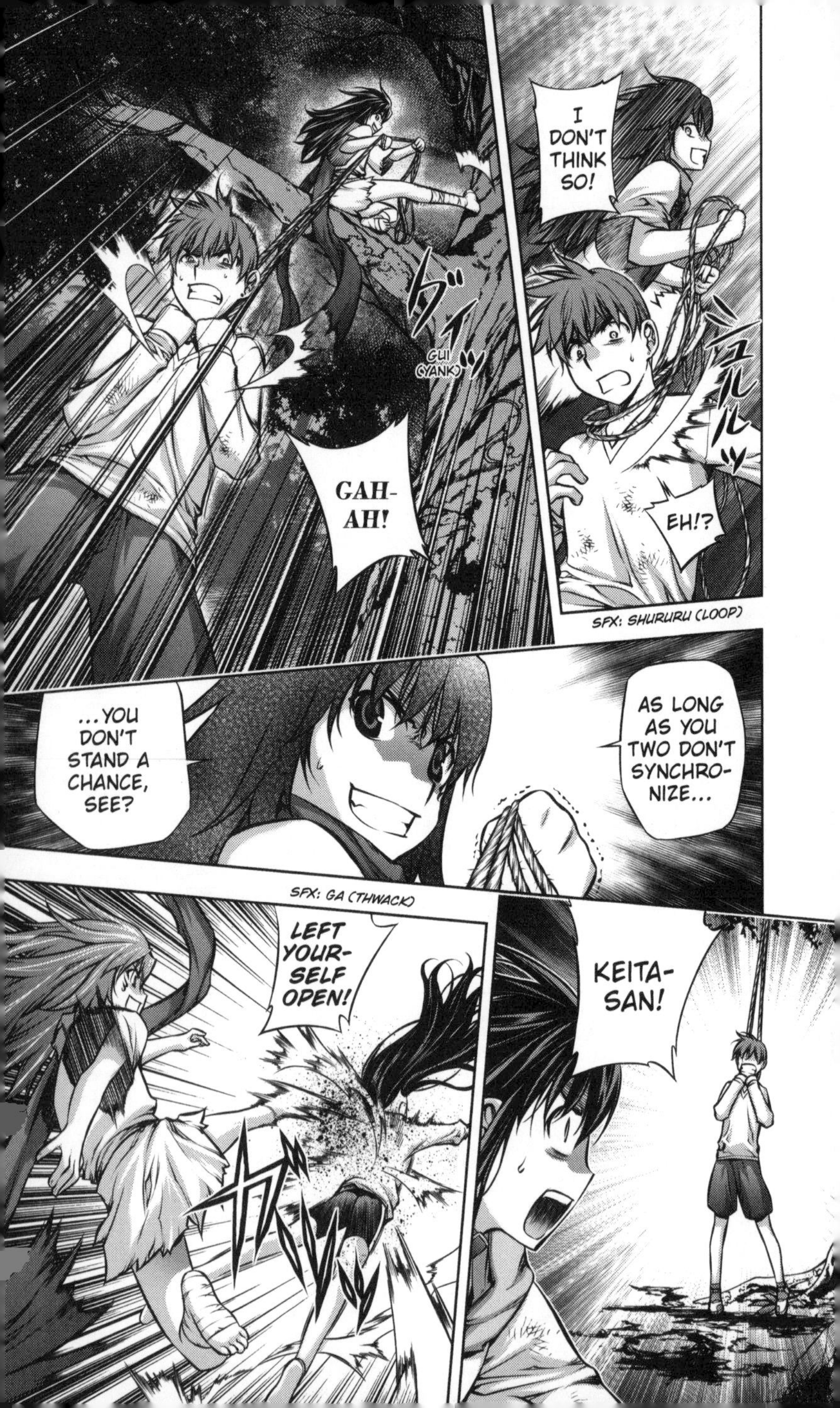

I DON'T THINK SO!
EH!?
SFX: SHURURU (LOOP)
GUI (YANK)
GAH-AH!
AS LONG AS YOU TWO DON'T SYNCHRONIZE...
...YOU DON'T STAND A CHANCE, SEE?
KEITA-SAN!
LEFT YOURSELF OPEN!
SFX: GA (THWACK)

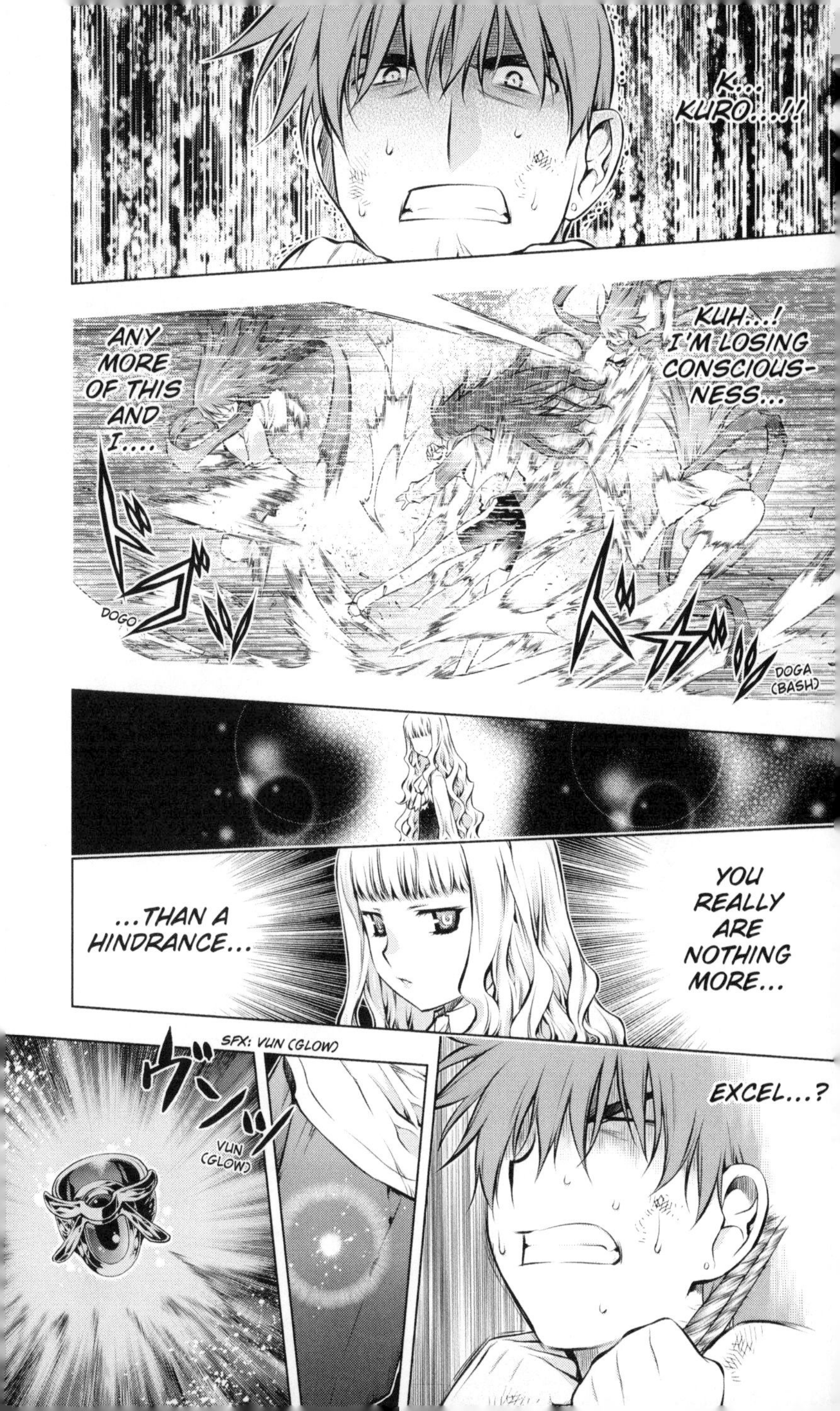
K... KURO...!!
KUH...! I'M LOSING CONSCIOUS-NESS...
ANY MORE OF THIS AND I....
DOGA (BASH)
DOGO
YOU REALLY ARE NOTHING MORE...
...THAN A HINDRANCE...
EXCEL...?
SFX: VUN (GLOW)
VUN (GLOW)

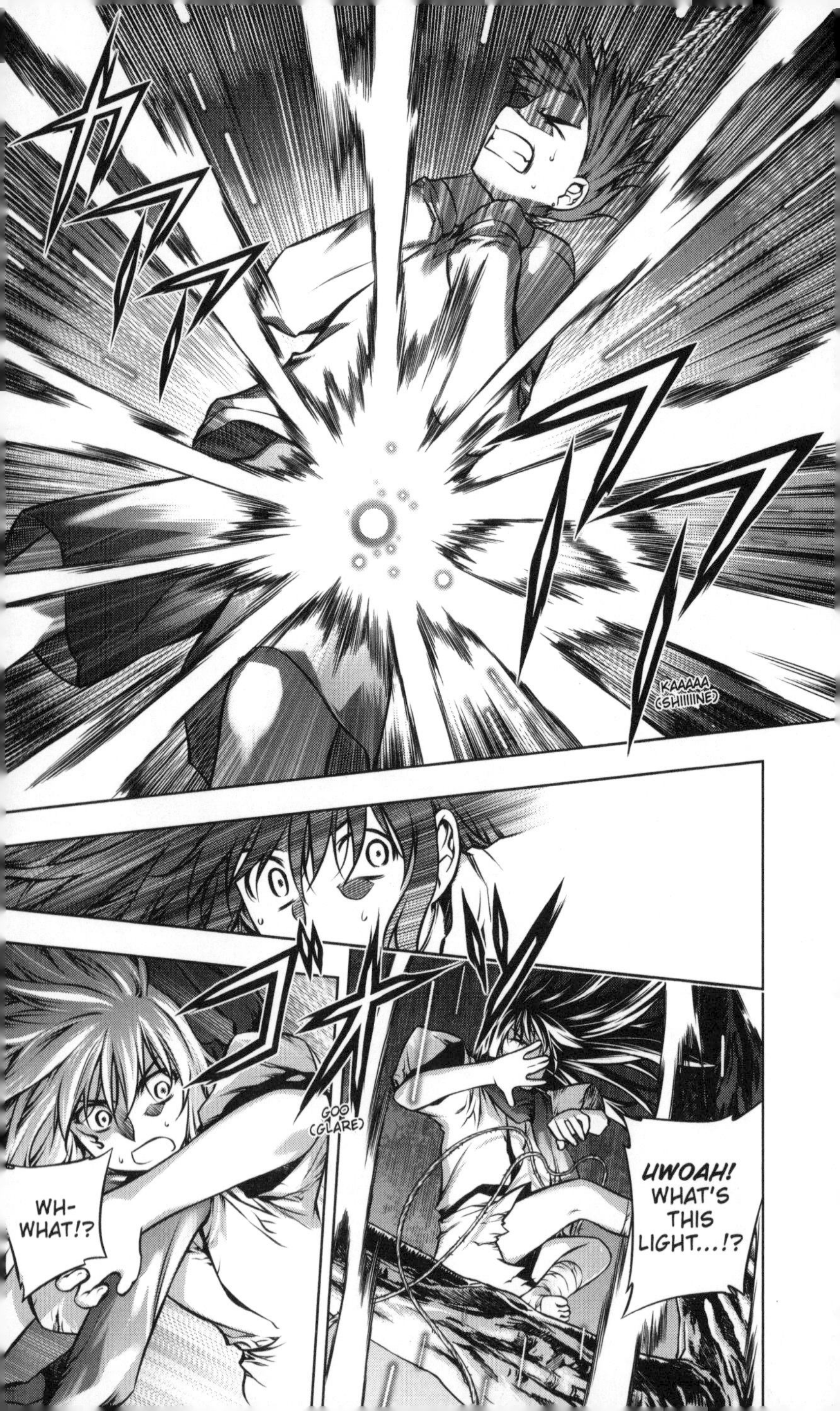

KAAAAA
(SHIIIIINE)
UWOAH! WHAT'S THIS LIGHT...!?
GOO
(GLARE)
WH- WHAT!?

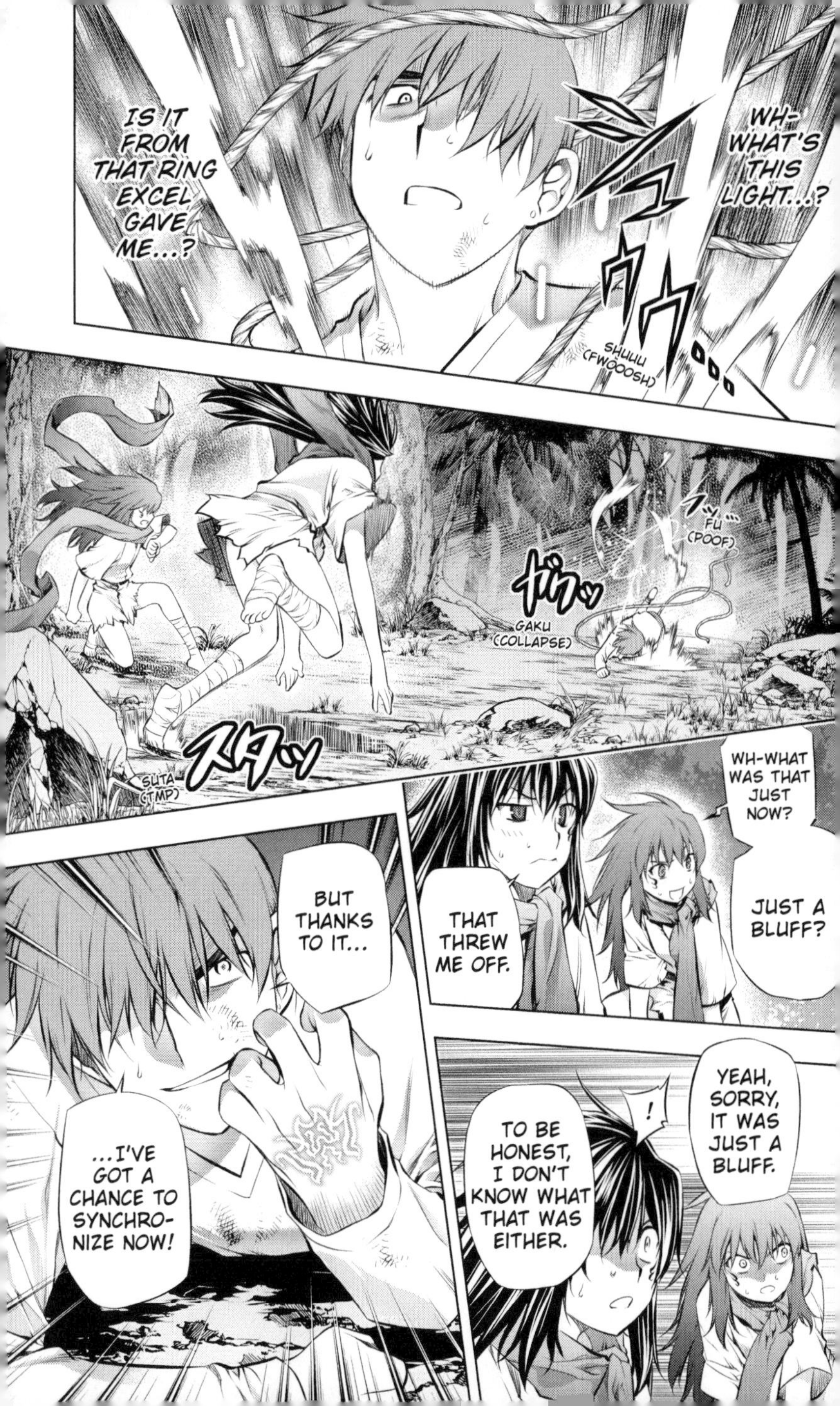
WH-WHAT'S THIS LIGHT...?
IS IT FROM THAT RING EXCEL GAVE ME...?
SHUUU (FWOOOSH)
FU (POOF)
ガクッ
GAKU (COLLAPSE)
スタッ
SUTA (TMP)
WH-WHAT WAS THAT JUST NOW?
JUST A BLUFF?
THAT THREW ME OFF.
YEAH, SORRY, IT WAS JUST A BLUFF.
!
TO BE HONEST, I DON'T KNOW WHAT THAT WAS EITHER.
BUT THANKS TO IT...
...I'VE GOT A CHANCE TO SYNCHRONIZE NOW!

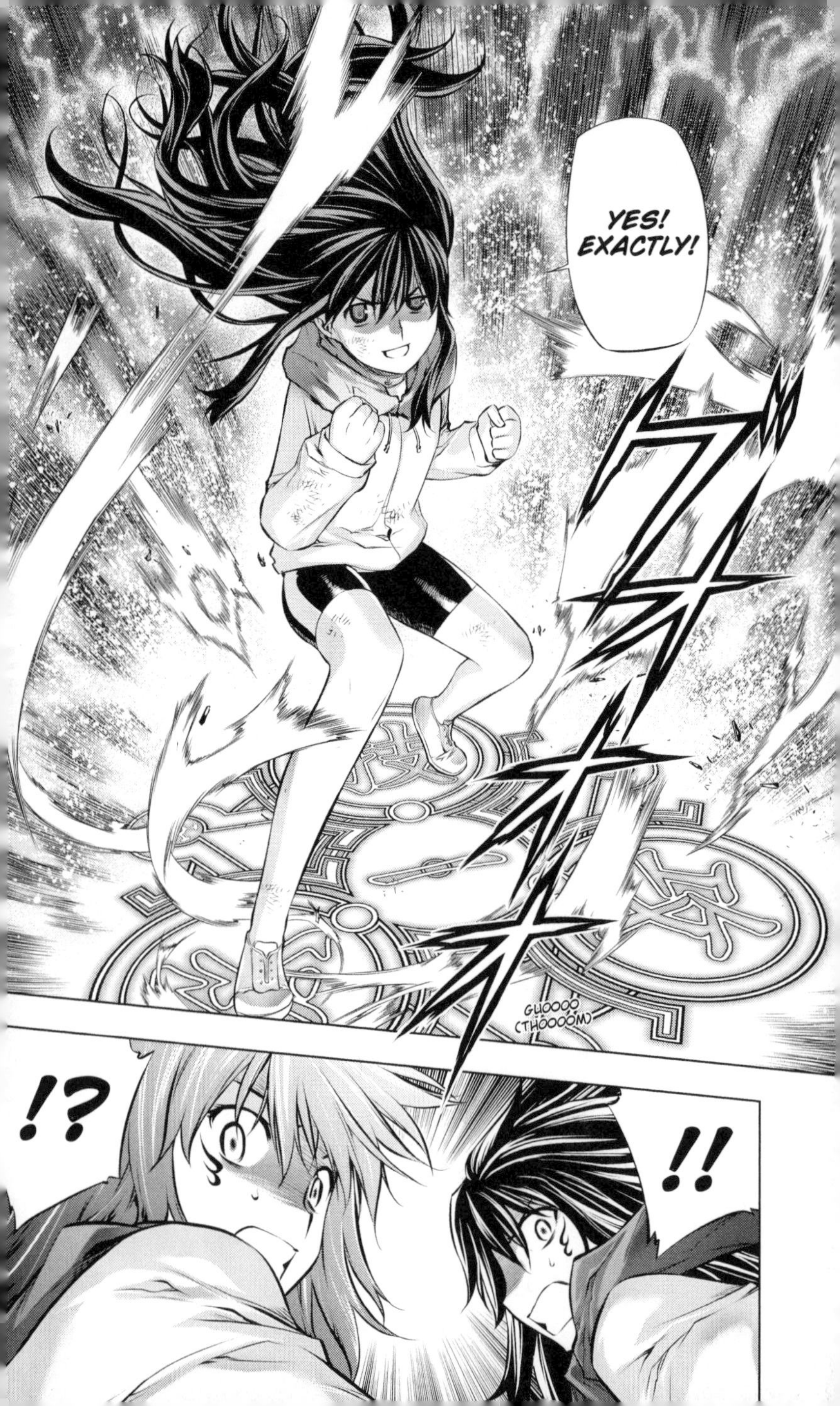
YES! EXACTLY!
GUOOOO (THOOOOM)
!!
!?

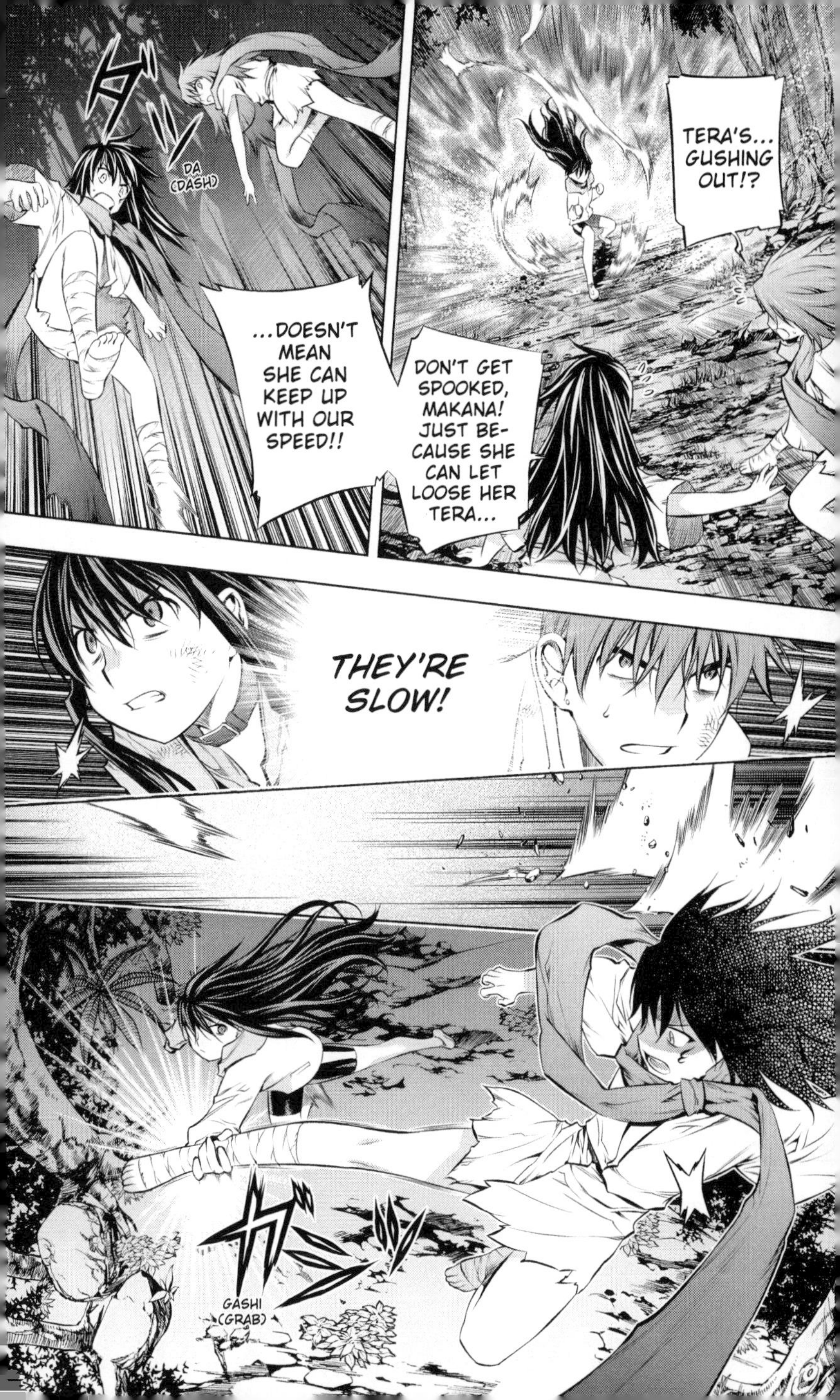
TERA'S... GUSHING OUT!?
DON'T GET SPOOKED, MAKANA! JUST BE-CAUSE SHE CAN LET LOOSE HER TERA...
...DOESN'T MEAN SHE CAN KEEP UP WITH OUR SPEED!!
DA (DASH)
THEY'RE SLOW!
GASHI (GRAB)

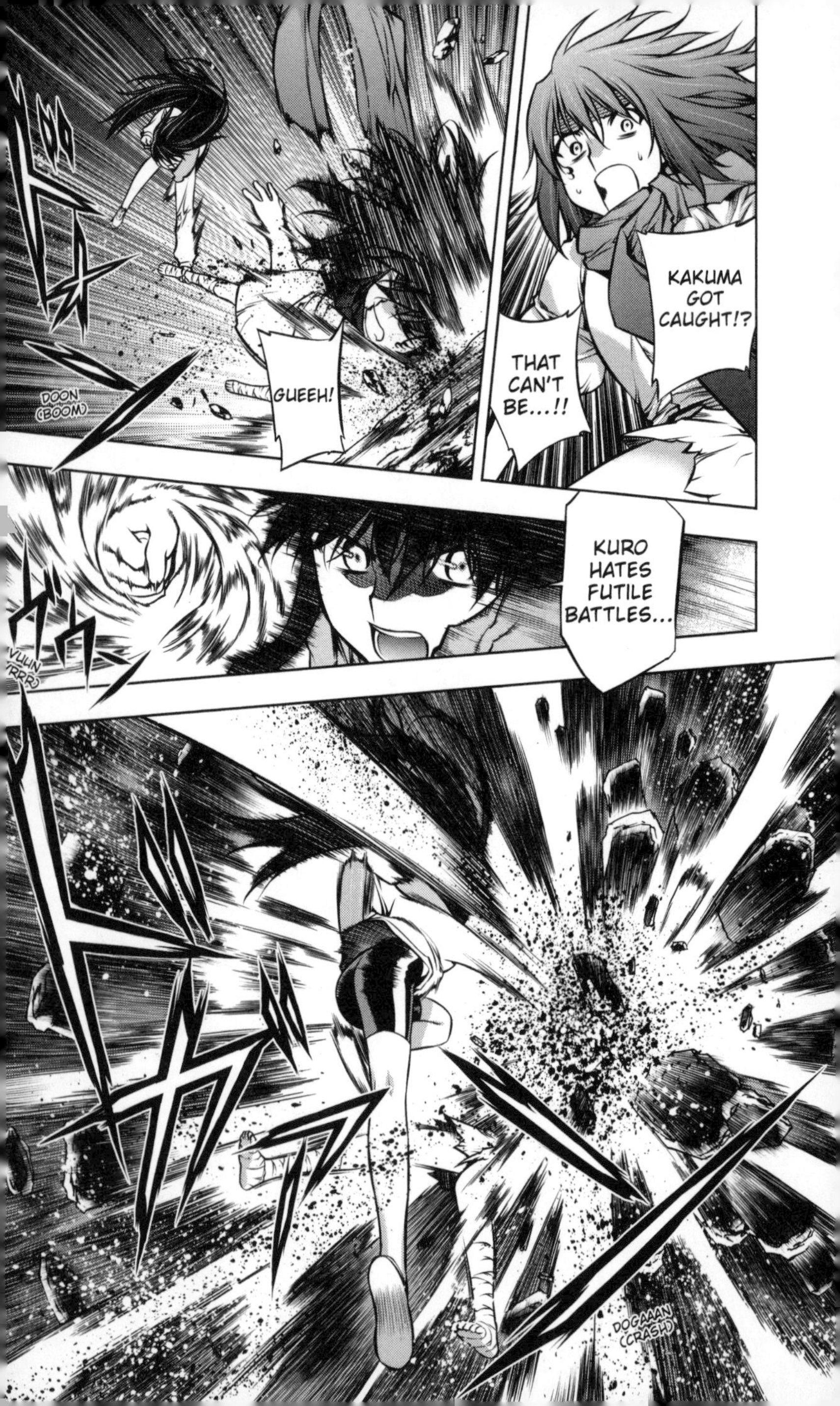
KAKUMA GOT CAUGHT!?
THAT CAN'T BE...!!
GUEEH!
DOON (BOOM)
KURO HATES FUTILE BATTLES...
VUUN (RRR)
DOGAAAN (CRASH)

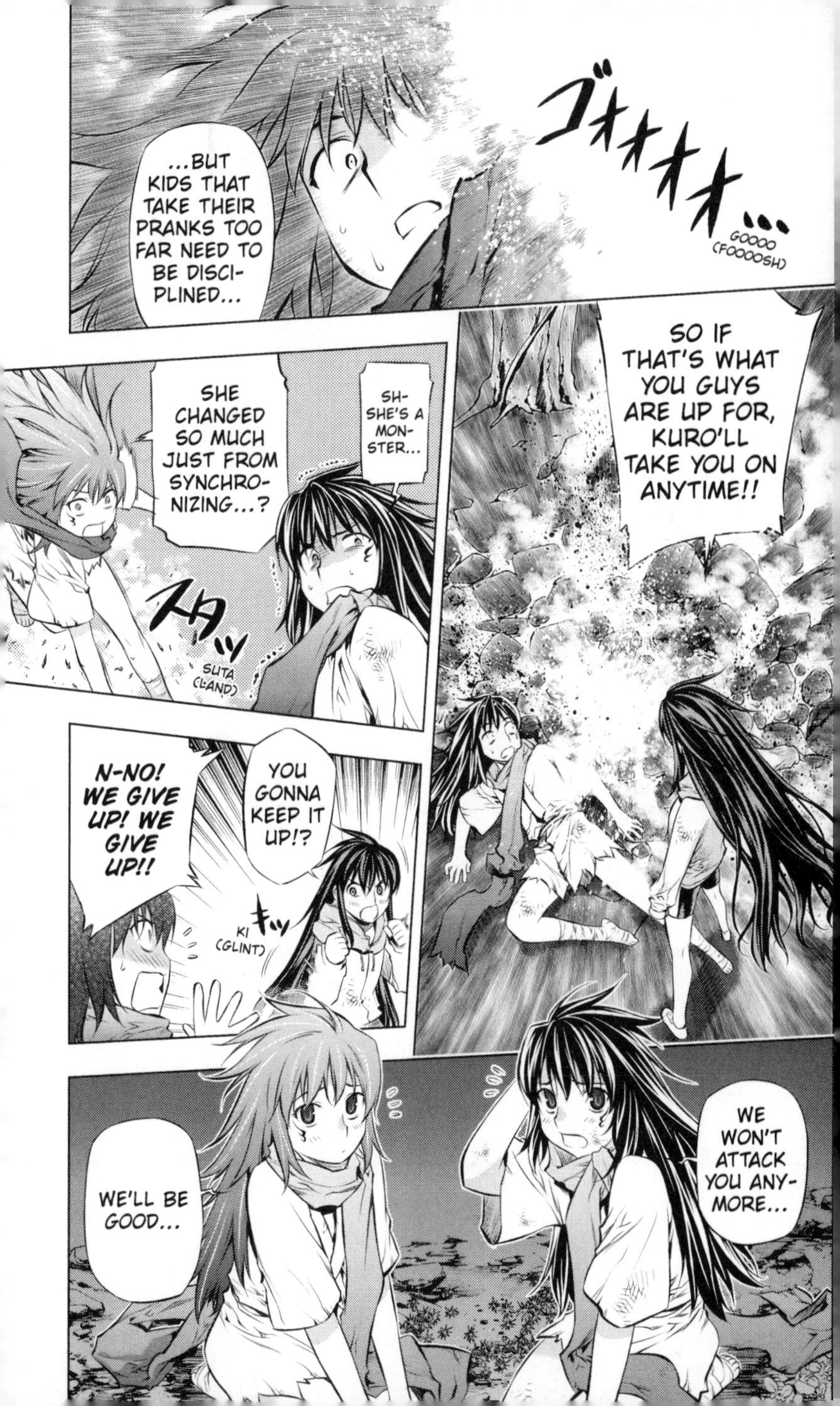
ゴォォォォ…
GOOOO (FOOOOSH)
...BUT KIDS THAT TAKE THEIR PRANKS TOO FAR NEED TO BE DISCIPLINED...
SO IF THAT'S WHAT YOU GUYS ARE UP FOR, KURO'LL TAKE YOU ON ANYTIME!!
SH-SHE'S A MONSTER...
SHE CHANGED SO MUCH JUST FROM SYNCHRONIZING...?
スタッ
SUTA (LAND)
YOU GONNA KEEP IT UP!?
キッ
KI (GLINT)
N-NO! WE GIVE UP! WE GIVE UP!!
WE WON'T ATTACK YOU ANYMORE...
WE'LL BE GOOD...

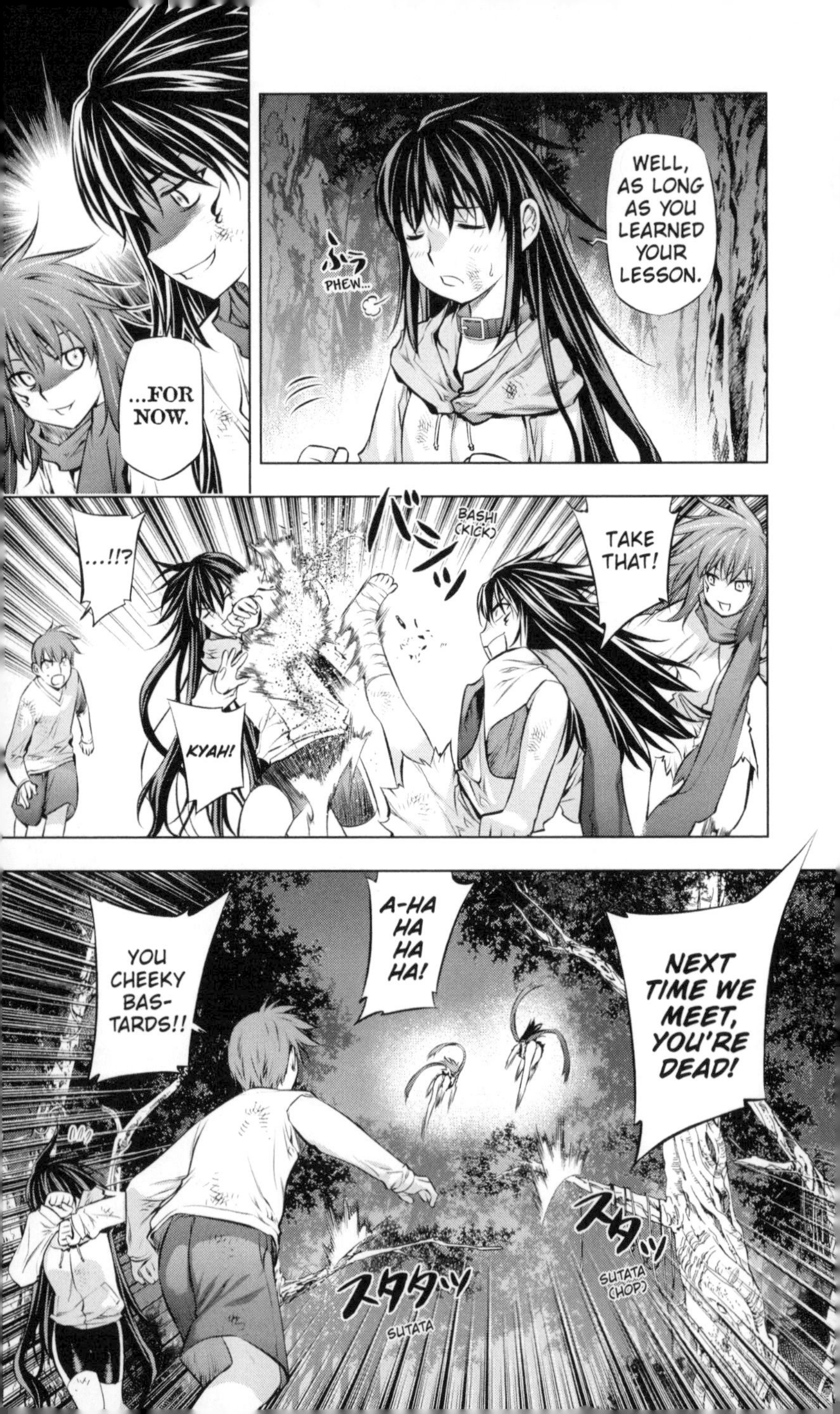
ふぅ
PHEW...
WELL, AS LONG AS YOU LEARNED YOUR LESSON.
...FOR NOW.
TAKE THAT!
バシッ
BASHI (KICK)
...!!?
KYAH!
NEXT TIME WE MEET, YOU'RE DEAD!
A-HA HA HA HA!
YOU CHEEKY BAS-TARDS!!
スタッ
SUTATA (HOP)
スタタッ
SUTATA

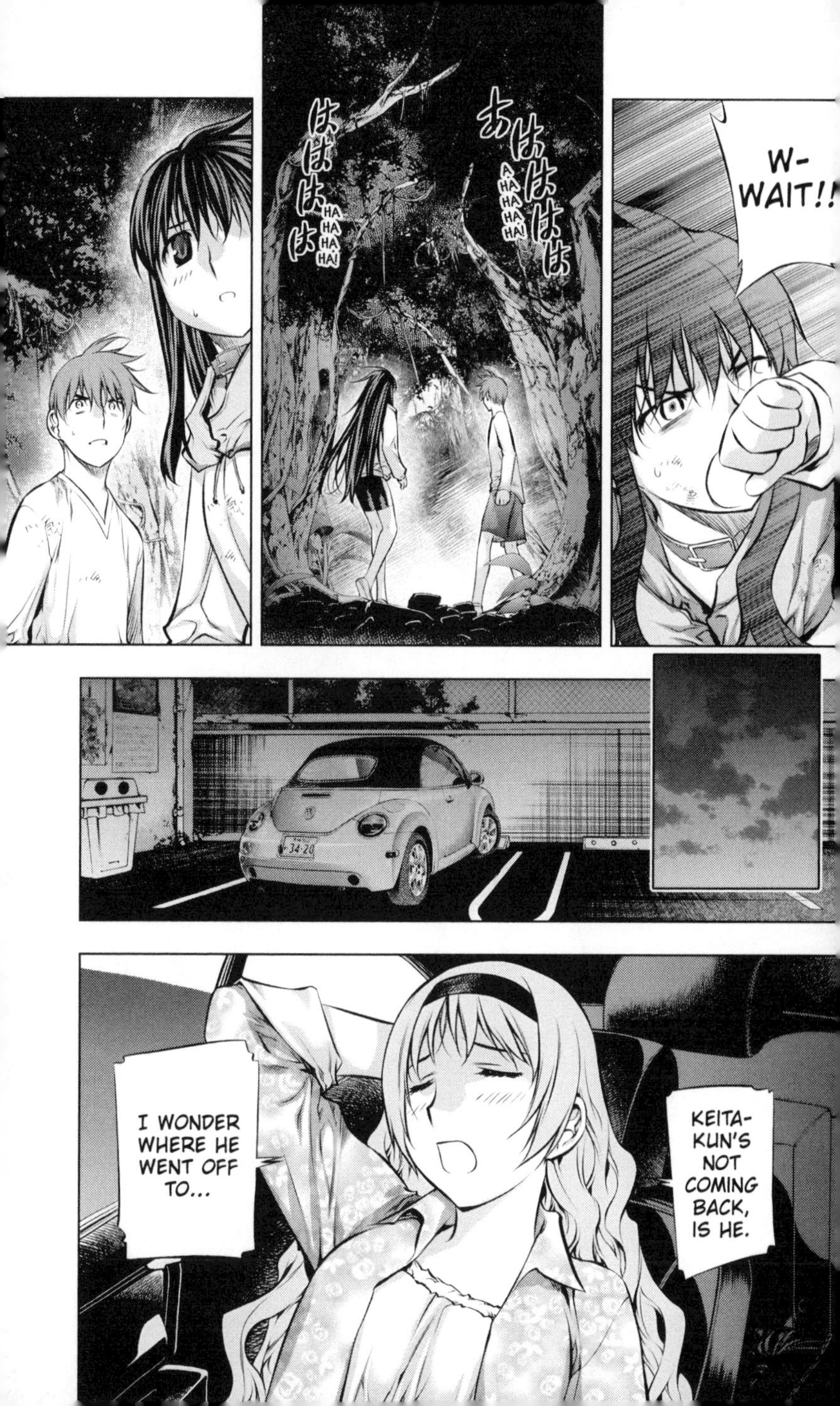
W-WAIT!!
あははは
AHAHAHAHA!
はははは
HAHAHAHA!
KEITA-KUN'S NOT COMING BACK, IS HE.
I WONDER WHERE HE WENT OFF TO...

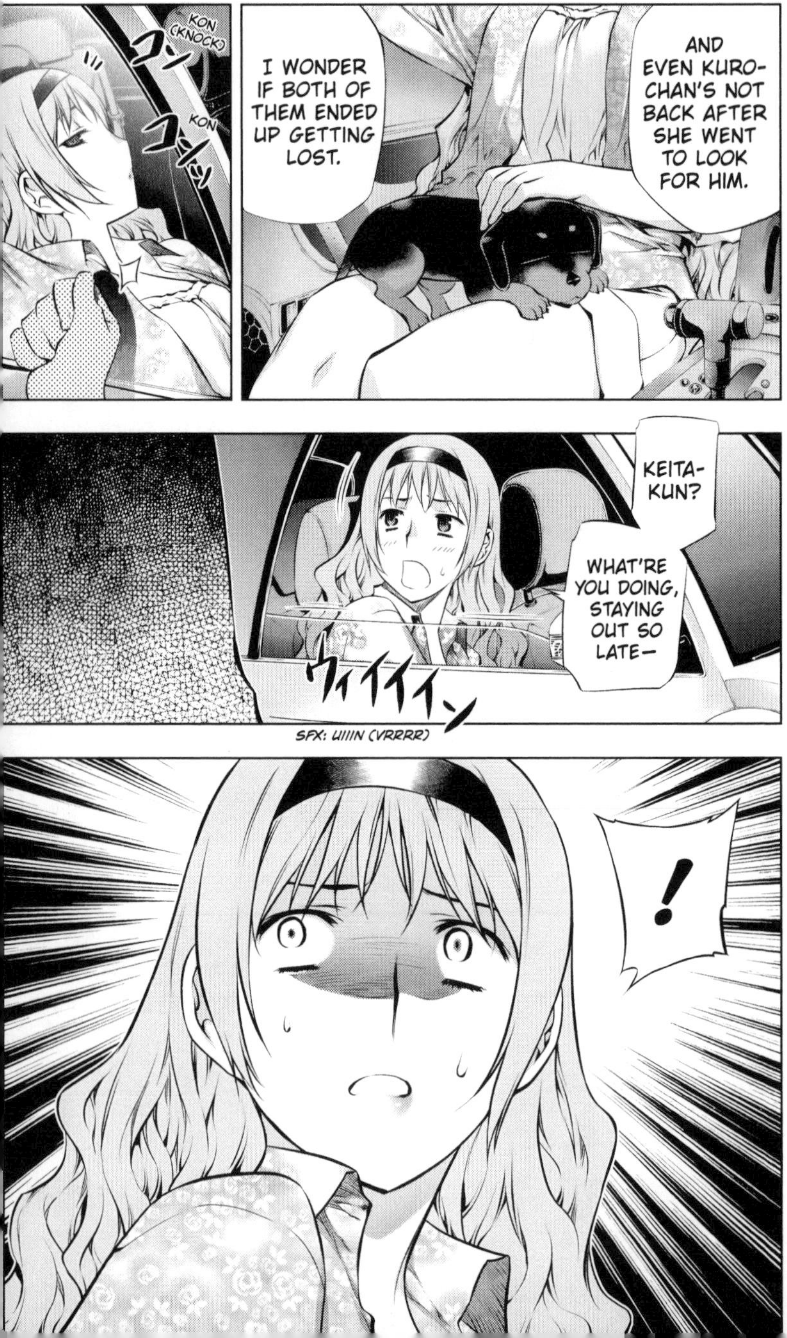
AND EVEN KURO-CHAN'S NOT BACK AFTER SHE WENT TO LOOK FOR HIM.
I WONDER IF BOTH OF THEM ENDED UP GETTING LOST.
コン
KON (KNOCK)
コンッ
KON
KEITA-KUN?
WHAT'RE YOU DOING, STAYING OUT SO LATE—
ウィイイイン
SFX: UIIIN (VRRRR)
!

技

四

BLACK GOD

which maintains balance in the world.

Nirai Kanai Arc

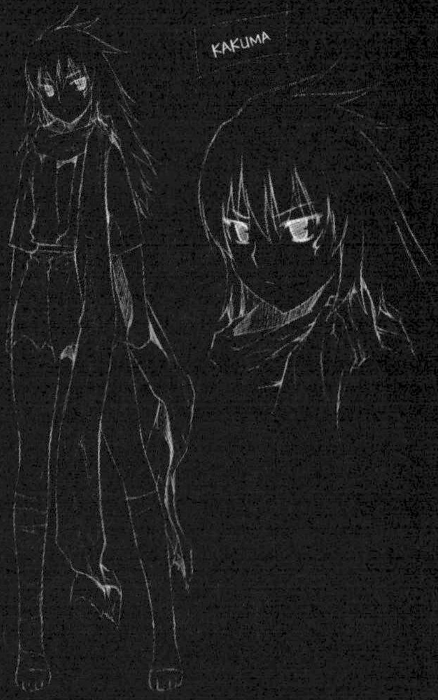
KAKUMA

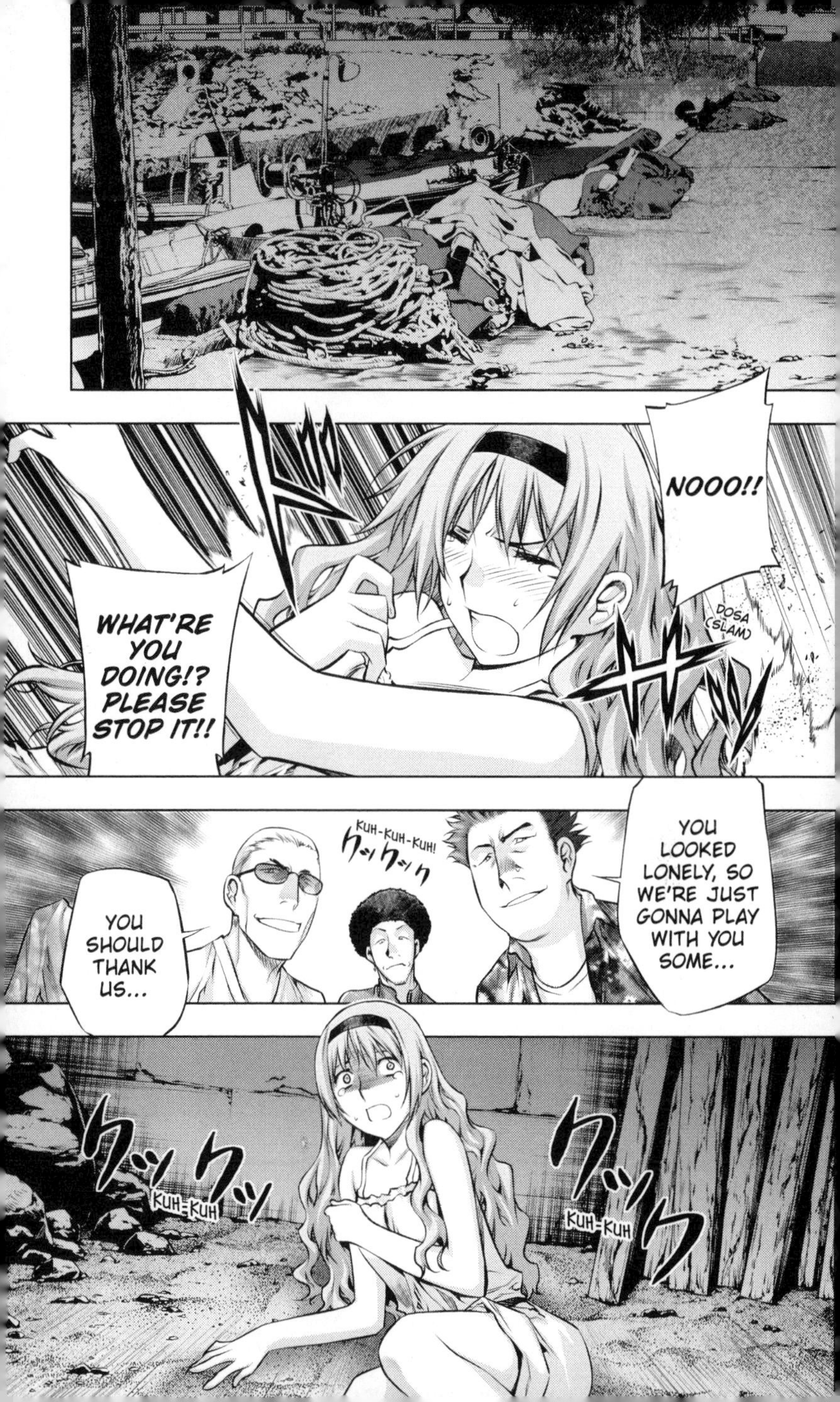
NOOO!!
DOSA (SLAM)
WHAT'RE YOU DOING!? PLEASE STOP IT!!
YOU LOOKED LONELY, SO WE'RE JUST GONNA PLAY WITH YOU SOME...
KUH-KUH-KUH!
YOU SHOULD THANK US...
KUH-KUH
KUH-KUH

FATE.24 MISTAKE •REUNION

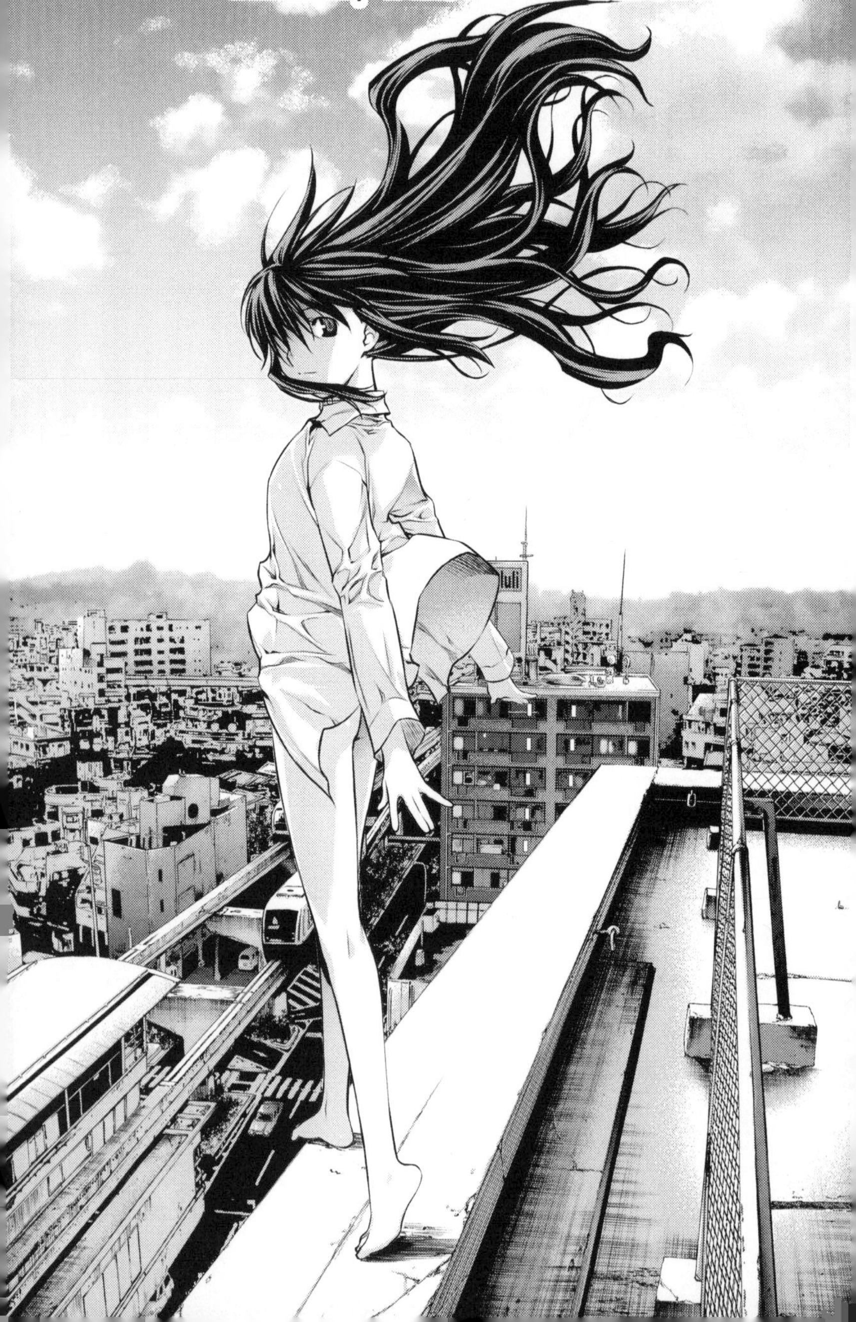

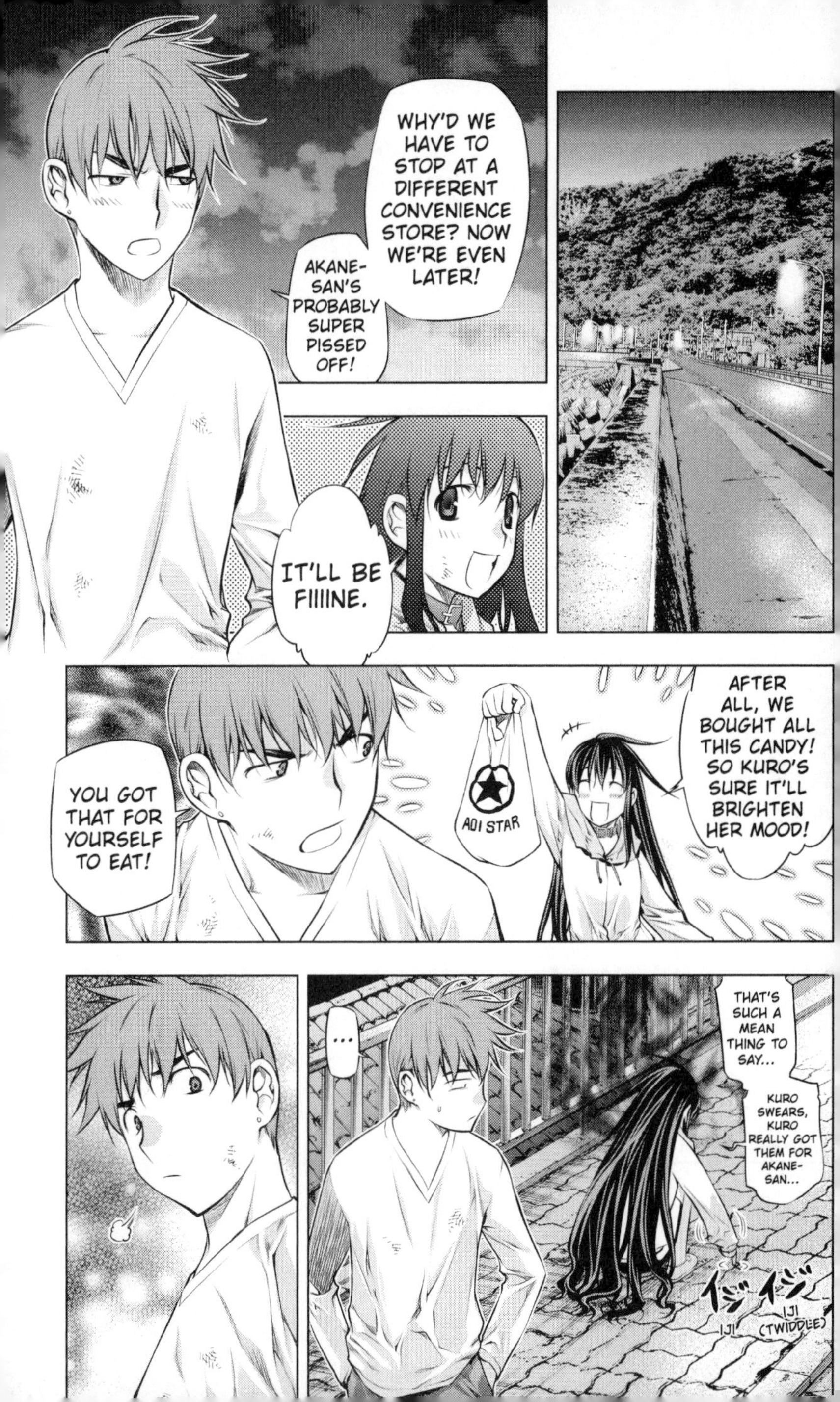
WHY'D WE HAVE TO STOP AT A DIFFERENT CONVENIENCE STORE? NOW WE'RE EVEN LATER!
AKANE-SAN'S PROBABLY SUPER PISSED OFF!
IT'LL BE FIIIINE.
AFTER ALL, WE BOUGHT ALL THIS CANDY! SO KURO'S SURE IT'LL BRIGHTEN HER MOOD!
AOI STAR
YOU GOT THAT FOR YOURSELF TO EAT!
THAT'S SUCH A MEAN THING TO SAY...
KURO SWEARS, KURO REALLY GOT THEM FOR AKANE-SAN...
...
イジ イジ
IJI IJI (TWIDDLE)

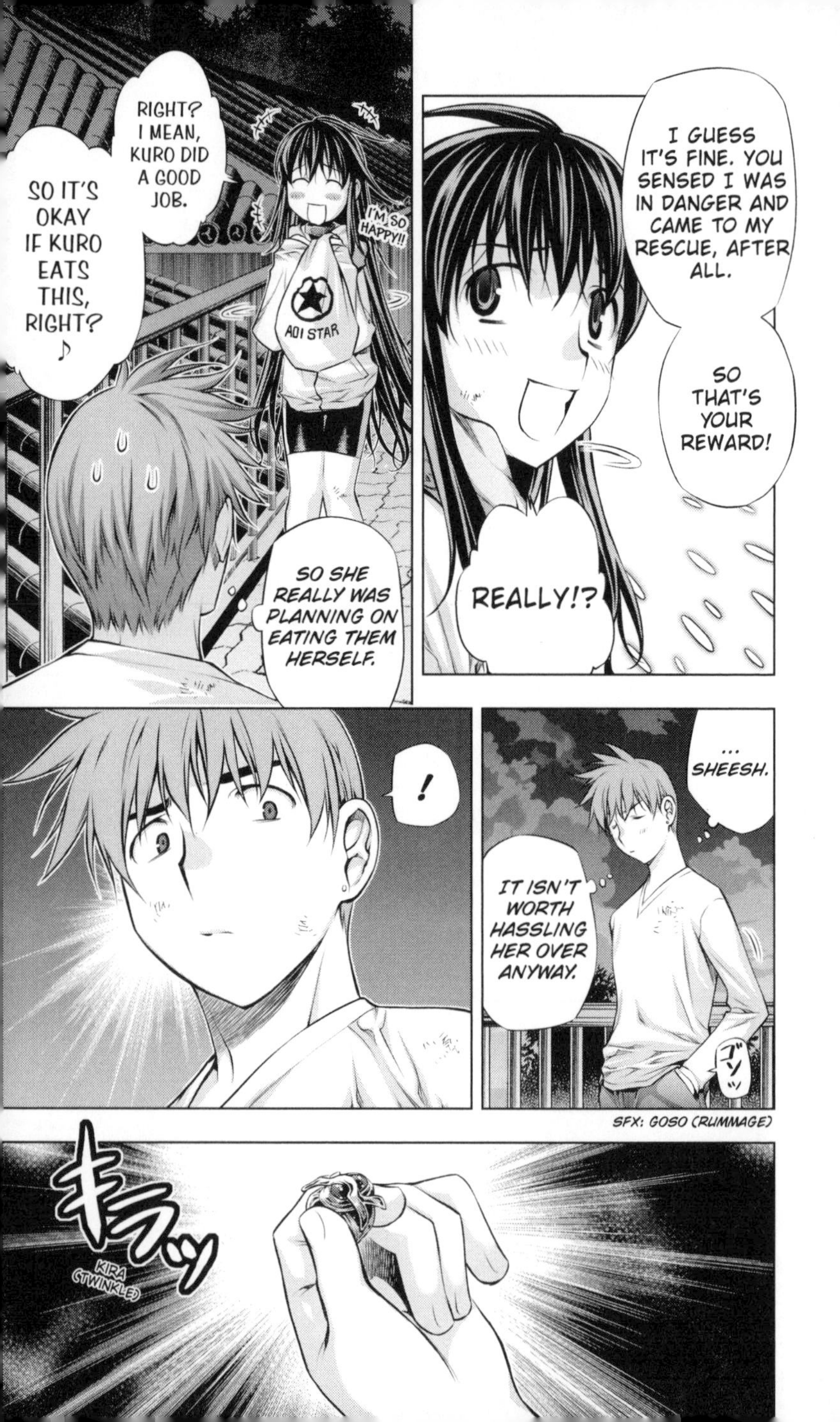
I GUESS IT'S FINE. YOU SENSED I WAS IN DANGER AND CAME TO MY RESCUE, AFTER ALL.
SO THAT'S YOUR REWARD!
REALLY!?
RIGHT? I MEAN, KURO DID A GOOD JOB.
SO IT'S OKAY IF KURO EATS THIS, RIGHT? ♪
I'M SO HAPPY!!
SO SHE REALLY WAS PLANNING ON EATING THEM HERSELF.
... SHEESH.
IT ISN'T WORTH HASSLING HER OVER ANYWAY.
SFX: GOSO (RUMMAGE)
!
KIRA (TWINKLE)

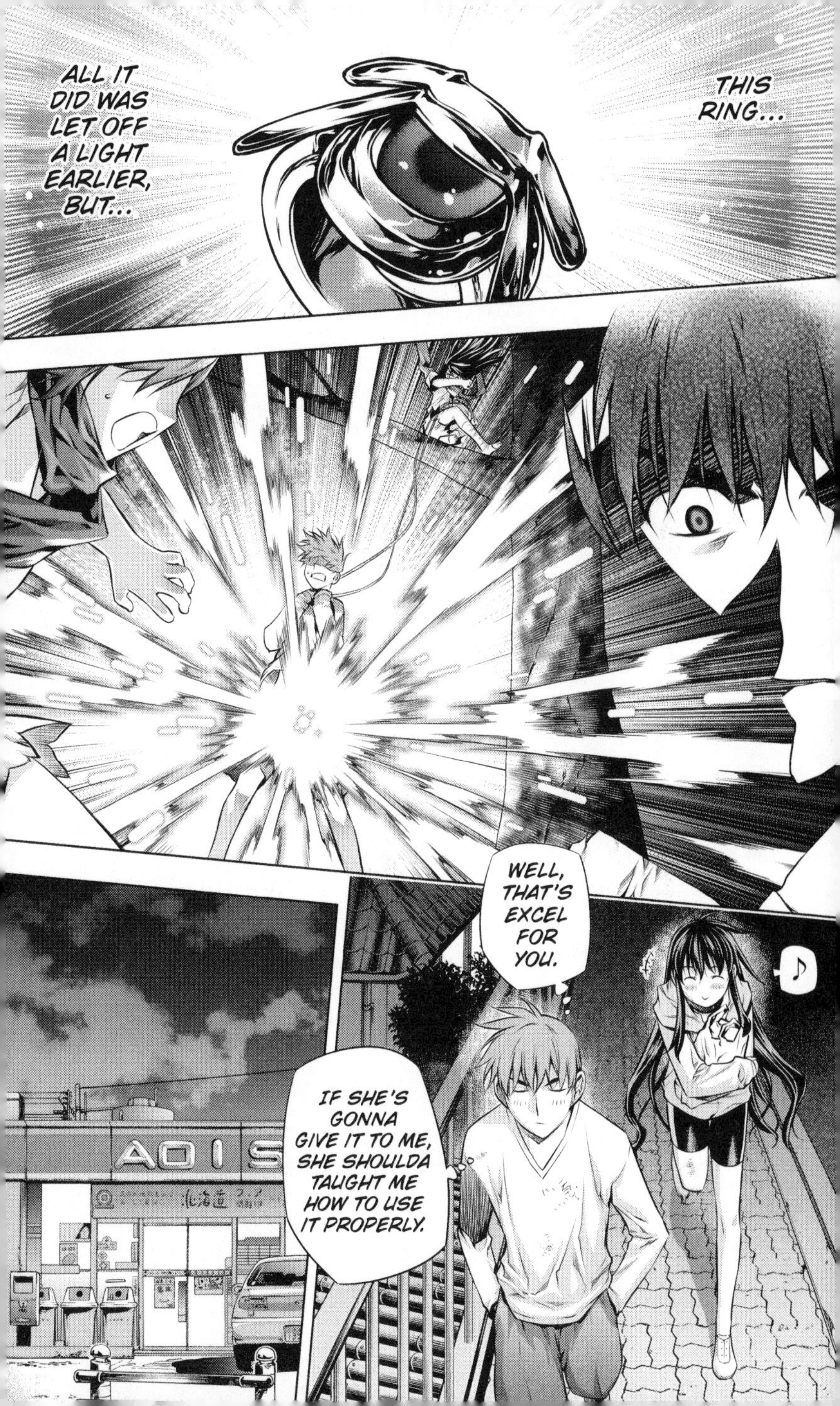
THIS RING...
ALL IT DID WAS LET OFF A LIGHT EARLIER, BUT...
WELL, THAT'S EXCEL FOR YOU.
IF SHE'S GONNA GIVE IT TO ME, SHE SHOULDA TAUGHT ME HOW TO USE IT PROPERLY.

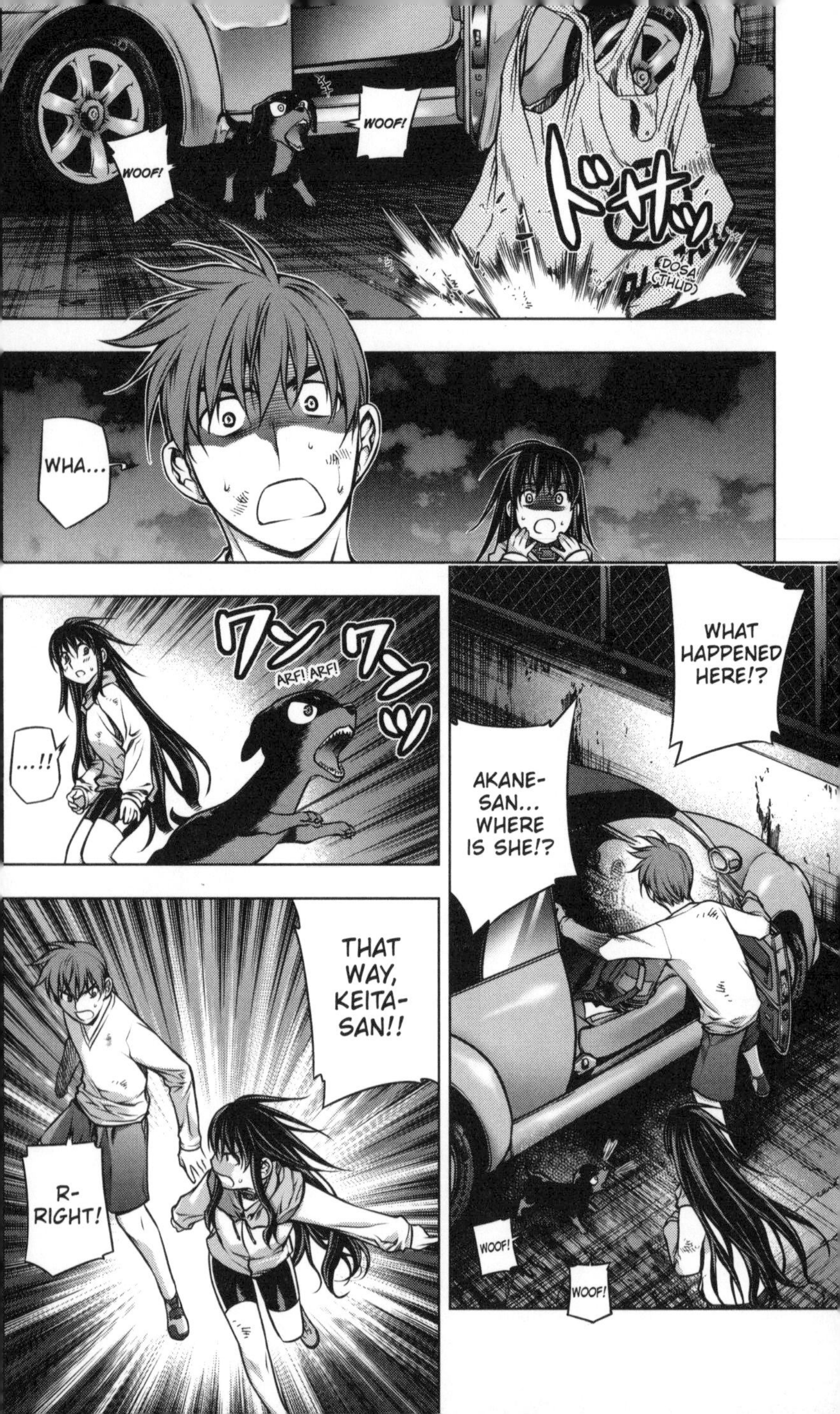

ドサッ
(DOSA (THUD))
WOOF!
WOOF!
WHA...
WHAT HAPPENED HERE!?
AKANE-SAN... WHERE IS SHE!?
WOOF!
WOOF!
ワンワンッ
ARF! ARF!
...!!
THAT WAY, KEITA-SAN!!
R-RIGHT!

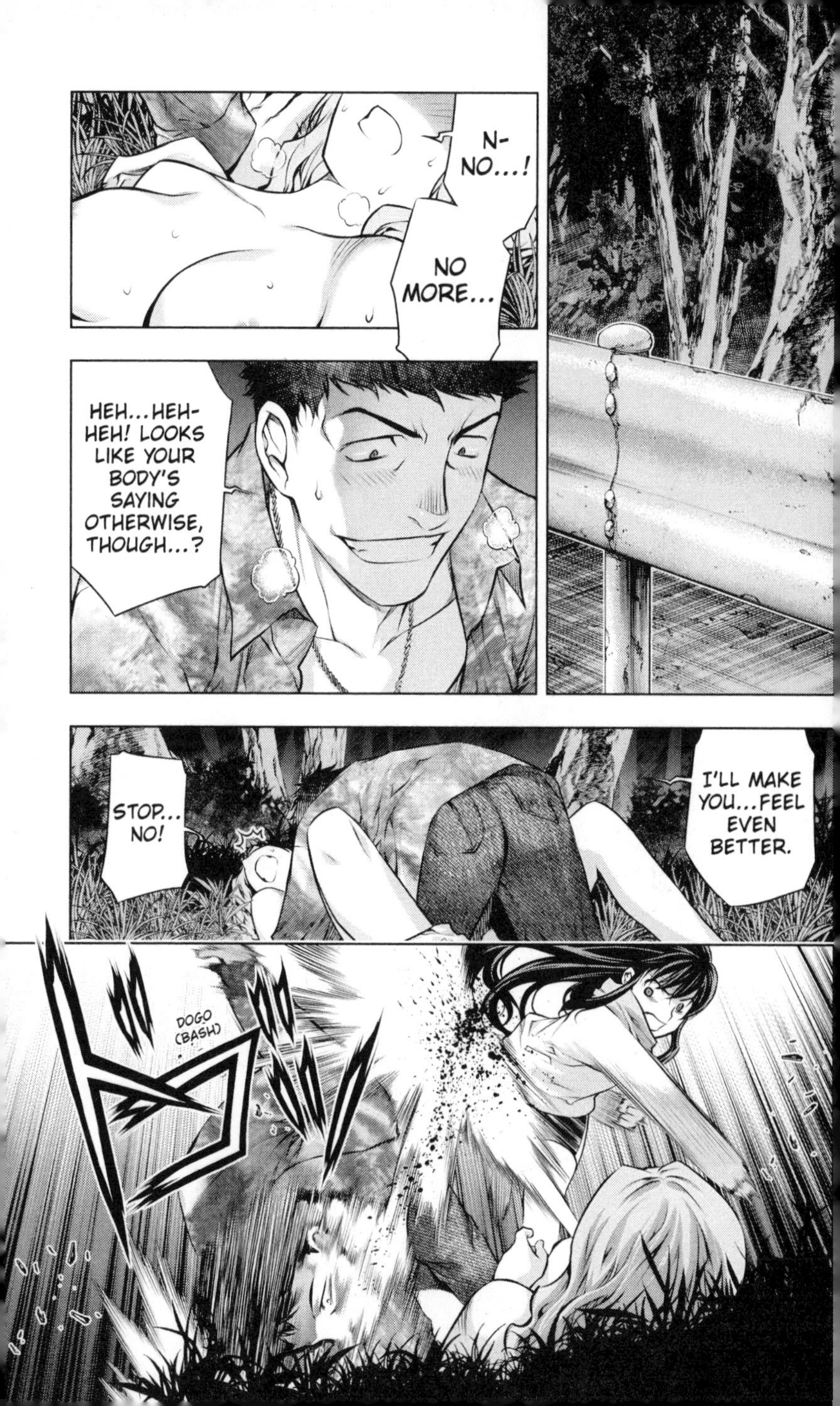
N- NO...!
NO MORE...
HEH...HEH-HEH! LOOKS LIKE YOUR BODY'S SAYING OTHERWISE, THOUGH...?
I'LL MAKE YOU...FEEL EVEN BETTER.
STOP... NO!
DOGO (BASH)

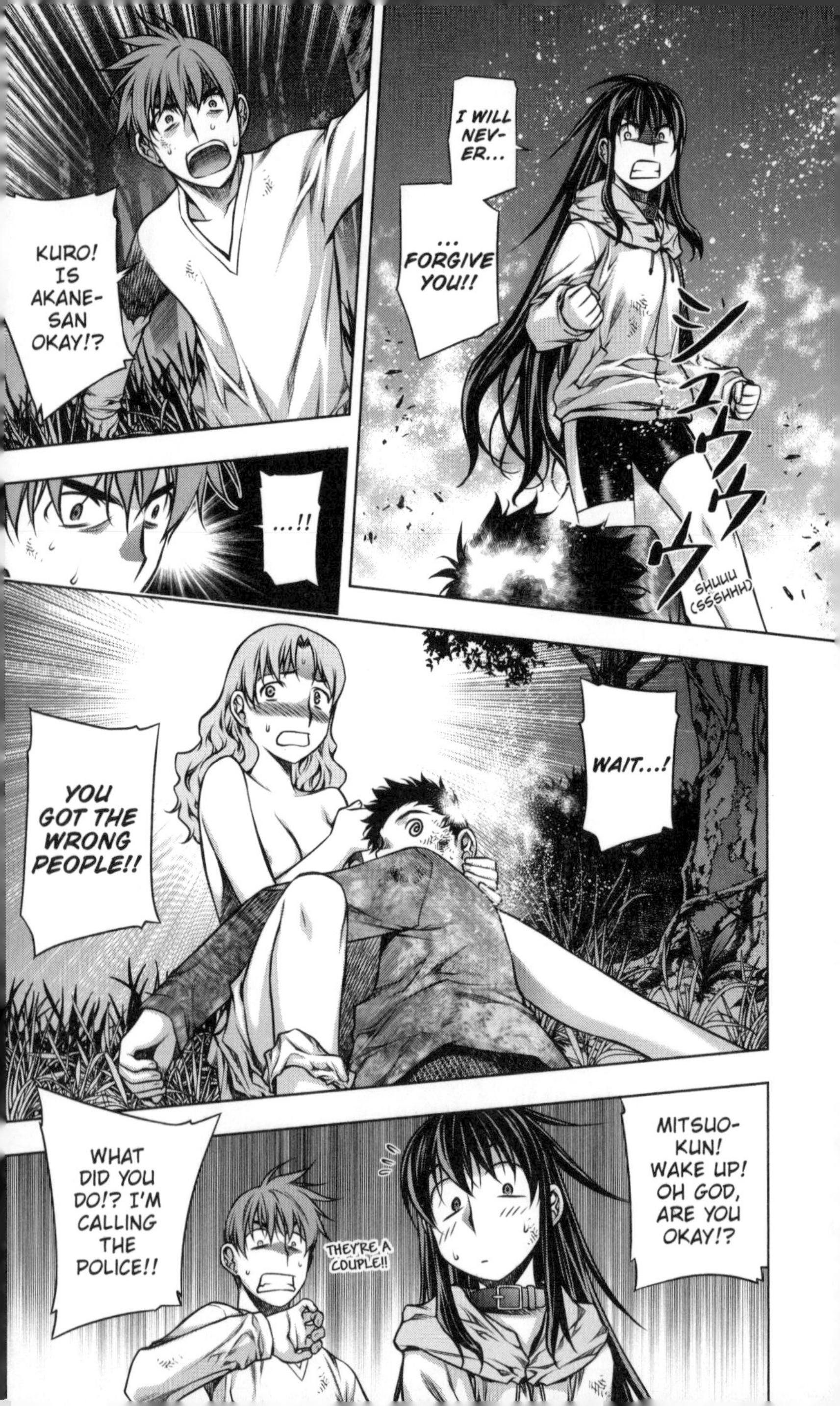
I WILL NEVER...
...FORGIVE YOU!!
シュウウウ
SHUUUU (SSSHHH)
KURO! IS AKANE-SAN OKAY!?
...!!
WAIT...!
YOU GOT THE WRONG PEOPLE!!
MITSUO-KUN! WAKE UP! OH GOD, ARE YOU OKAY!?
THEY'RE A COUPLE!!
WHAT DID YOU DO!? I'M CALLING THE POLICE!!

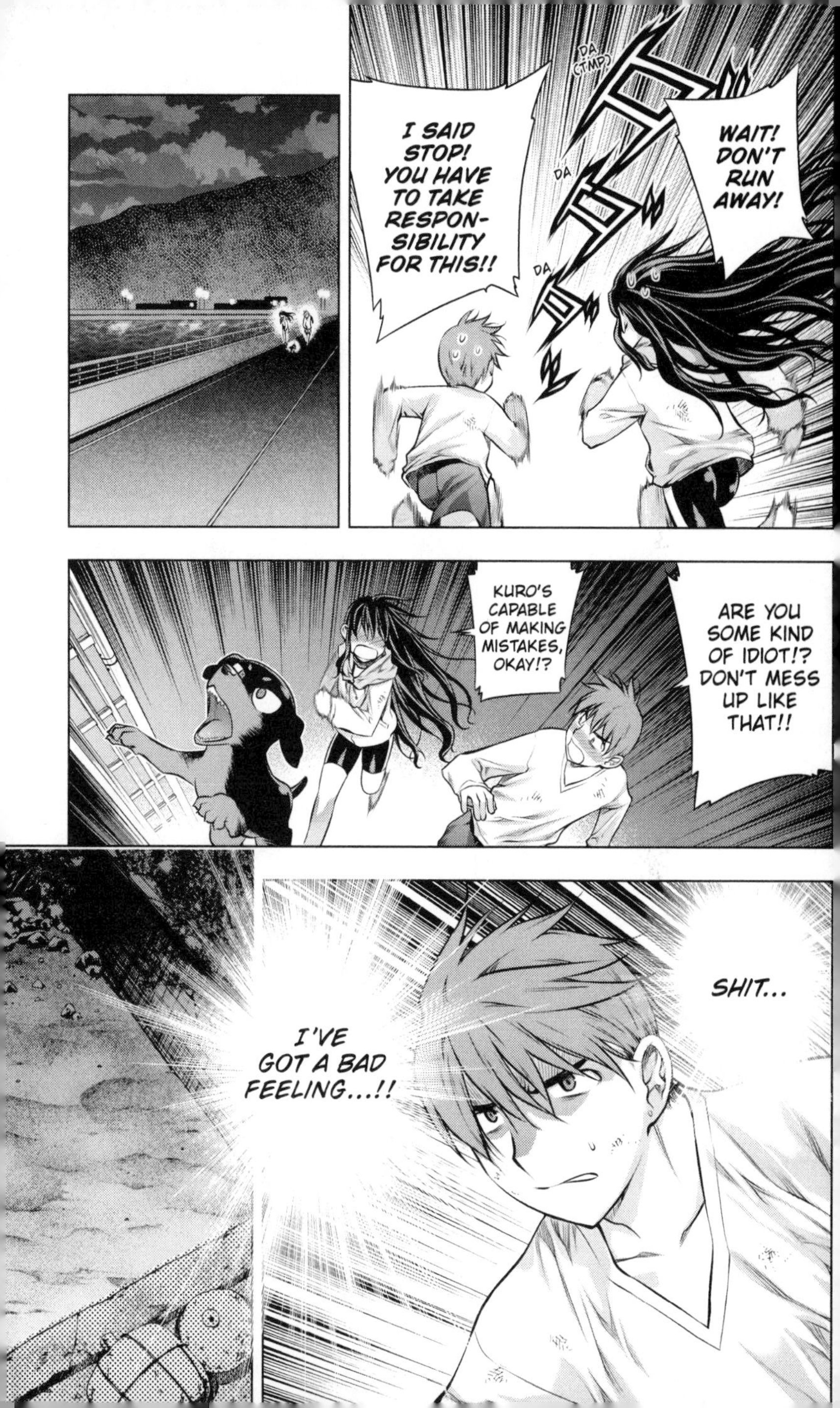
DA (TMP)
WAIT! DON'T RUN AWAY!
DA
DA
I SAID STOP! YOU HAVE TO TAKE RESPON-SIBILITY FOR THIS!!
ARE YOU SOME KIND OF IDIOT!? DON'T MESS UP LIKE THAT!!
KURO'S CAPABLE OF MAKING MISTAKES, OKAY!?
SHIT...
I'VE GOT A BAD FEELING...!!

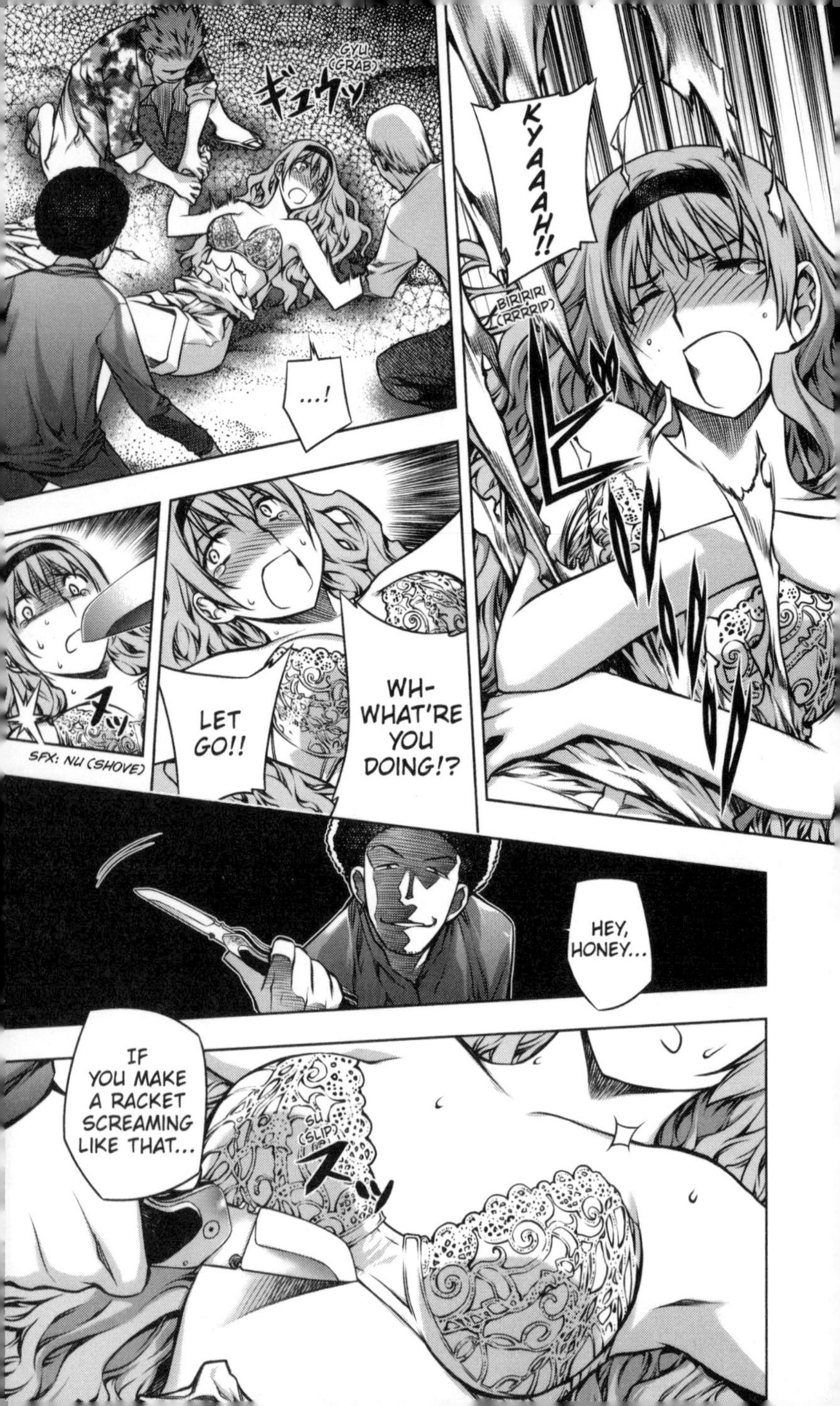

KYAAAAH!!
BIRIRIRI (RRRRIP)
GYU (GRAB)
...!
WH-WHAT'RE YOU DOING!?
LET GO!!
SFX: NU (SHOVE)
HEY, HONEY...
IF YOU MAKE A RACKET SCREAMING LIKE THAT...
SU (SLIP)

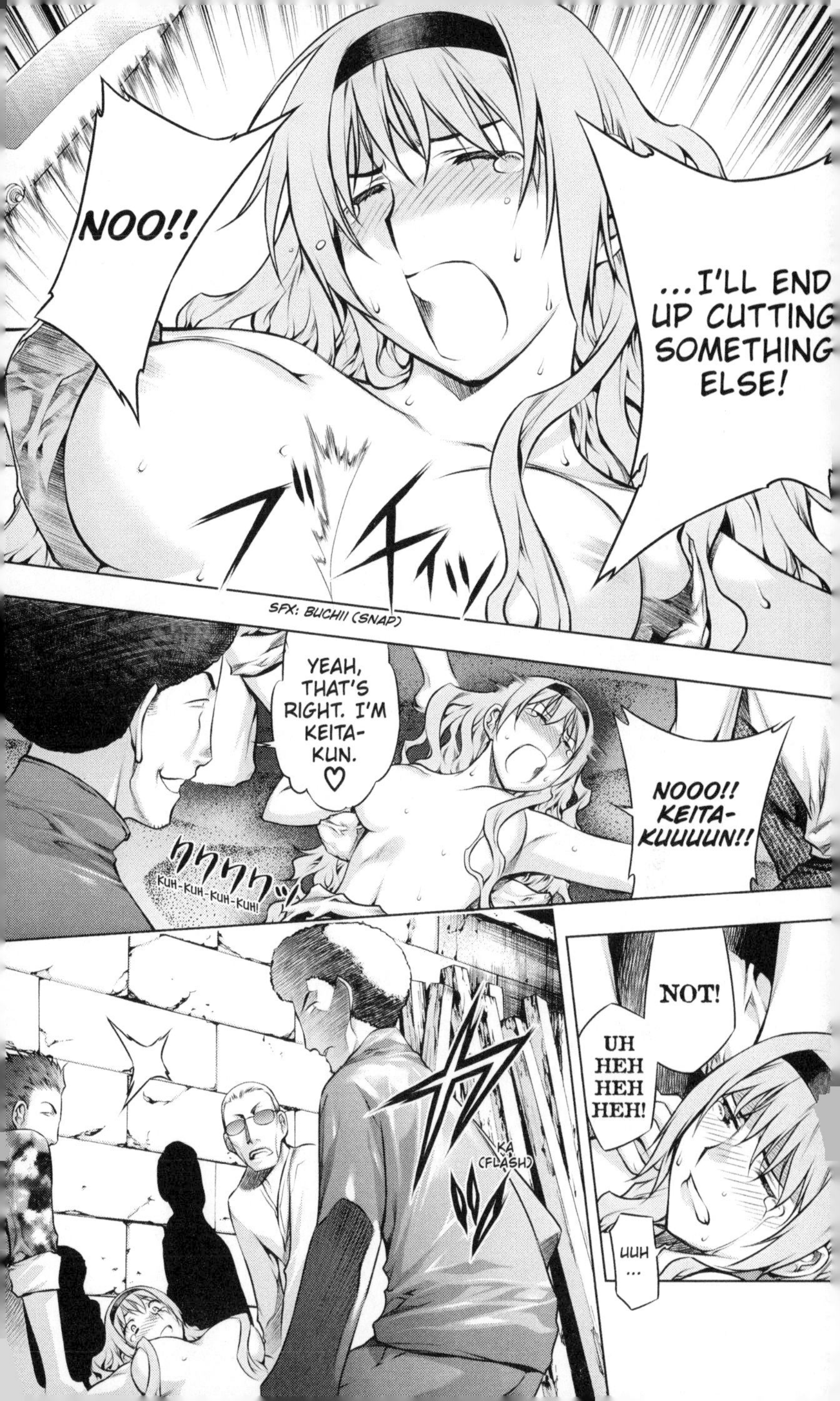
...I'LL END UP CUTTING SOMETHING ELSE!
NOO!!
SFX: BUCHII (SNAP)
NOOO!! KEITA-KUUUUN!!
YEAH, THAT'S RIGHT. I'M KEITA-KUN. ♡
KUH-KUH-KUH-KUH!
NOT!
UH HEH HEH HEH!
UUH ...
KA (FLASH)

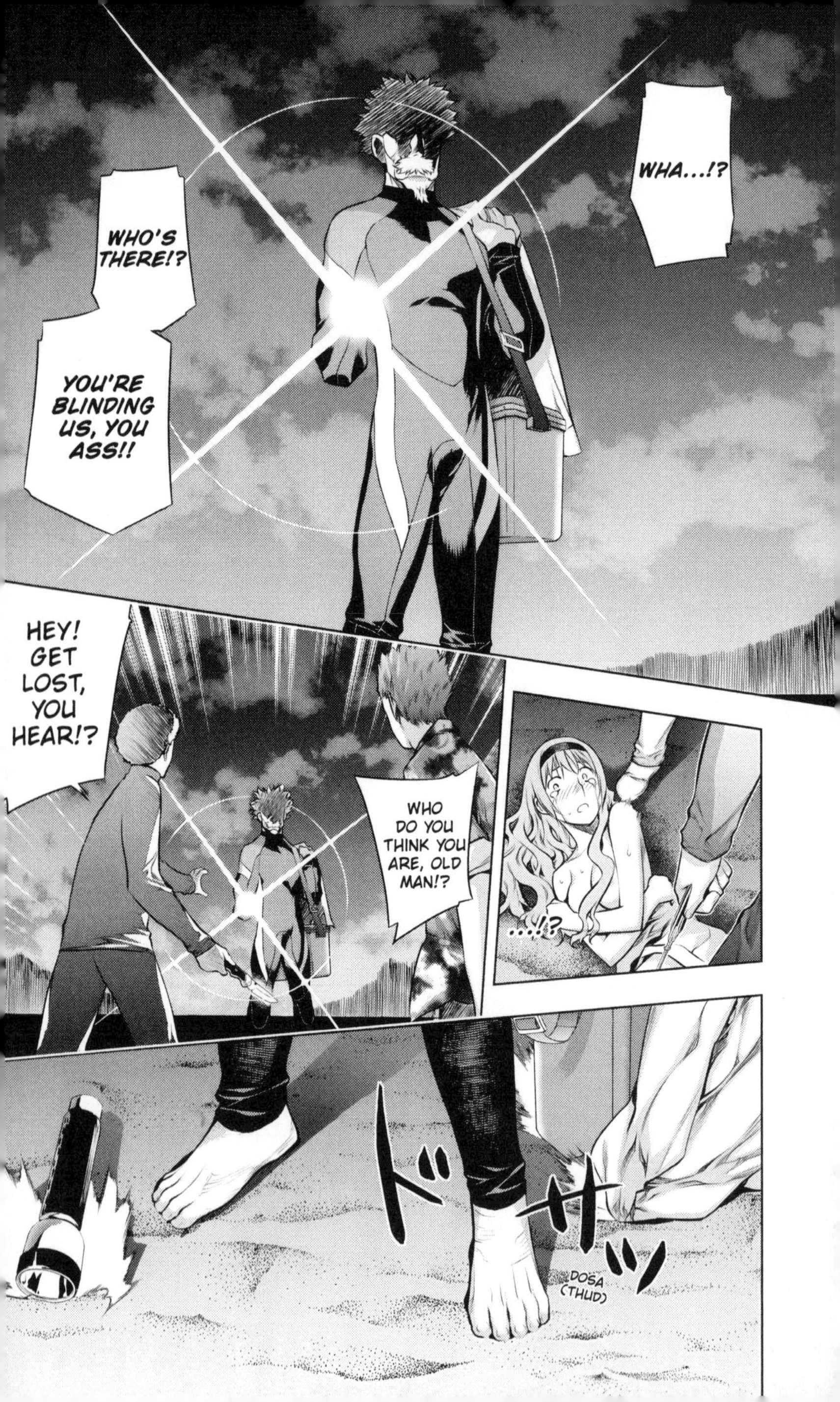
WHA...!?
WHO'S THERE!?
YOU'RE BLINDING US, YOU ASS!!
...!?
WHO DO YOU THINK YOU ARE, OLD MAN!?
HEY! GET LOST, YOU HEAR!?
ドサッ
DOSA (THUD)

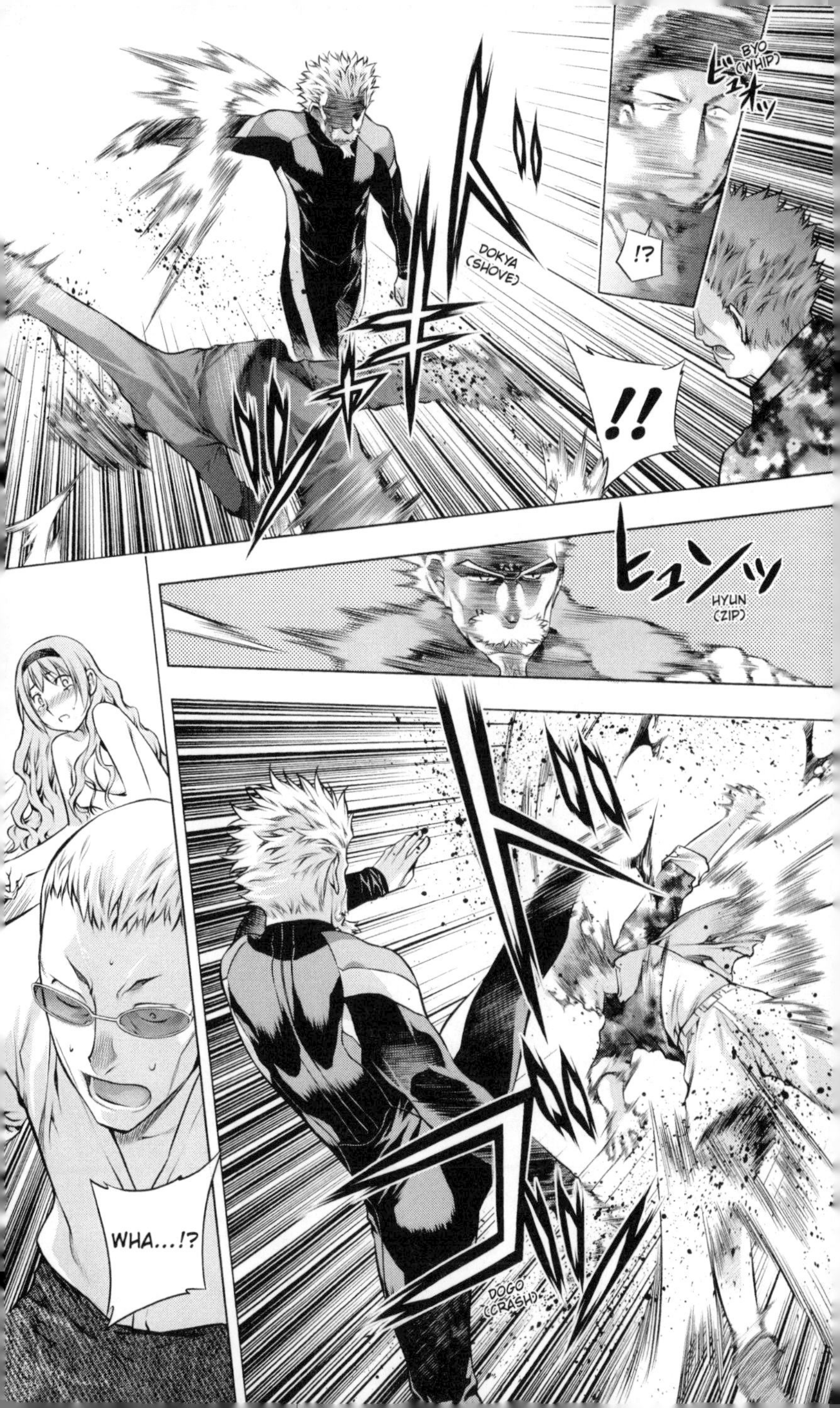
BYO (WHIP)
!?
!!
DOKYA (SHOVE)
ヒュンッ
HYUN (ZIP)
DOGO (CRASH)
WHA...!?

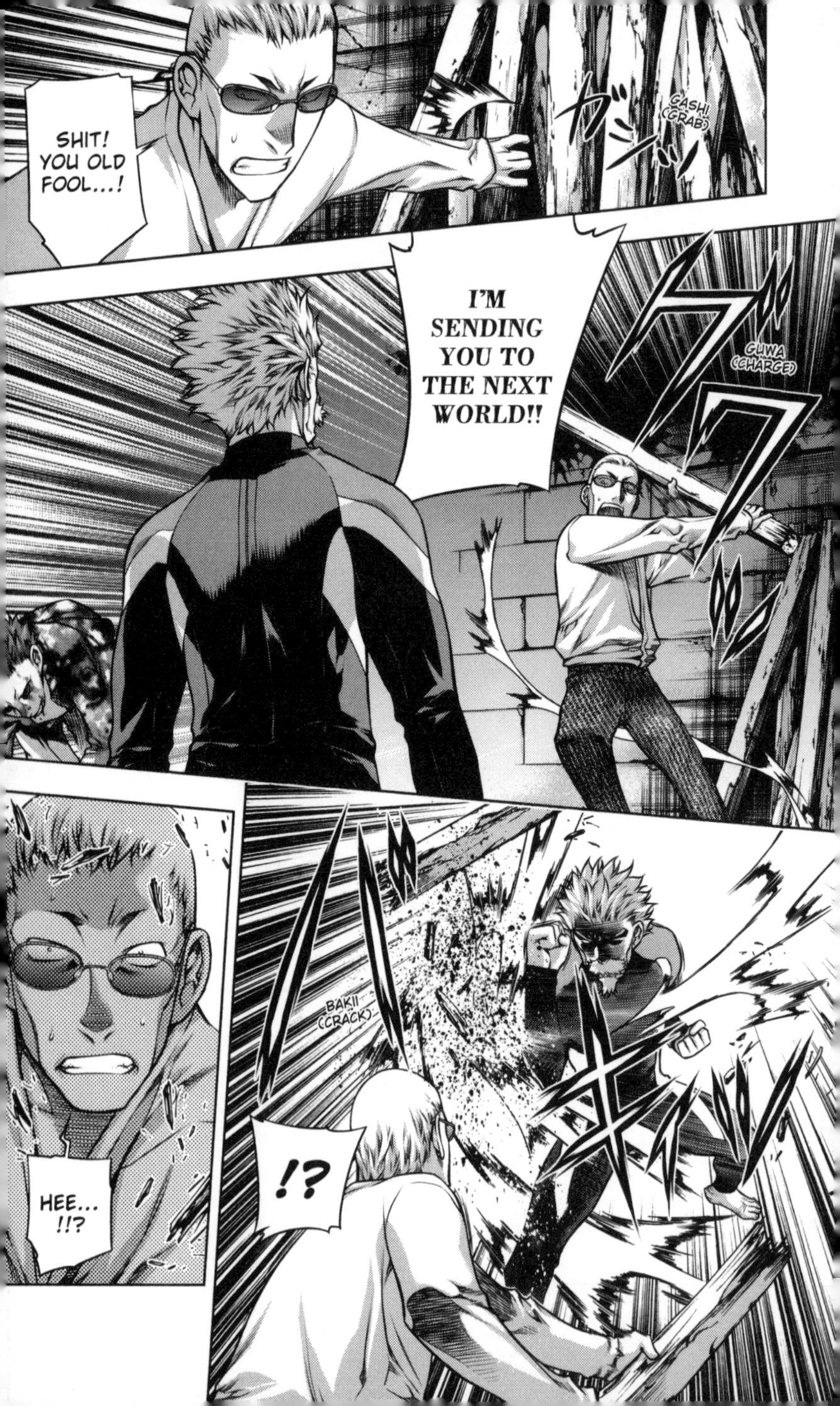

GASHI! (GRAB)
SHIT! YOU OLD FOOL...!
I'M SENDING YOU TO THE NEXT WORLD!!
GUWA (CHARGE)
BAKI! (CRACK)
!?
HEE... !!?

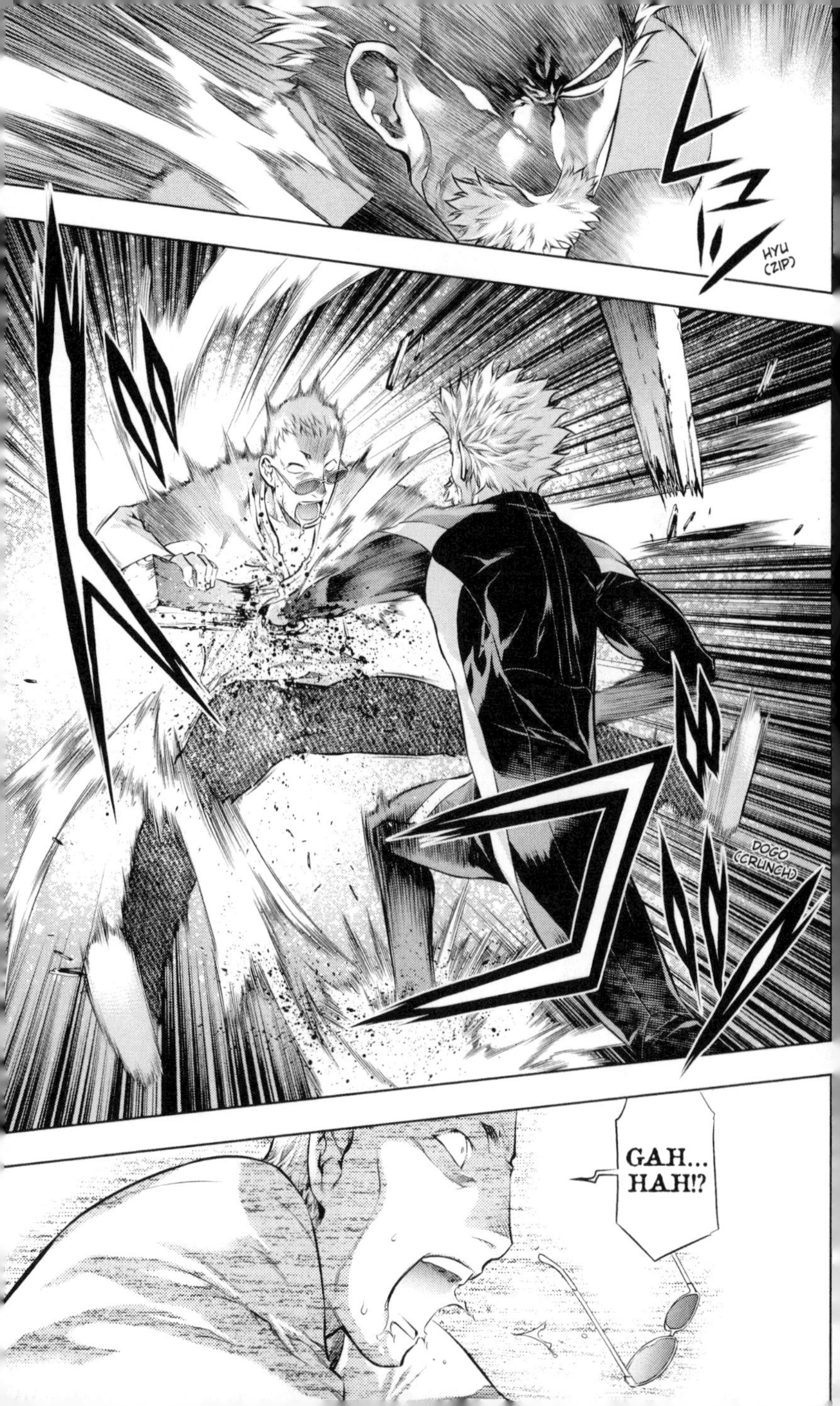
HYU
(ZIP)
DOGO
(CRUNCH)
GAH... HAH!?

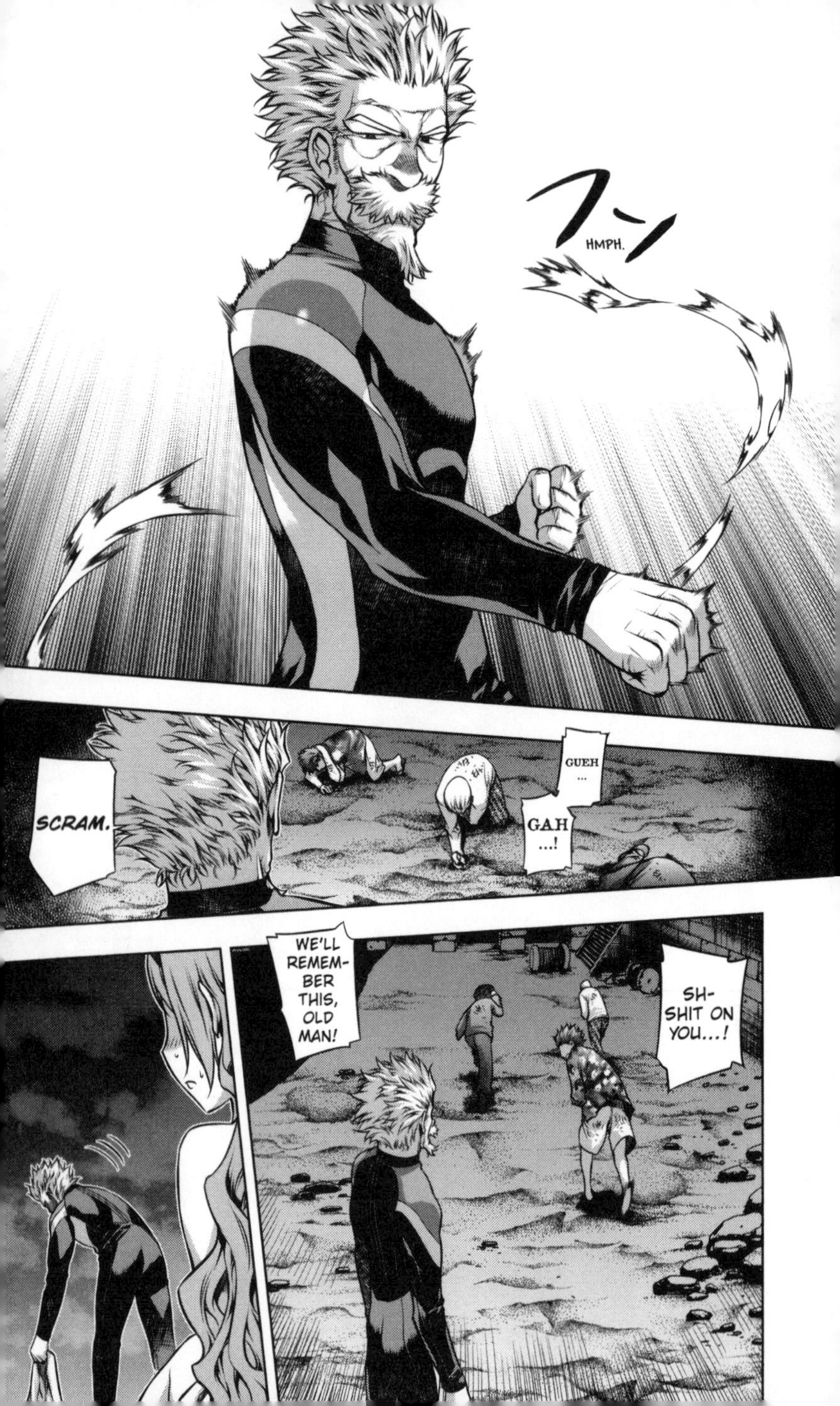
フン
HMPH.
GUEH ...
GAH ...!
SCRAM.
SH- SHIT ON YOU...!
WE'LL REMEMBER THIS, OLD MAN!

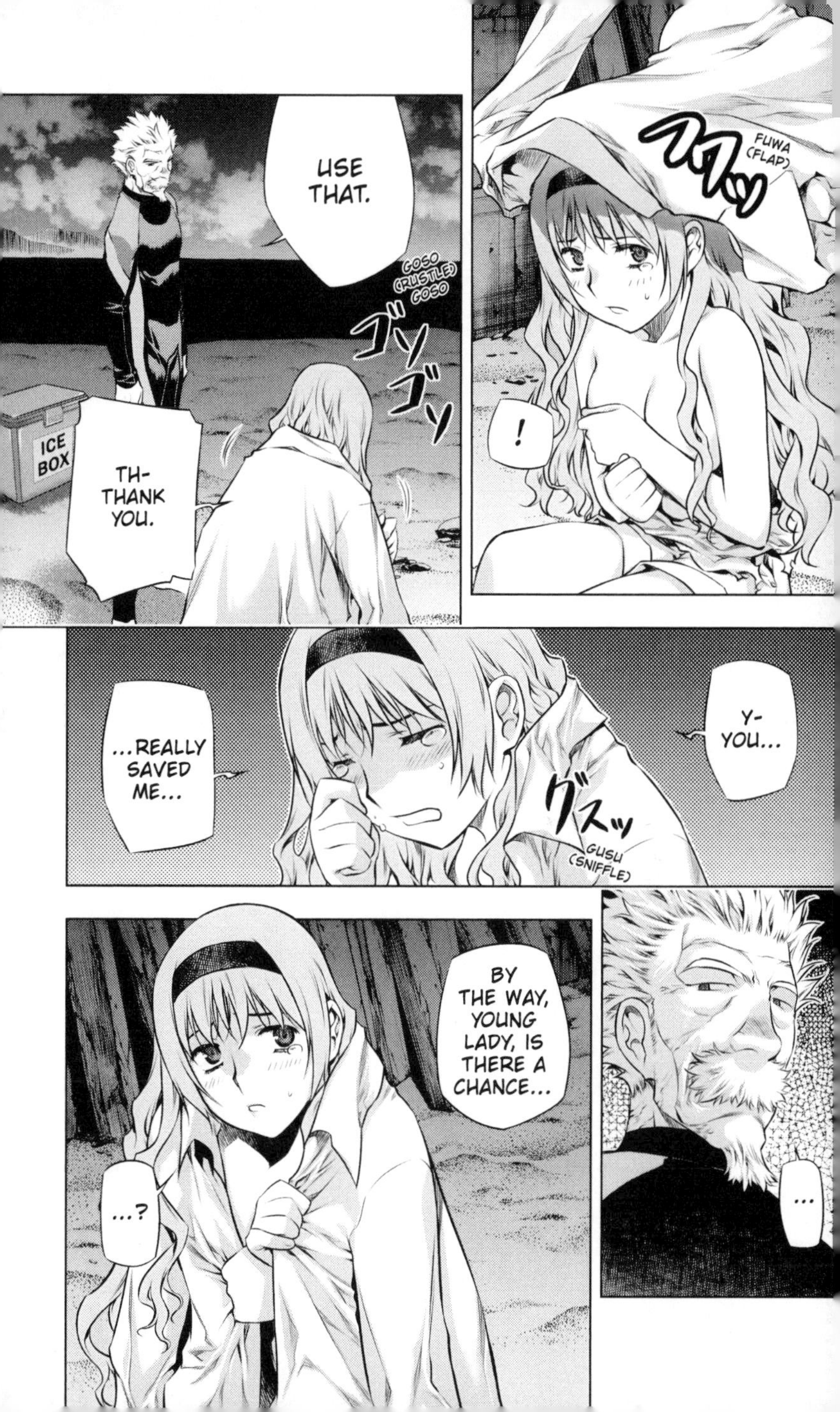
FUWA (FLAP)
!
USE THAT.
ゴソゴソ
GOSO (RUSTLE) GOSO
ICE BOX
TH-THANK YOU.
Y-YOU...
グスッ
GUSU (SNIFFLE)
...REALLY SAVED ME...
...
BY THE WAY, YOUNG LADY, IS THERE A CHANCE...
...?

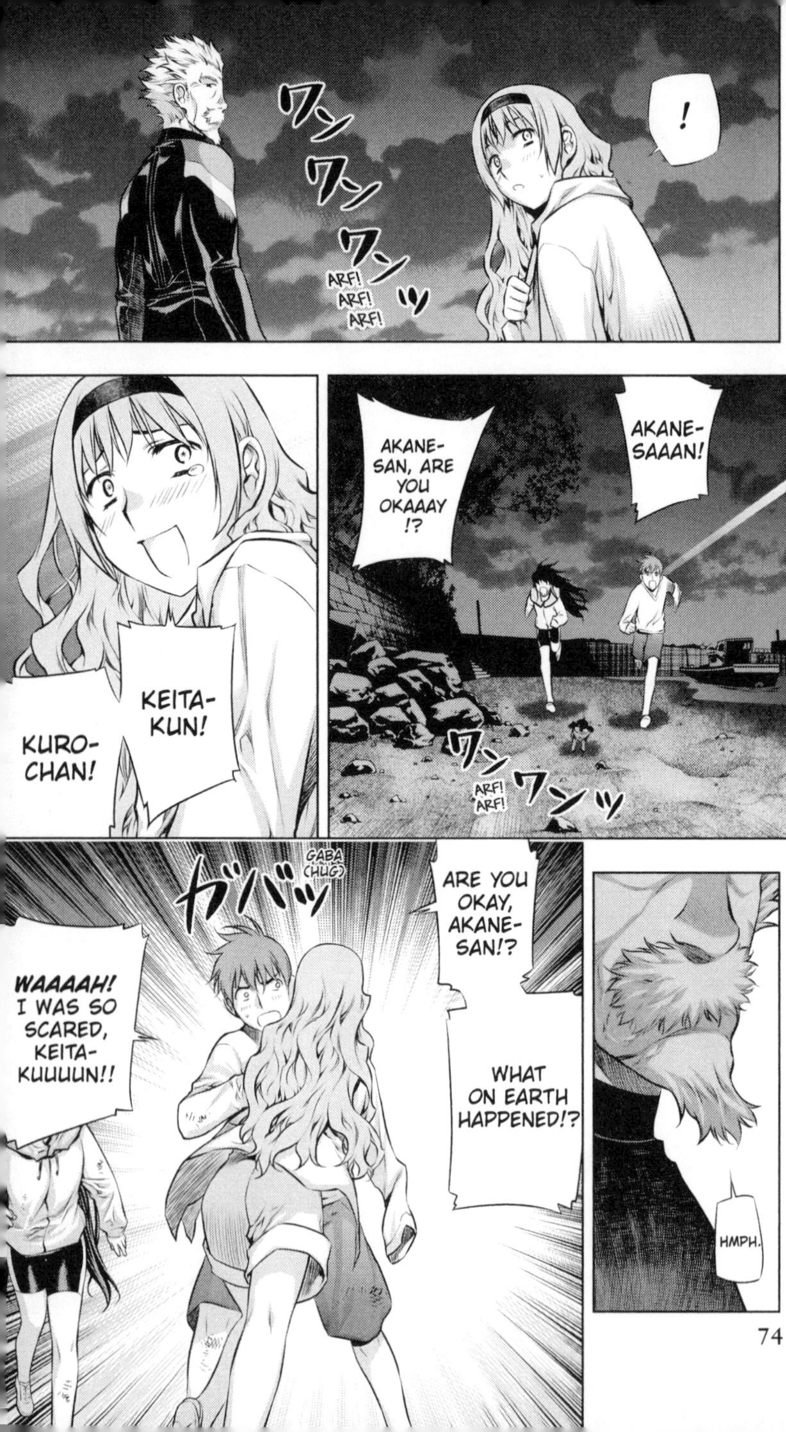
!
ワンワンワンッ
ARF! ARF! ARF!
AKANE-SAAAN!
AKANE-SAN, ARE YOU OKAAAY!?
ワンワンッ
ARF! ARF!
KEITA-KUN!
KURO-CHAN!
HMPH.
ARE YOU OKAY, AKANE-SAN!?
WHAT ON EARTH HAPPENED!?
ガバッ
GABA (HUG)
WAAAAH! I WAS SO SCARED, KEITA-KUUUUN!!

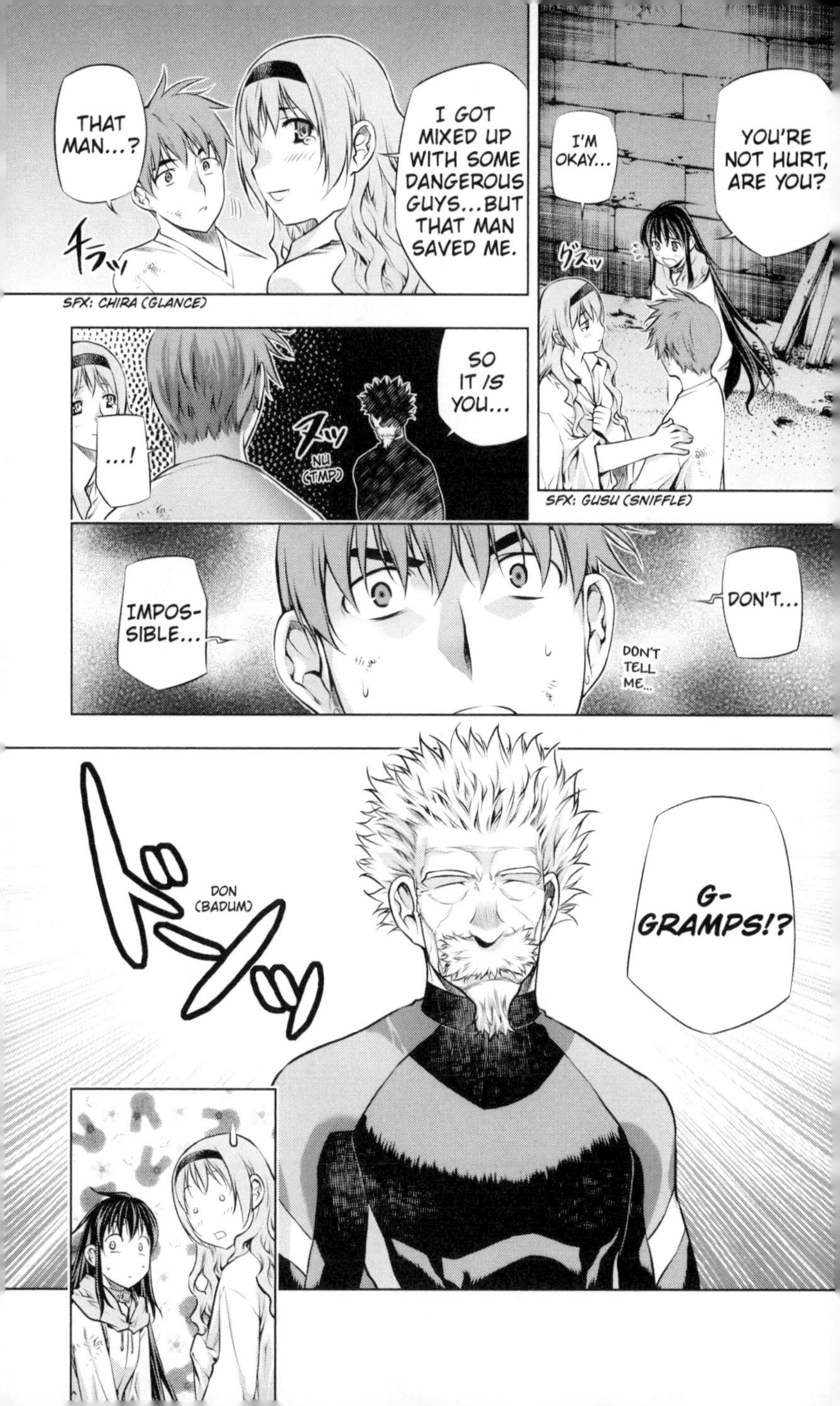
YOU'RE NOT HURT, ARE YOU?
I'M OKAY...
SFX: GUSU (SNIFFLE)
I GOT MIXED UP WITH SOME DANGEROUS GUYS...BUT THAT MAN SAVED ME.
THAT MAN...?
SFX: CHIRA (GLANCE)
SO IT IS YOU...
NU (TMP)
...!
DON'T...
DON'T TELL ME...
IMPOSSIBLE...
G-GRAMPS!?
DON (BADUM)

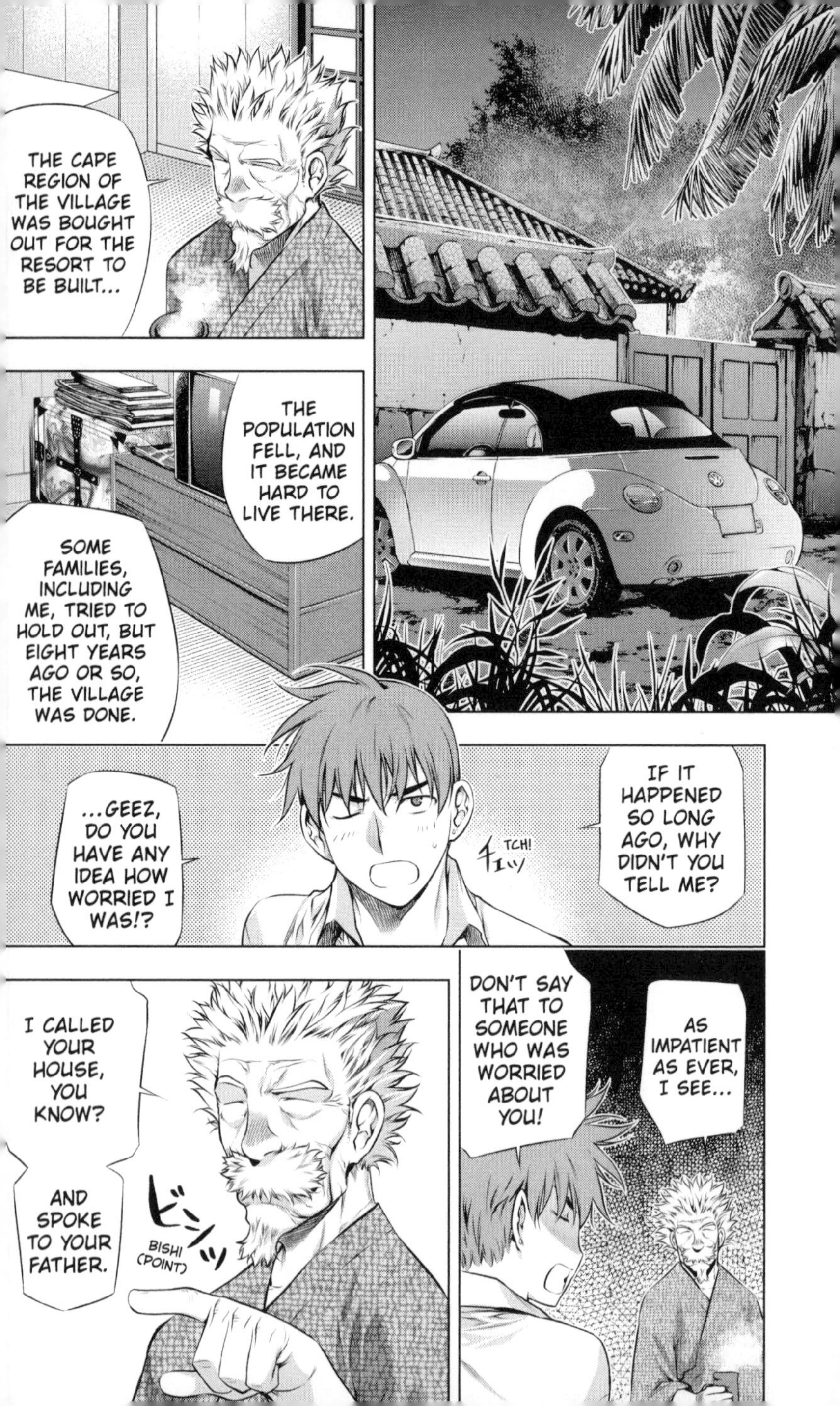

THE CAPE REGION OF THE VILLAGE WAS BOUGHT OUT FOR THE RESORT TO BE BUILT...
THE POPULATION FELL, AND IT BECAME HARD TO LIVE THERE.
SOME FAMILIES, INCLUDING ME, TRIED TO HOLD OUT, BUT EIGHT YEARS AGO OR SO, THE VILLAGE WAS DONE.
IF IT HAPPENED SO LONG AGO, WHY DIDN'T YOU TELL ME?
TCH!
...GEEZ, DO YOU HAVE ANY IDEA HOW WORRIED I WAS!?
AS IMPATIENT AS EVER, I SEE...
DON'T SAY THAT TO SOMEONE WHO WAS WORRIED ABOUT YOU!
I CALLED YOUR HOUSE, YOU KNOW?
AND SPOKE TO YOUR FATHER.
BISHI (POINT)

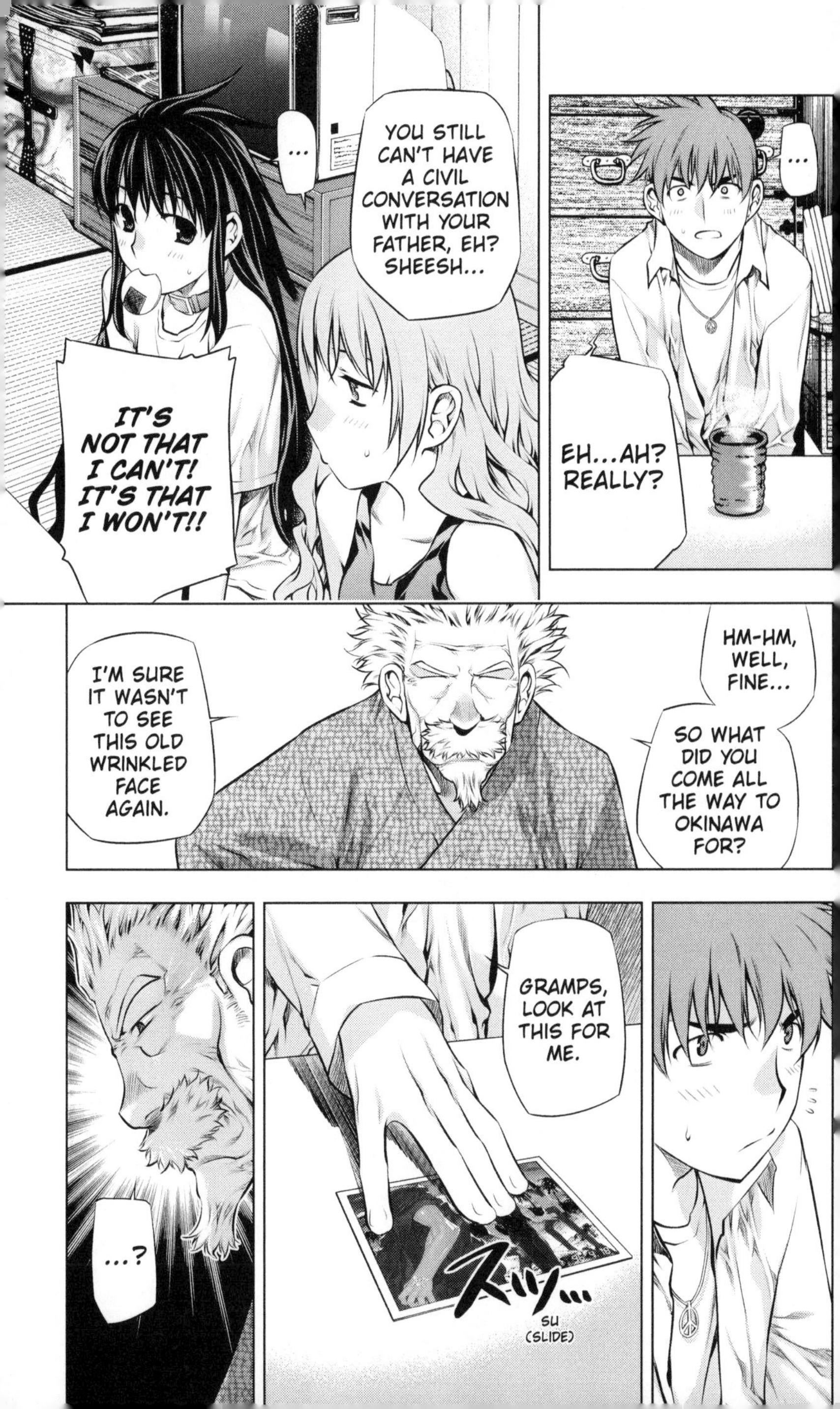
...
EH...AH? REALLY?
YOU STILL CAN'T HAVE A CIVIL CONVERSATION WITH YOUR FATHER, EH? SHEESH...
...
IT'S NOT THAT I CAN'T! IT'S THAT I WON'T!!
HM-HM, WELL, FINE...
SO WHAT DID YOU COME ALL THE WAY TO OKINAWA FOR?
I'M SURE IT WASN'T TO SEE THIS OLD WRINKLED FACE AGAIN.
GRAMPS, LOOK AT THIS FOR ME.
スッ...
SU (SLIDE)
...?

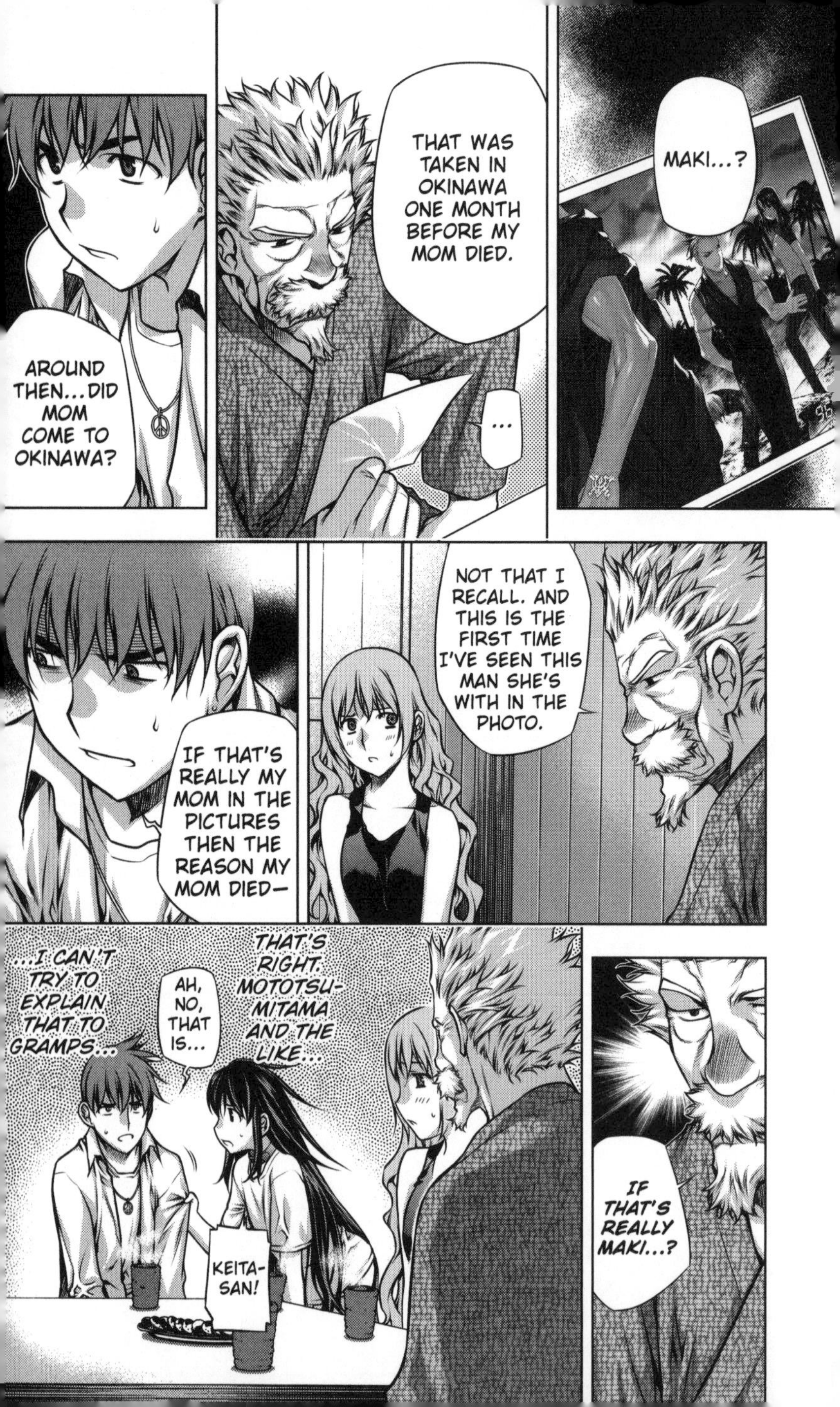
MAKI...?
THAT WAS TAKEN IN OKINAWA ONE MONTH BEFORE MY MOM DIED.
...
AROUND THEN...DID MOM COME TO OKINAWA?
NOT THAT I RECALL. AND THIS IS THE FIRST TIME I'VE SEEN THIS MAN SHE'S WITH IN THE PHOTO.
IF THAT'S REALLY MY MOM IN THE PICTURES THEN THE REASON MY MOM DIED—
IF THAT'S REALLY MAKI...?
THAT'S RIGHT. MOTOTSU-MITAMA AND THE LIKE...
AH, NO, THAT IS...
...I CAN'T TRY TO EXPLAIN THAT TO GRAMPS...
KEITA-SAN!

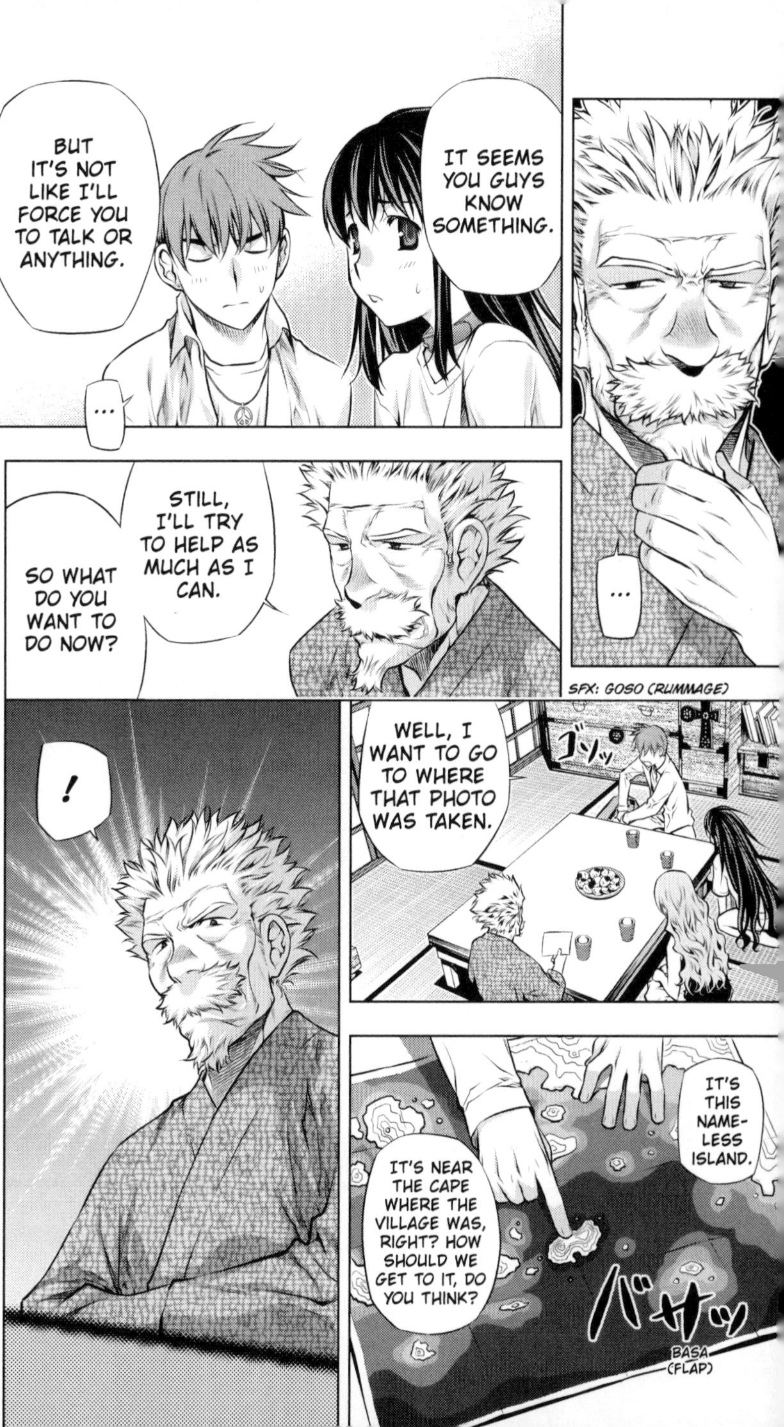
...
IT SEEMS YOU GUYS KNOW SOMETHING.
BUT IT'S NOT LIKE I'LL FORCE YOU TO TALK OR ANYTHING.
...
STILL, I'LL TRY TO HELP AS MUCH AS I CAN.
SO WHAT DO YOU WANT TO DO NOW?
ゴソッ
SFX: GOSO (RUMMAGE)
WELL, I WANT TO GO TO WHERE THAT PHOTO WAS TAKEN.
IT'S THIS NAMELESS ISLAND.
IT'S NEAR THE CAPE WHERE THE VILLAGE WAS, RIGHT? HOW SHOULD WE GET TO IT, DO YOU THINK?
バサッ
BASA (FLAP)
!

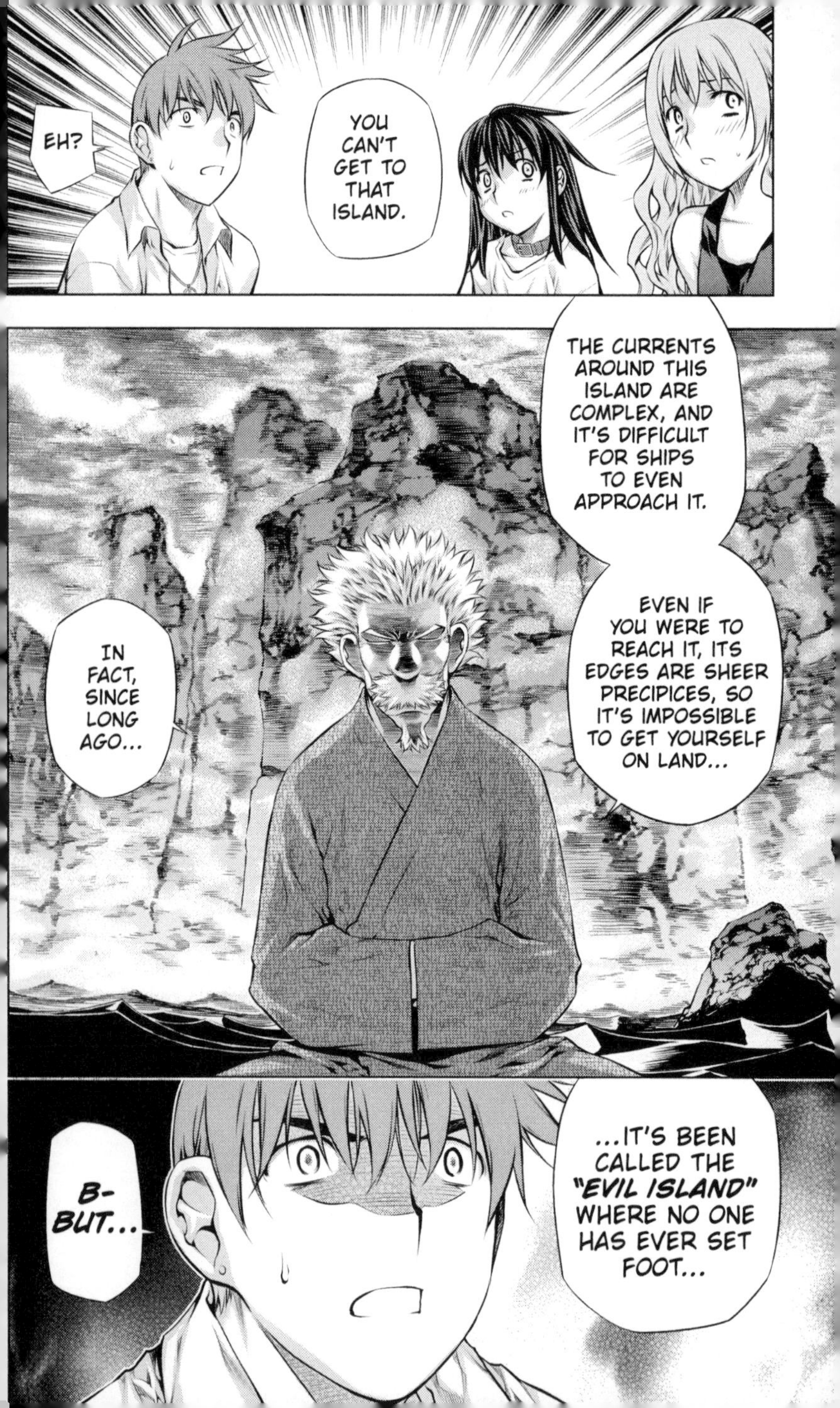
YOU CAN'T GET TO THAT ISLAND.
EH?
THE CURRENTS AROUND THIS ISLAND ARE COMPLEX, AND IT'S DIFFICULT FOR SHIPS TO EVEN APPROACH IT.
EVEN IF YOU WERE TO REACH IT, ITS EDGES ARE SHEER PRECIPICES, SO IT'S IMPOSSIBLE TO GET YOURSELF ON LAND...
IN FACT, SINCE LONG AGO...
...IT'S BEEN CALLED THE *"EVIL ISLAND"* WHERE NO ONE HAS EVER SET FOOT...
B-BUT...

FATE.25 Sense • Cowardice

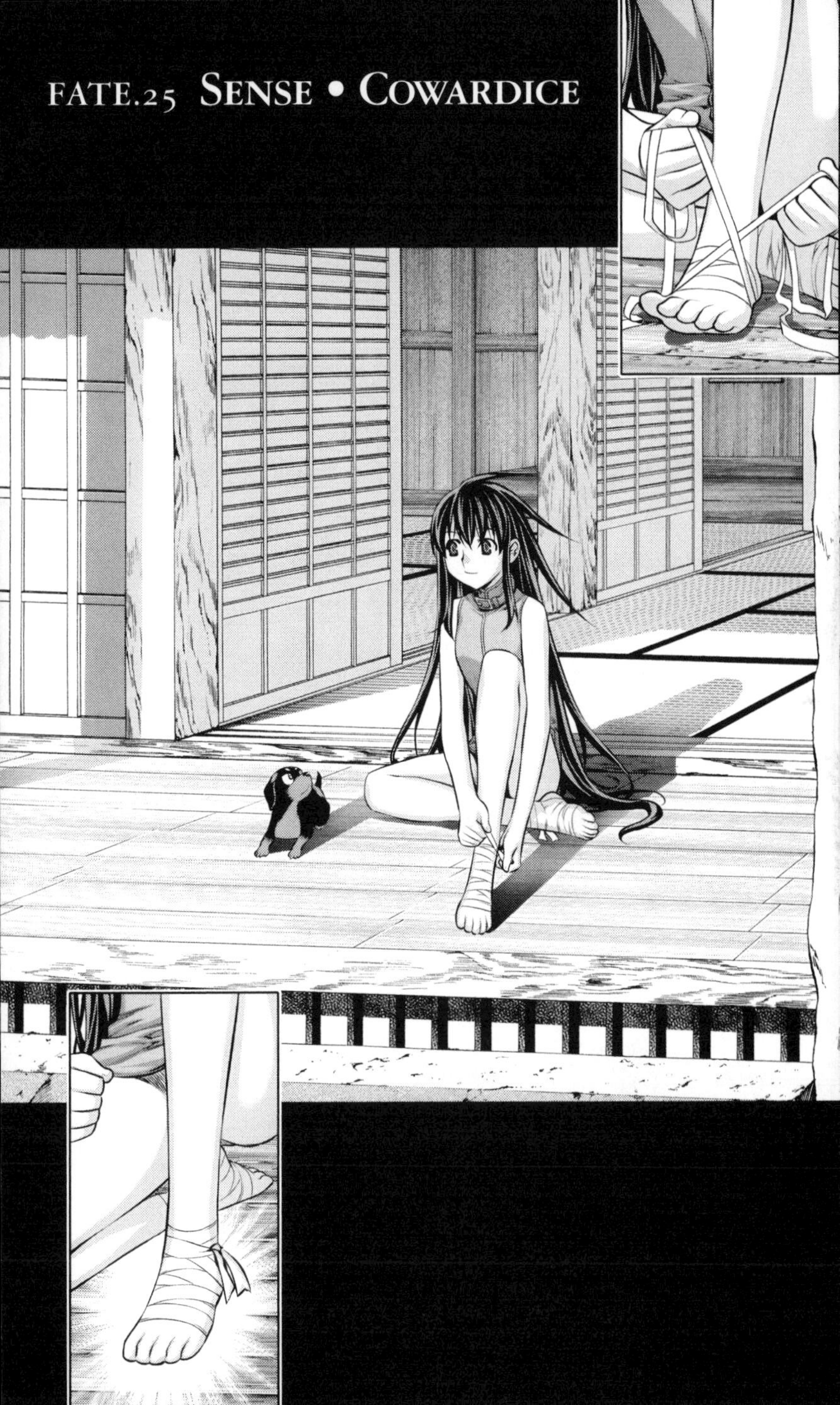

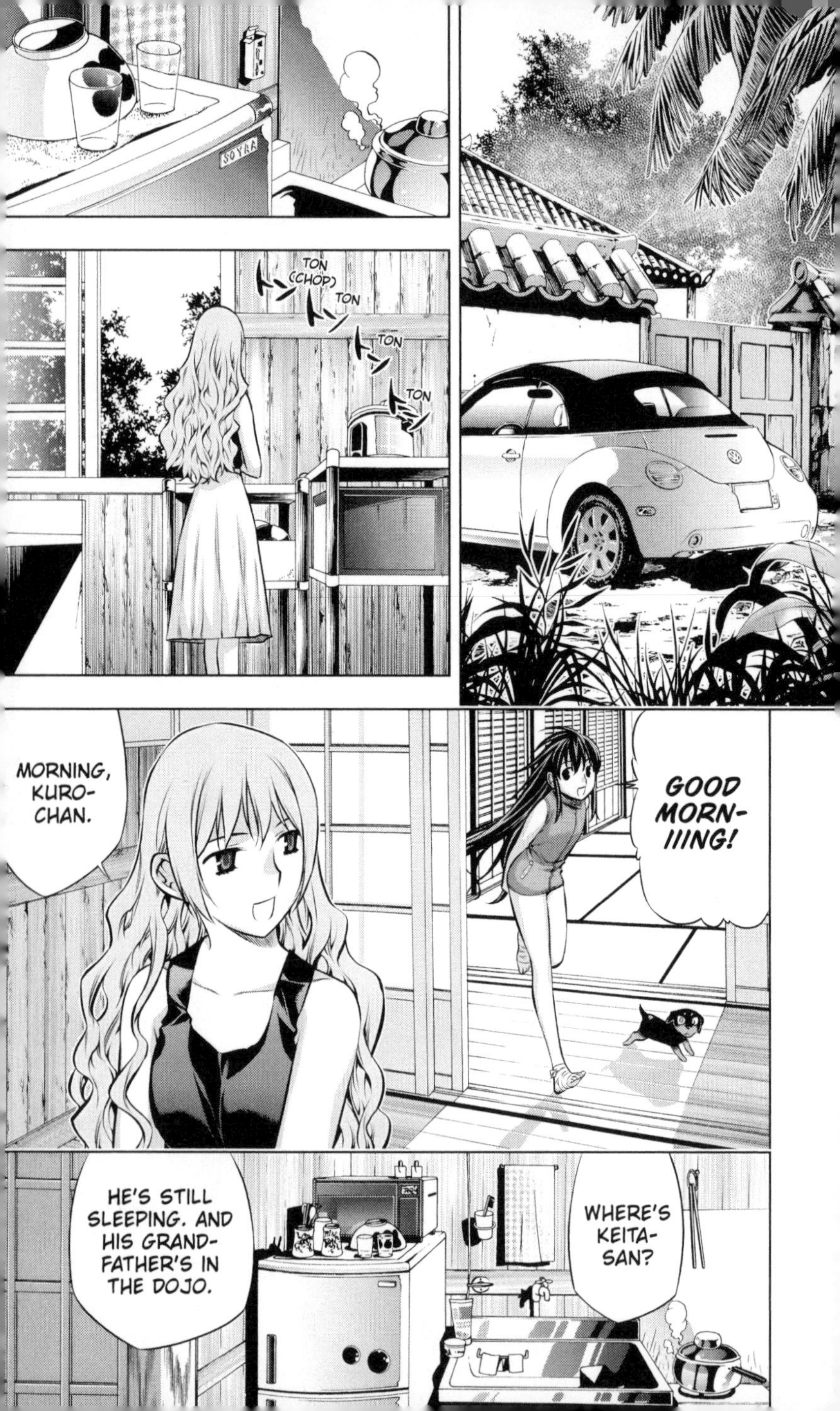

TON (CHOP)
TON
TON
TON
GOOD MORN-IIING!
MORNING, KURO-CHAN.
WHERE'S KEITA-SAN?
HE'S STILL SLEEPING. AND HIS GRAND-FATHER'S IN THE DOJO.

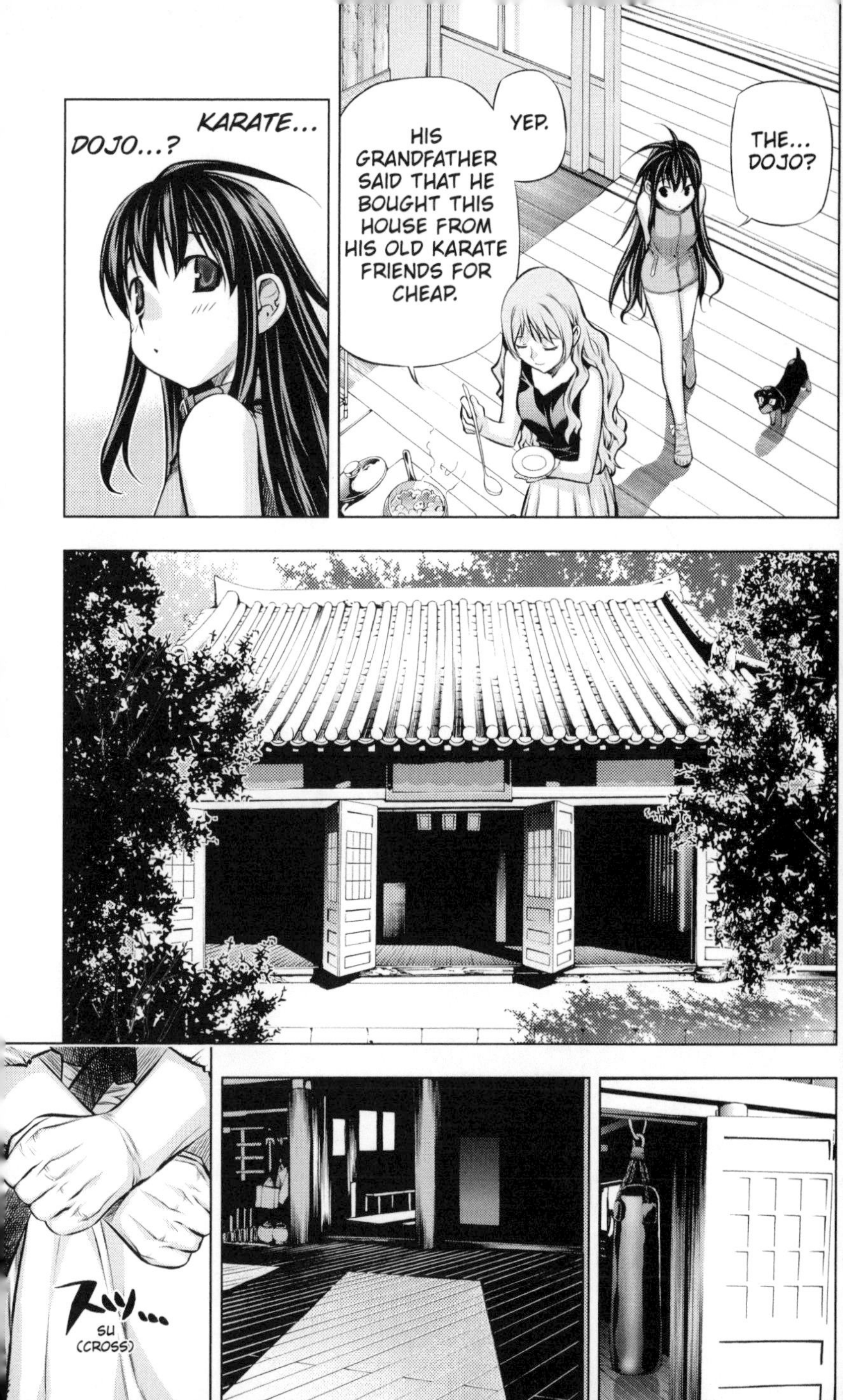
THE... DOJO?
YEP.
HIS GRANDFATHER SAID THAT HE BOUGHT THIS HOUSE FROM HIS OLD KARATE FRIENDS FOR CHEAP.
KARATE...
DOJO...?
スッ...
SU (CROSS)

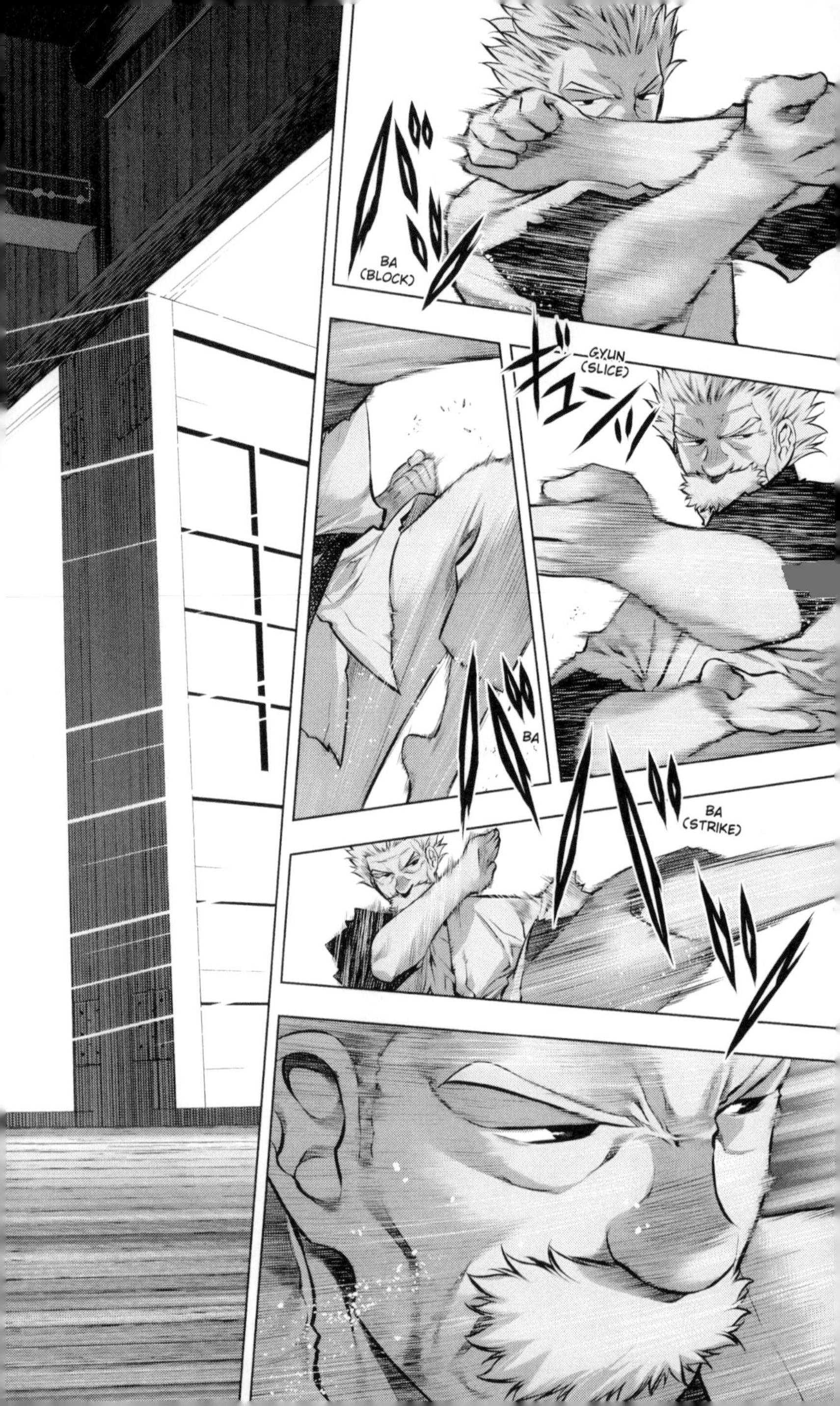
BA
(BLOCK)
GYUN
(SLICE)
BA
BA
(STRIKE)

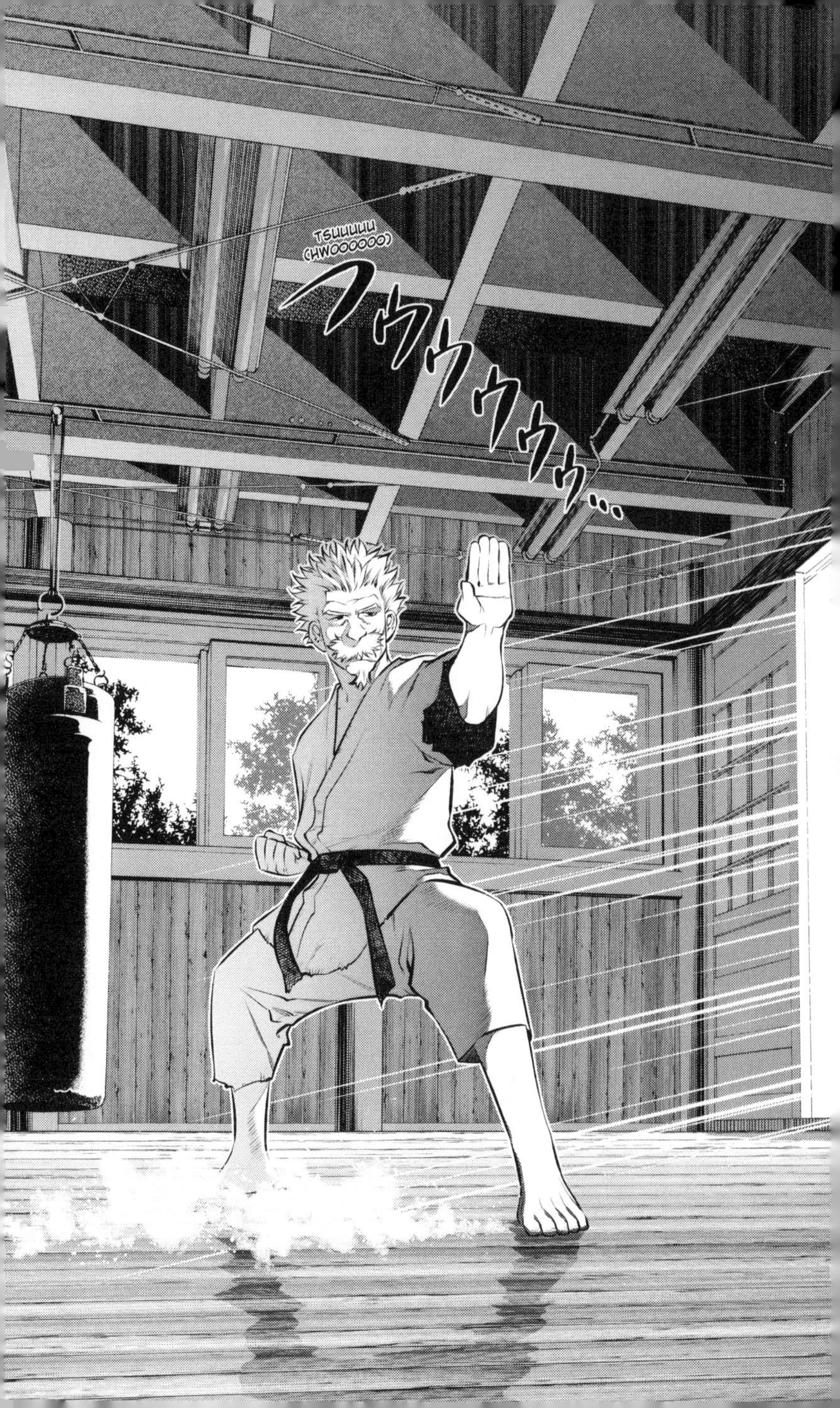
TSUUUUU
(HWOOOOOO)
フゥゥゥゥゥ…

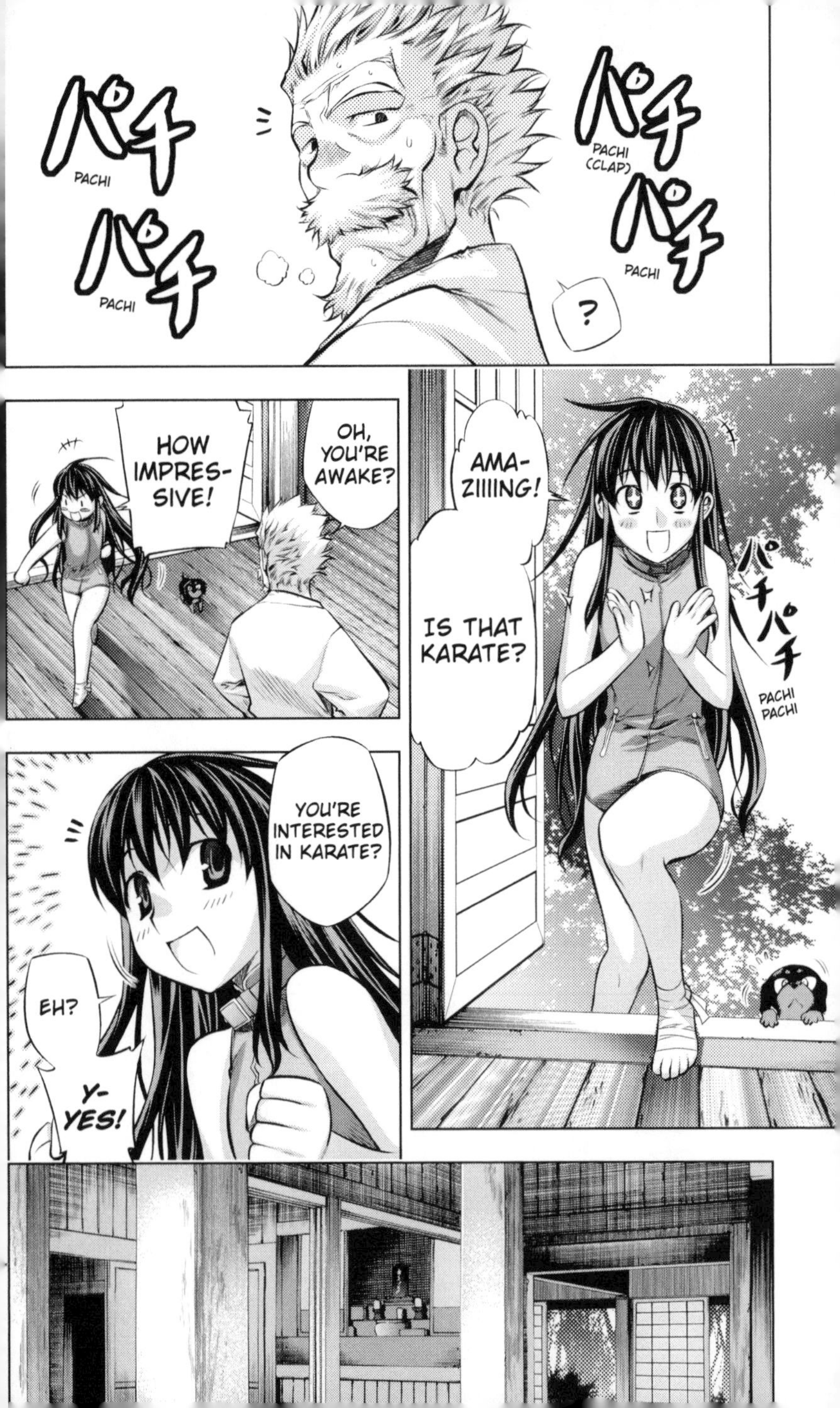

パチ
PACHI (CLAP)
パチ
PACHI
?
パチ
PACHI
パチ
PACHI
AMA-ZIIIING!
IS THAT KARATE?
パチパチ
PACHI PACHI
OH, YOU'RE AWAKE?
HOW IMPRES-SIVE!
YOU'RE INTERESTED IN KARATE?
EH?
Y-YES!

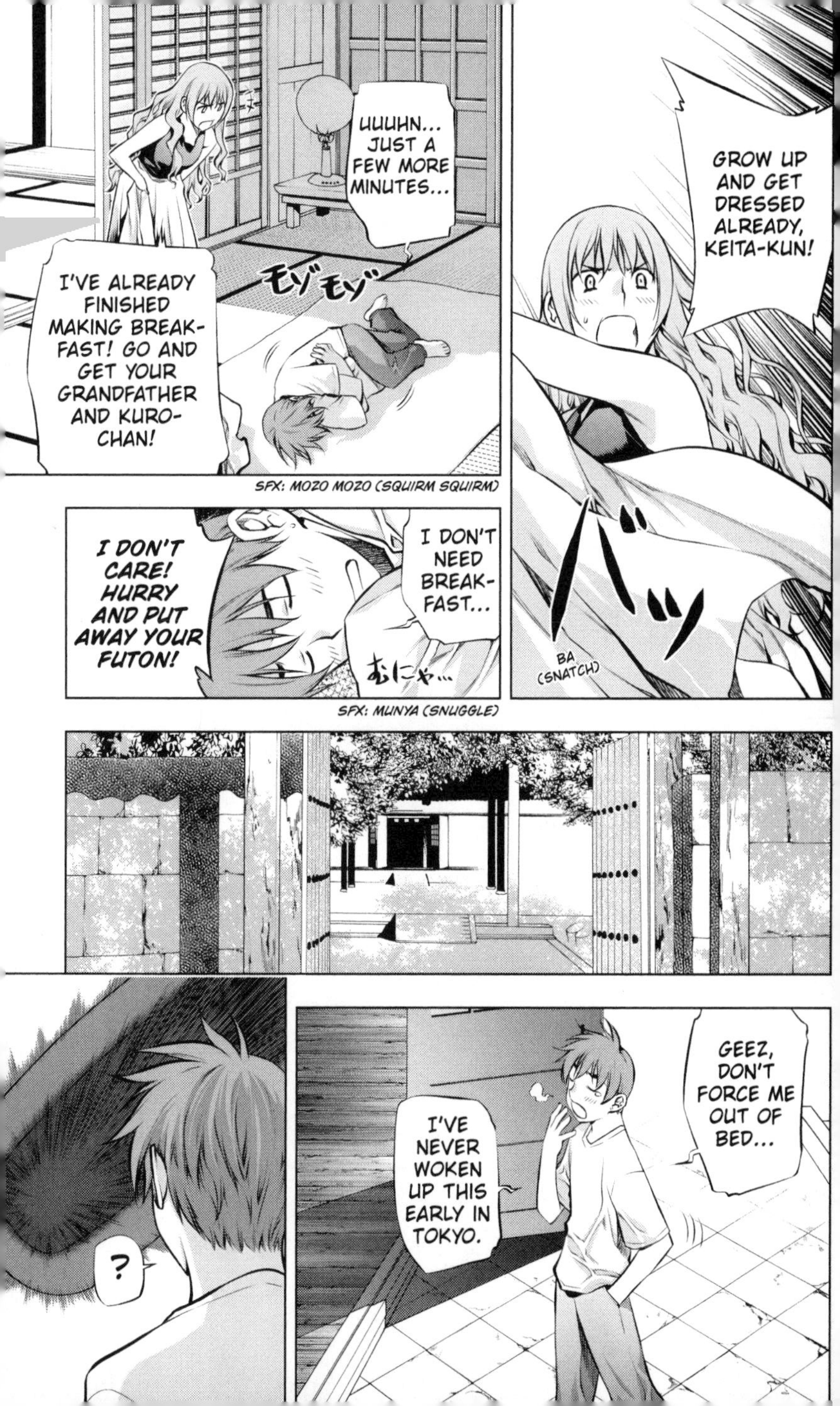
GROW UP AND GET DRESSED ALREADY, KEITA-KUN!
バッ
BA (SNATCH)
UUUHN... JUST A FEW MORE MINUTES...
I'VE ALREADY FINISHED MAKING BREAK-FAST! GO AND GET YOUR GRANDFATHER AND KURO-CHAN!
モゾモゾ
SFX: MOZO MOZO (SQUIRM SQUIRM)
I DON'T NEED BREAK-FAST...
I DON'T CARE! HURRY AND PUT AWAY YOUR FUTON!
むにゃ...
SFX: MUNYA (SNUGGLE)
GEEZ, DON'T FORCE ME OUT OF BED...
I'VE NEVER WOKEN UP THIS EARLY IN TOKYO.
?

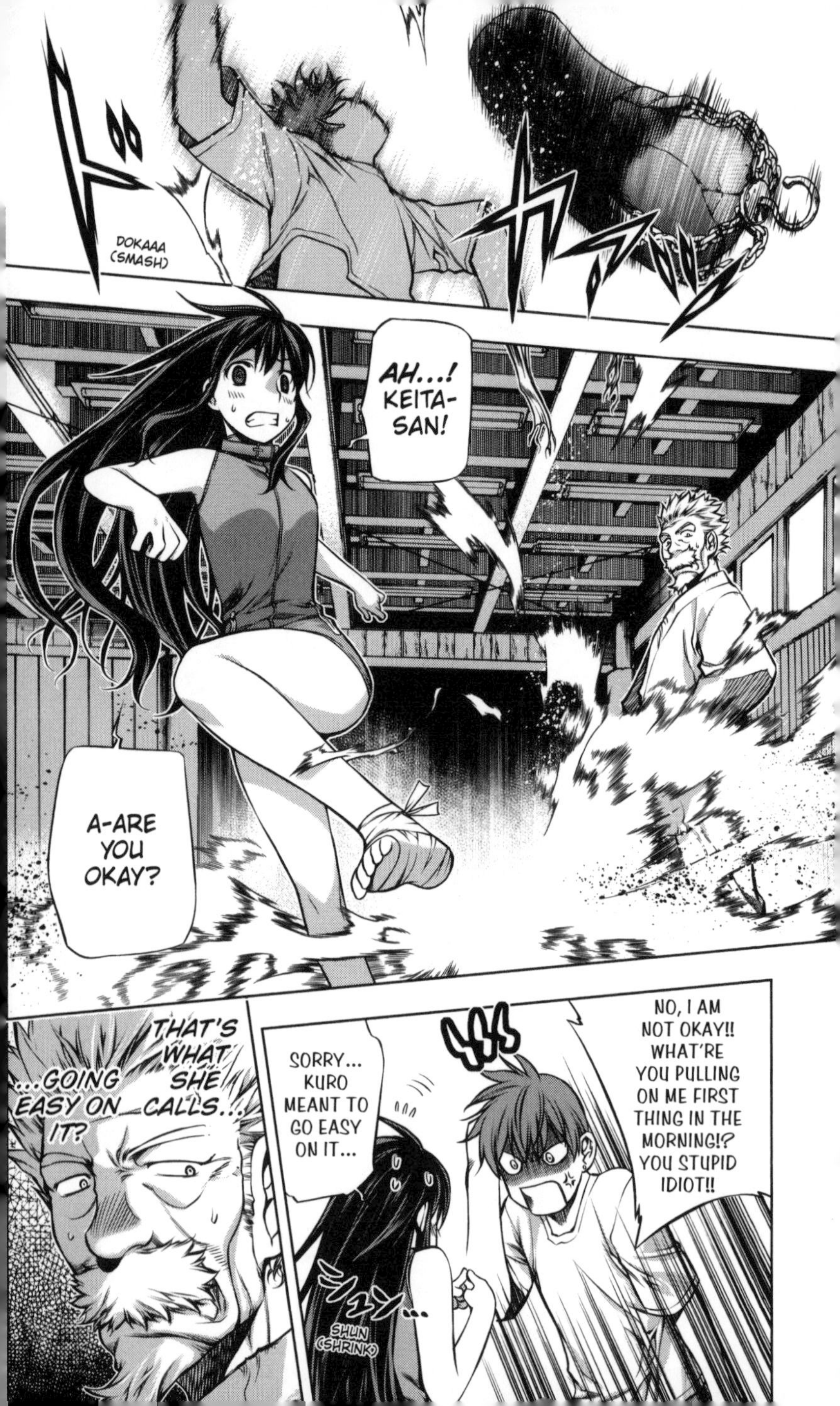
DOKAAA (SMASH)
AH...! KEITA-SAN!
A-ARE YOU OKAY?
NO, I AM NOT OKAY!! WHAT'RE YOU PULLING ON ME FIRST THING IN THE MORNING!? YOU STUPID IDIOT!!
SORRY... KURO MEANT TO GO EASY ON IT...
SHUN (SHRINK)
THAT'S WHAT SHE CALLS...
...GOING EASY ON IT?

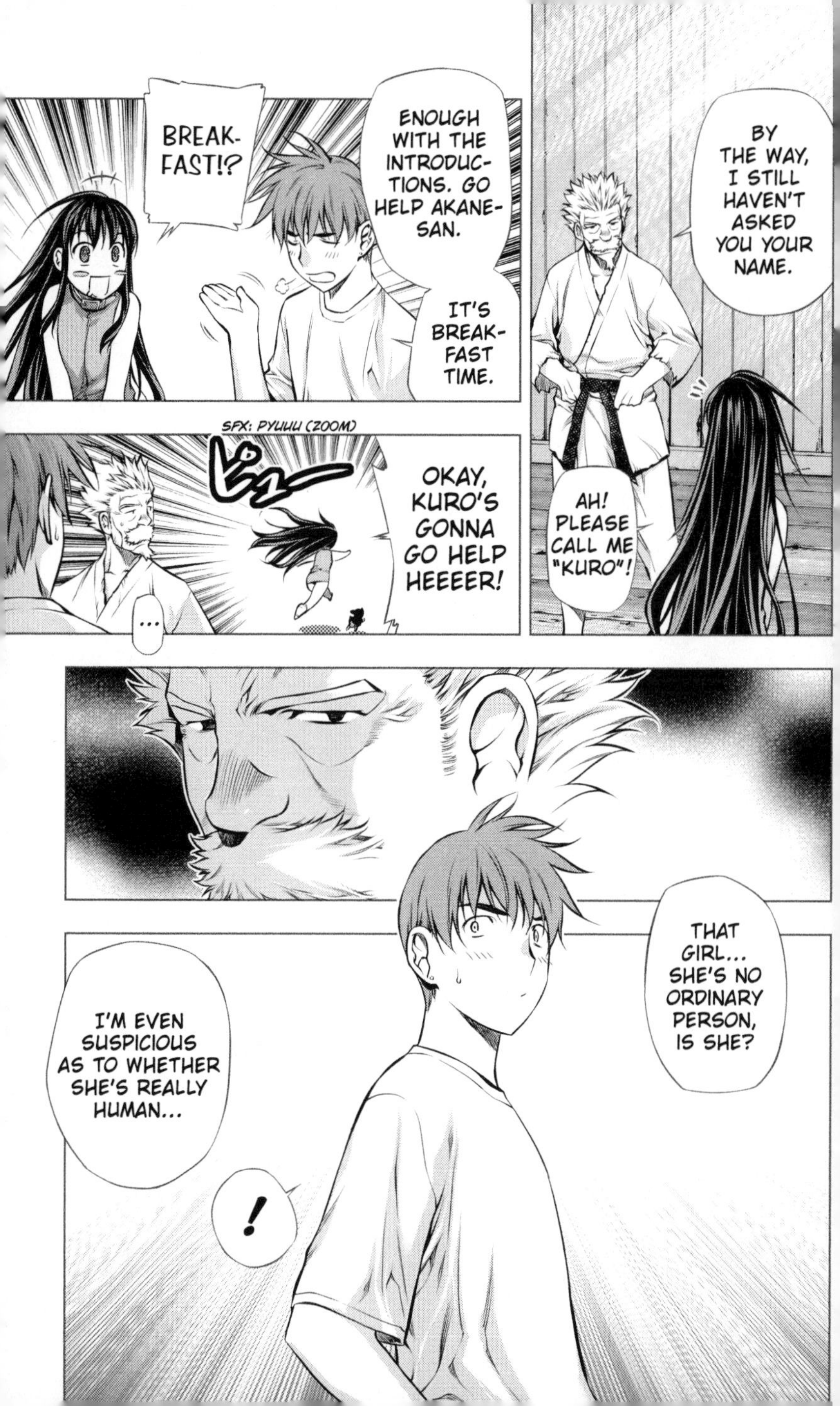
BY THE WAY, I STILL HAVEN'T ASKED YOU YOUR NAME.
AH! PLEASE CALL ME "KURO"!
ENOUGH WITH THE INTRODUCTIONS. GO HELP AKANE-SAN.
IT'S BREAKFAST TIME.
BREAKFAST!?
SFX: PYUUU (ZOOM)
OKAY, KURO'S GONNA GO HELP HEEEER!
...
THAT GIRL... SHE'S NO ORDINARY PERSON, IS SHE?
I'M EVEN SUSPICIOUS AS TO WHETHER SHE'S REALLY HUMAN...
!

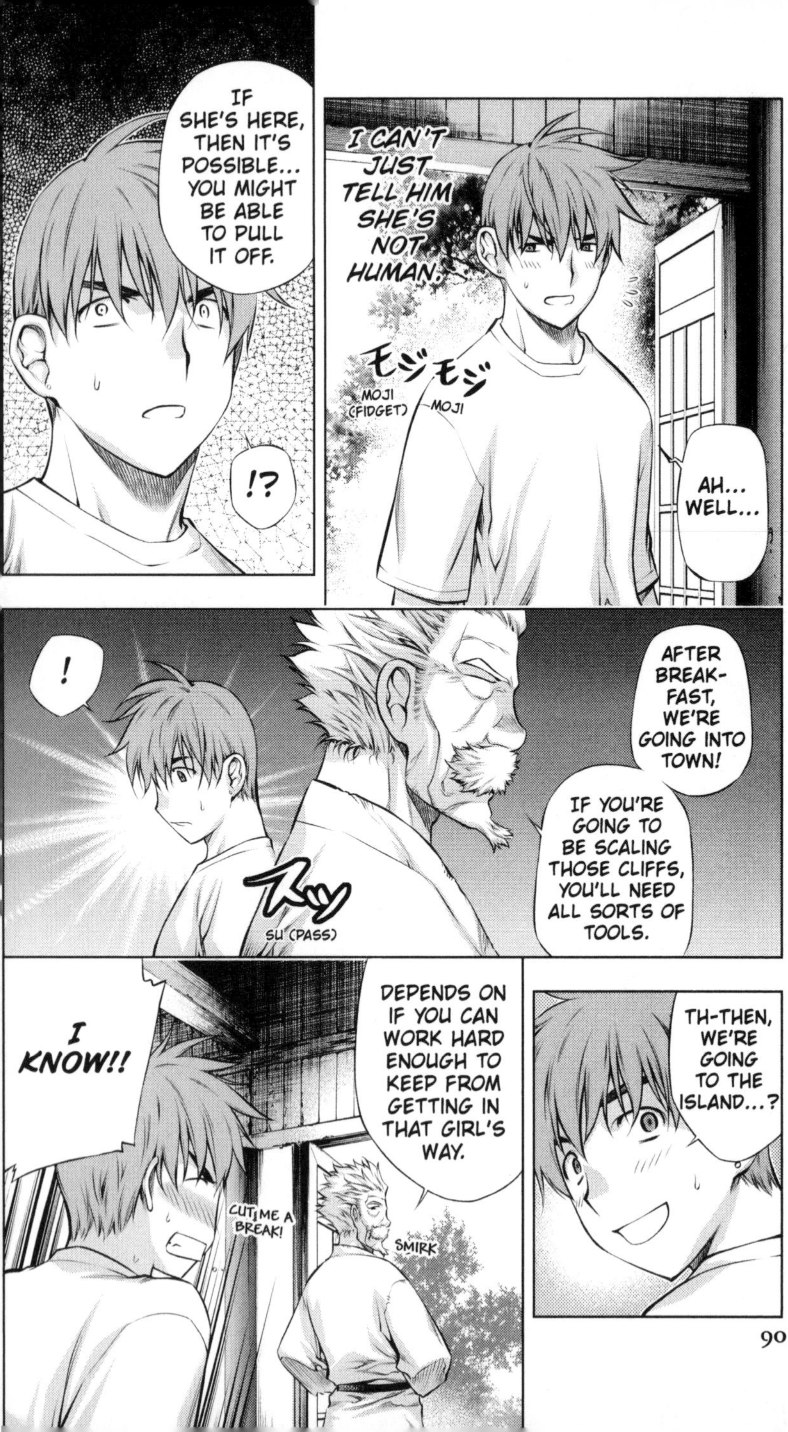

I CAN'T JUST TELL HIM SHE'S NOT HUMAN.
モジモジ
MOJI (FIDGET) MOJI
AH... WELL...
IF SHE'S HERE, THEN IT'S POSSIBLE... YOU MIGHT BE ABLE TO PULL IT OFF.
!?
AFTER BREAK-FAST, WE'RE GOING INTO TOWN!
IF YOU'RE GOING TO BE SCALING THOSE CLIFFS, YOU'LL NEED ALL SORTS OF TOOLS.
スッ
SU (PASS)
!
TH-THEN, WE'RE GOING TO THE ISLAND...?
DEPENDS ON IF YOU CAN WORK HARD ENOUGH TO KEEP FROM GETTING IN THAT GIRL'S WAY.
I KNOW!!
CUT ME A BREAK!
SMIRK

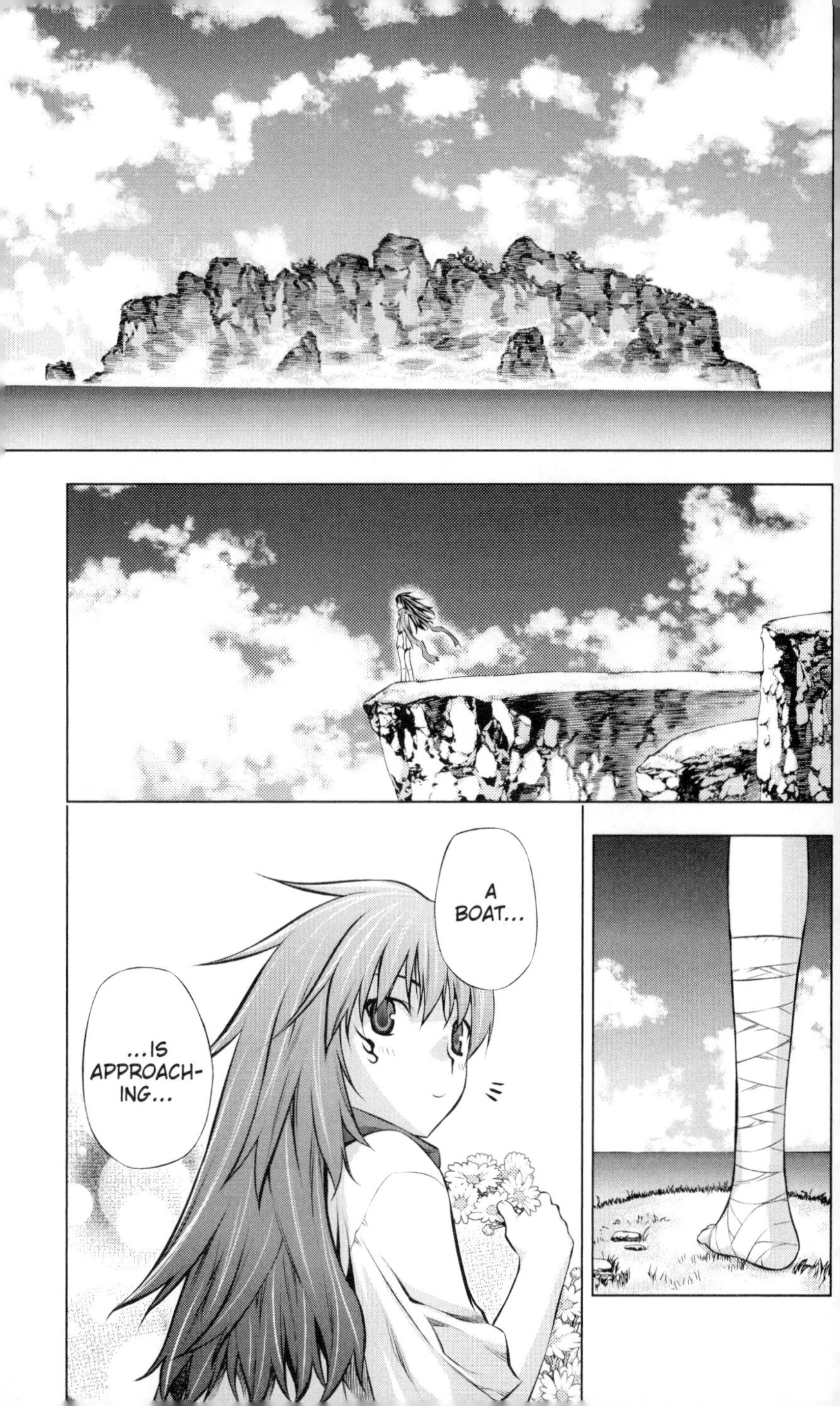
A BOAT...
...IS APPROACH-ING...

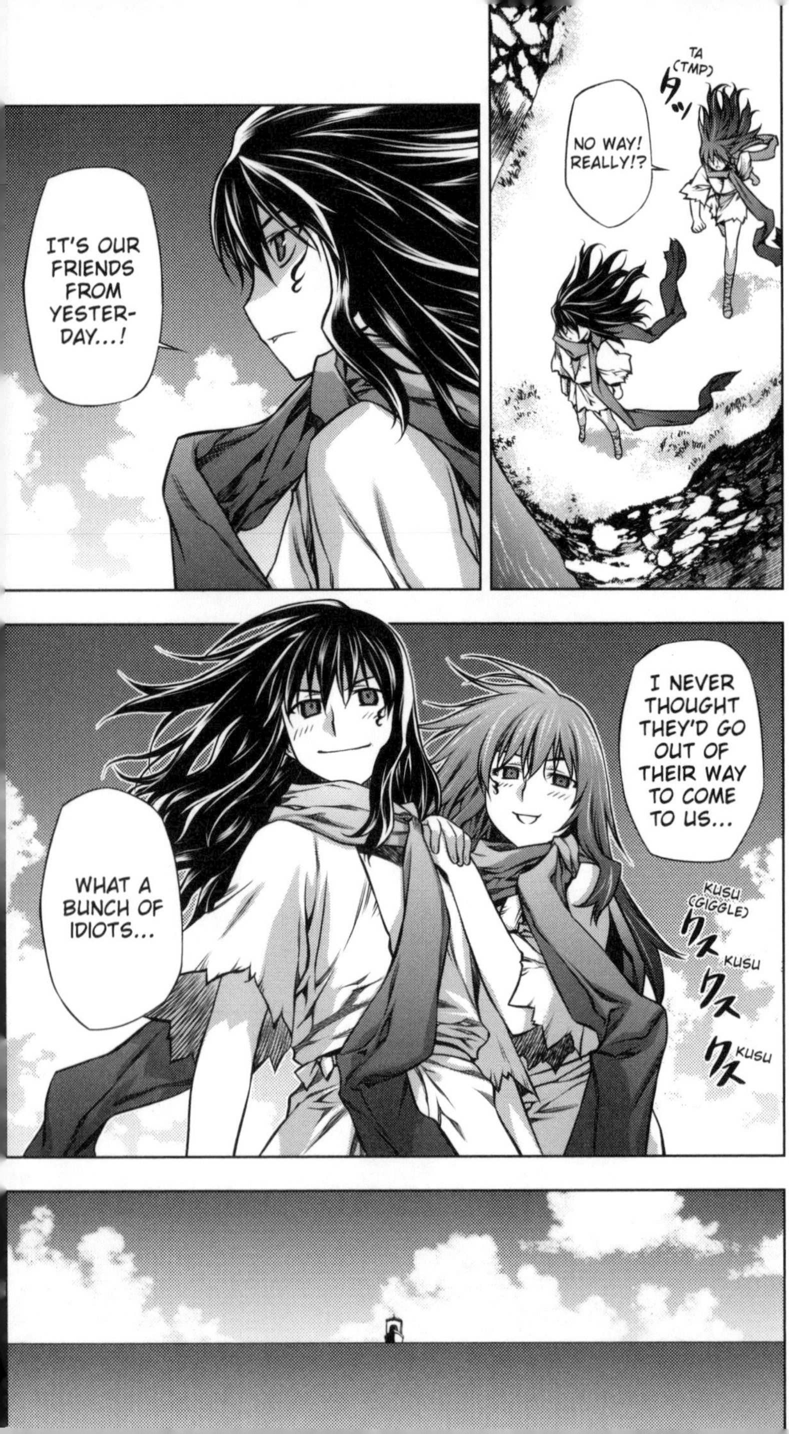

TA (TMP)
タッ
NO WAY! REALLY!?
IT'S OUR FRIENDS FROM YESTER-DAY...!
I NEVER THOUGHT THEY'D GO OUT OF THEIR WAY TO COME TO US...
KUSU (GIGGLE)
クス
KUSU
クス
KUSU
クス
WHAT A BUNCH OF IDIOTS...

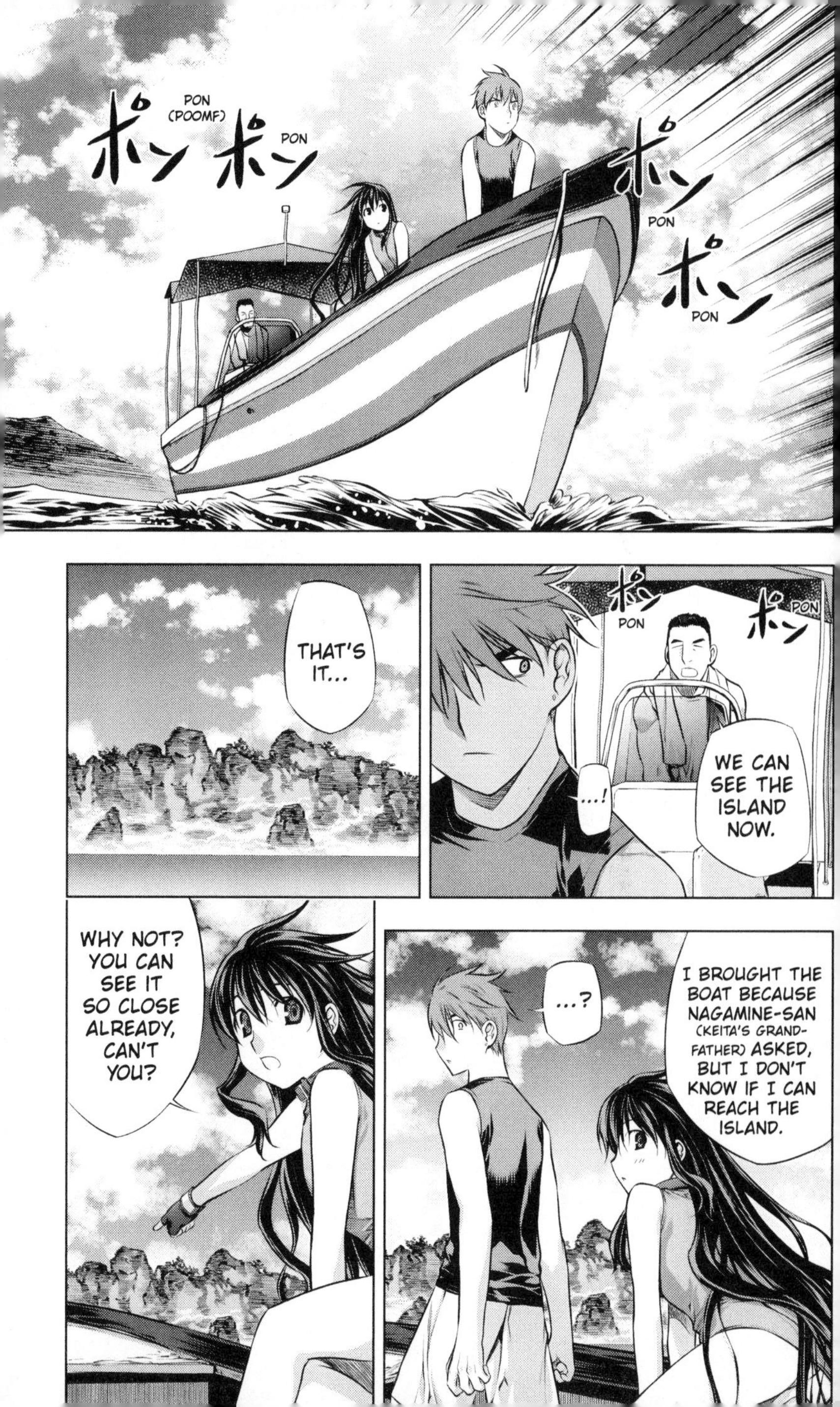

ポン
PON
ポン
PON
PON
(POOMF)
ポン
ポン
PON
ポン
PON
ポン
PON
WE CAN SEE THE ISLAND NOW.
...!
THAT'S IT...
I BROUGHT THE BOAT BECAUSE NAGAMINE-SAN (KEITA'S GRANDFATHER) ASKED, BUT I DON'T KNOW IF I CAN REACH THE ISLAND.
...?
WHY NOT? YOU CAN SEE IT SO CLOSE ALREADY, CAN'T YOU?

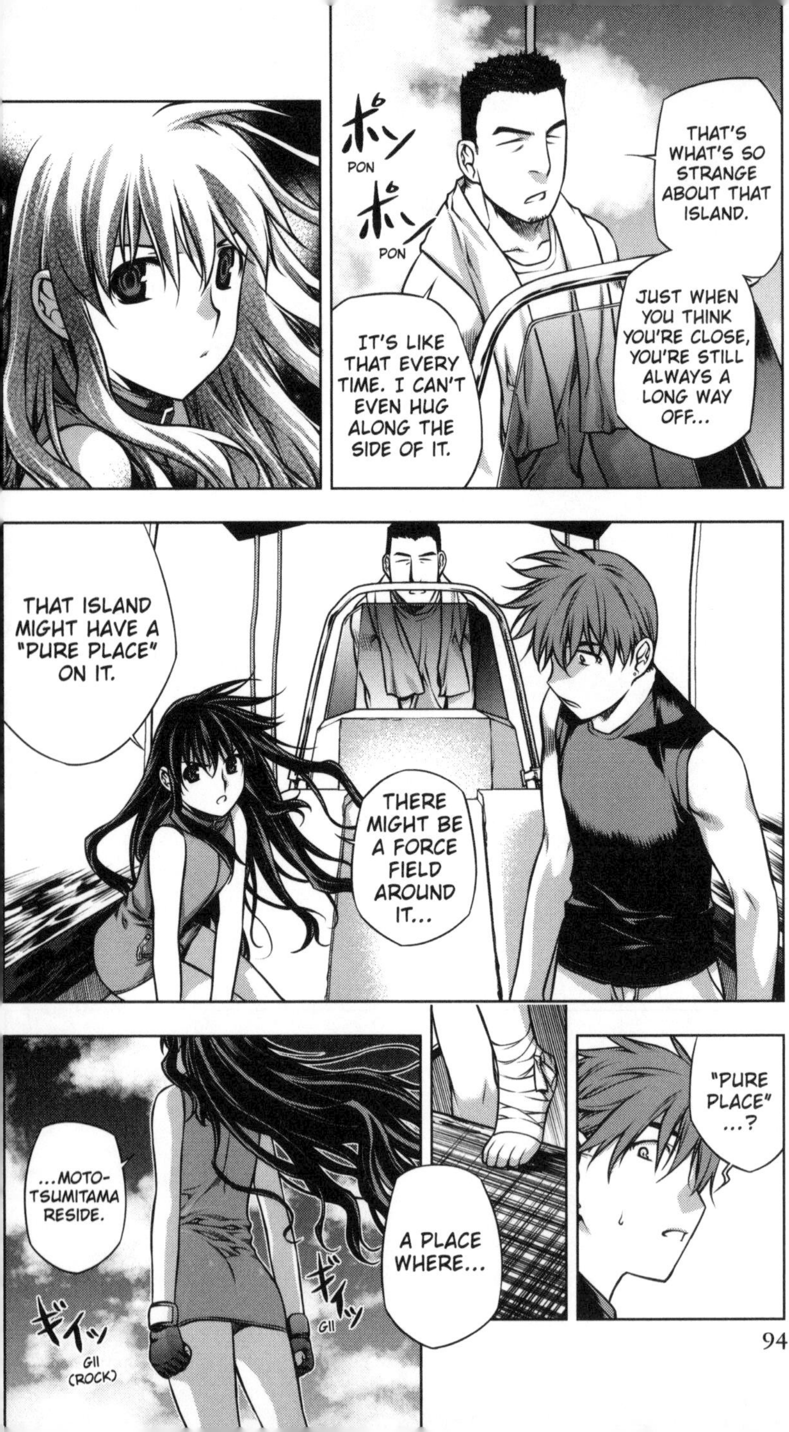
ポン
PON
ポン
PON
THAT'S WHAT'S SO STRANGE ABOUT THAT ISLAND.
JUST WHEN YOU THINK YOU'RE CLOSE, YOU'RE STILL ALWAYS A LONG WAY OFF...
IT'S LIKE THAT EVERY TIME. I CAN'T EVEN HUG ALONG THE SIDE OF IT.
THAT ISLAND MIGHT HAVE A "PURE PLACE" ON IT.
THERE MIGHT BE A FORCE FIELD AROUND IT...
"PURE PLACE" ...?
A PLACE WHERE...
...MOTO-TSUMITAMA RESIDE.
ギイッ
GII
ギイッ
GII (ROCK)

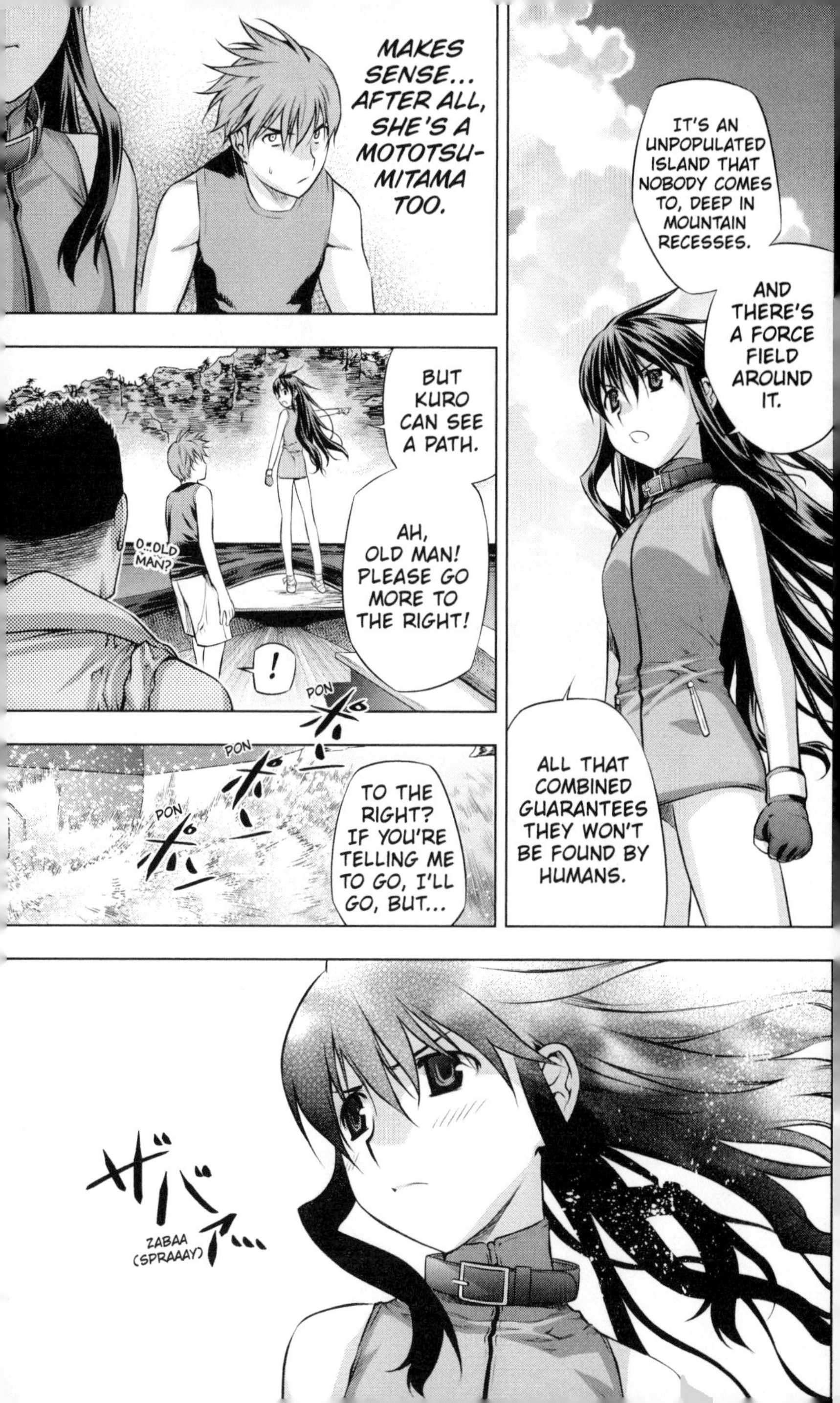
IT'S AN UNPOPULATED ISLAND THAT NOBODY COMES TO, DEEP IN MOUNTAIN RECESSES.
AND THERE'S A FORCE FIELD AROUND IT.
ALL THAT COMBINED GUARANTEES THEY WON'T BE FOUND BY HUMANS.
MAKES SENSE... AFTER ALL, SHE'S A MOTOTSU-MITAMA TOO.
BUT KURO CAN SEE A PATH.
AH, OLD MAN! PLEASE GO MORE TO THE RIGHT!
O...OLD MAN?
!
PON
PON
PON
TO THE RIGHT? IF YOU'RE TELLING ME TO GO, I'LL GO, BUT...
ザバァ...
ZABAA (SPRAAAY)

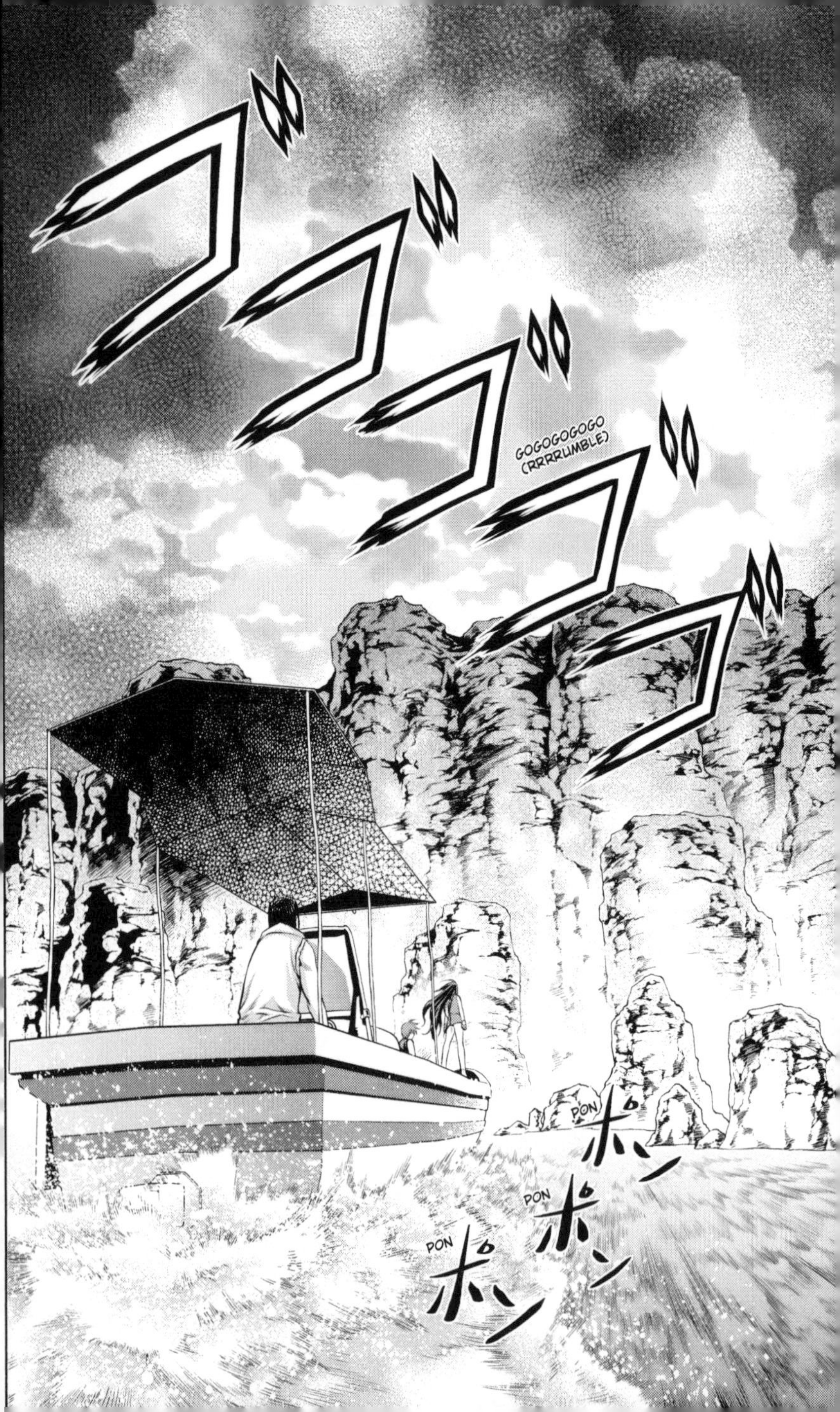
ゴゴゴゴゴ
GOGOGOGOGO
(RRRRUMBLE)
ポン
PON
ポン
PON
ポン
PON

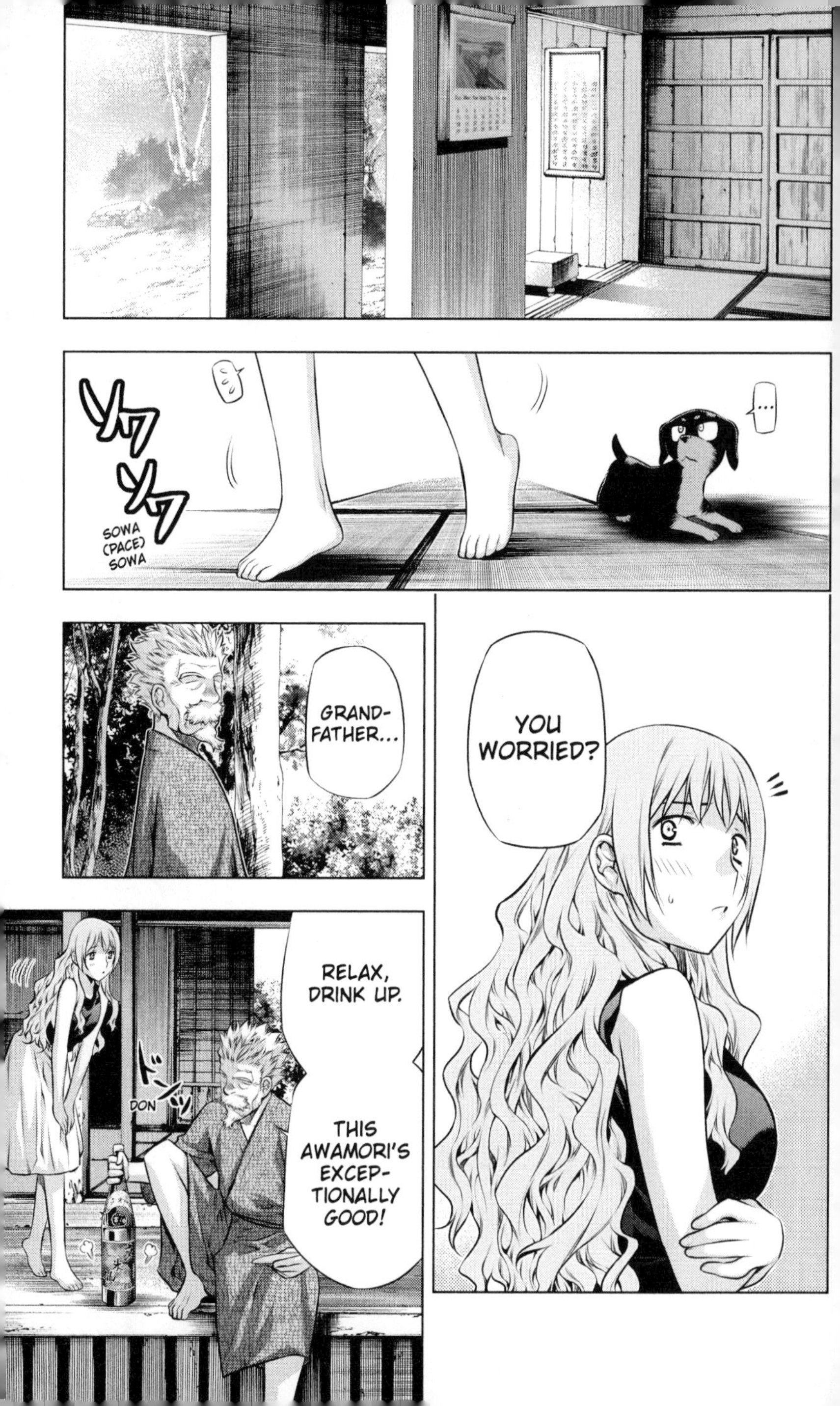
ソワソワ
SOWA (PACE) SOWA
…
YOU WORRIED?
GRAND-FATHER…
ド
DON
RELAX, DRINK UP.
THIS AWAMORI'S EXCEP-TIONALLY GOOD!

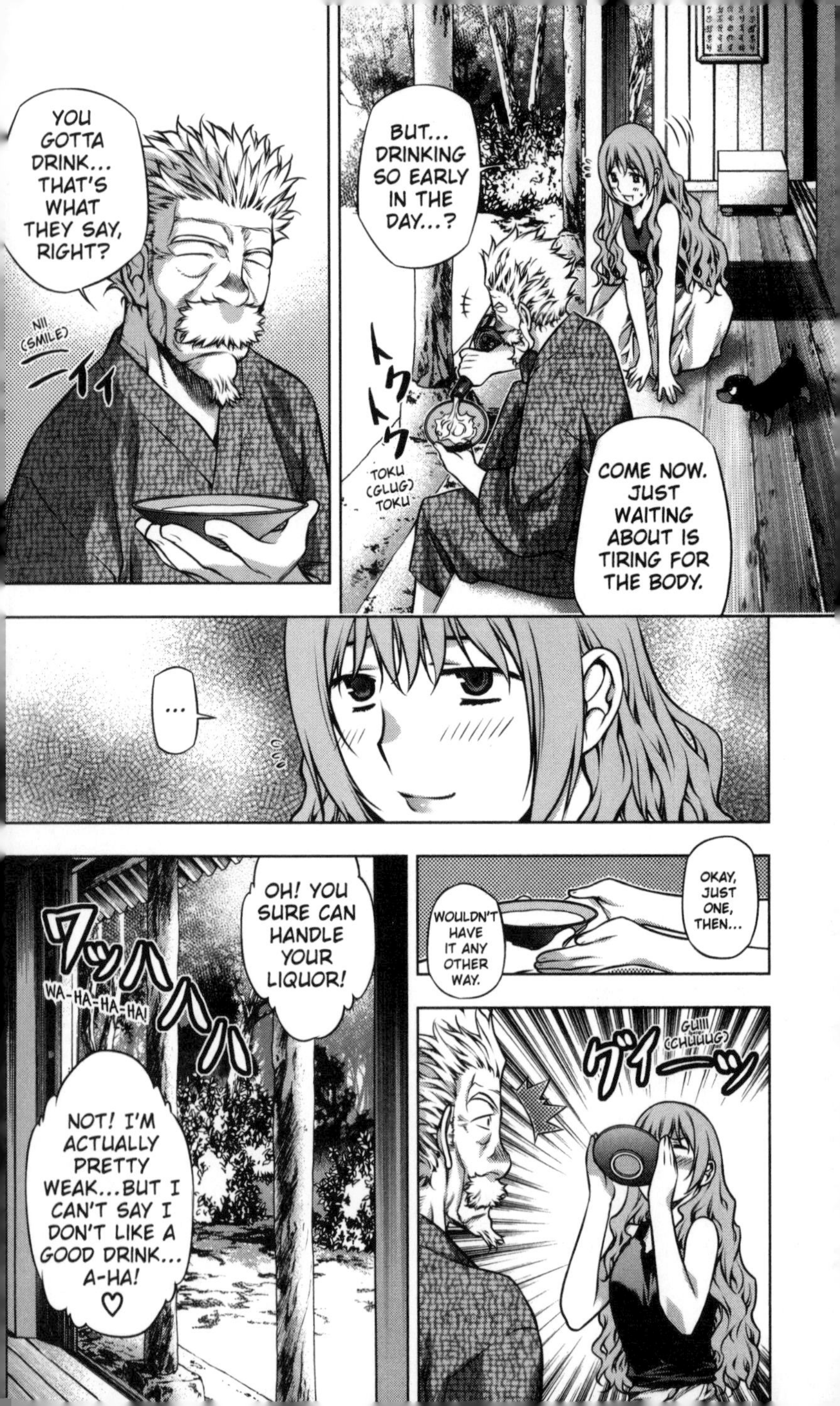
BUT... DRINKING SO EARLY IN THE DAY...?
トクトク
TOKU (GLUG) TOKU
COME NOW. JUST WAITING ABOUT IS TIRING FOR THE BODY.
YOU GOTTA DRINK... THAT'S WHAT THEY SAY, RIGHT?
NII (SMILE)
ニイィ
...
OKAY, JUST ONE, THEN...
WOULDN'T HAVE IT ANY OTHER WAY.
GUIII (CHUUUG)
グイーッ
OH! YOU SURE CAN HANDLE YOUR LIQUOR!
ワッハハハ
WA-HA-HA-HA!
NOT! I'M ACTUALLY PRETTY WEAK...BUT I CAN'T SAY I DON'T LIKE A GOOD DRINK... A-HA! ♡

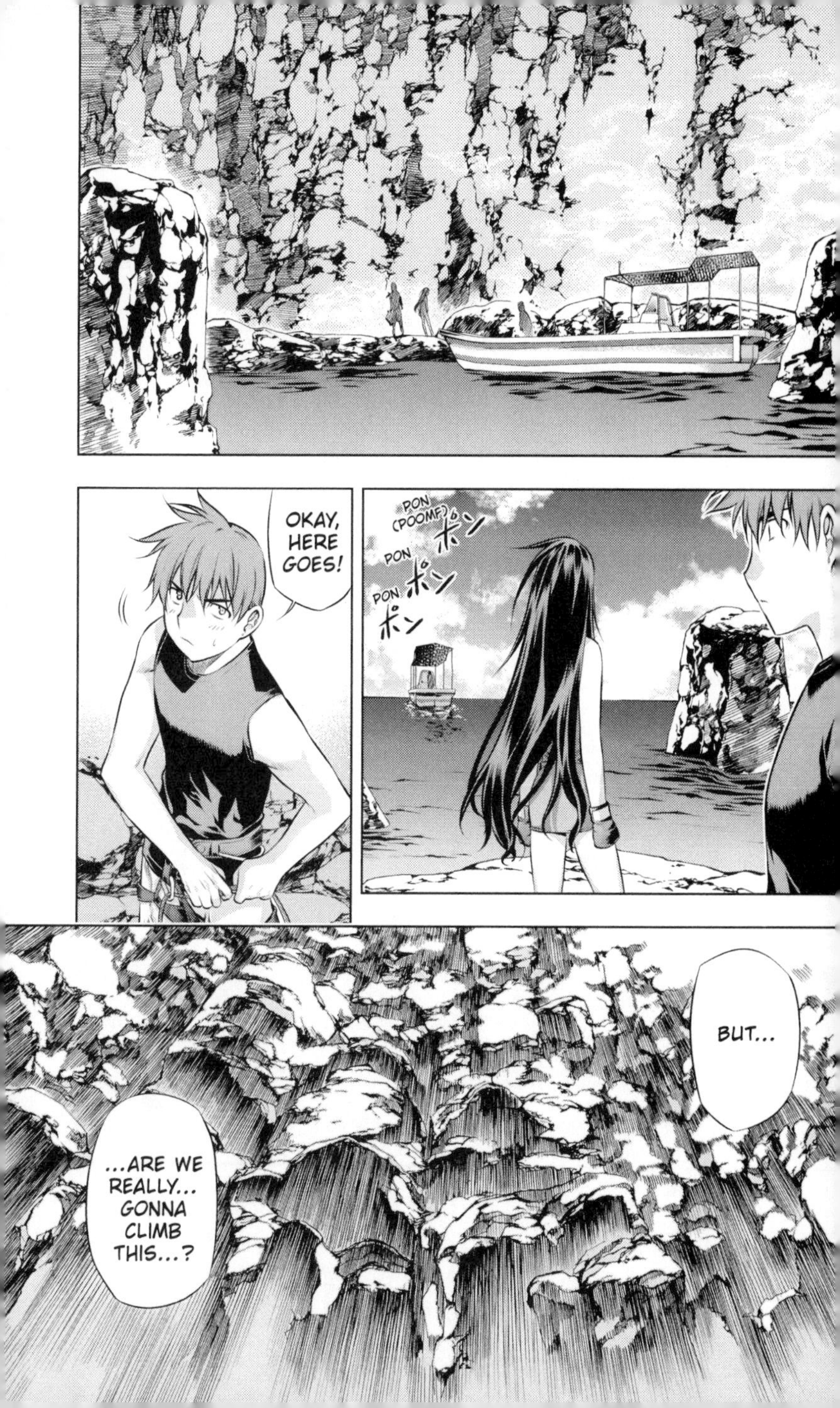
PON (POOMF) ポン
PON ポン
PON ポン
OKAY, HERE GOES!
BUT...
...ARE WE REALLY... GONNA CLIMB THIS...?

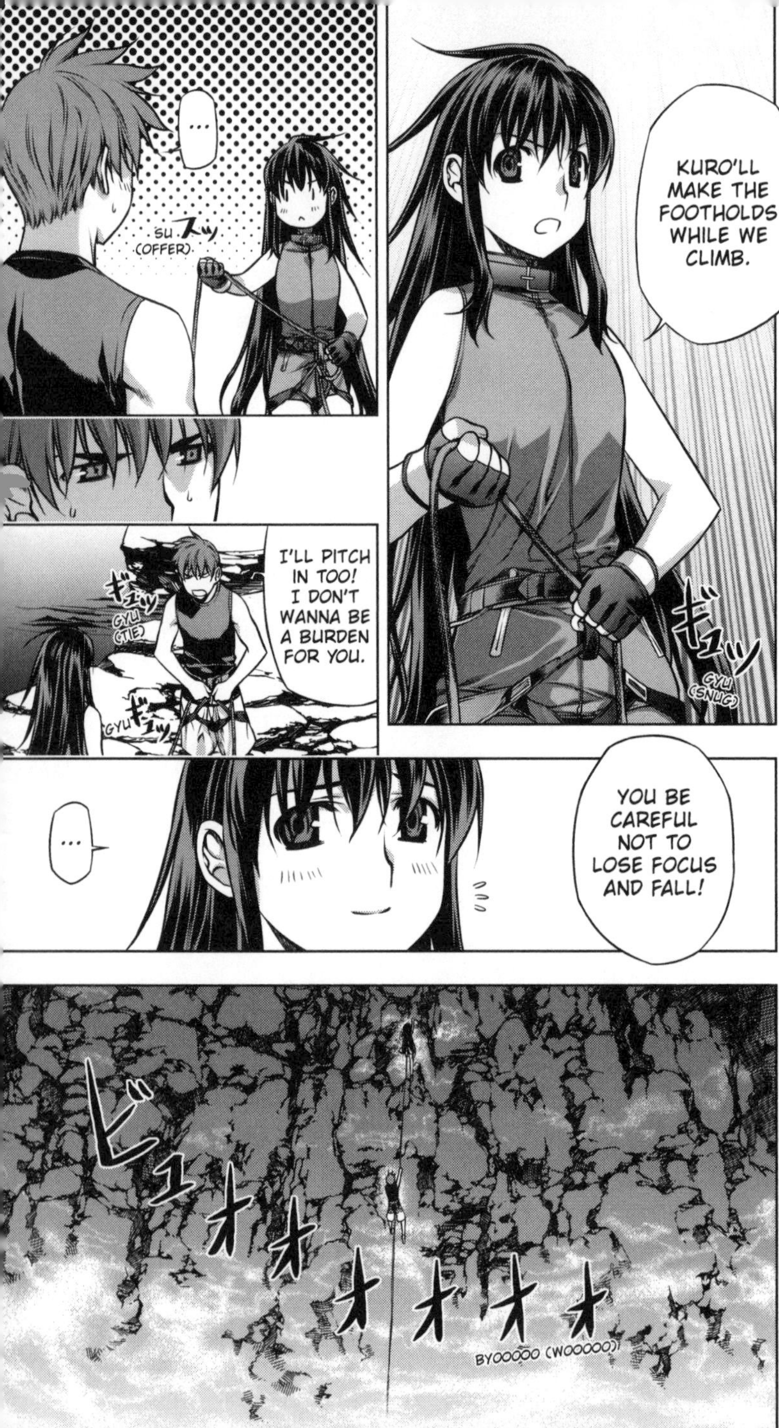

KURO'LL MAKE THE FOOTHOLDS WHILE WE CLIMB.
ギュッ
GYU (SNUG)
...
スッ
SU (OFFER)
I'LL PITCH IN TOO! I DON'T WANNA BE A BURDEN FOR YOU.
ギュッ
GYU (TIE)
ギュッ
GYU
YOU BE CAREFUL NOT TO LOSE FOCUS AND FALL!
...
ビュオオオオオオ
BYOOOOO (WOOOOO)

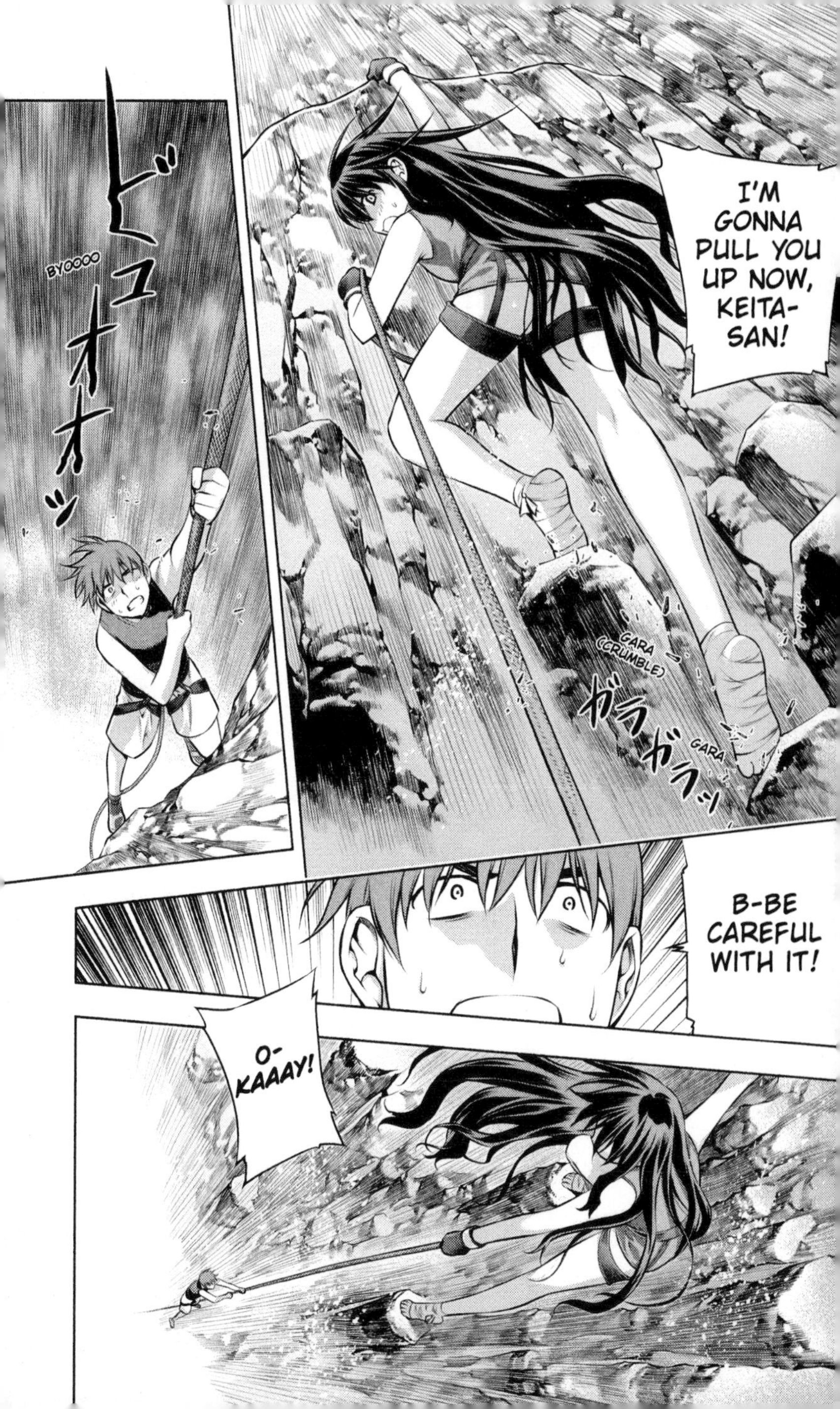
I'M GONNA PULL YOU UP NOW, KEITA-SAN!
GARA (CRUMBLE)
ガラガラッ
GARA
ビュオオッ
BYOOOO
B-BE CAREFUL WITH IT!
O-KAAAY!

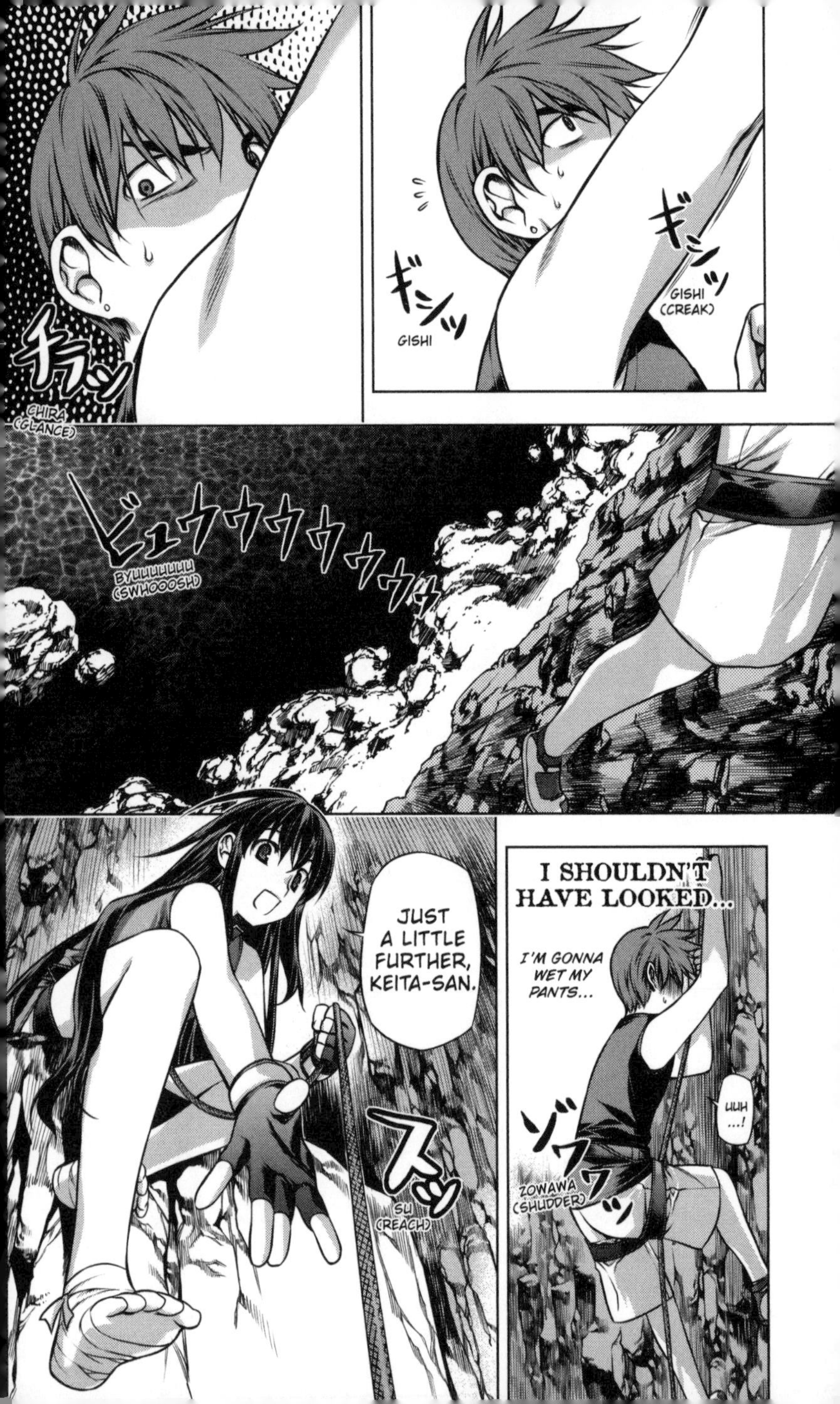
ギシッ
GISHI (CREAK)
ギシッ
GISHI
チラッ
CHIRA (GLANCE)
ビュウウウウウウウ
BYUUUUUUU (SWHOOOSH)
I SHOULDN'T HAVE LOOKED...
I'M GONNA WET MY PANTS...
UUH ...!
ゾワワッ
ZOWAWA (SHUDDER)
JUST A LITTLE FURTHER, KEITA-SAN.
スッ
SU (REACH)

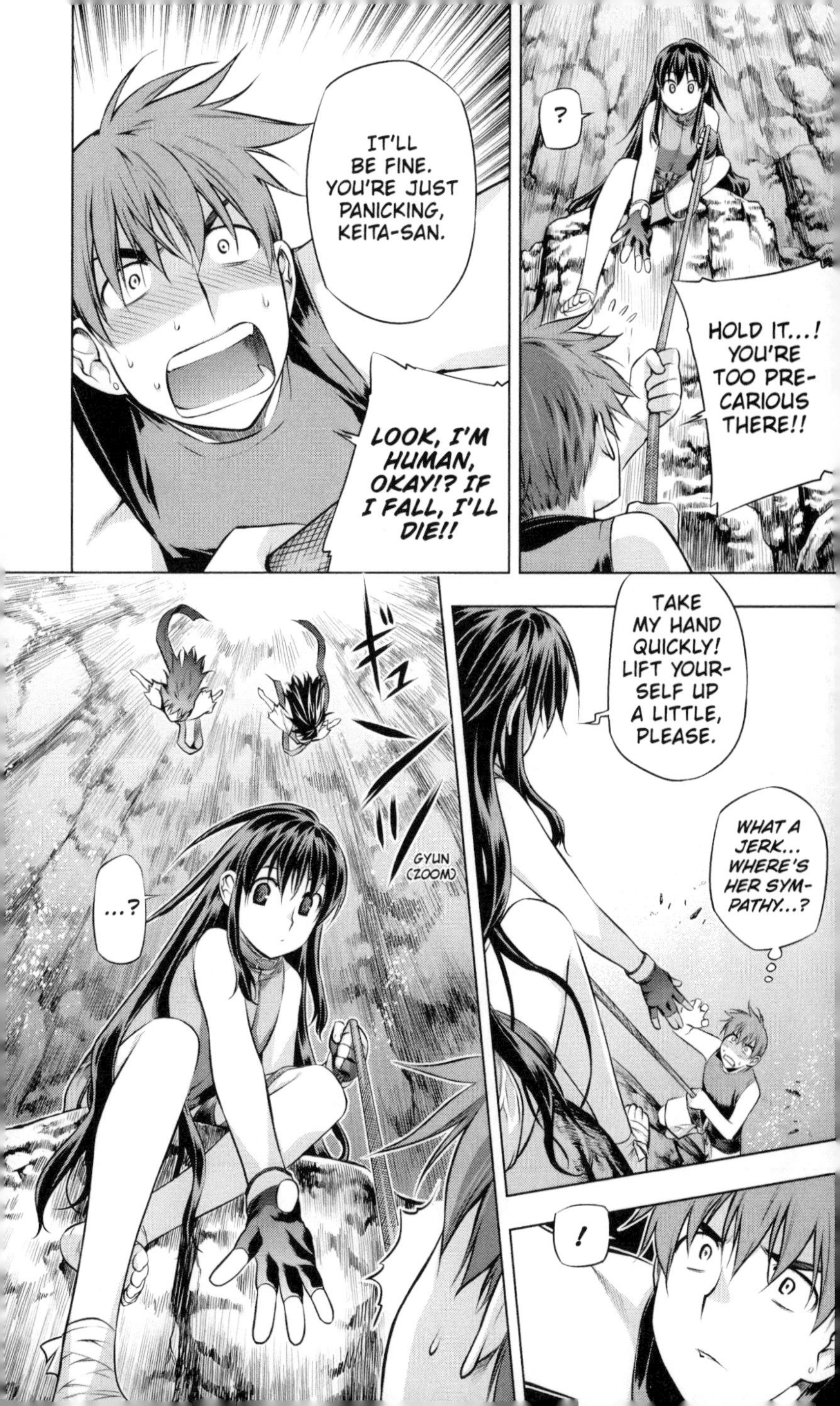

?
HOLD IT...! YOU'RE TOO PRE-CARIOUS THERE!!
IT'LL BE FINE. YOU'RE JUST PANICKING, KEITA-SAN.
LOOK, I'M HUMAN, OKAY!? IF I FALL, I'LL DIE!!
TAKE MY HAND QUICKLY! LIFT YOURSELF UP A LITTLE, PLEASE.
WHAT A JERK... WHERE'S HER SYMPATHY...?
!
GYUN (ZOOM)
...?

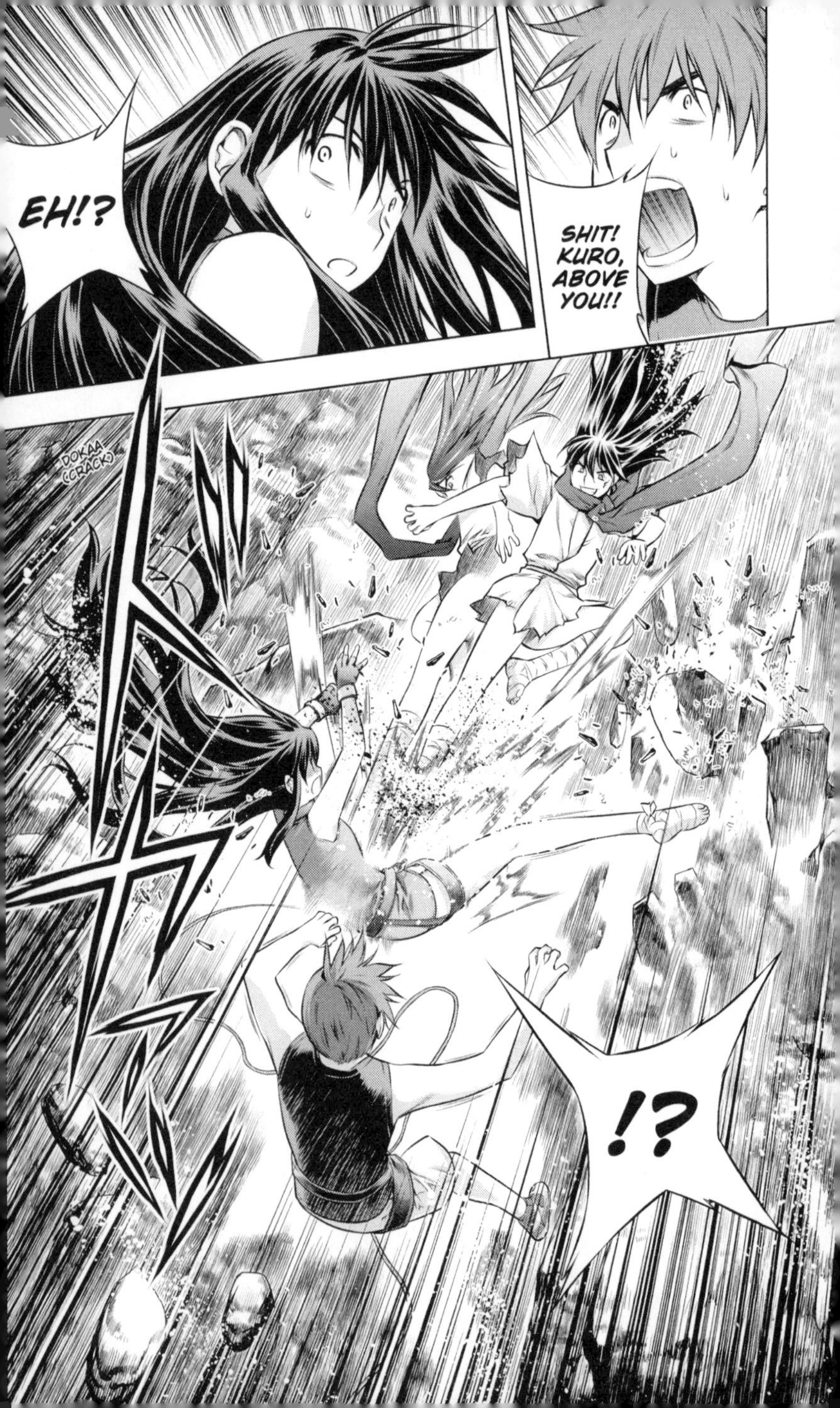
SHIT! KURO, ABOVE YOU!!
EH!?
DOKAA (CRACK)
!?

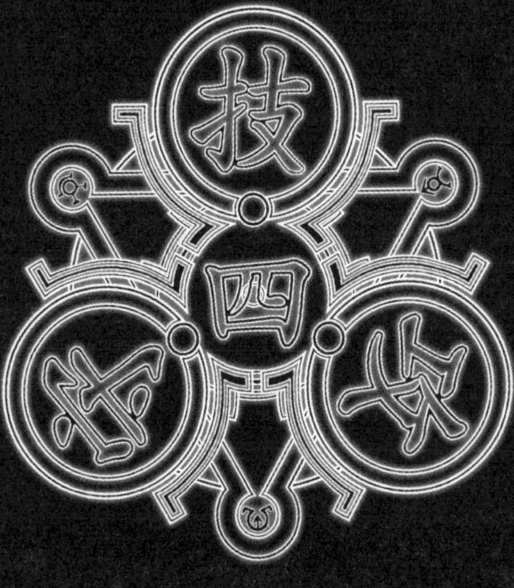
技
四

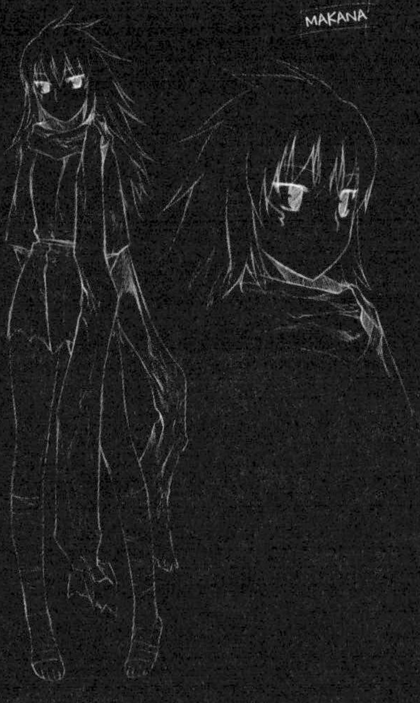
MAKANA

BLACK GOD
which maintains balance in the world.

Nirai Kanai Arc

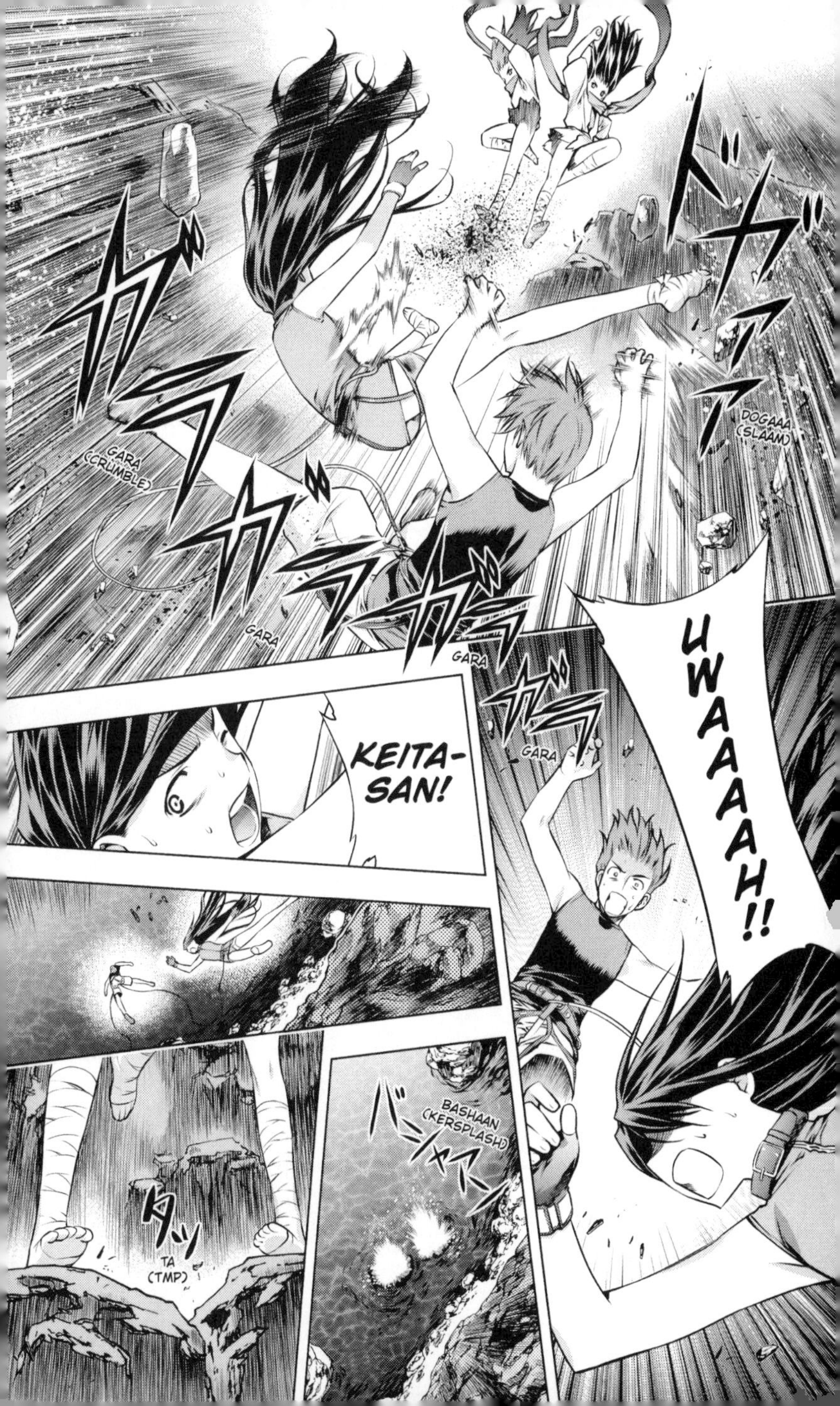
DOGAAA (SLAAM)
GARA (CRUMBLE)
GARA
GARA
GARA
UWAAAAAH!!
KEITA-SAN!
BASHAAN (KERSPLASH)
TA (TMP)

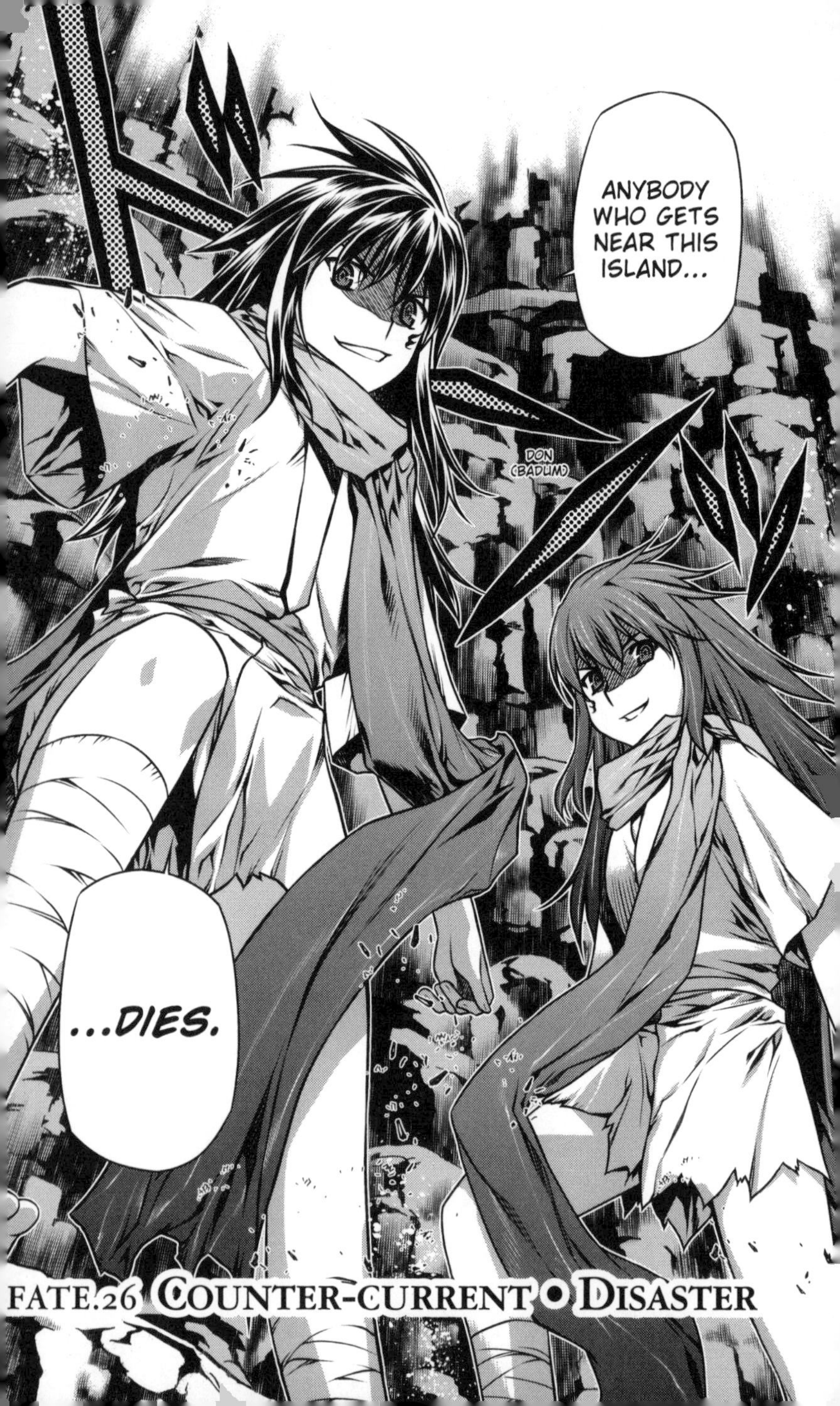
ANYBODY WHO GETS NEAR THIS ISLAND...
DON (BADUM)
...DIES.
FATE.26 COUNTER-CURRENT • DISASTER

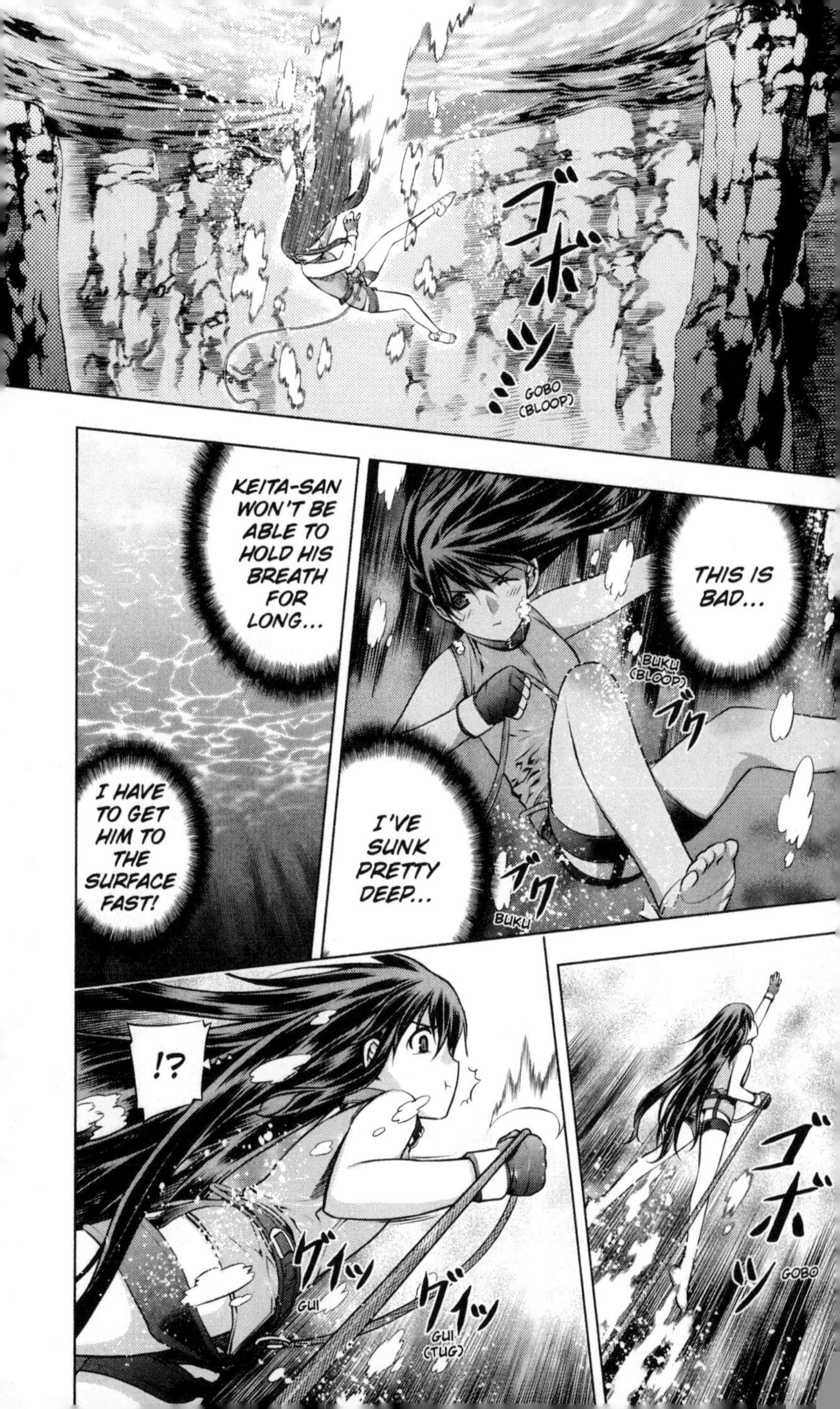

ゴボッ
GOBO (BLOOP)
THIS IS BAD...
BUKU (BLOOP)
ブク
I'VE SUNK PRETTY DEEP...
ブク
BUKU
KEITA-SAN WON'T BE ABLE TO HOLD HIS BREATH FOR LONG...
I HAVE TO GET HIM TO THE SURFACE FAST!
ゴボッ
GOBO
!?
グイッ
GUI
グイッ
GUI (TUG)

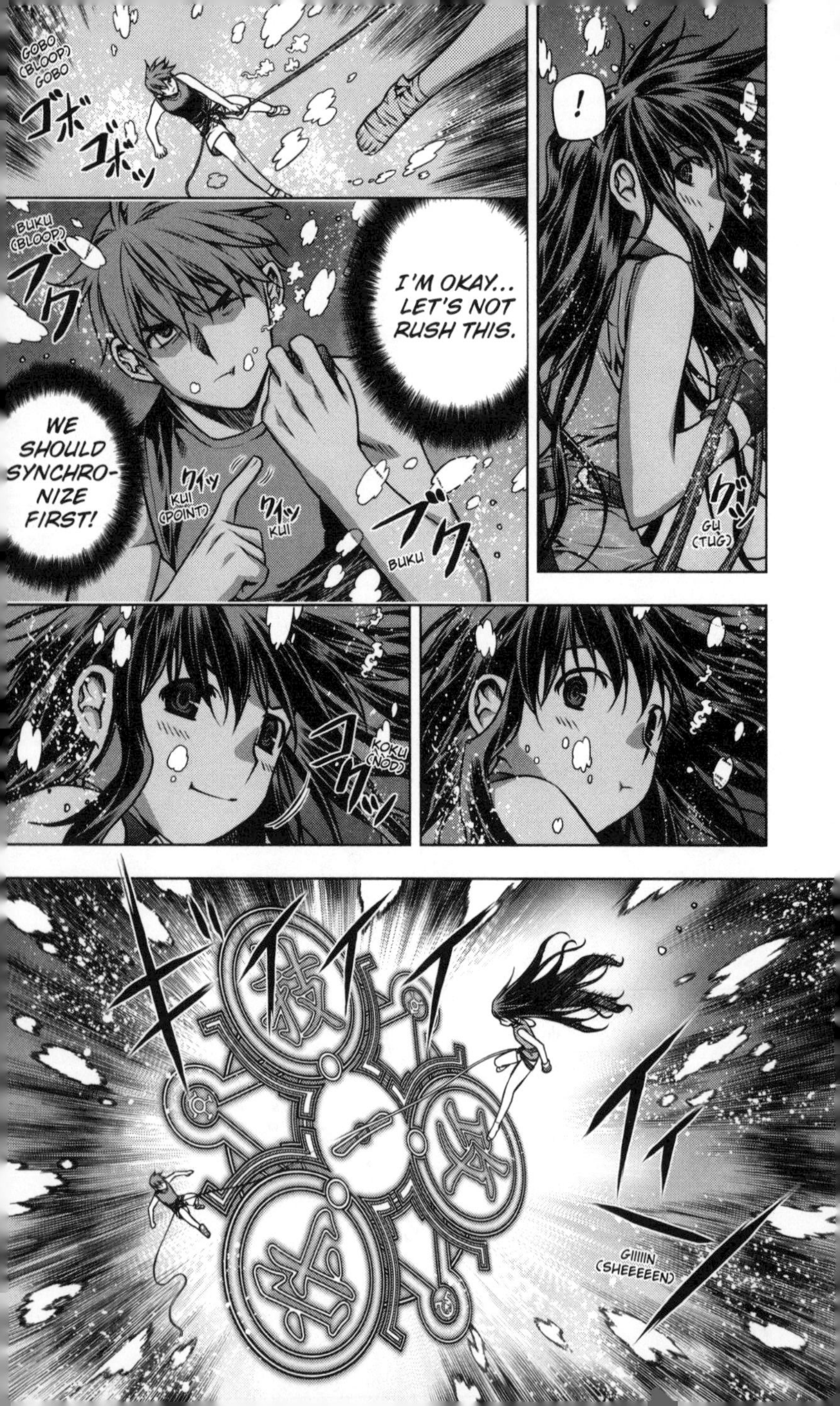
!
グッ
GU (TUG)
GOBO (BLOOP) GOBO
ゴボ ゴボッ
I'M OKAY... LET'S NOT RUSH THIS.
ブク
BUKU (BLOOP)
ブク
BUKU
クイッ
KUI (POINT)
クイッ
KUI
WE SHOULD SYNCHRONIZE FIRST!
コクッ
KOKU (NOD)
GIIIIN (SHEEEEEN)

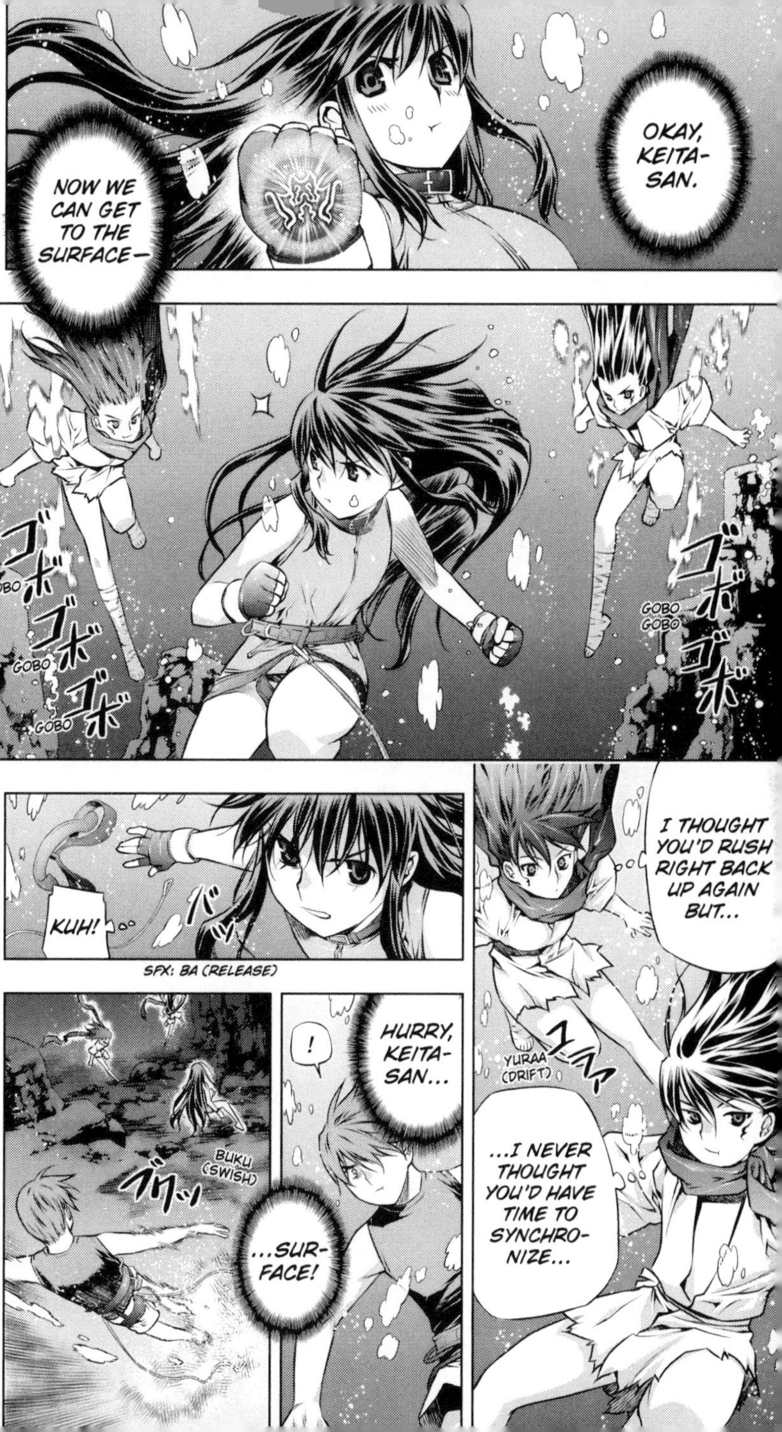
OKAY, KEITA-SAN.
NOW WE CAN GET TO THE SURFACE—
ゴボゴボ
GOBO GOBO
ゴボ
GOBO
ゴボ
GOBO
ゴボ
GOBO
I THOUGHT YOU'D RUSH RIGHT BACK UP AGAIN BUT...
ユラ〜
YURAA (DRIFT)
...I NEVER THOUGHT YOU'D HAVE TIME TO SYNCHRO-NIZE...
バッ
KUH!
SFX: BA (RELEASE)
!
HURRY, KEITA-SAN...
...SUR-FACE!
ブワッ
BUKU (SWISH)

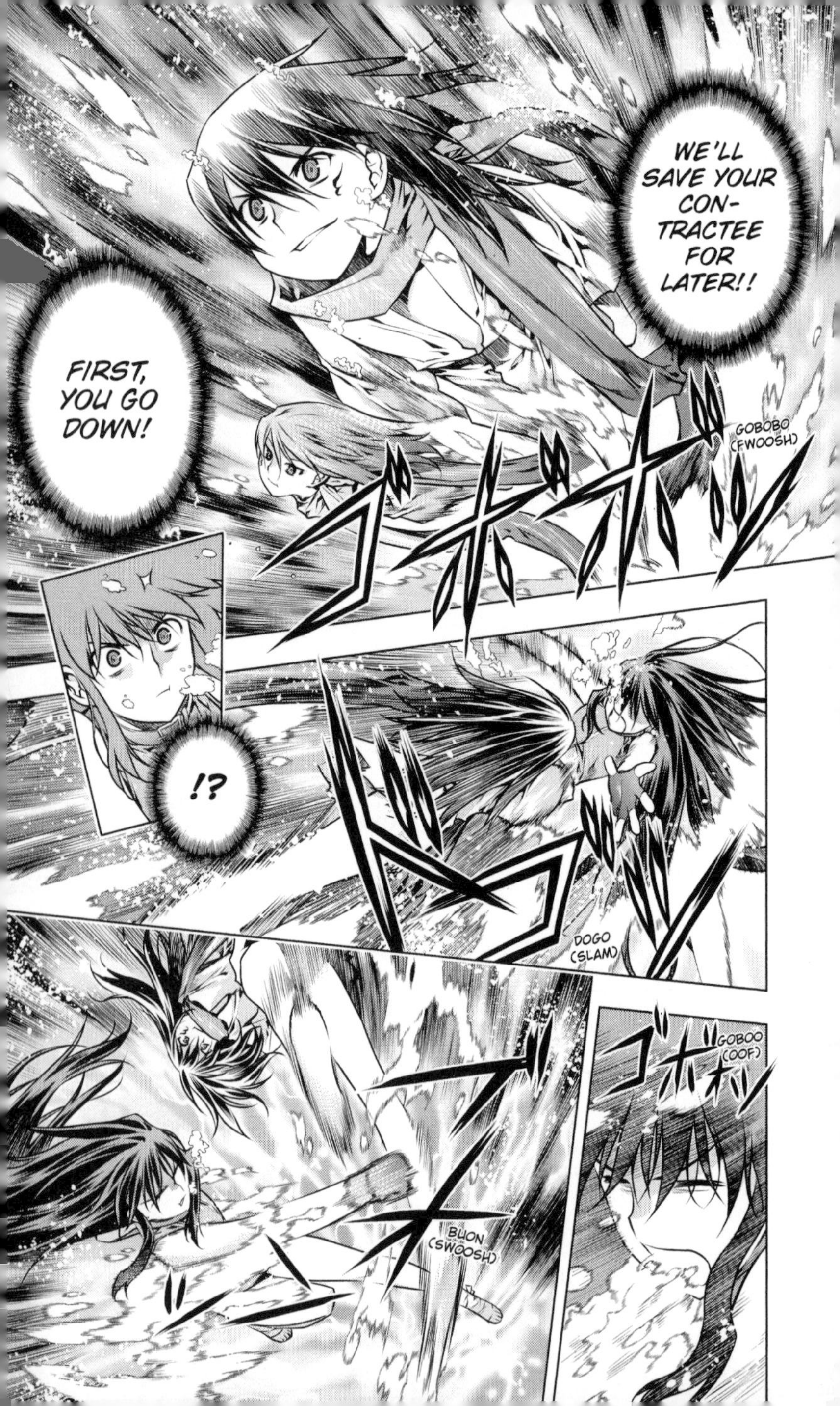
WE'LL SAVE YOUR CON-TRACTEE FOR LATER!!
FIRST, YOU GO DOWN!
GOBOBO (FWOOSH)
DOGO (SLAM)
!?
GOBOO (OOF)
BUON (SWOOSH)

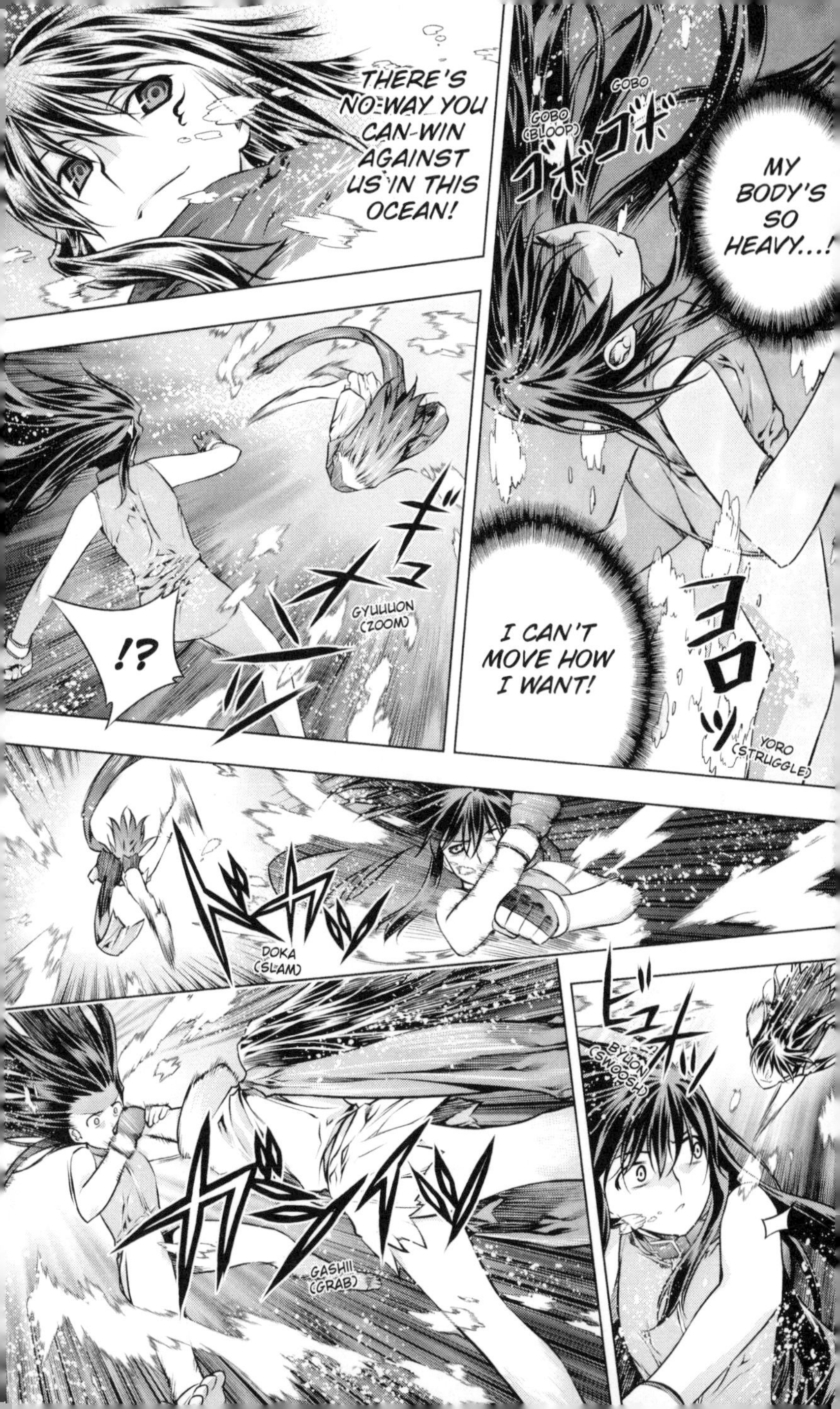
GOBO GOBO (BLOOP)
ゴボゴボ
MY BODY'S SO HEAVY...!
I CAN'T MOVE HOW I WANT!
ヨロッ
YORO (STRUGGLE)
THERE'S NO WAY YOU CAN WIN AGAINST US IN THIS OCEAN!
GYUUUON (ZOOM)
!?
DOKA (SLAM)
BYUON (SWOOSH)
GASHII (GRAB)

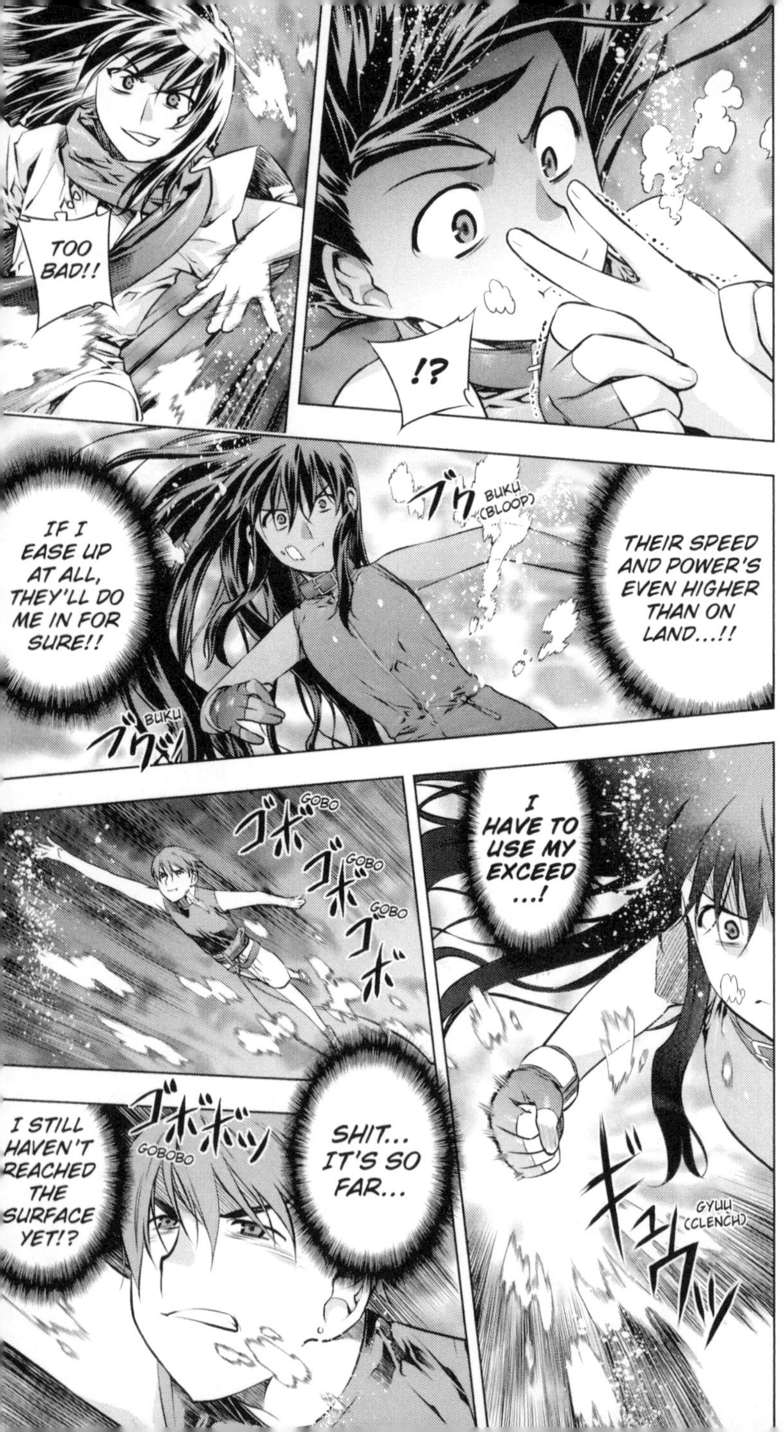
!?
TOO BAD!!
THEIR SPEED AND POWER'S EVEN HIGHER THAN ON LAND...!!
ブク
BUKU (BLOOP)
IF I EASE UP AT ALL, THEY'LL DO ME IN FOR SURE!!
ブクッ
BUKU
I HAVE TO USE MY EXCEED ...!
ギュウッ
GYUU (CLENCH)
ゴボ
GOBO
ゴボ
GOBO
ゴボ
GOBO
SHIT... IT'S SO FAR...
ゴボボッ
GOBOBO
I STILL HAVEN'T REACHED THE SURFACE YET!?

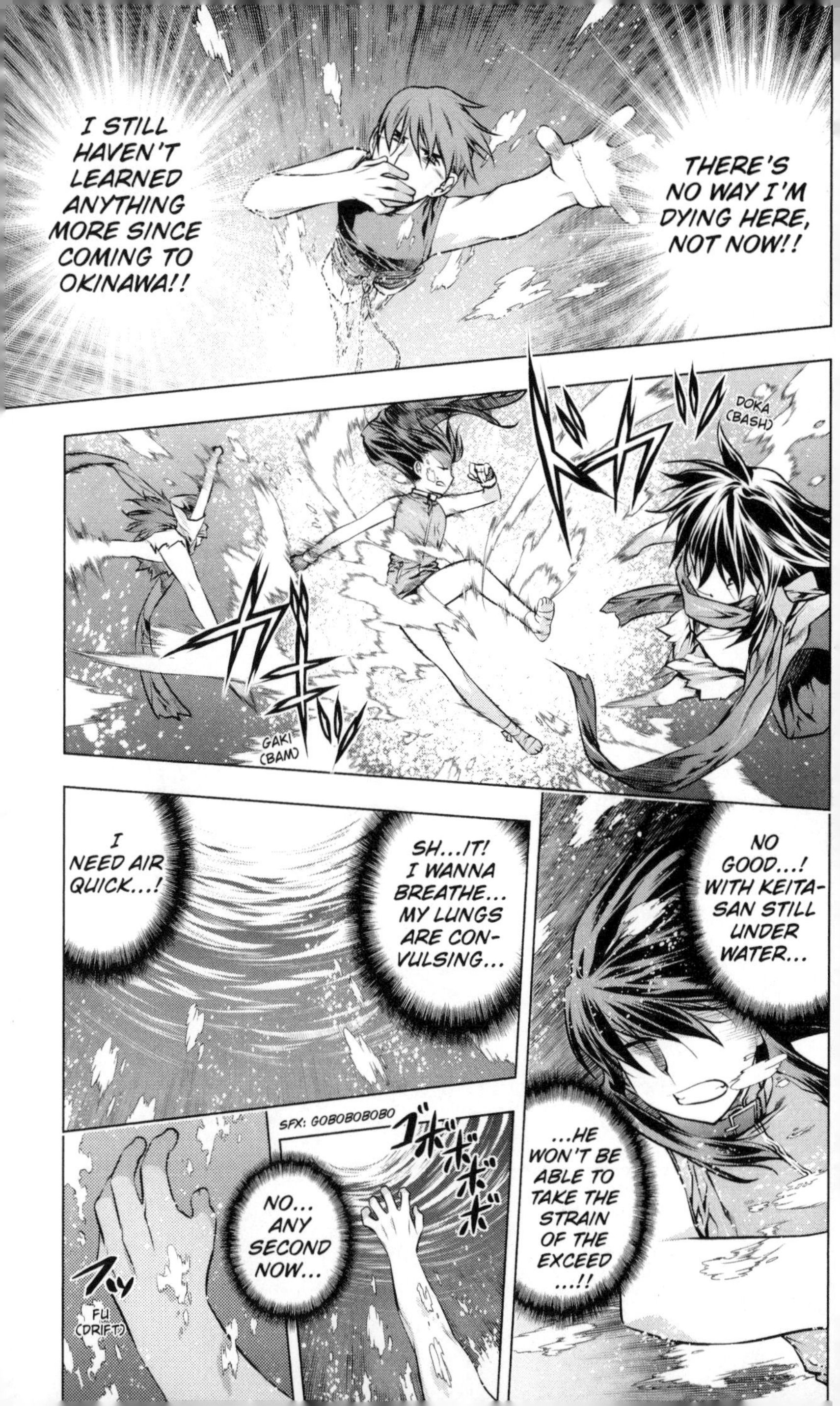
THERE'S NO WAY I'M DYING HERE, NOT NOW!!
I STILL HAVEN'T LEARNED ANYTHING MORE SINCE COMING TO OKINAWA!!
DOKA (BASH)
GAKI (BAM)
NO GOOD...! WITH KEITA-SAN STILL UNDER WATER...
...HE WON'T BE ABLE TO TAKE THE STRAIN OF THE EXCEED ...!!
SH...IT! I WANNA BREATHE... MY LUNGS ARE CON-VULSING...
I NEED AIR QUICK...!
SFX: GOBOBOBOBO
NO... ANY SECOND NOW...
FU (DRIFT)

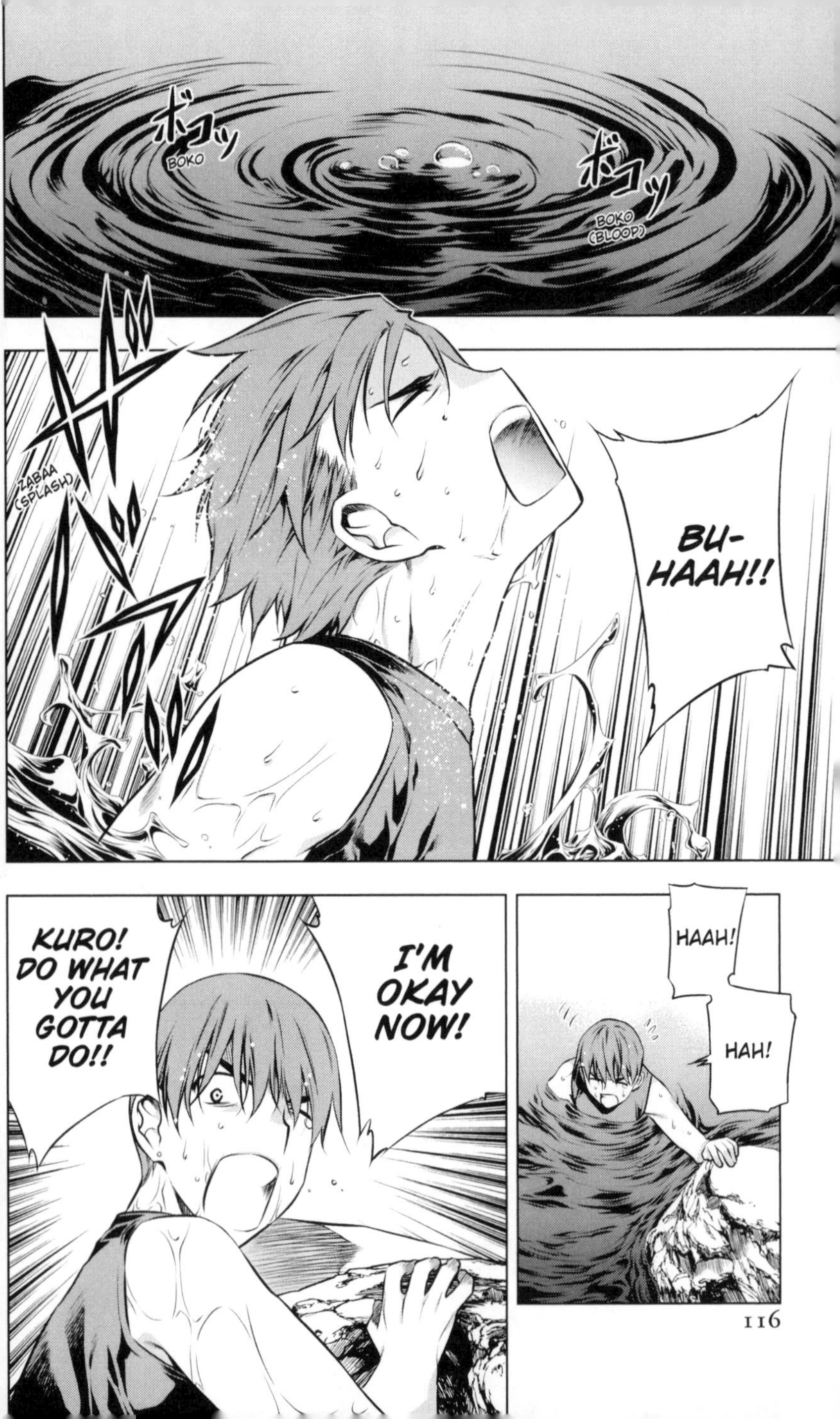
ボコッ
BOKO (BLOOP)
ボコッ
BOKO
BU-HAAH!!
ZABAA (SPLASH)
HAAH!
HAH!
I'M OKAY NOW!
KURO! DO WHAT YOU GOTTA DO!!

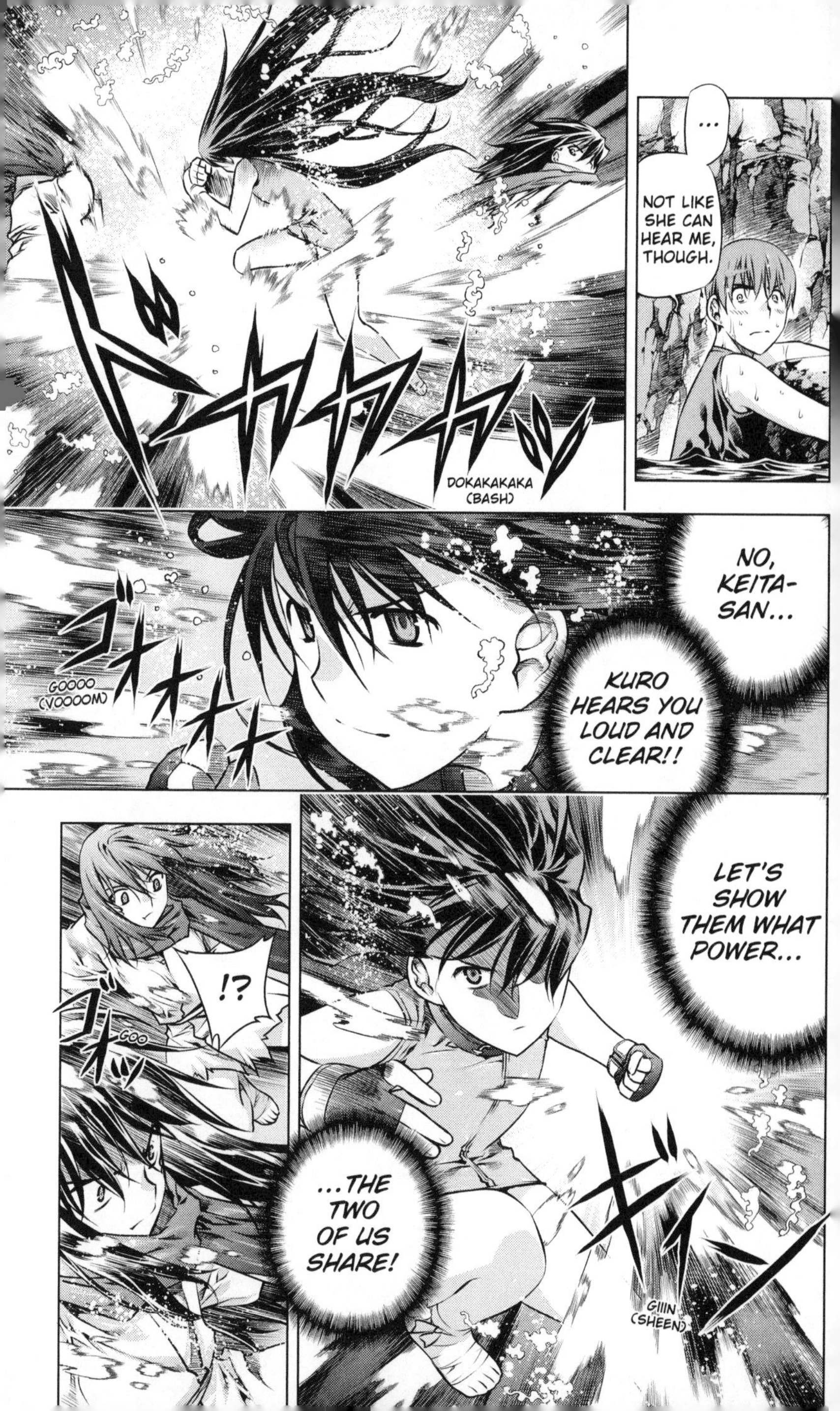
...
NOT LIKE SHE CAN HEAR ME, THOUGH.
DOKAKAKAKA (BASH)
NO, KEITA-SAN...
KURO HEARS YOU LOUD AND CLEAR!!
GOOOO (VOOOOM)
LET'S SHOW THEM WHAT POWER...
...THE TWO OF US SHARE!
GIIIN (SHEEN)
!?
GOO

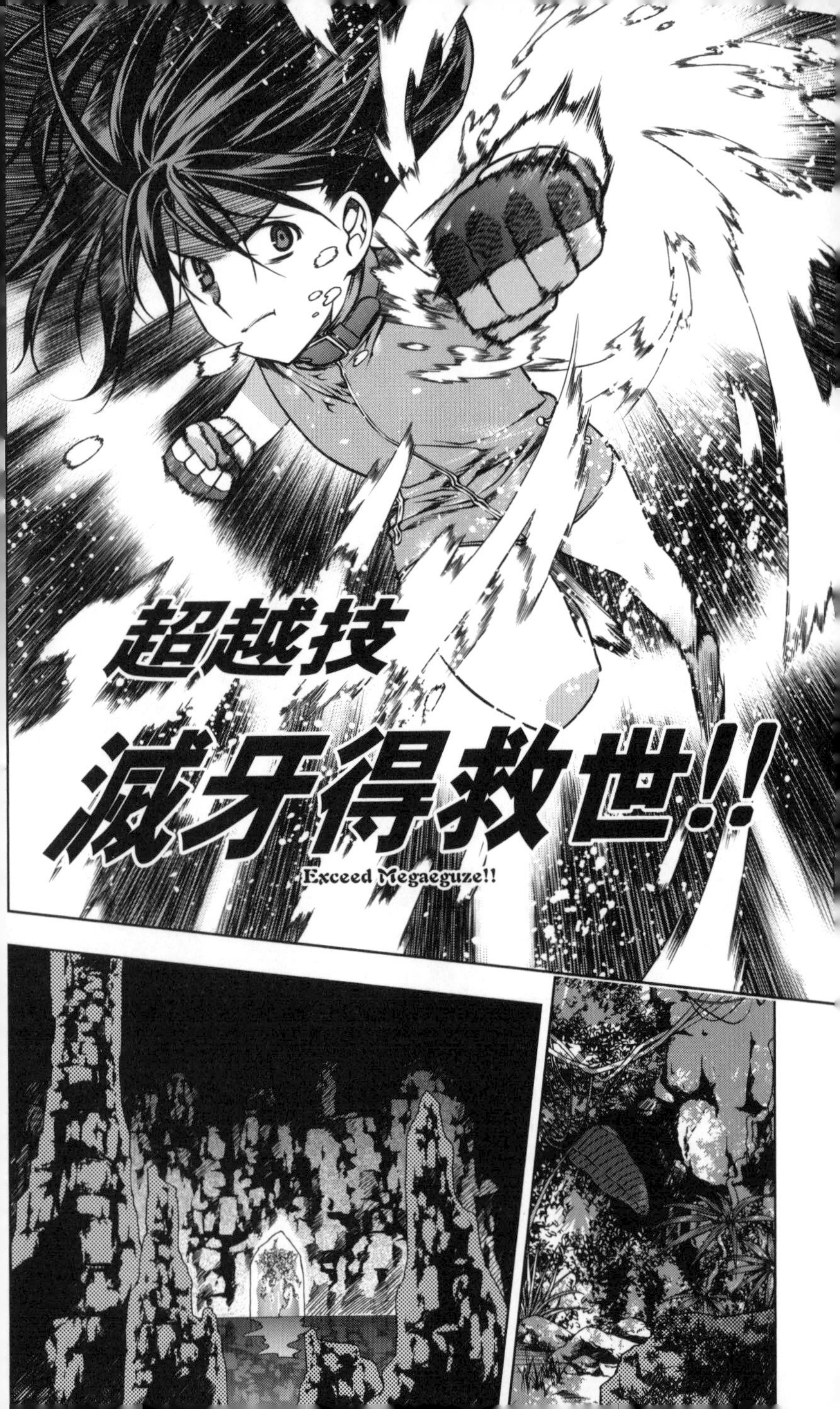
超越技
滅牙得救世!!
Exceed Megaeguze!!

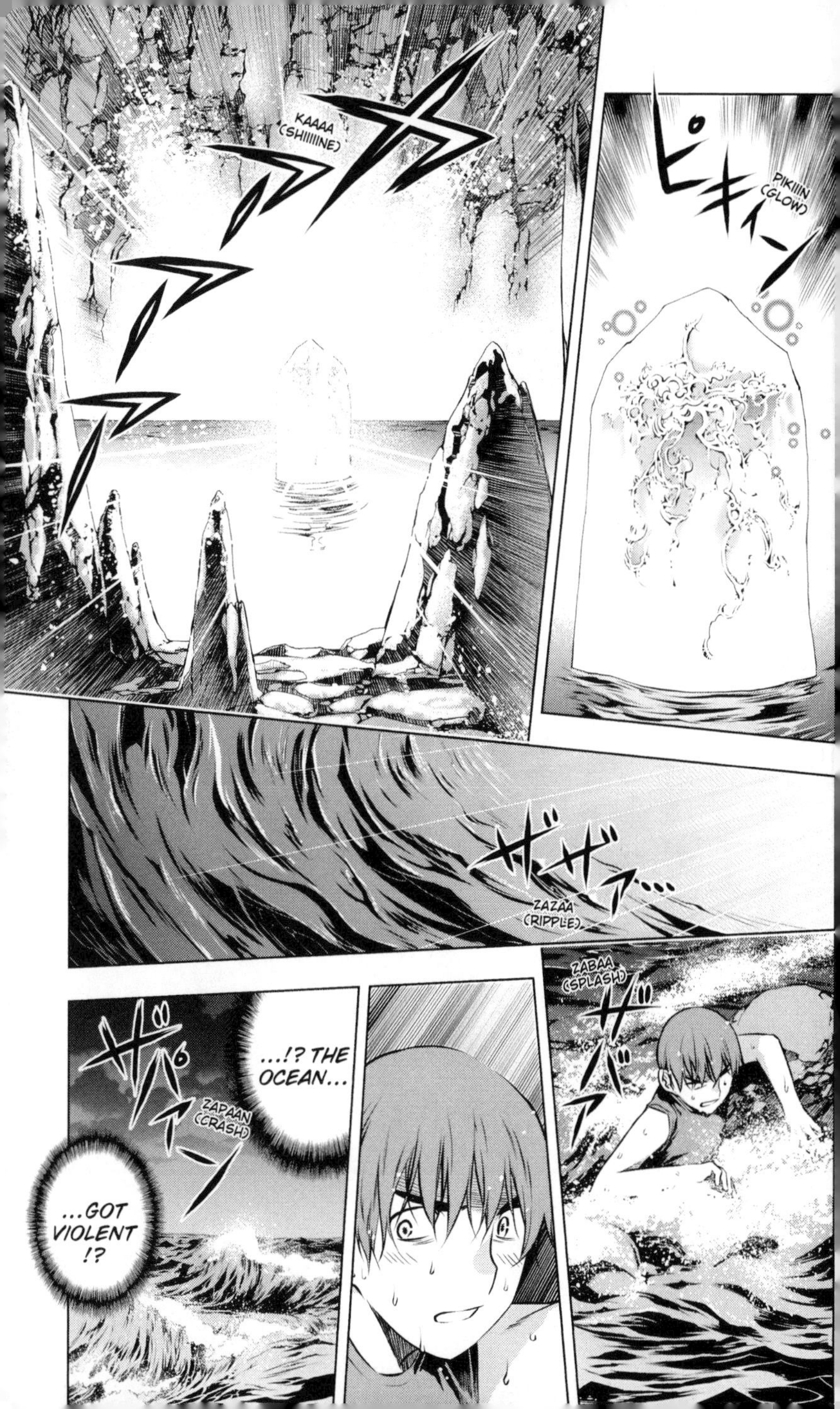
ピキィーン
PIKIIIN (GLOW)
カァァァ
KAAAA (SHIIIINE)
ザザァ…
ZAZAA (RIPPLE)
ザバァ
ZABAA (SPLASH)
...!? THE OCEAN...
ザパァーン
ZAPAAN (CRASH)
...GOT VIOLENT !?

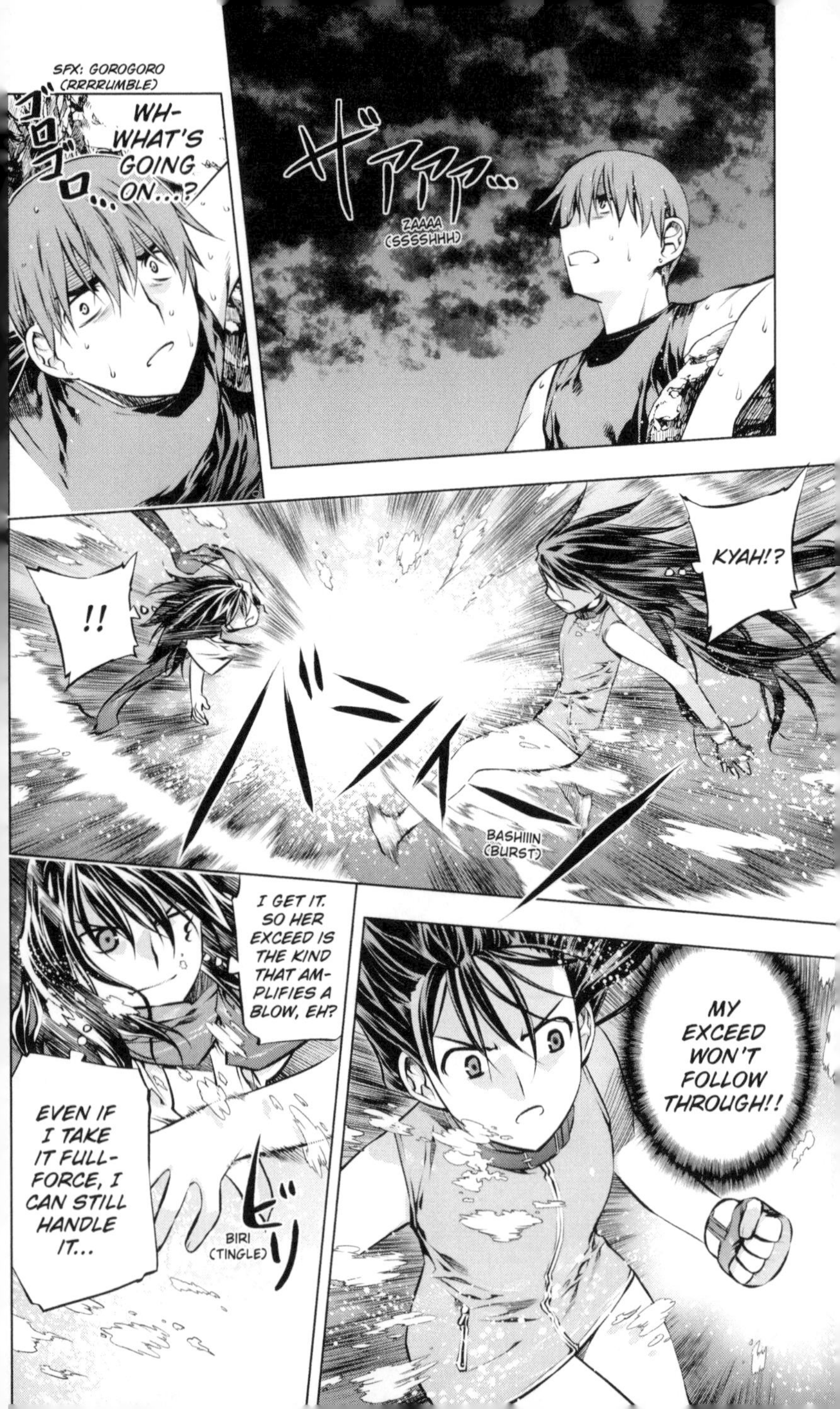

ザァァァ..
ZAAAA (SSSSHHH)
SFX: GOROGORO (RRRRUMBLE)
ゴロゴロ...
WH- WHAT'S GOING ON...?
KYAH!?
!!
バシィーン
BASHIIIN (BURST)
MY EXCEED WON'T FOLLOW THROUGH!!
I GET IT. SO HER EXCEED IS THE KIND THAT AMPLIFIES A BLOW, EH?
EVEN IF I TAKE IT FULL-FORCE, I CAN STILL HANDLE IT...
ビリ
BIRI (TINGLE)

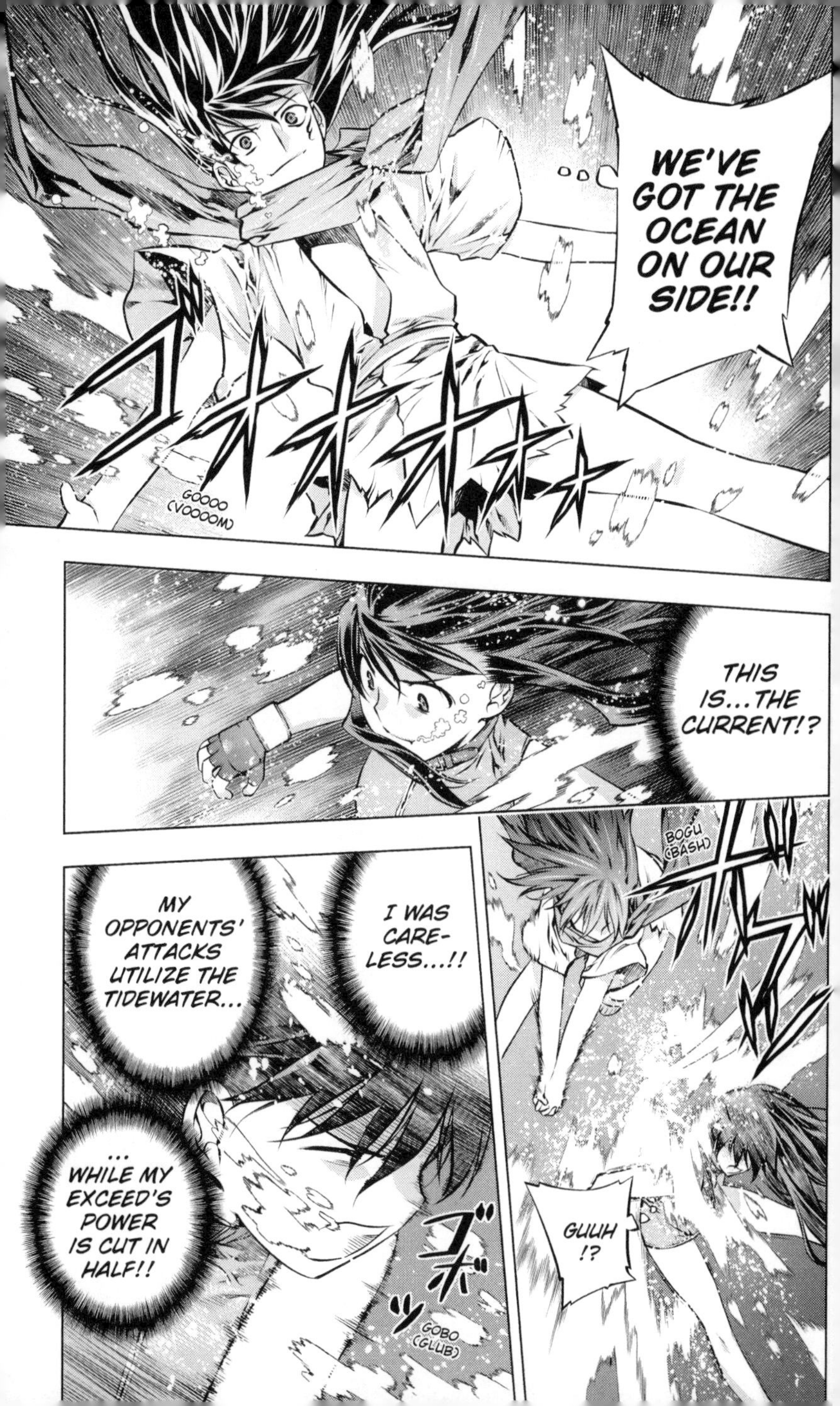
WE'VE GOT THE OCEAN ON OUR SIDE!!
GOOOO (VOOOOM)
THIS IS...THE CURRENT!?
BOGU (BASH)
GUUH !?
I WAS CARE-LESS...!!
MY OPPONENTS' ATTACKS UTILIZE THE TIDEWATER...
... WHILE MY EXCEED'S POWER IS CUT IN HALF!!
GOBO (GLUB)

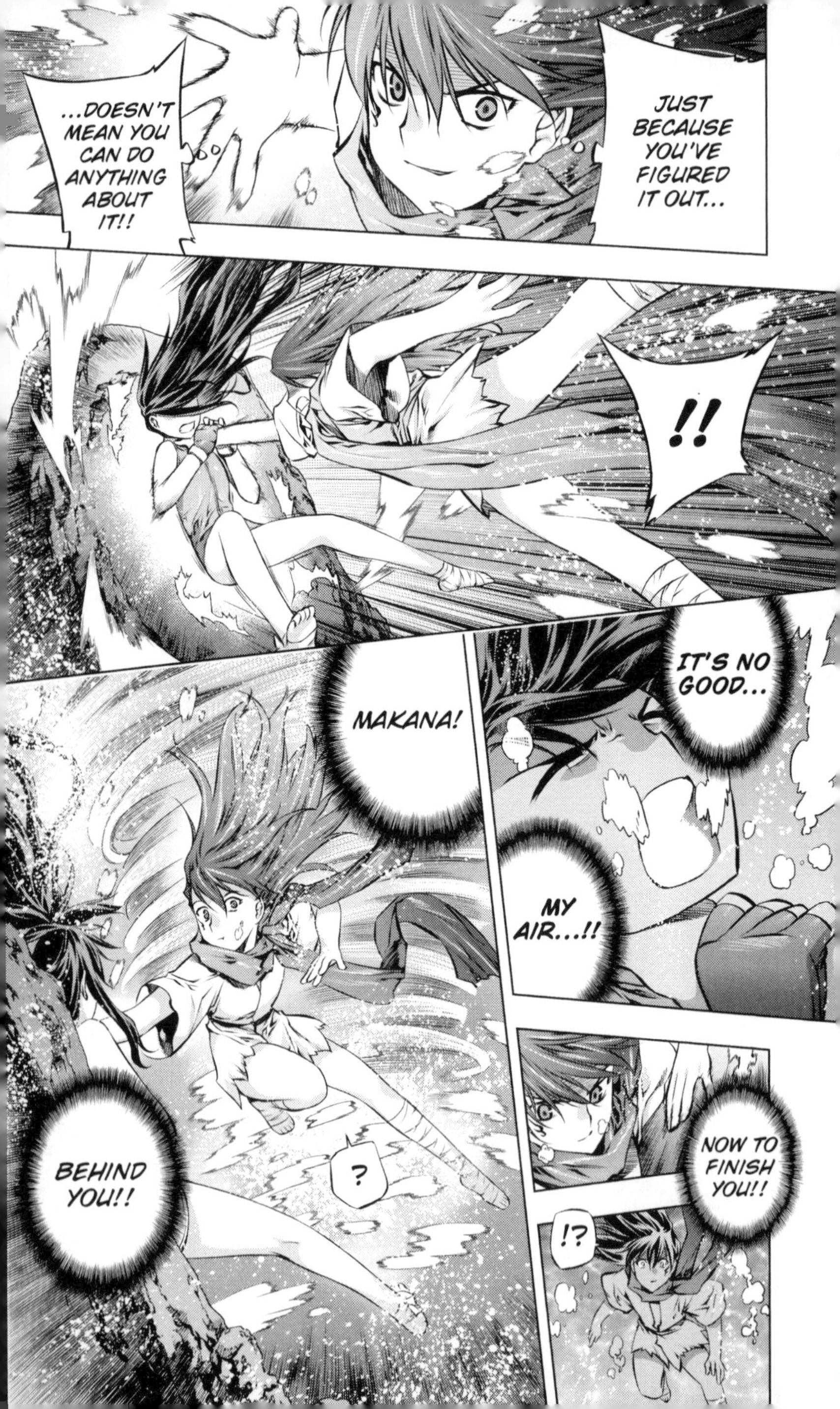
JUST BECAUSE YOU'VE FIGURED IT OUT...
...DOESN'T MEAN YOU CAN DO ANYTHING ABOUT IT!!
!!
IT'S NO GOOD...
MY AIR...!!
NOW TO FINISH YOU!!
!?
MAKANA!
?
BEHIND YOU!!

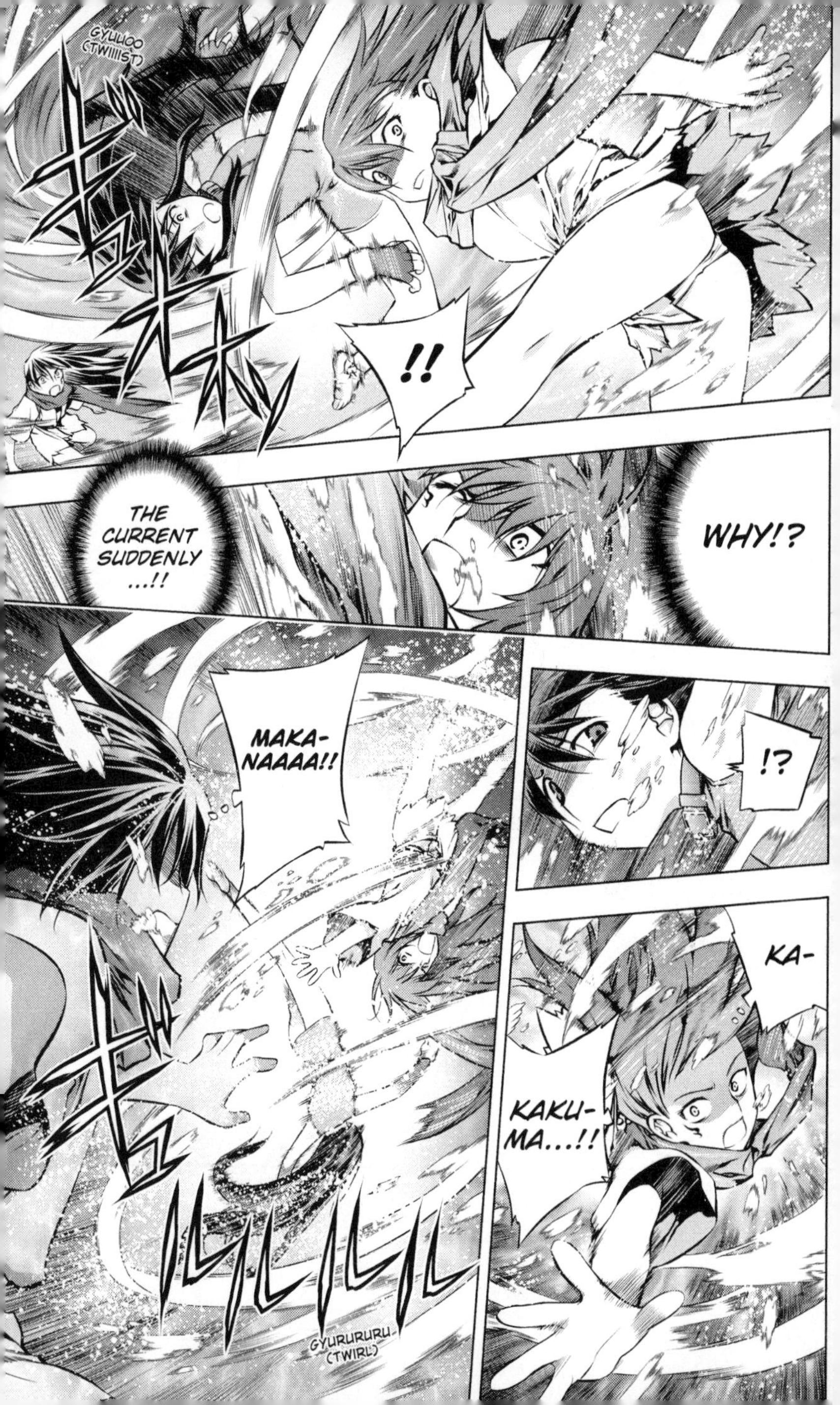
GYUUUOO (TWIIIIST)
!!
WHY!?
THE CURRENT SUDDENLY ...!!
!?
KA-
KAKU-MA...!!
MAKA-NAAAA!!
GYURURURU (TWIRL)

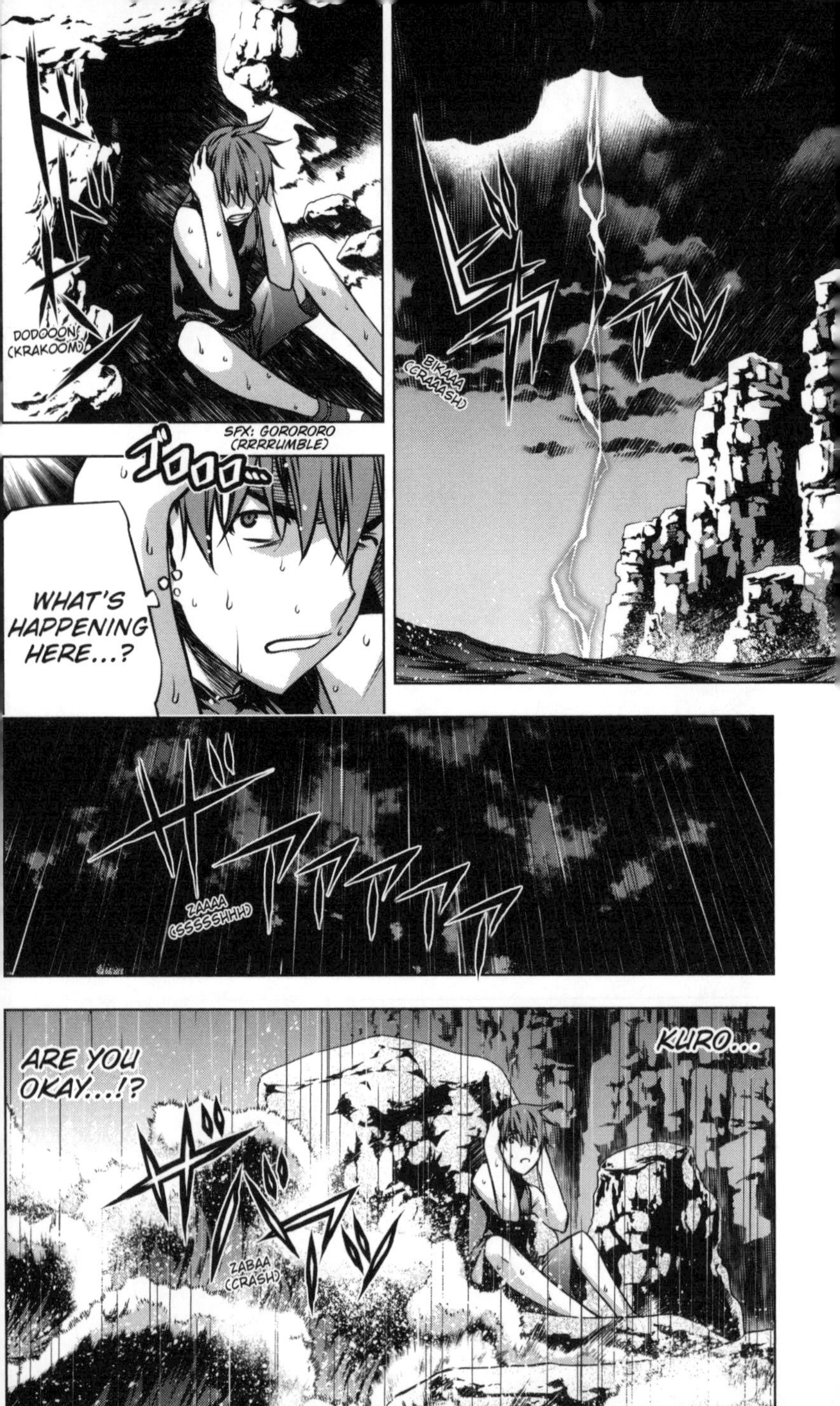
BIKAAA (CRAAASH)
DODOOON (KRAKOOM)
SFX: GOROROR (RRRRUMBLE)
WHAT'S HAPPENING HERE...?
ZAAAA (SSSSSHHH)
KURO...
ARE YOU OKAY...!?
ZABAA (CRASH)

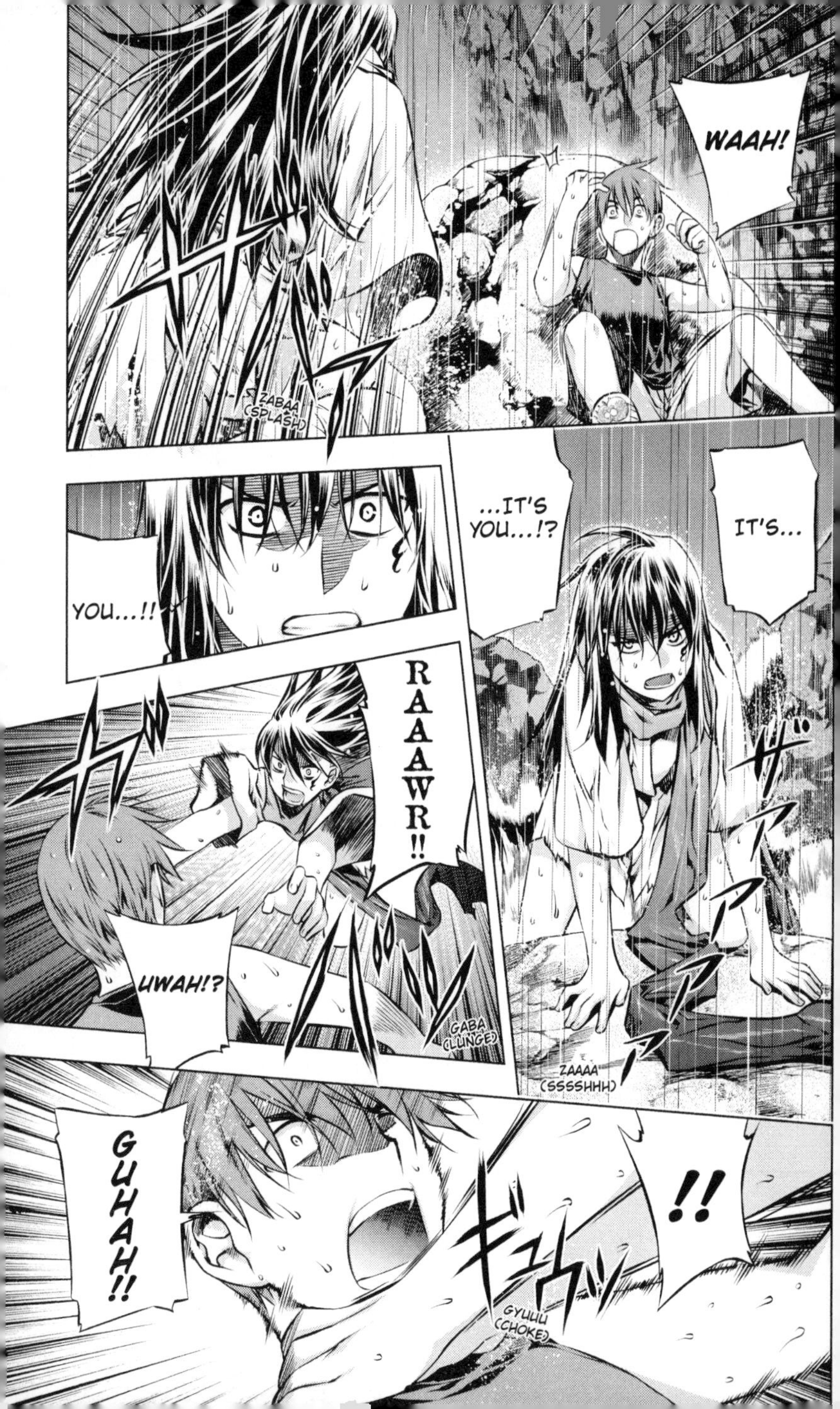
WAAH!
ZABAA (SPLASH)
IT'S...
...IT'S YOU...!?
ZAAAA (SSSSHHH)
YOU...!!
RAAAWR!!
UWAH!?
GABA (LUNGE)
!!
GYUUU (CHOKE)
GUHAH!!

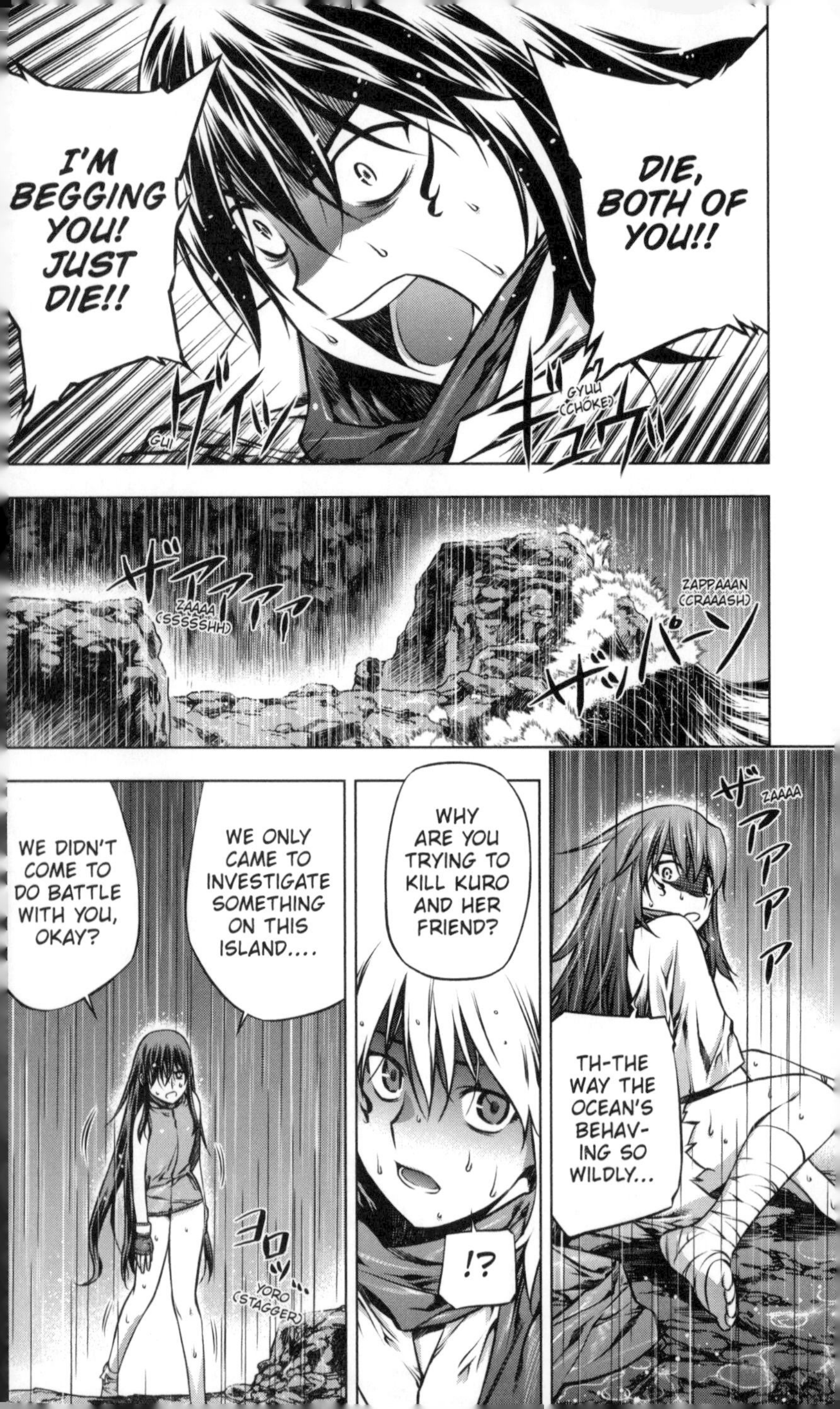
DIE, BOTH OF YOU!!
I'M BEGGING YOU! JUST DIE!!
GYUU (CHOKE)
GUI
ZAPPAAAN (CRAAASH)
ZAAAA (SSSSSHH)
ZAAAA
TH-THE WAY THE OCEAN'S BEHAV-ING SO WILDLY...
WHY ARE YOU TRYING TO KILL KURO AND HER FRIEND?
!?
WE ONLY CAME TO INVESTIGATE SOMETHING ON THIS ISLAND....
WE DIDN'T COME TO DO BATTLE WITH YOU, OKAY?
YORO (STAGGER)

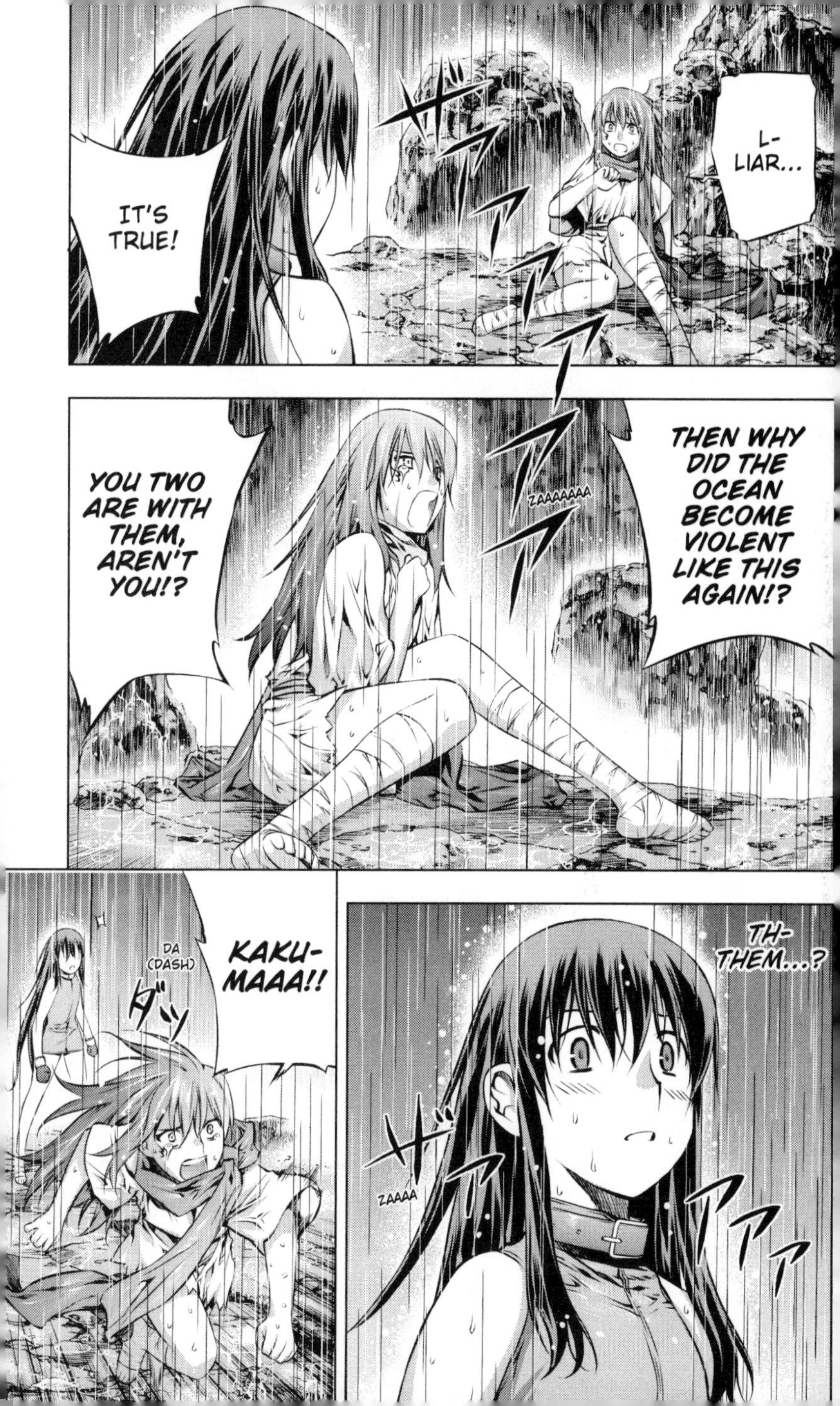
L- LIAR...
IT'S TRUE!
THEN WHY DID THE OCEAN BECOME VIOLENT LIKE THIS AGAIN!?
ZAAAAAAA
YOU TWO ARE WITH THEM, AREN'T YOU!?
TH- THEM...?
ZAAAA
KAKU- MAAA!!
DA (DASH)

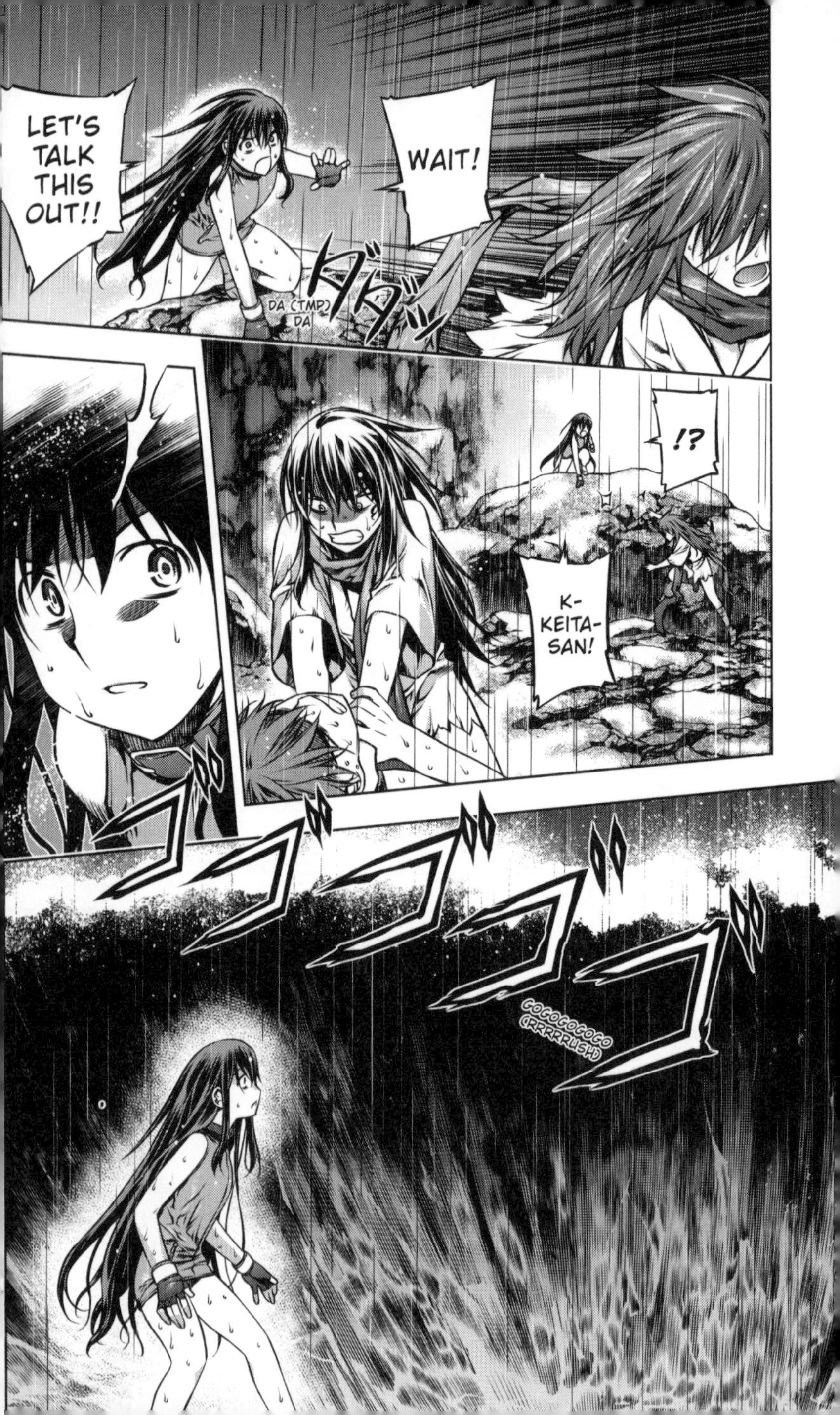
WAIT!
LET'S TALK THIS OUT!!
ダダッ
DA (TMP) DA
!?
K-KEITA-SAN!
ゴゴゴゴゴ
GOGOGOGOGO (RRRRRUSH)

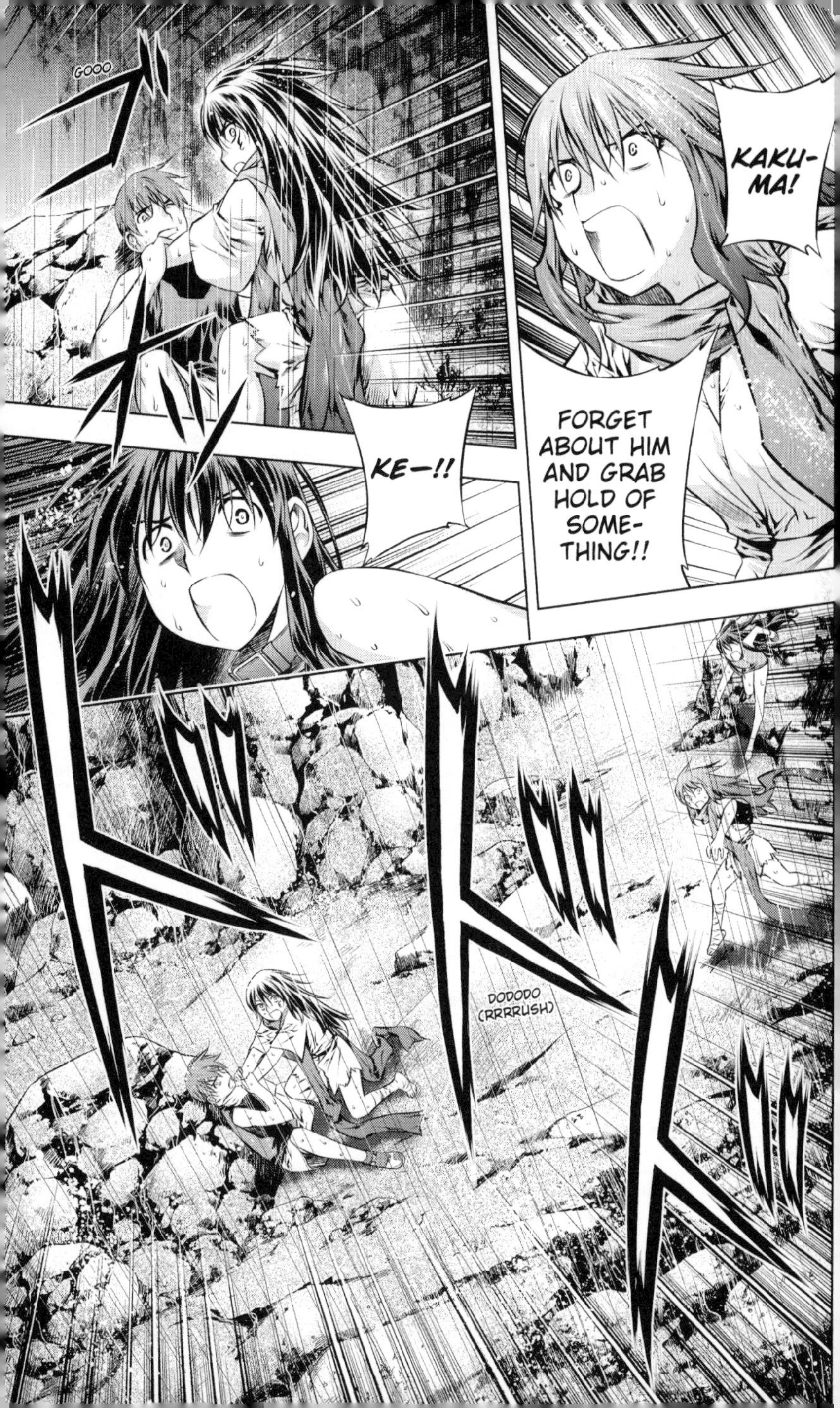
KAKU-MA!
FORGET ABOUT HIM AND GRAB HOLD OF SOME-THING!!
GOOO
KE—!!
DODODO (RRRUSH)

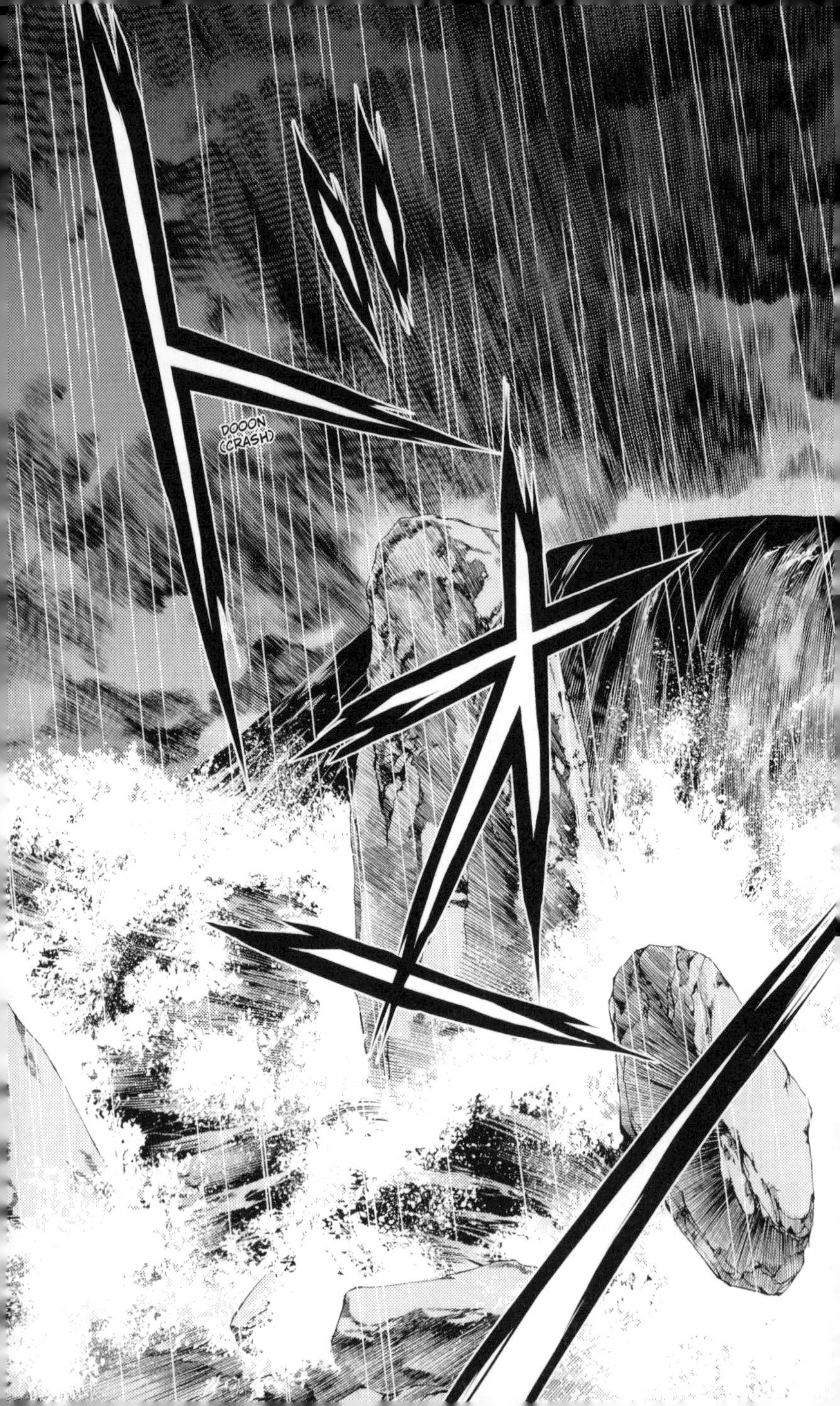
DOOON
(CRASH)

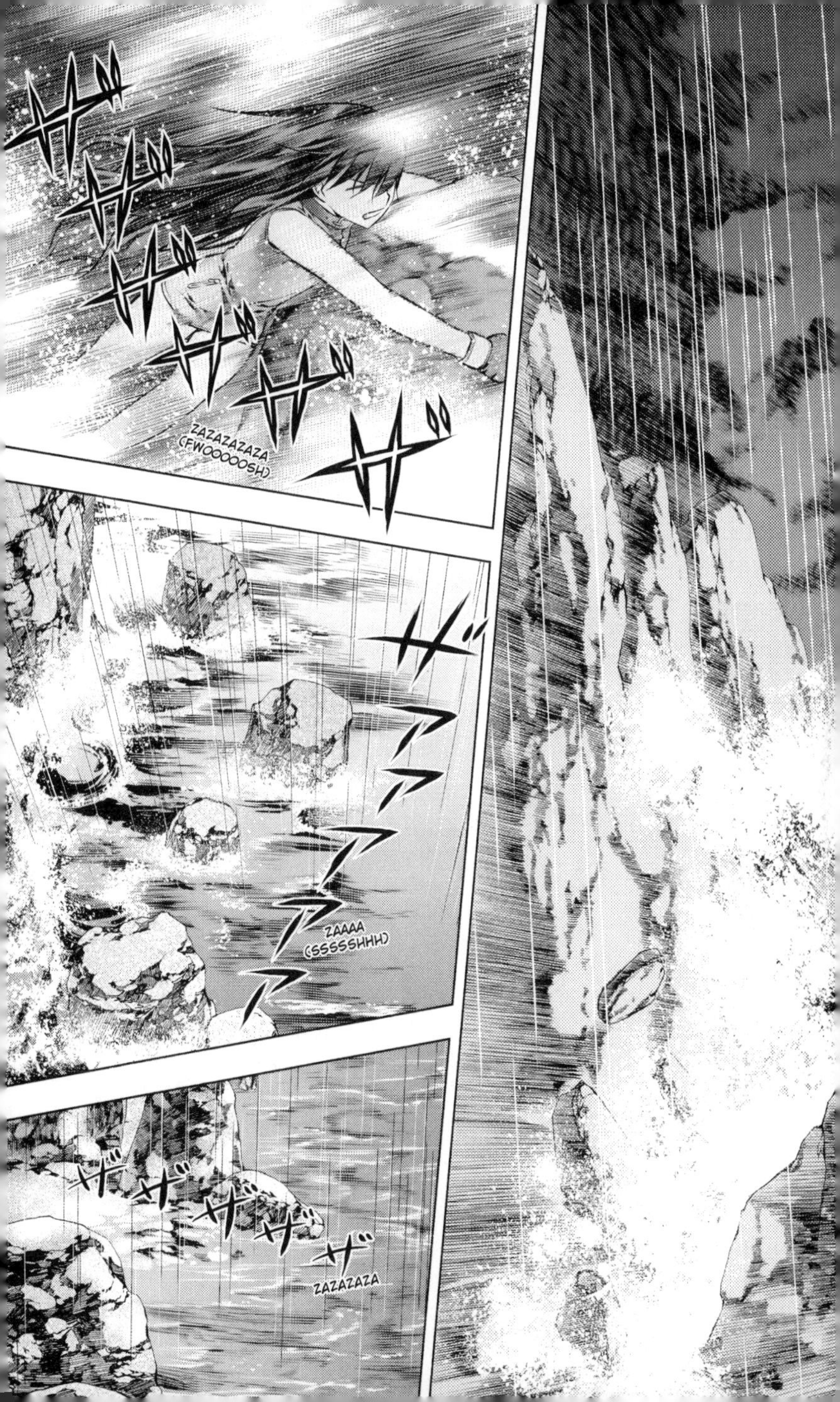
ZAZAZAZAZA
(FWOOOOOSH)
ZAAAA
(SSSSSHHH)
ZAZAZAZA

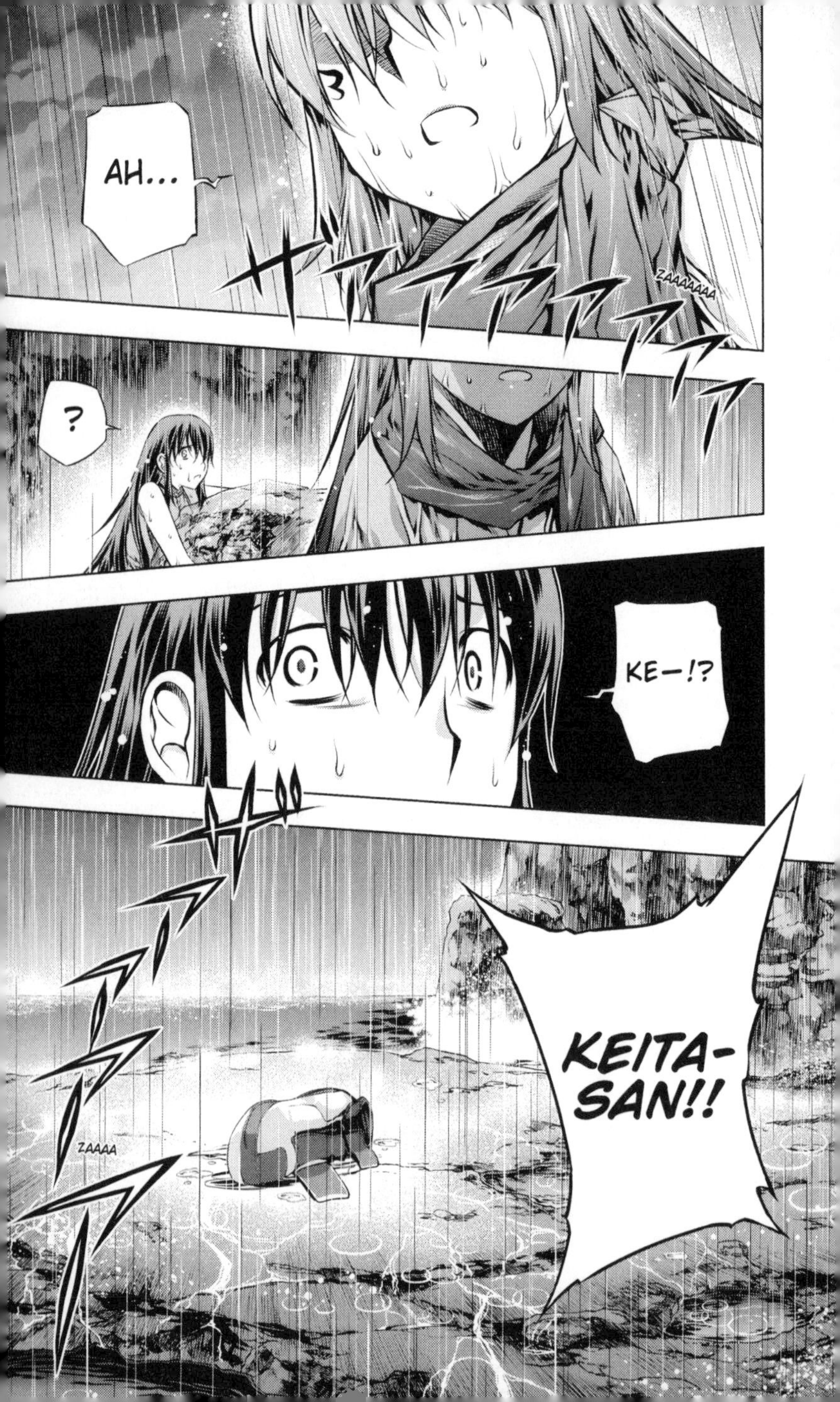
AH...
ZAAAAAAAA
?
KE—!?
KEITA-SAN!!
ZAAAA

技

四

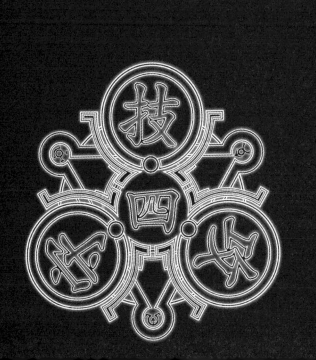

KEITA'S GRAMPS

BLACK GOD
which maintains
balance in the world.

Nirai Kanai Arc

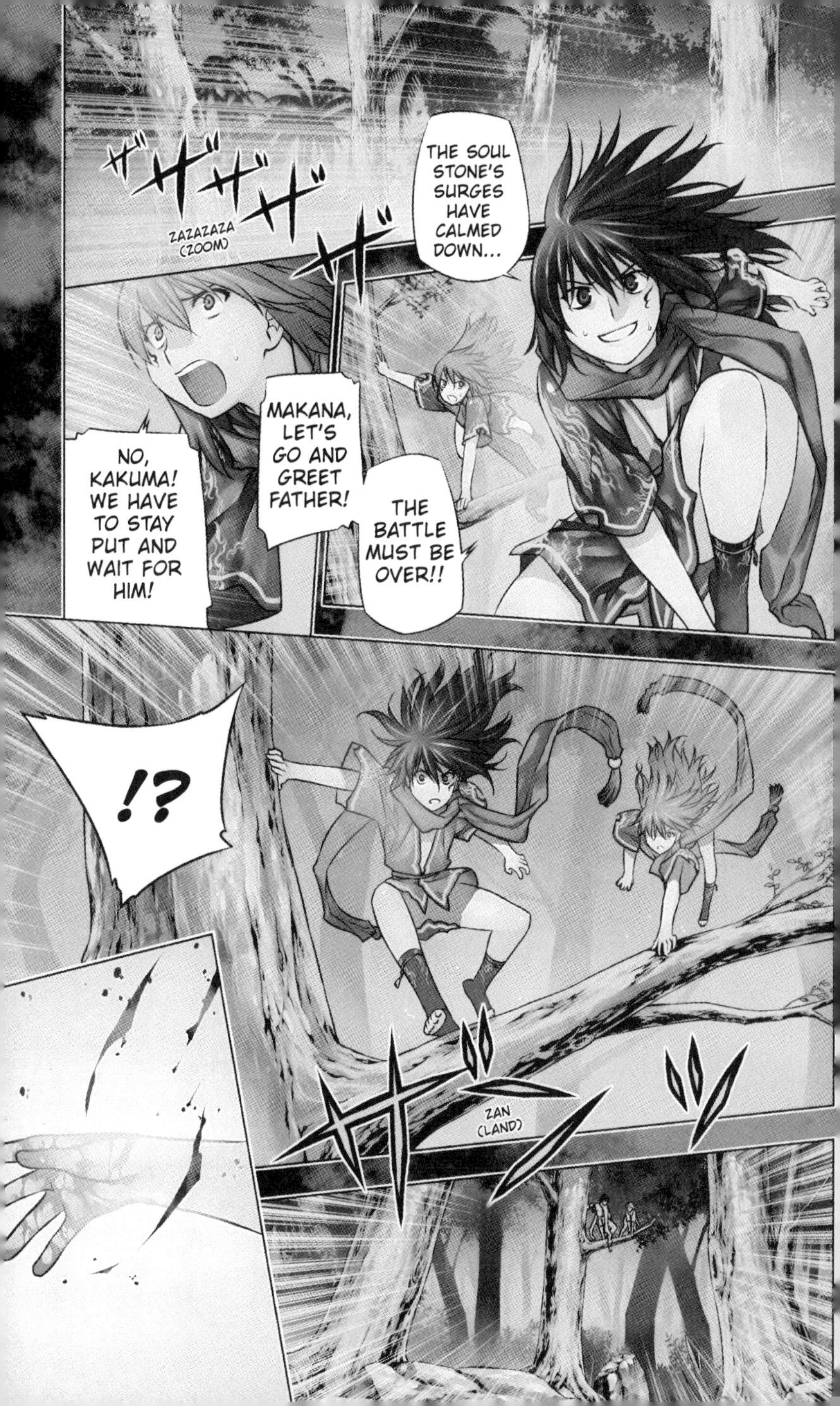
THE SOUL STONE'S SURGES HAVE CALMED DOWN...
ZAZAZAZA (ZOOM)
MAKANA, LET'S GO AND GREET FATHER!
THE BATTLE MUST BE OVER!!
NO, KAKUMA! WE HAVE TO STAY PUT AND WAIT FOR HIM!
!?
ZAN (LAND)

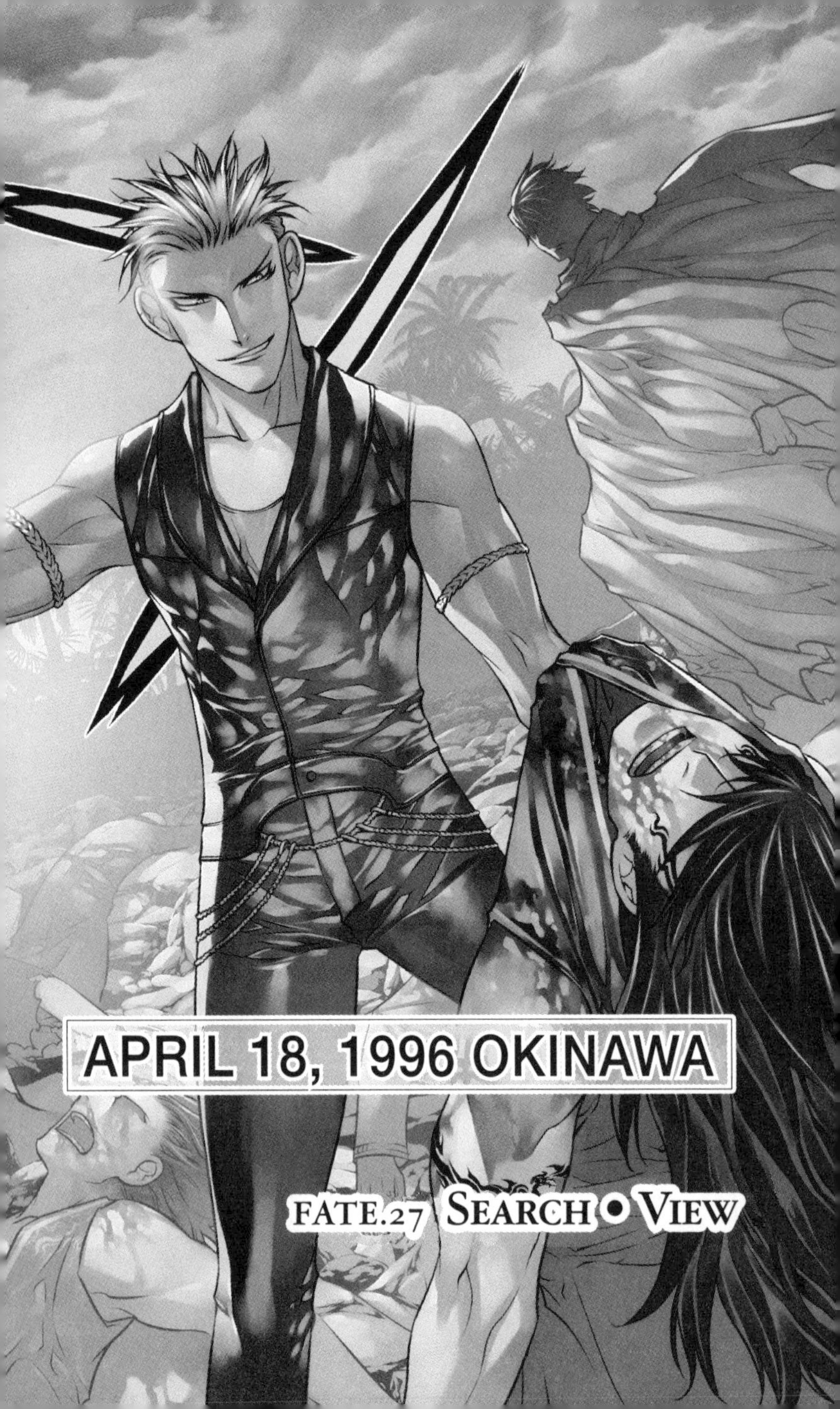
APRIL 18, 1996 OKINAWA
FATE.27 SEARCH • VIEW

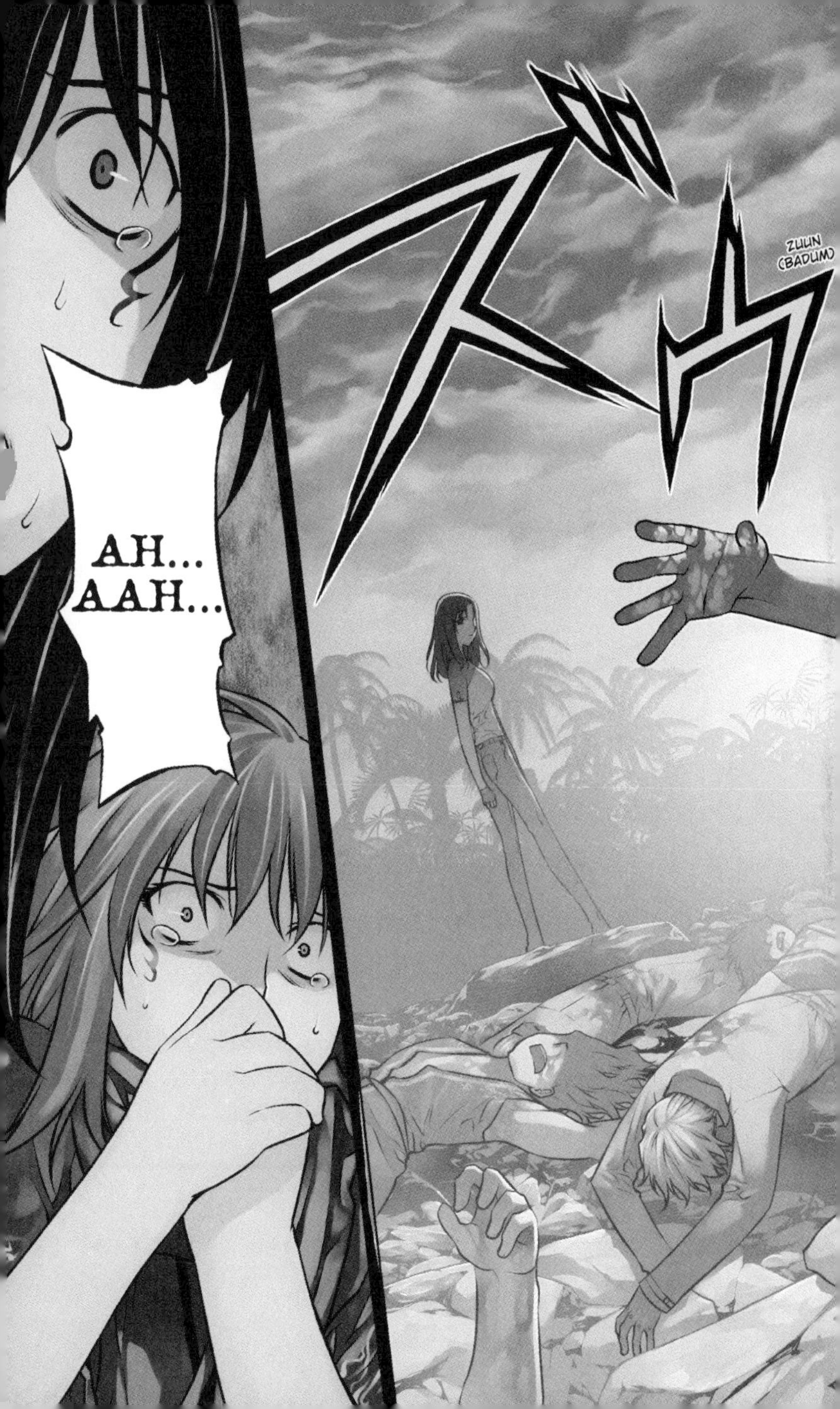
ZUUN (BADUM)
AH... AAH...

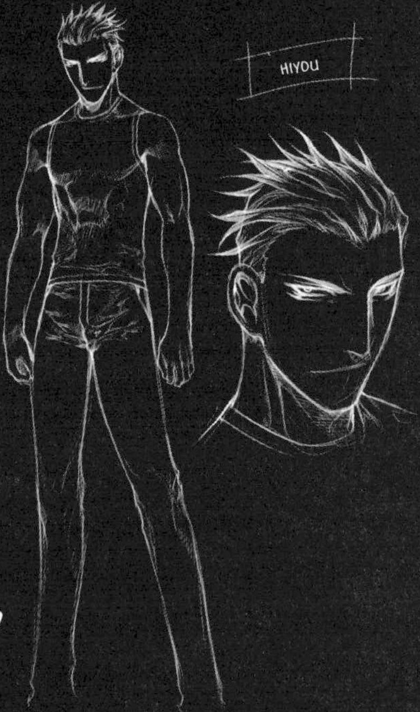
HIYOU

BLACK GOD
which maintains balance in the world.
Nirai Kanai Arc

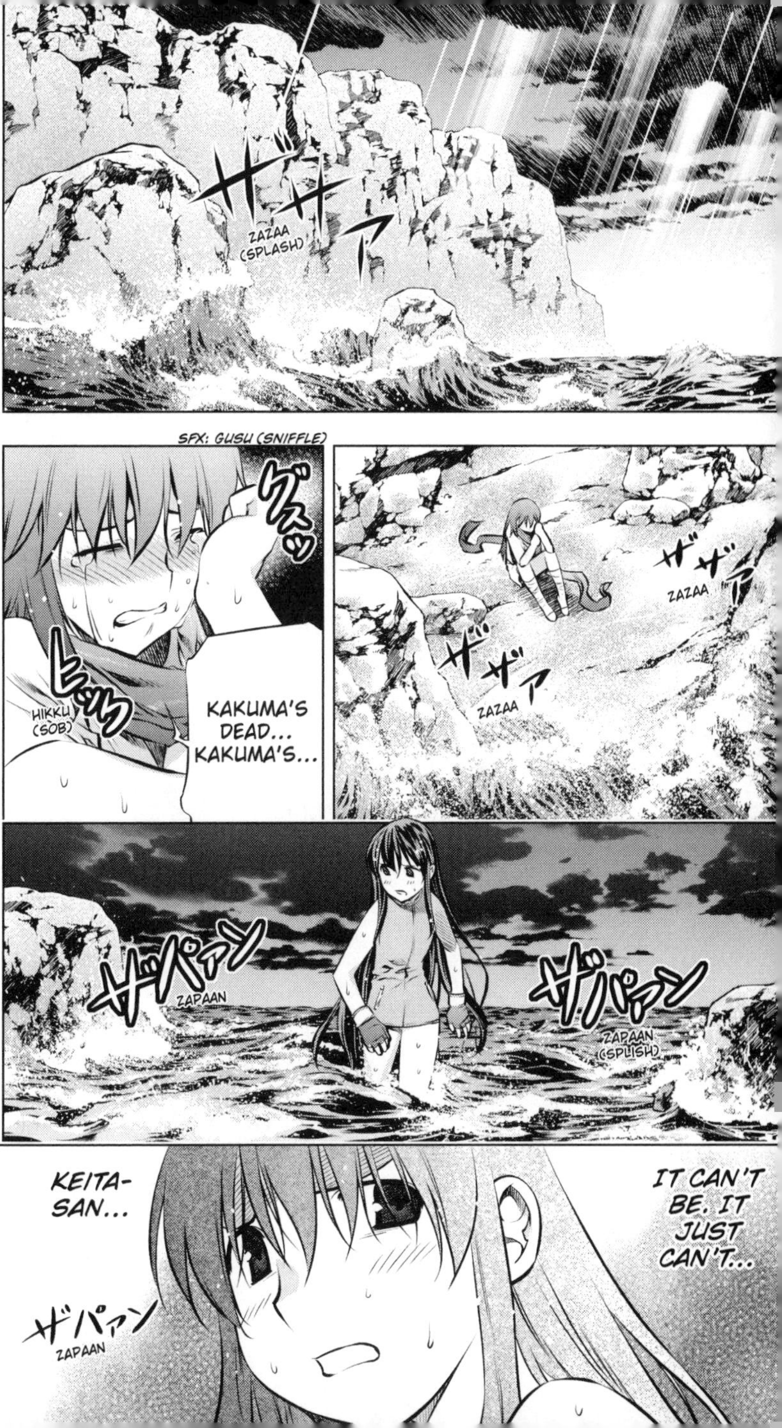
ザザァ
ZAZAA (SPLASH)
ザザァ
ZAZAA
ザザァ
ZAZAA
SFX: GUSU (SNIFFLE)
グスッ
ヒック
HIKKU (SOB)
KAKUMA'S DEAD... KAKUMA'S...
ザパァン
ZAPAAN (SPLISH)
ザパァン
ZAPAAN
IT CAN'T BE. IT JUST CAN'T...
KEITA-SAN...
ザパァン
ZAPAAN

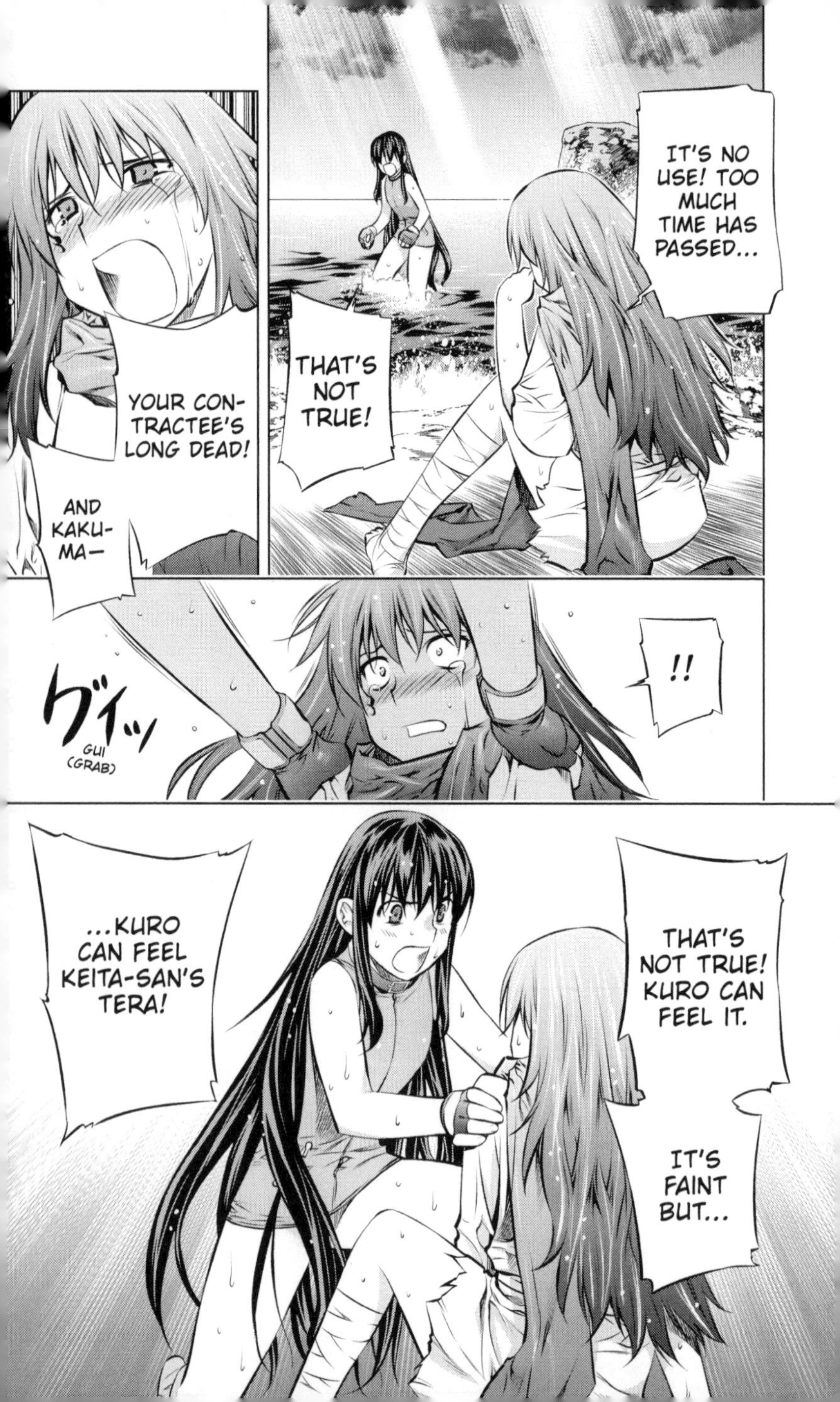

IT'S NO USE! TOO MUCH TIME HAS PASSED...
THAT'S NOT TRUE!
YOUR CON-TRACTEE'S LONG DEAD!
AND KAKU-MA—
!!
グイッ
GUI (GRAB)
THAT'S NOT TRUE! KURO CAN FEEL IT.
IT'S FAINT BUT...
...KURO CAN FEEL KEITA-SAN'S TERA!

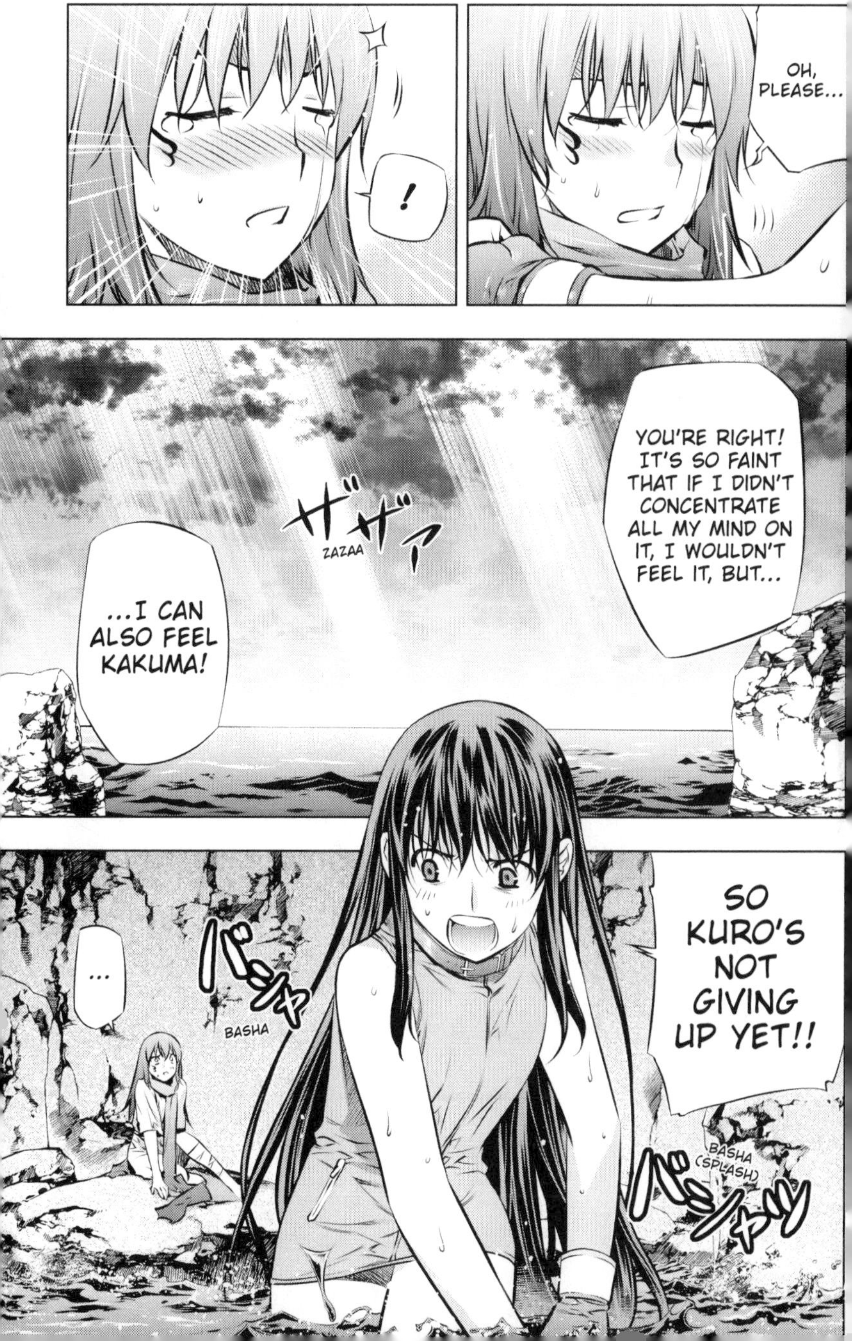
OH, PLEASE...
!
YOU'RE RIGHT! IT'S SO FAINT THAT IF I DIDN'T CONCENTRATE ALL MY MIND ON IT, I WOULDN'T FEEL IT, BUT...
ザザア
ZAZAA
...I CAN ALSO FEEL KAKUMA!
SO KURO'S NOT GIVING UP YET!!
BASHA (SPLASH)
BASHA
...

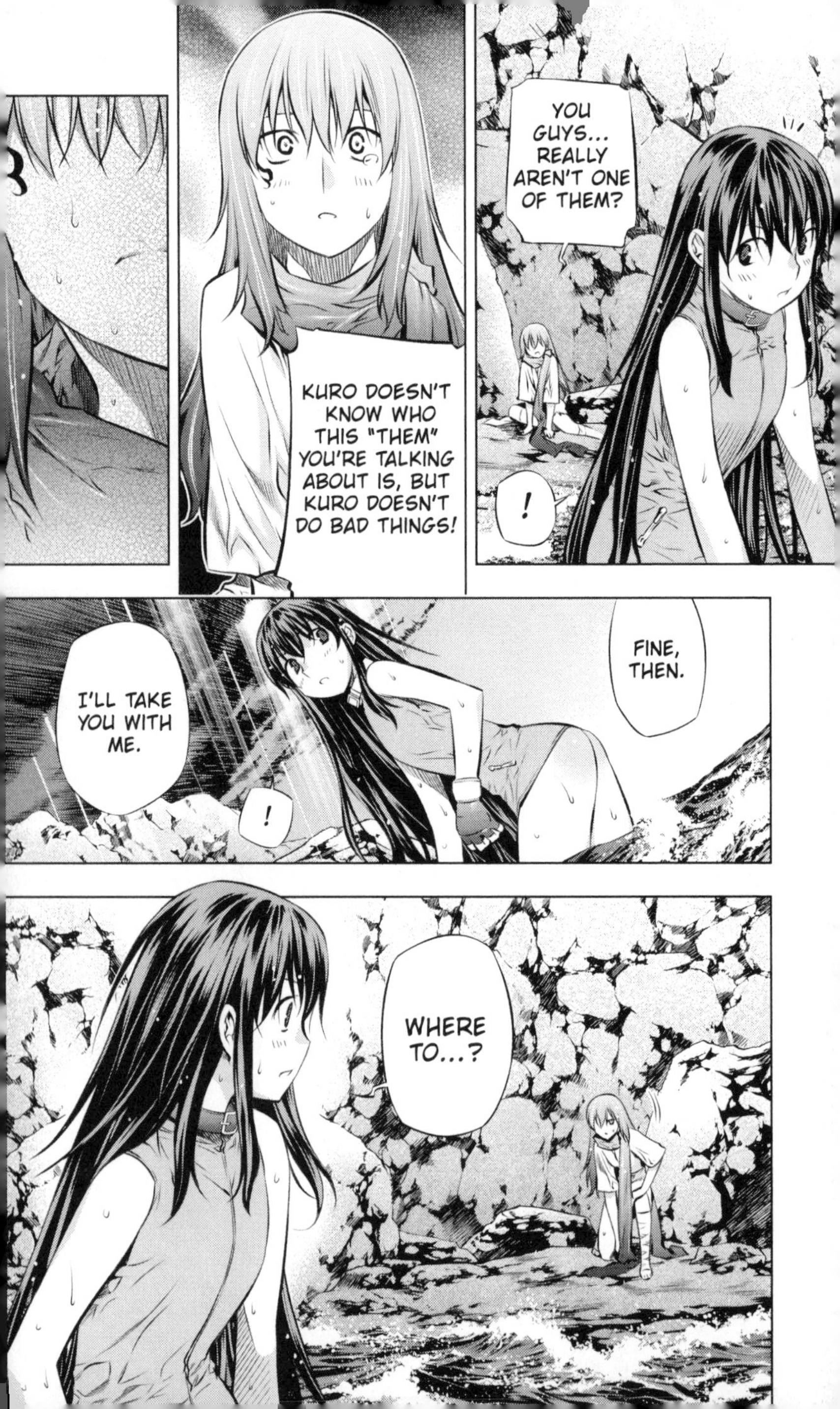
YOU GUYS... REALLY AREN'T ONE OF THEM?
!
KURO DOESN'T KNOW WHO THIS "THEM" YOU'RE TALKING ABOUT IS, BUT KURO DOESN'T DO BAD THINGS!
FINE, THEN.
I'LL TAKE YOU WITH ME.
!
WHERE TO...?

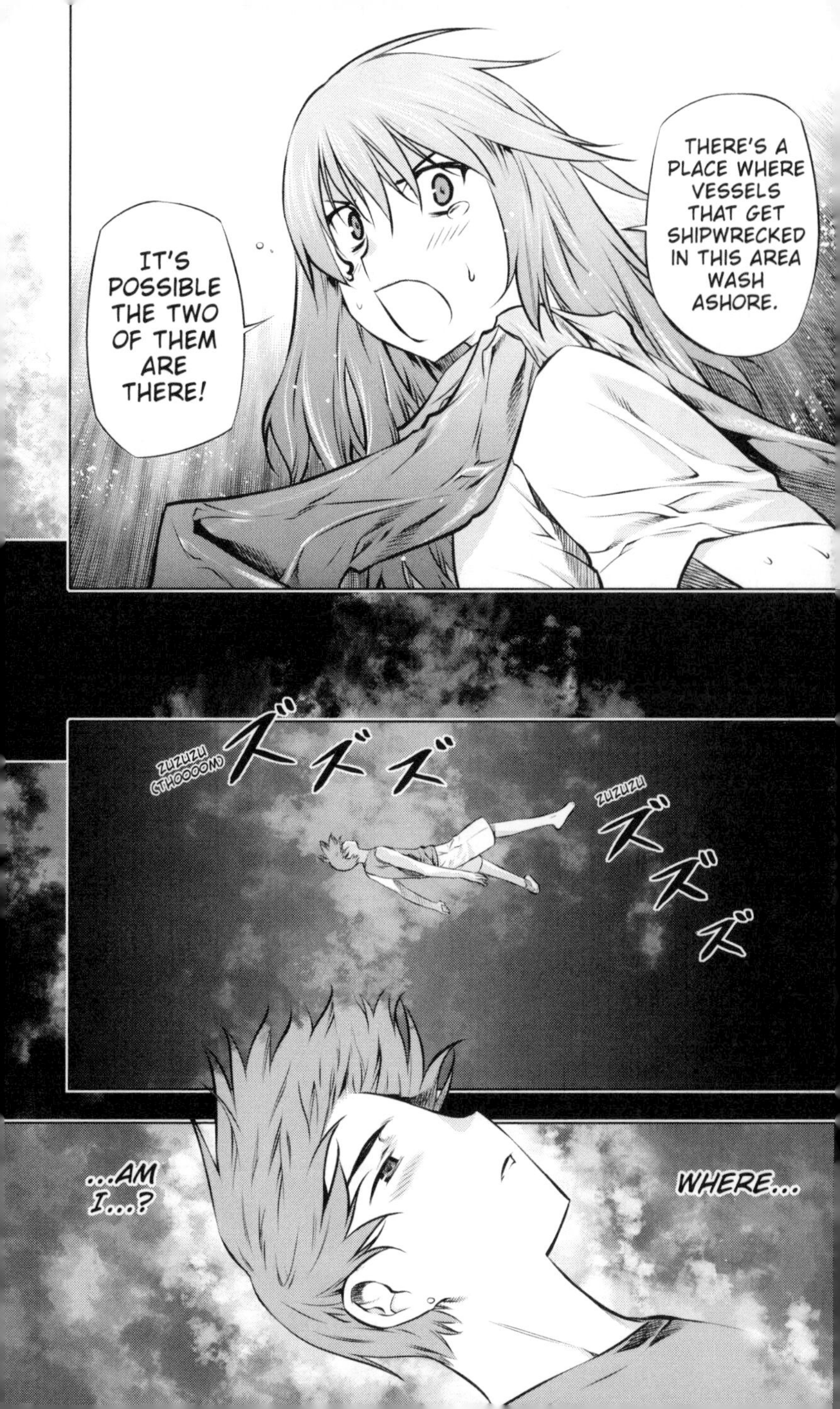
THERE'S A PLACE WHERE VESSELS THAT GET SHIPWRECKED IN THIS AREA WASH ASHORE.
IT'S POSSIBLE THE TWO OF THEM ARE THERE!
ZUZUZU (THOOOOM)
ZUZUZU
WHERE...
...AM I...?

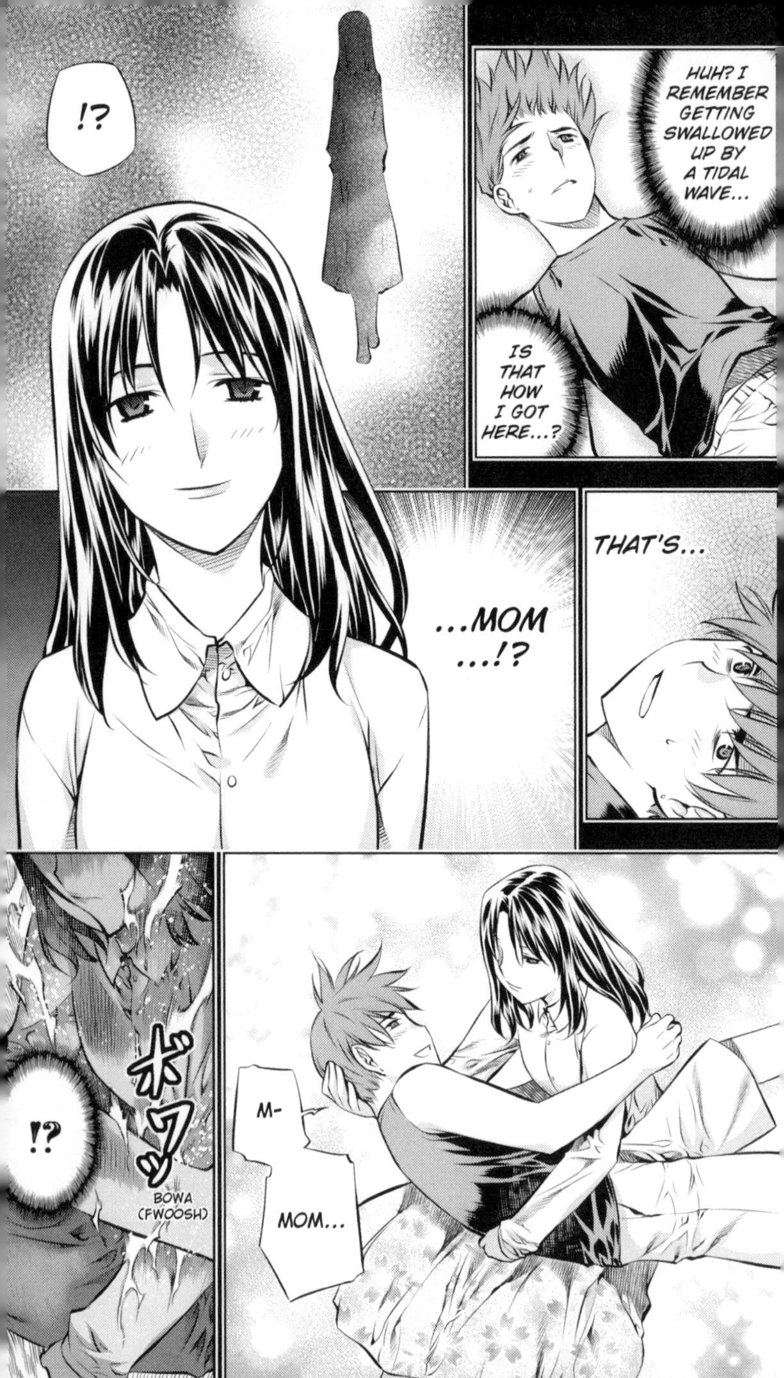
HUH? I REMEMBER GETTING SWALLOWED UP BY A TIDAL WAVE...
IS THAT HOW I GOT HERE...?
THAT'S...
!?
...MOM ...!?
M-
MOM...
ボワッ
BOWA (FWOOSH)
!?

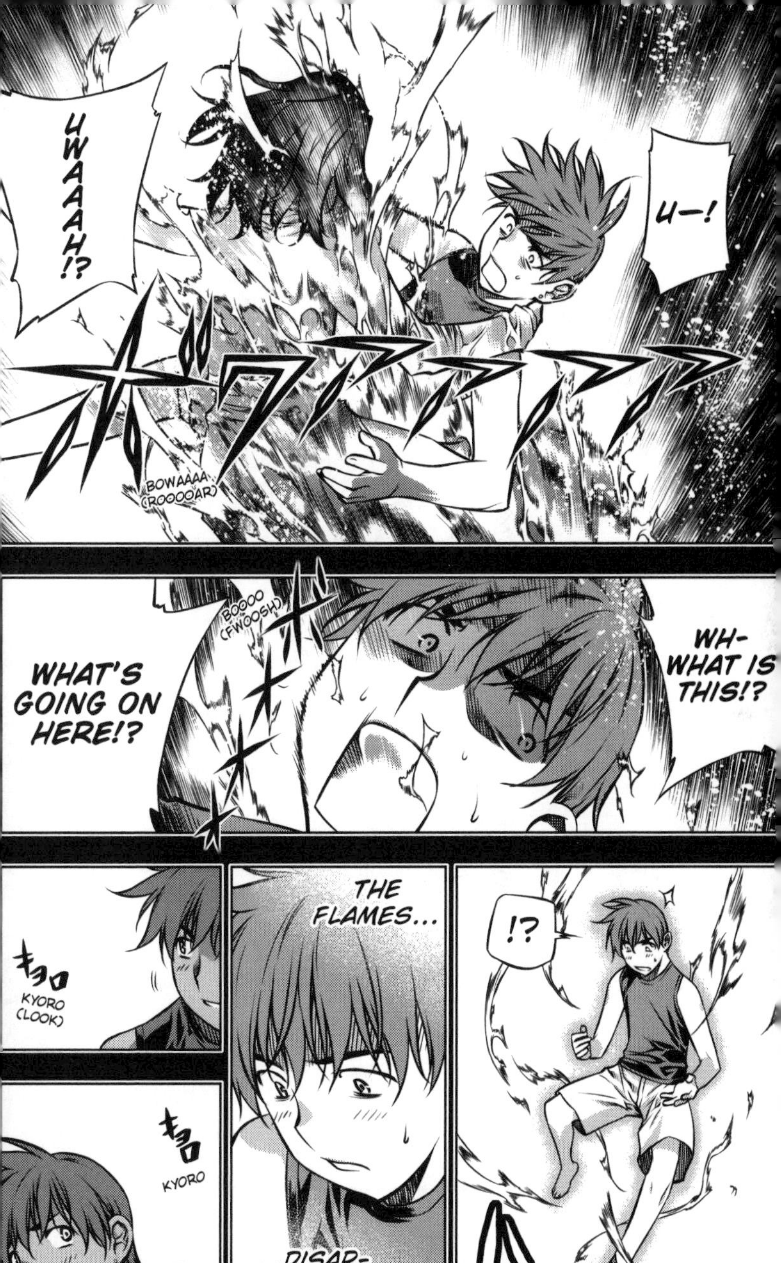
U—!
UWAAAAH!?
BOWAAAA (ROOOOAR)
WH-WHAT IS THIS!?
BOOOO (FWOOSH)
WHAT'S GOING ON HERE!?
!?
HA
THE FLAMES...
...DISAP-PEARED...!?
キョロ
KYORO (LOOK)
キョロ
KYORO

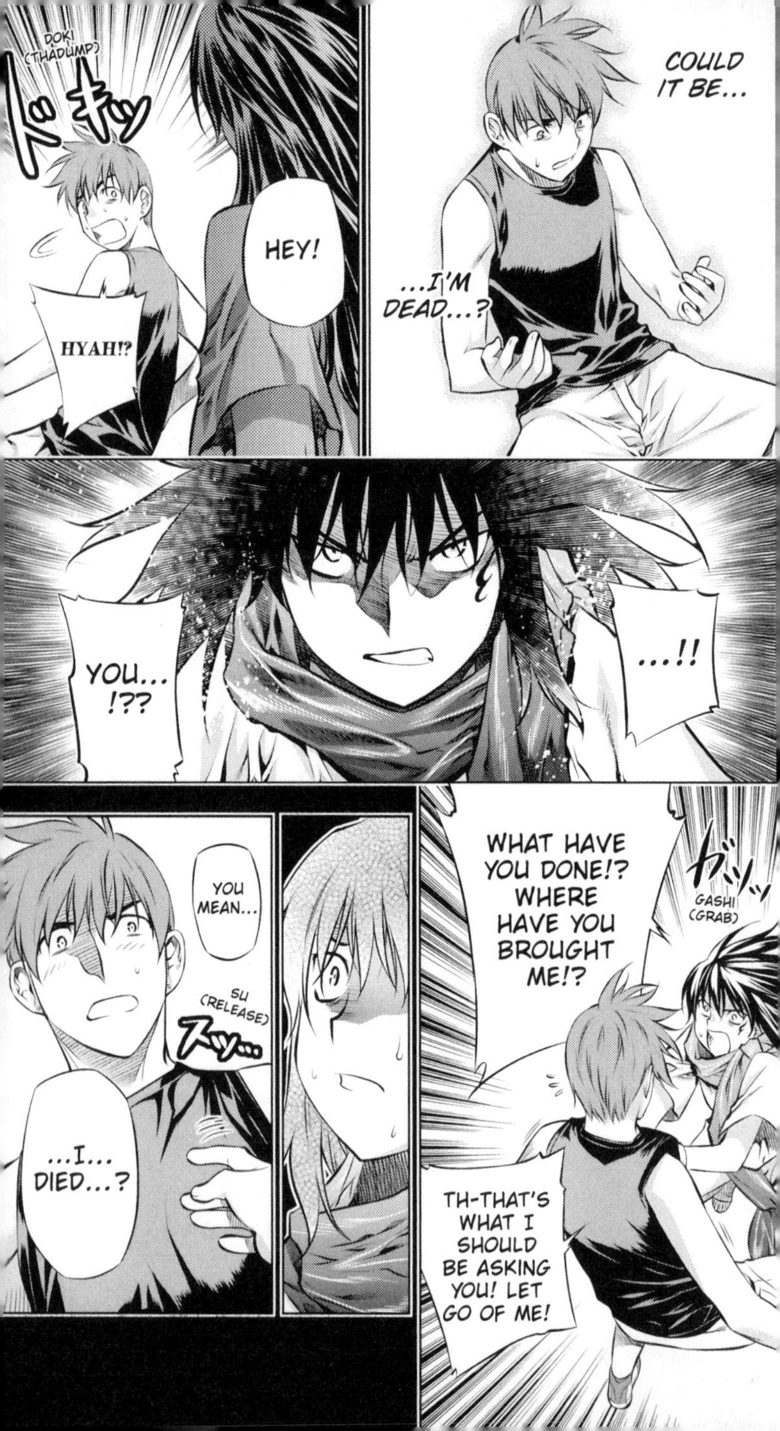
COULD IT BE...
...I'M DEAD...?
HEY!
DOKI (THADUMP)
HYAH!?
...!!
YOU... !??
WHAT HAVE YOU DONE!? WHERE HAVE YOU BROUGHT ME!?
GASHI (GRAB)
TH-THAT'S WHAT I SHOULD BE ASKING YOU! LET GO OF ME!
YOU MEAN...
SU (RELEASE)
...I... DIED...?

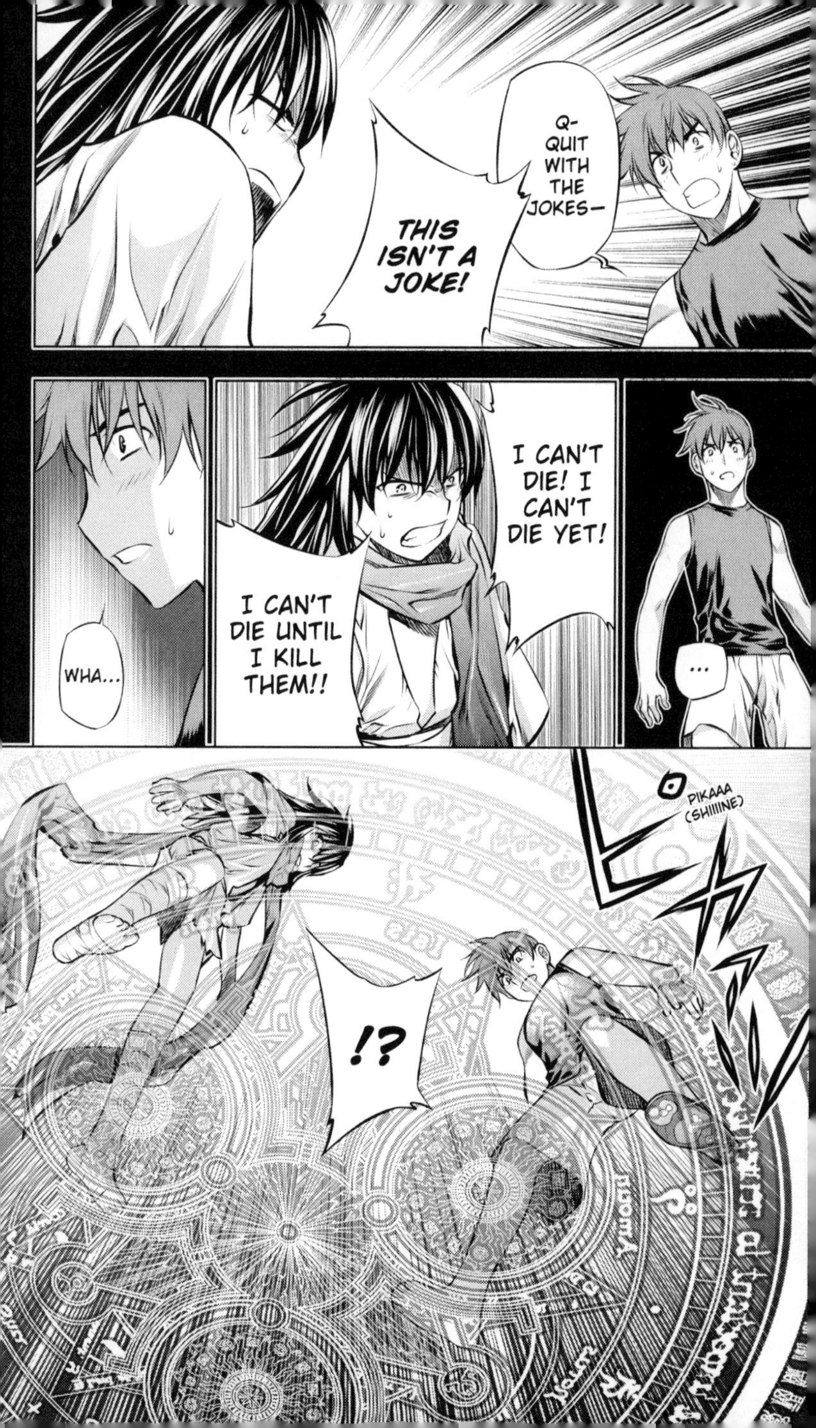
Q-QUIT WITH THE JOKES—
THIS ISN'T A JOKE!
...
I CAN'T DIE! I CAN'T DIE YET!
I CAN'T DIE UNTIL I KILL THEM!!
WHA...
PIKAAA (SHIIIINE)
!?

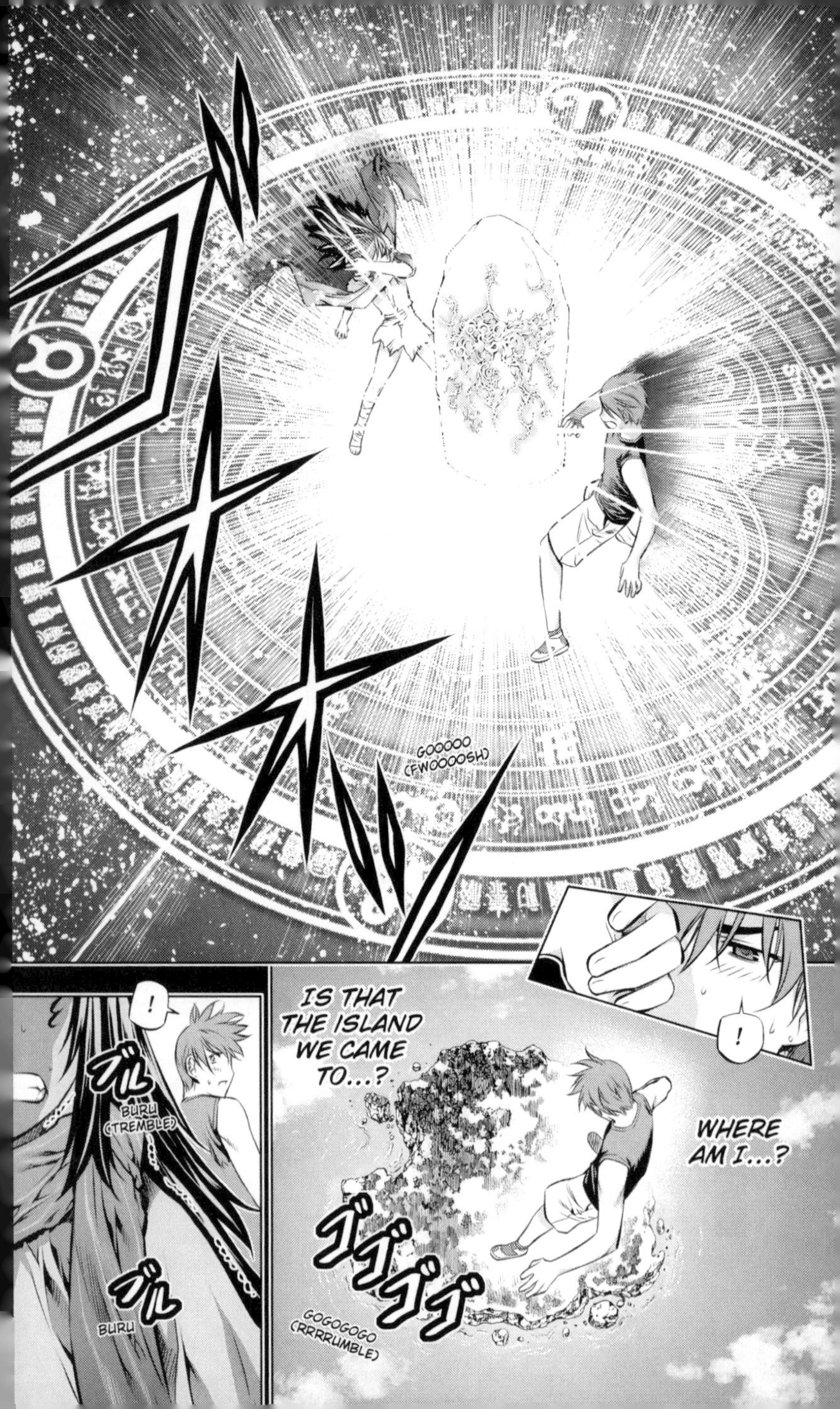
GOOOOO
(FWOOOOSH)
!
WHERE AM I...?
IS THAT THE ISLAND WE CAME TO...?
ゴゴゴゴ
GOGOGOGO
(RRRRUMBLE)
!
ブル
BURU
(TREMBLE)
ブル
BURU

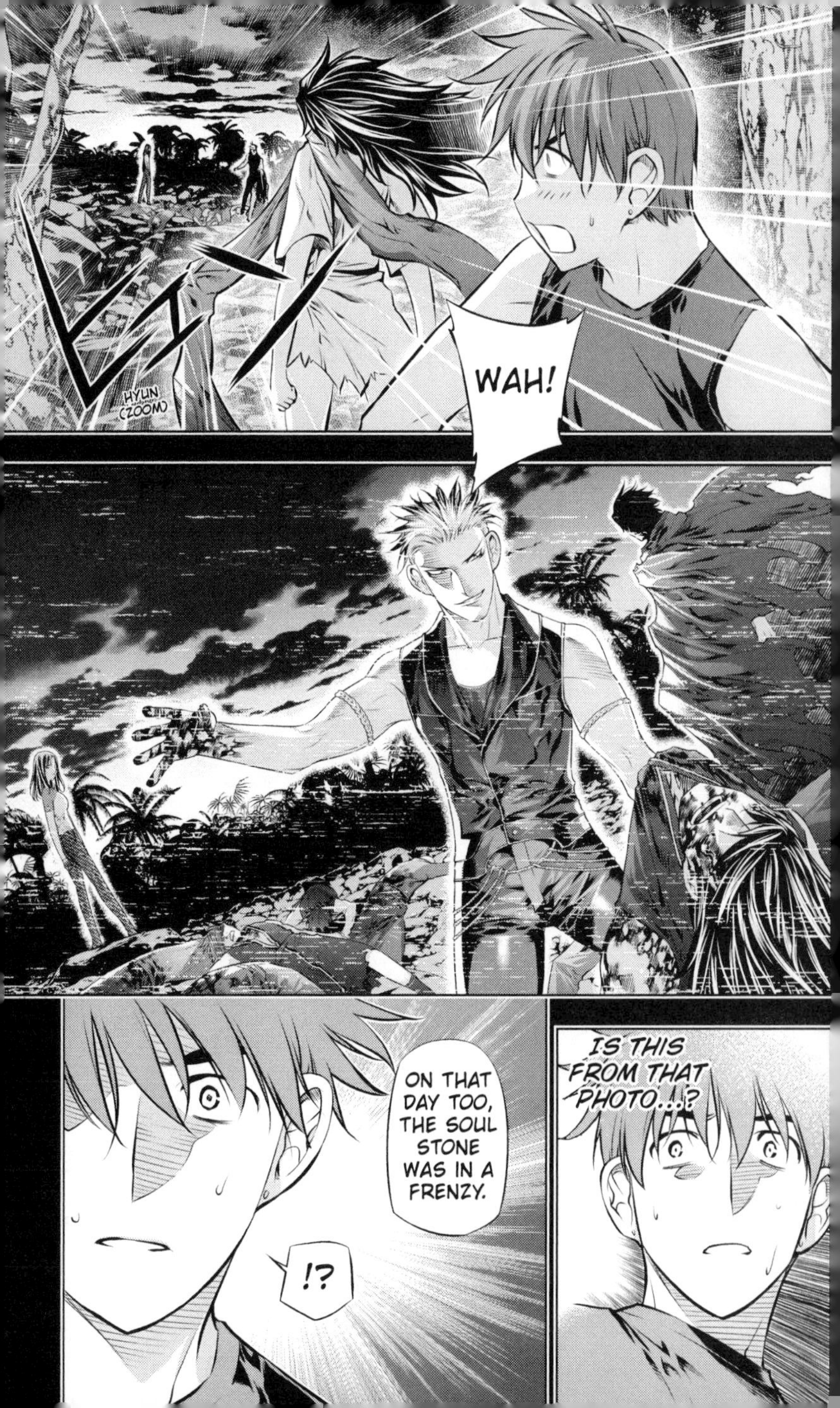
WAH!
HYUN (ZOOM)
IS THIS FROM THAT PHOTO...?
ON THAT DAY TOO, THE SOUL STONE WAS IN A FRENZY.
!?

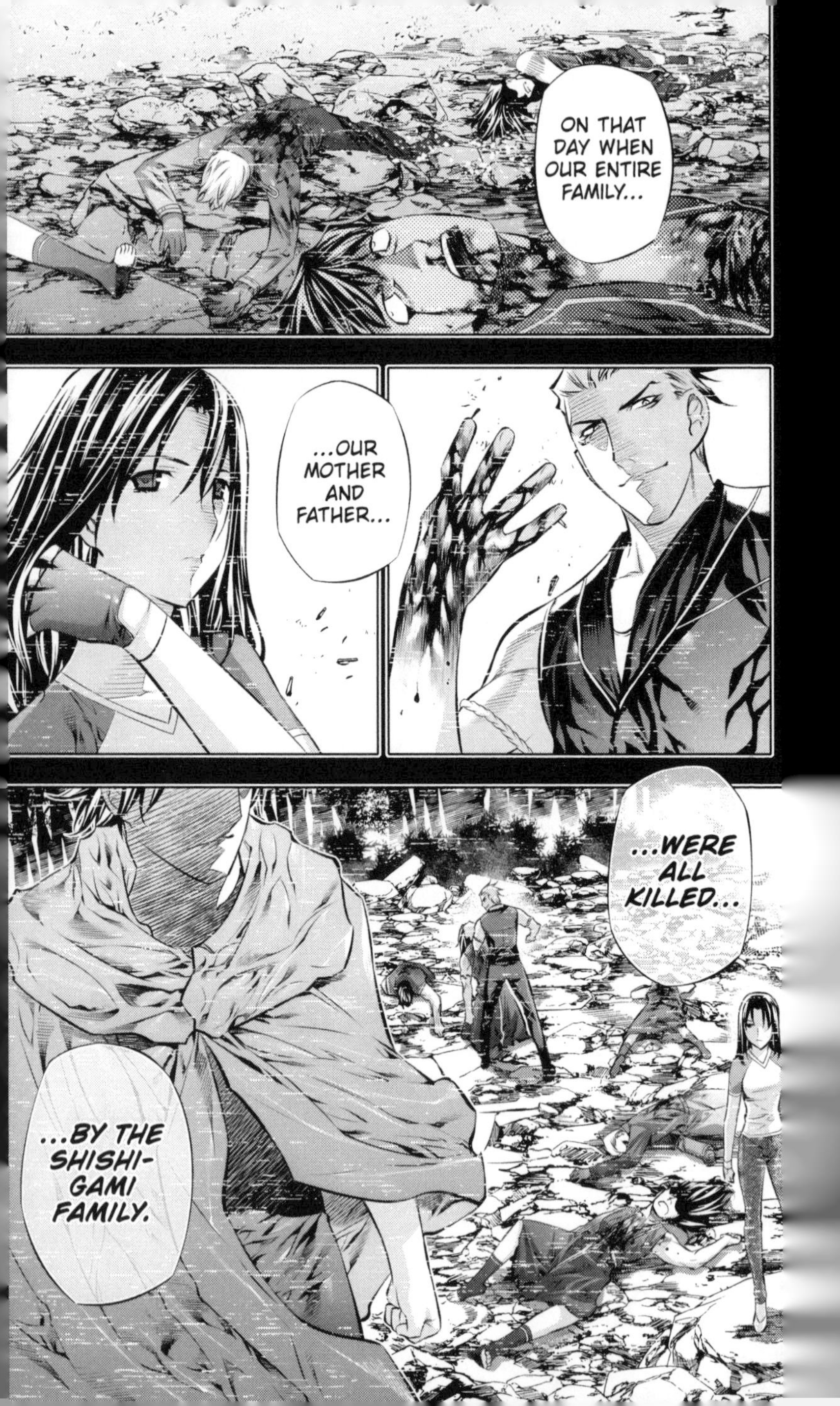
ON THAT DAY WHEN OUR ENTIRE FAMILY...
...OUR MOTHER AND FATHER...
...WERE ALL KILLED...
...BY THE SHISHI-GAMI FAMILY.

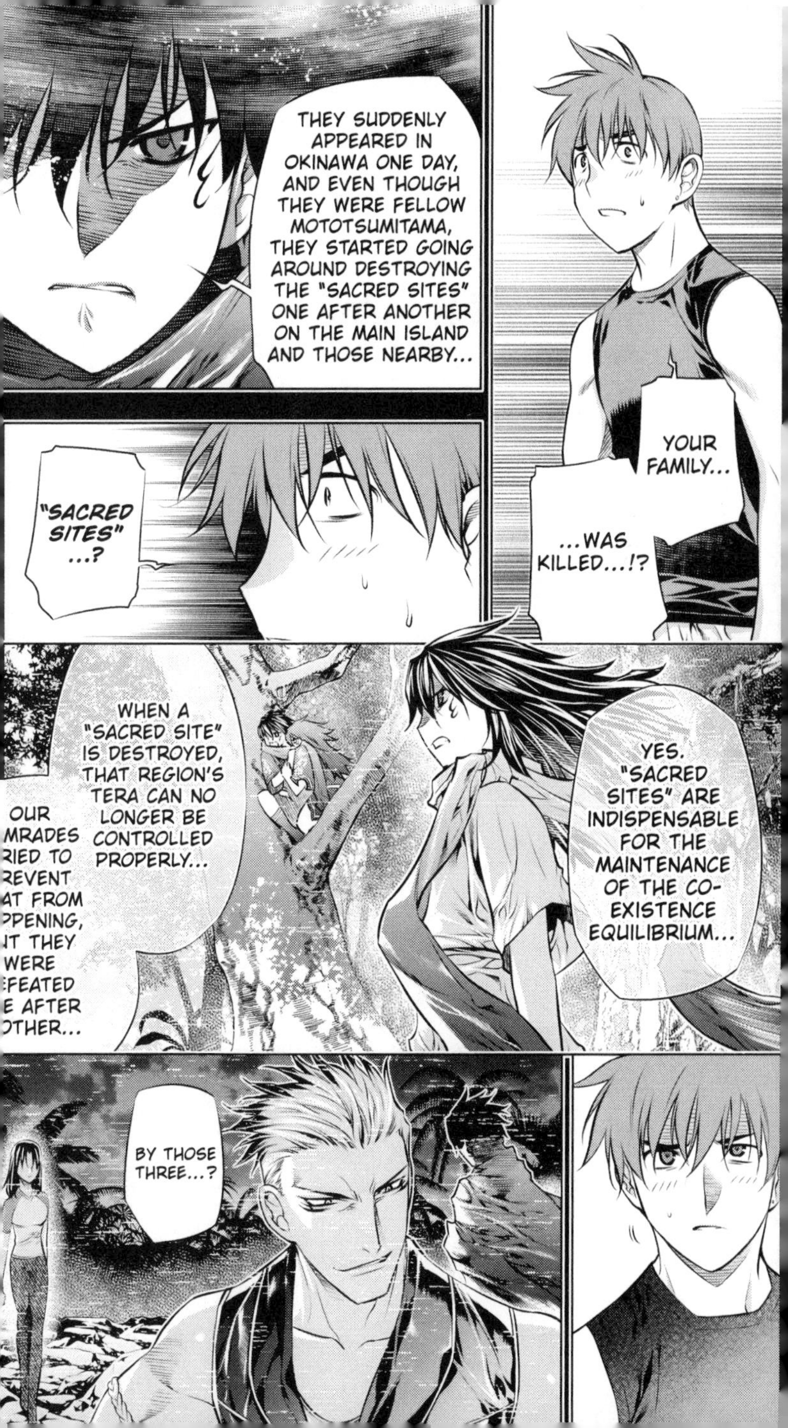
YOUR FAMILY...
...WAS KILLED...!?
THEY SUDDENLY APPEARED IN OKINAWA ONE DAY, AND EVEN THOUGH THEY WERE FELLOW MOTOTSUMITAMA, THEY STARTED GOING AROUND DESTROYING THE "SACRED SITES" ONE AFTER ANOTHER ON THE MAIN ISLAND AND THOSE NEARBY...
"SACRED SITES" ...?
YES. "SACRED SITES" ARE INDISPENSABLE FOR THE MAINTENANCE OF THE CO-EXISTENCE EQUILIBRIUM...
WHEN A "SACRED SITE" IS DESTROYED, THAT REGION'S TERA CAN NO LONGER BE CONTROLLED PROPERLY...
OUR MRADES RIED TO REVENT AT FROM PPENING, IT THEY WERE EFEATED E AFTER OTHER...
BY THOSE THREE...?

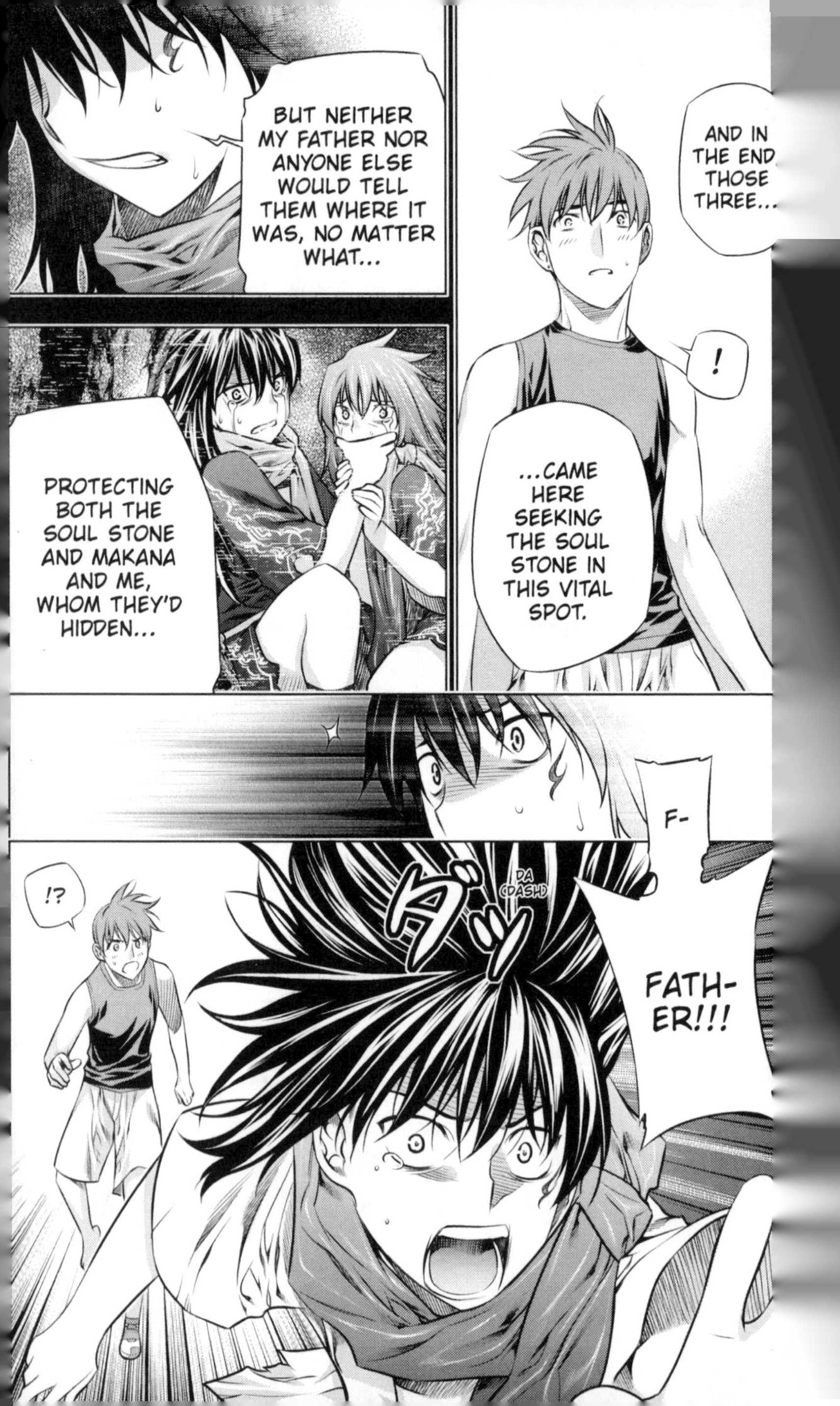
AND IN THE END THOSE THREE...
!
...CAME HERE SEEKING THE SOUL STONE IN THIS VITAL SPOT.
BUT NEITHER MY FATHER NOR ANYONE ELSE WOULD TELL THEM WHERE IT WAS, NO MATTER WHAT...
PROTECTING BOTH THE SOUL STONE AND MAKANA AND ME, WHOM THEY'D HIDDEN...
F-
DA (DASH)
FATH-ER!!!
!?

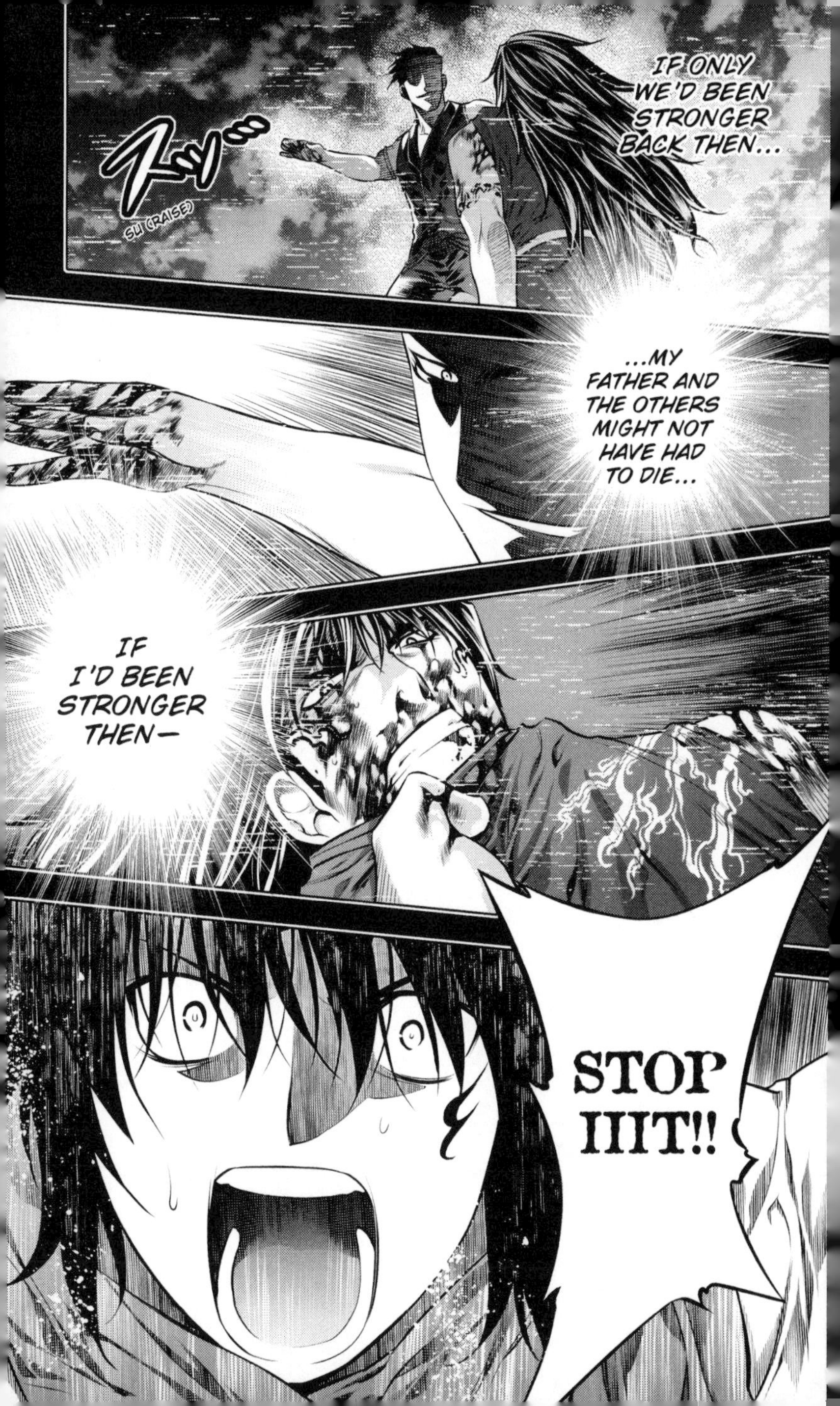
IF ONLY WE'D BEEN STRONGER BACK THEN...
SU (RAISE)
...MY FATHER AND THE OTHERS MIGHT NOT HAVE HAD TO DIE...
IF I'D BEEN STRONGER THEN—
STOP IIIT!!

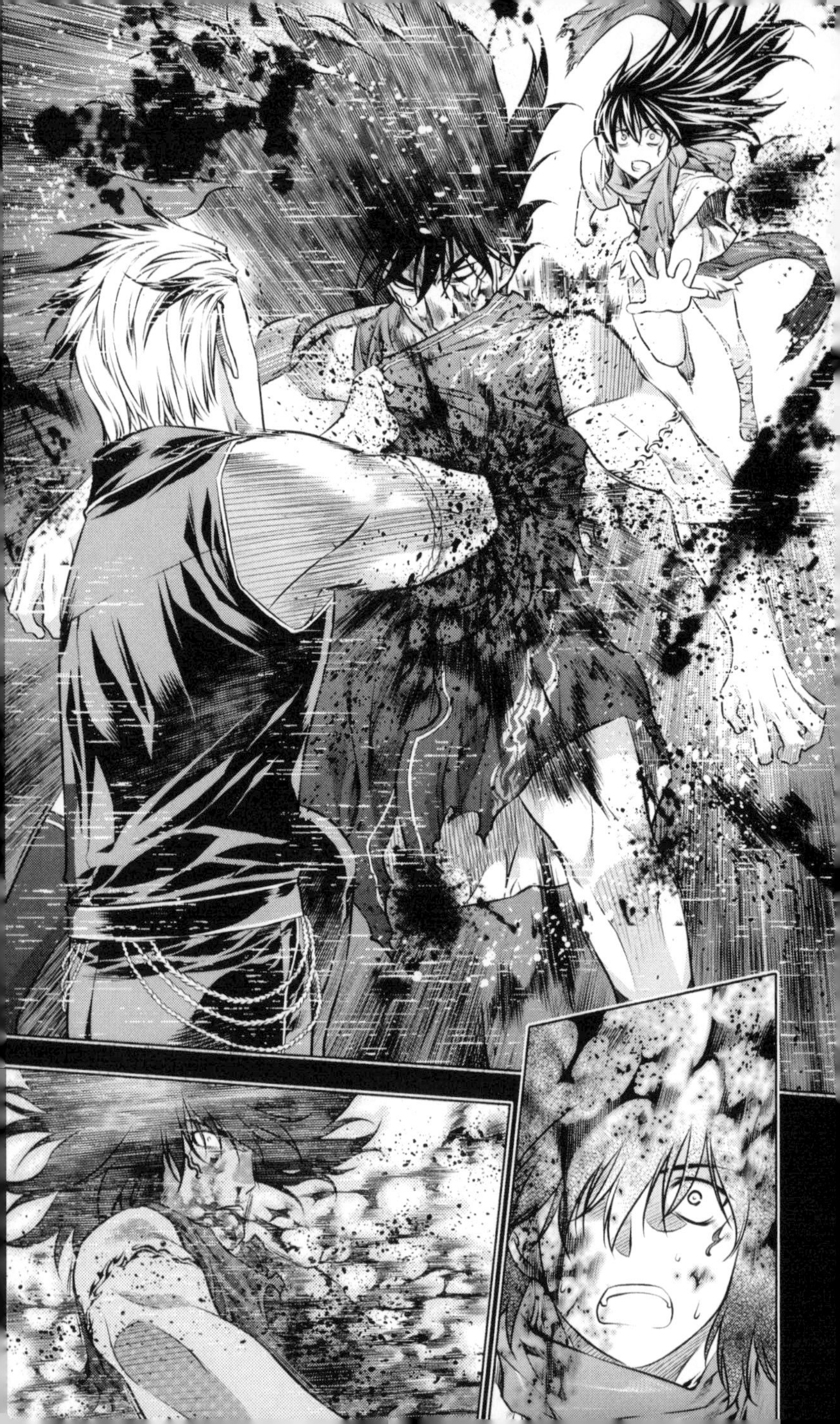

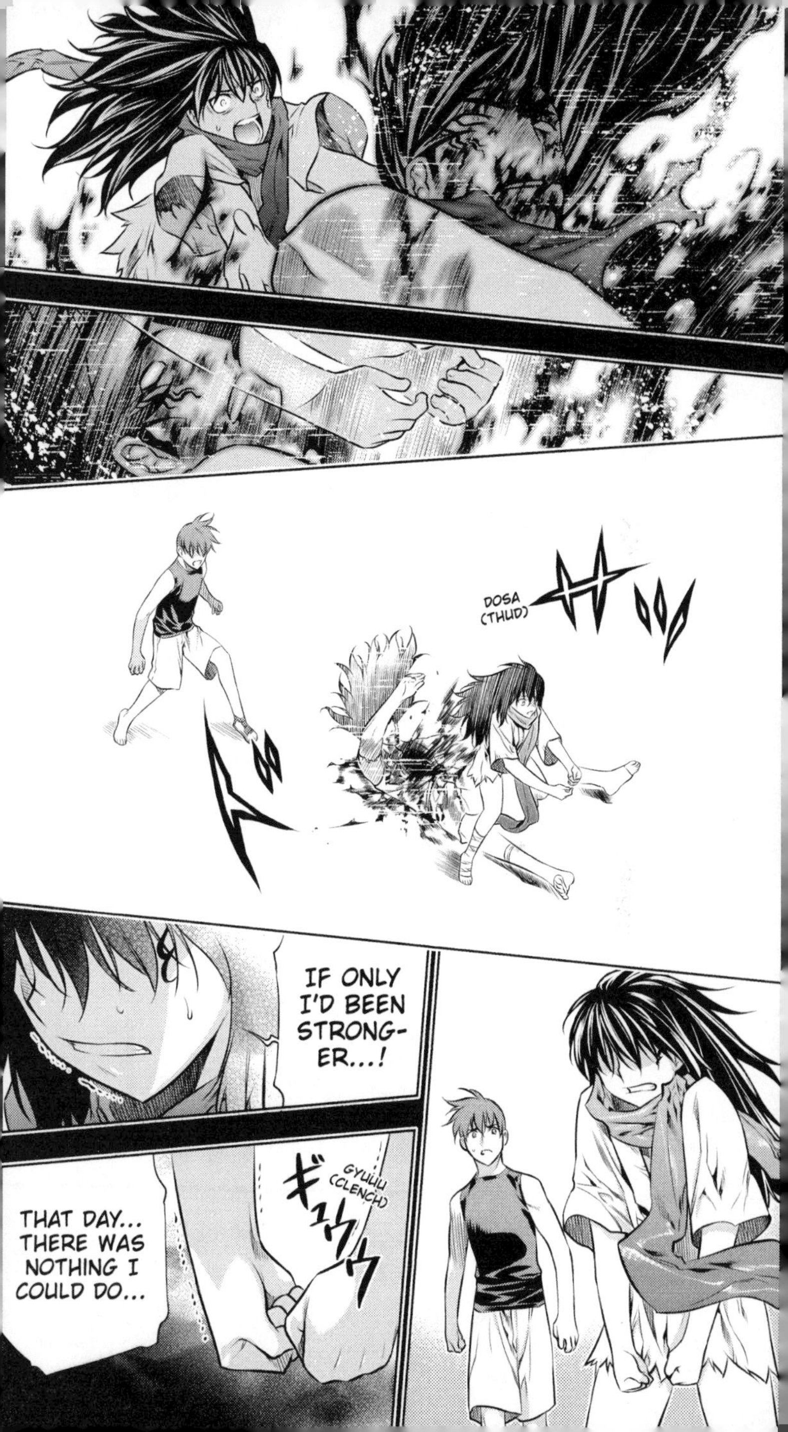
DOSA (THUD)
IF ONLY I'D BEEN STRONGER...!
GYUUU (CLENCH)
THAT DAY... THERE WAS NOTHING I COULD DO...

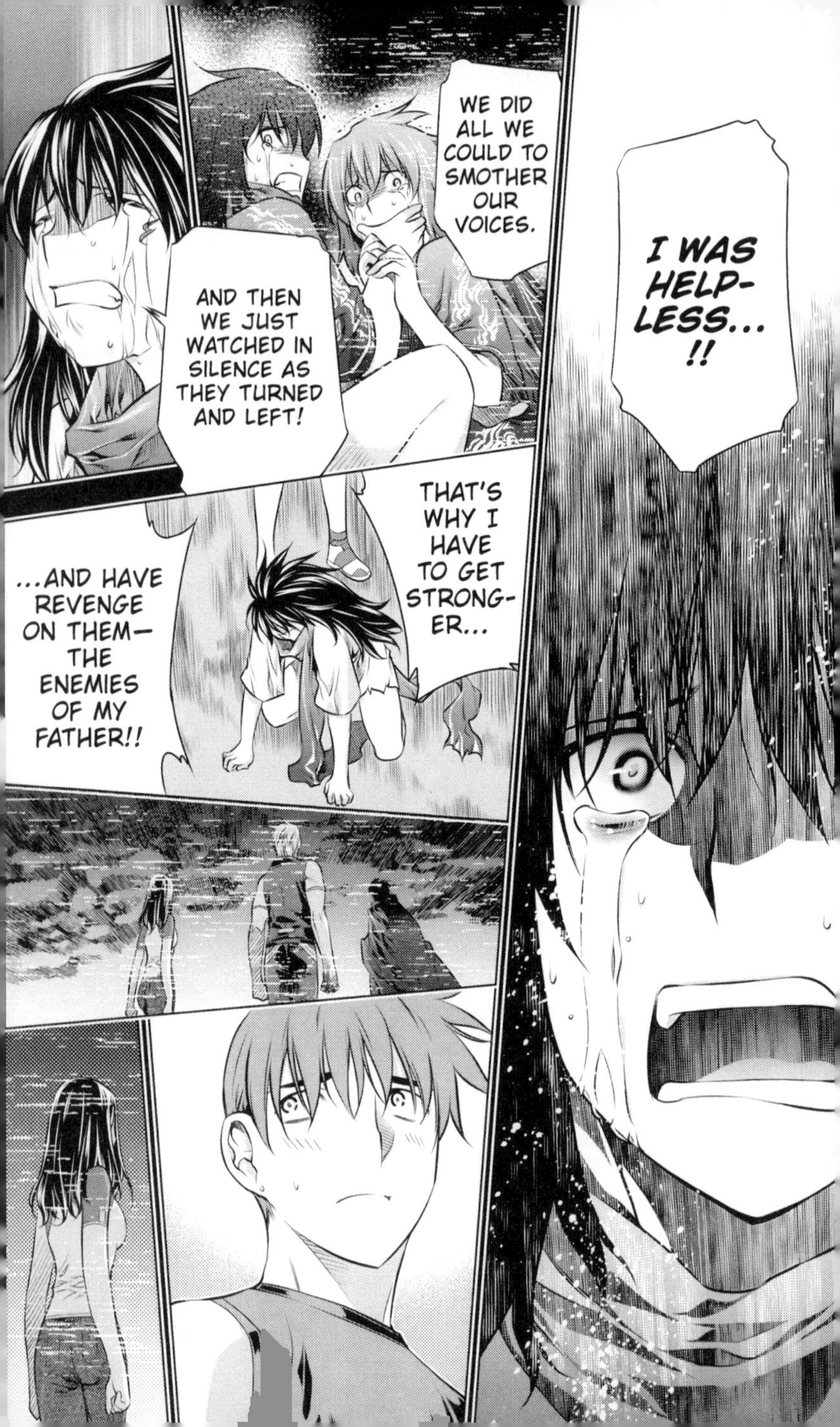
I WAS HELPLESS...!!
WE DID ALL WE COULD TO SMOTHER OUR VOICES.
AND THEN WE JUST WATCHED IN SILENCE AS THEY TURNED AND LEFT!
THAT'S WHY I HAVE TO GET STRONGER...
...AND HAVE REVENGE ON THEM—THE ENEMIES OF MY FATHER!!

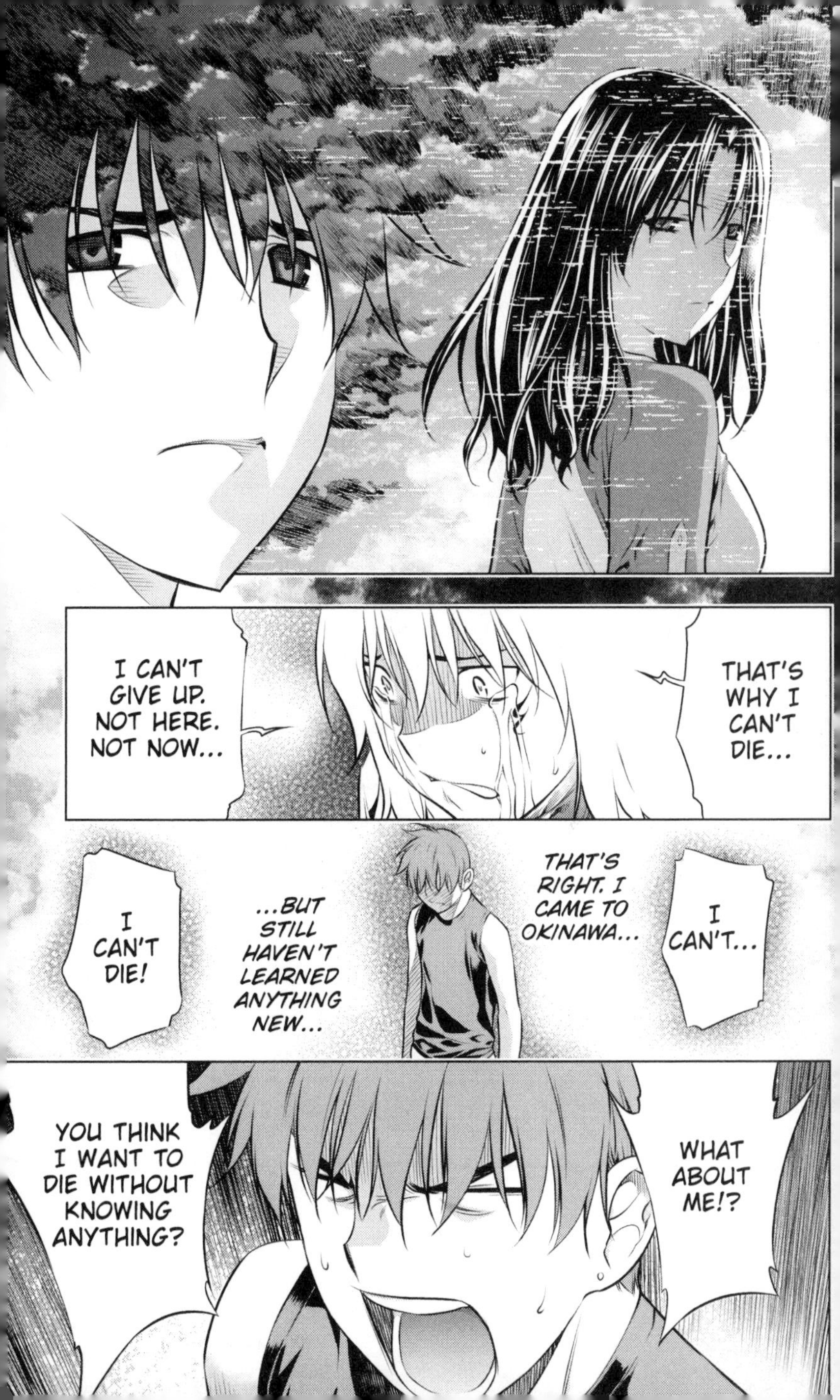
THAT'S WHY I CAN'T DIE...
I CAN'T GIVE UP. NOT HERE. NOT NOW...
I CAN'T...
THAT'S RIGHT. I CAME TO OKINAWA...
...BUT STILL HAVEN'T LEARNED ANYTHING NEW...
I CAN'T DIE!
WHAT ABOUT ME!?
YOU THINK I WANT TO DIE WITHOUT KNOWING ANYTHING?

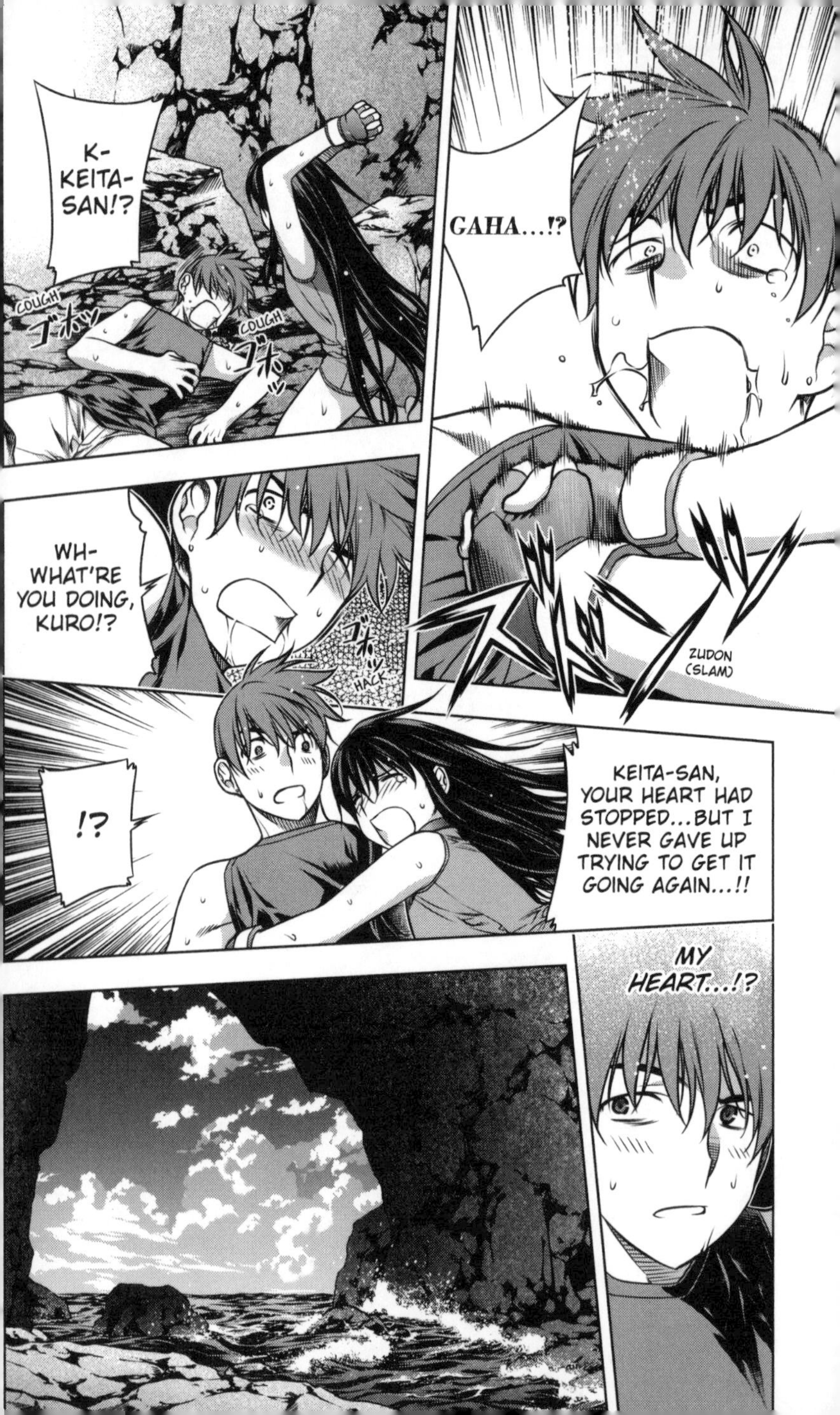
GAHA...!?
K-KEITA-SAN!?
COUGH
ゴホッ
COUGH
ゴホッ
ZUDON (SLAM)
WH-WHAT'RE YOU DOING, KURO!?
ゴホッ
HACK
KEITA-SAN, YOUR HEART HAD STOPPED...BUT I NEVER GAVE UP TRYING TO GET IT GOING AGAIN...!!
!?
MY HEART...!?

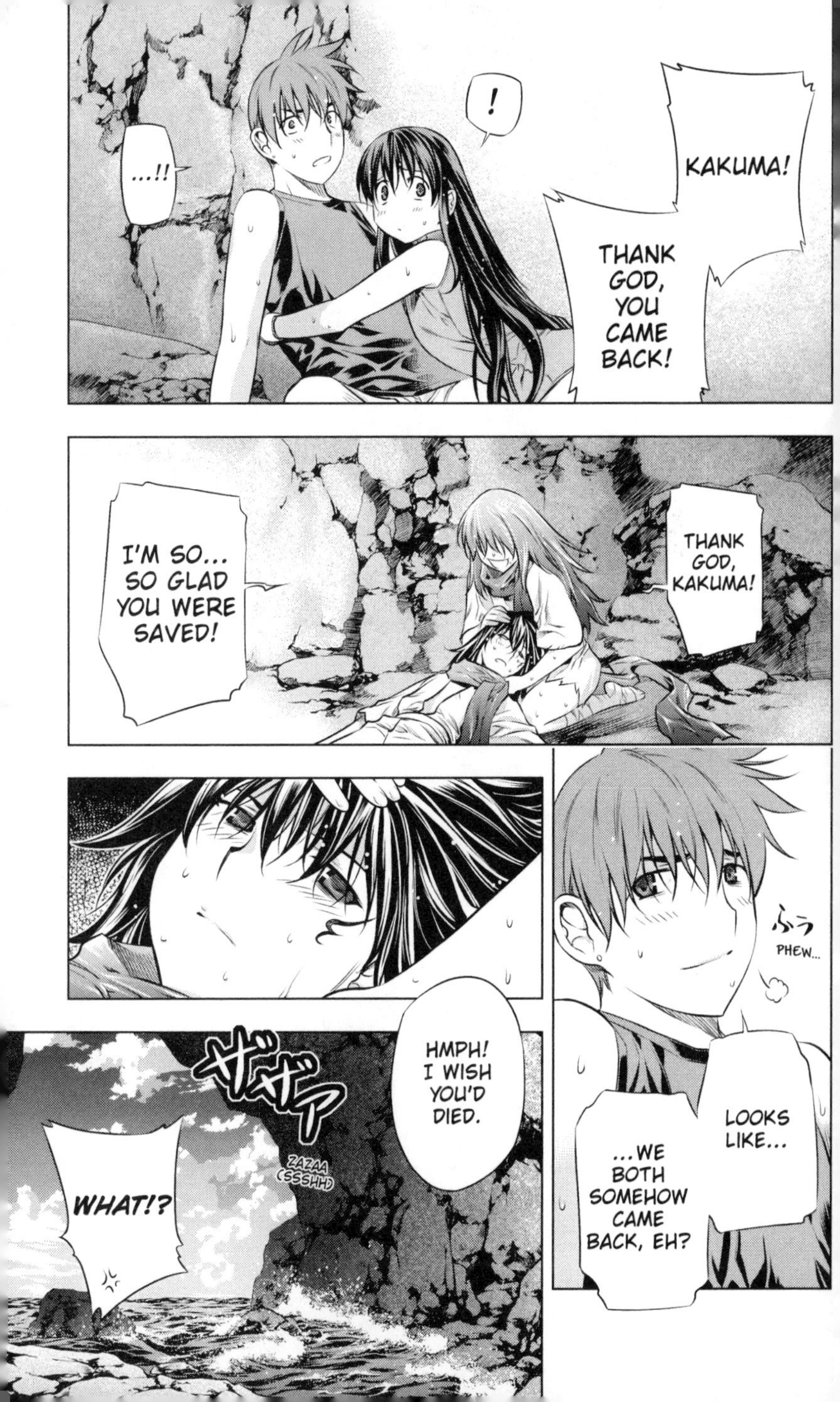

KAKUMA!
THANK GOD, YOU CAME BACK!
!
...!!
THANK GOD, KAKUMA!
I'M SO... SO GLAD YOU WERE SAVED!
ふう
PHEW...
LOOKS LIKE...
...WE BOTH SOMEHOW CAME BACK, EH?
HMPH! I WISH YOU'D DIED.
ザザァ
ZAZAA (SSSHHD)
WHAT!?

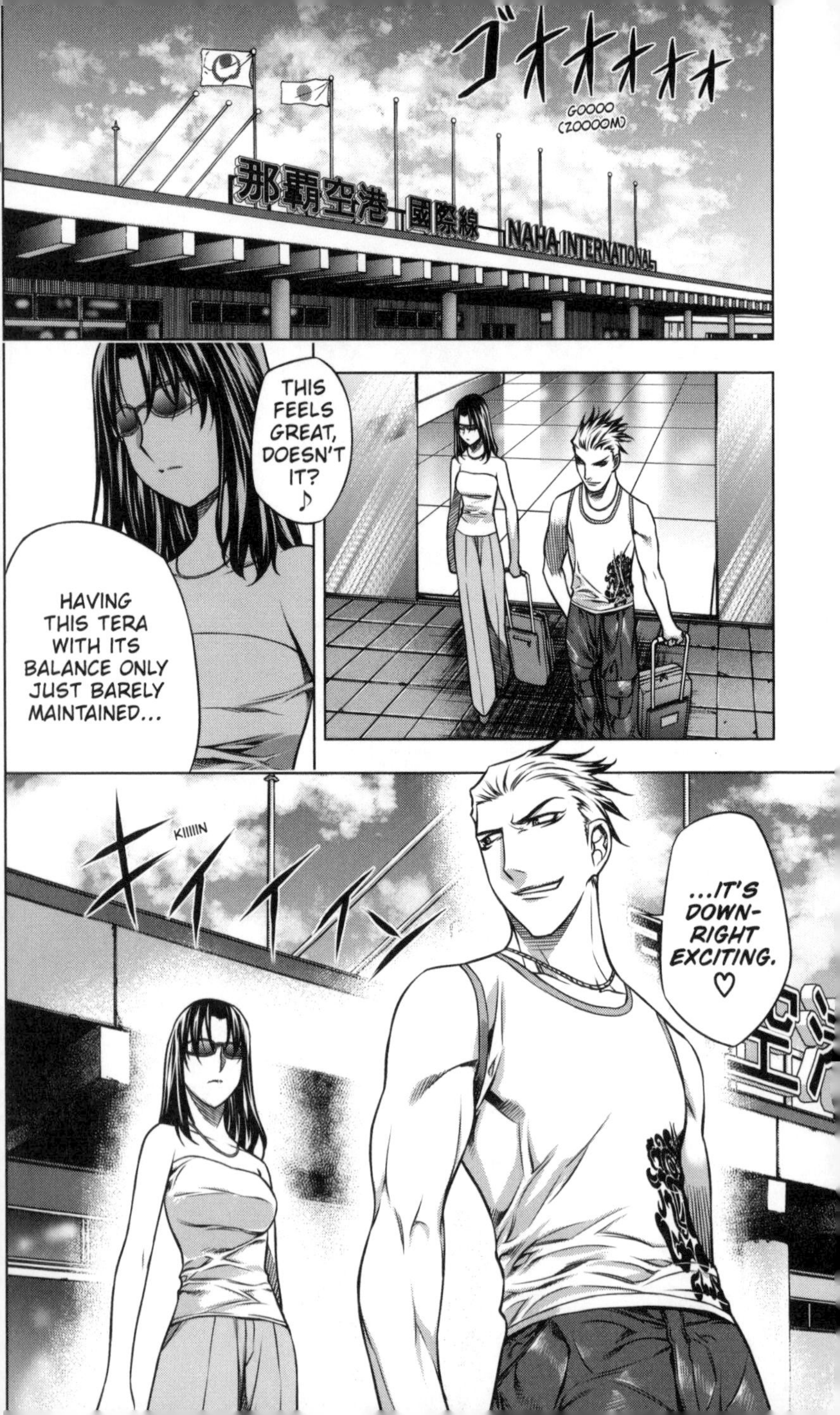

ゴオオオオオ
GOOOO (ZOOOOM)
那覇空港 國際線 NAHA INTERNATIONAL
THIS FEELS GREAT, DOESN'T IT? ♪
HAVING THIS TERA WITH ITS BALANCE ONLY JUST BARELY MAINTAINED...
...IT'S DOWN-RIGHT EXCITING. ♡
キイイイン
KIIIIIN

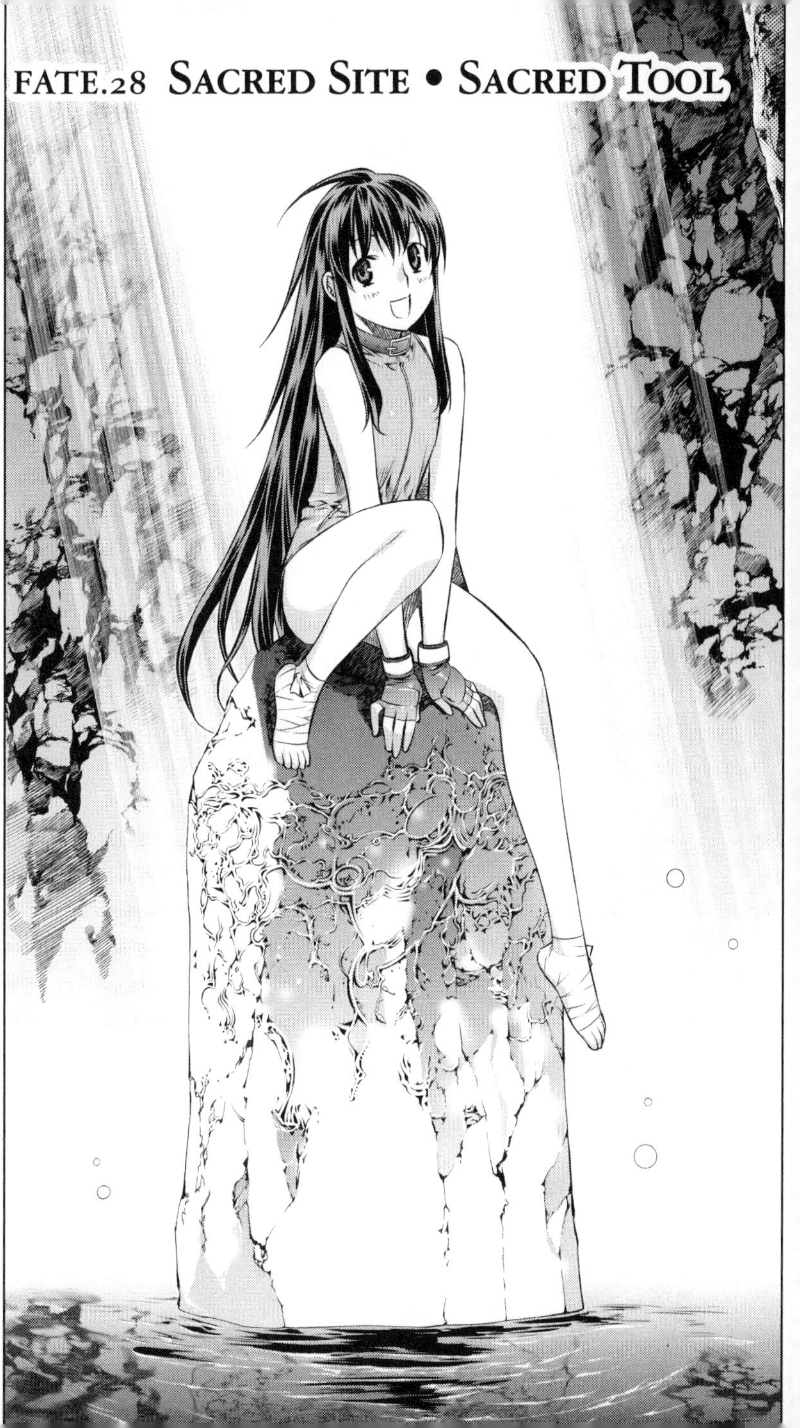
FATE.28 SACRED SITE • SACRED TOOL

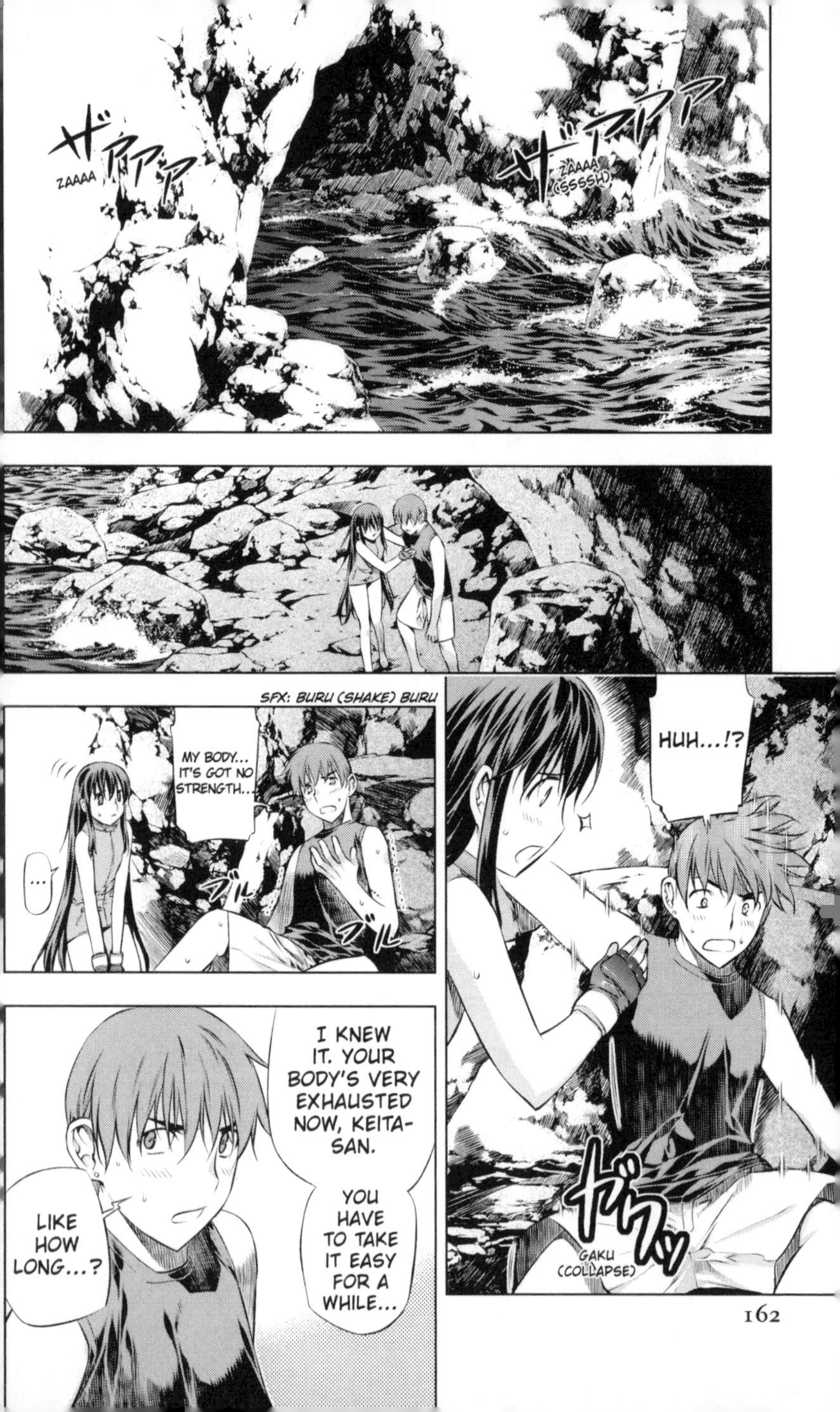
ZAAAA (SSSSH)
ZAAAA
HUH...!?
GAKU (COLLAPSE)
SFX: BURU (SHAKE) BURU
MY BODY... IT'S GOT NO STRENGTH...
...
I KNEW IT. YOUR BODY'S VERY EXHAUSTED NOW, KEITA-SAN.
YOU HAVE TO TAKE IT EASY FOR A WHILE...
LIKE HOW LONG...?

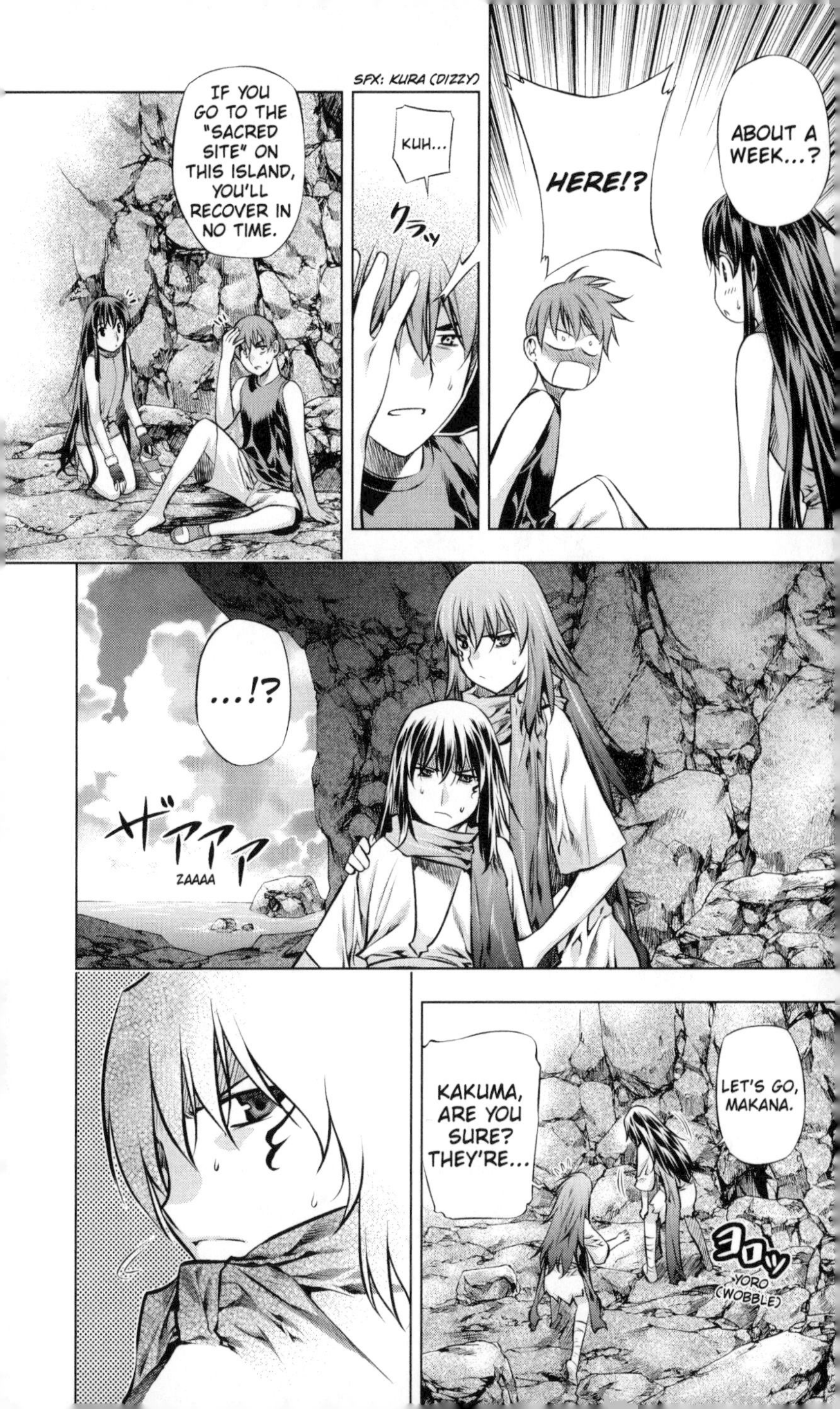
ABOUT A WEEK...?
HERE!?
KUH...
SFX: KURA (DIZZY)
IF YOU GO TO THE "SACRED SITE" ON THIS ISLAND, YOU'LL RECOVER IN NO TIME.
...!?
ZAAAA
LET'S GO, MAKANA.
YORO (WOBBLE)
KAKUMA, ARE YOU SURE? THEY'RE...

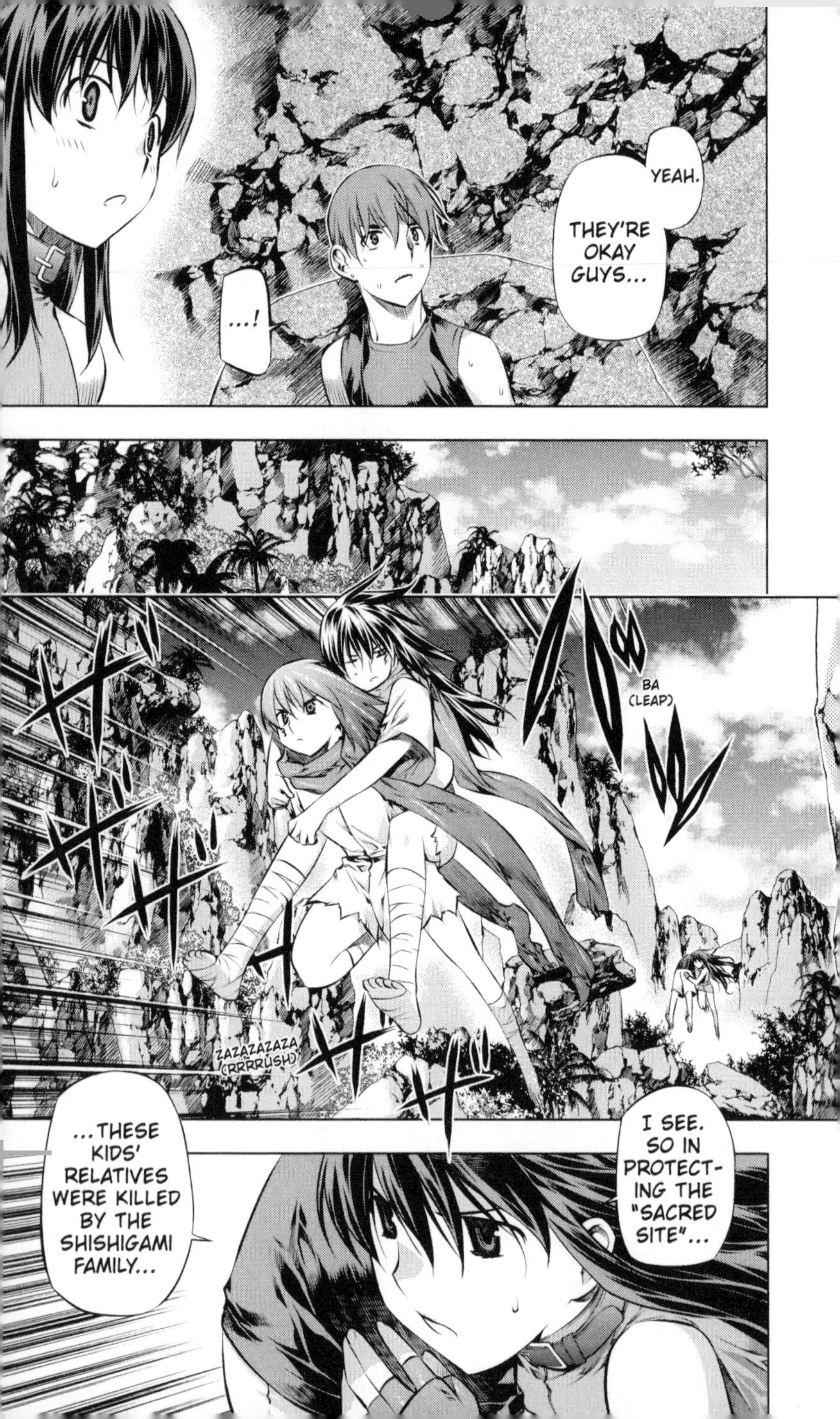
YEAH.
THEY'RE OKAY GUYS...
...!
BA (LEAP)
ZAZAZAZAZA (RRRRUSH)
I SEE. SO IN PROTECT-ING THE "SACRED SITE"...
...THESE KIDS' RELATIVES WERE KILLED BY THE SHISHIGAMI FAMILY...

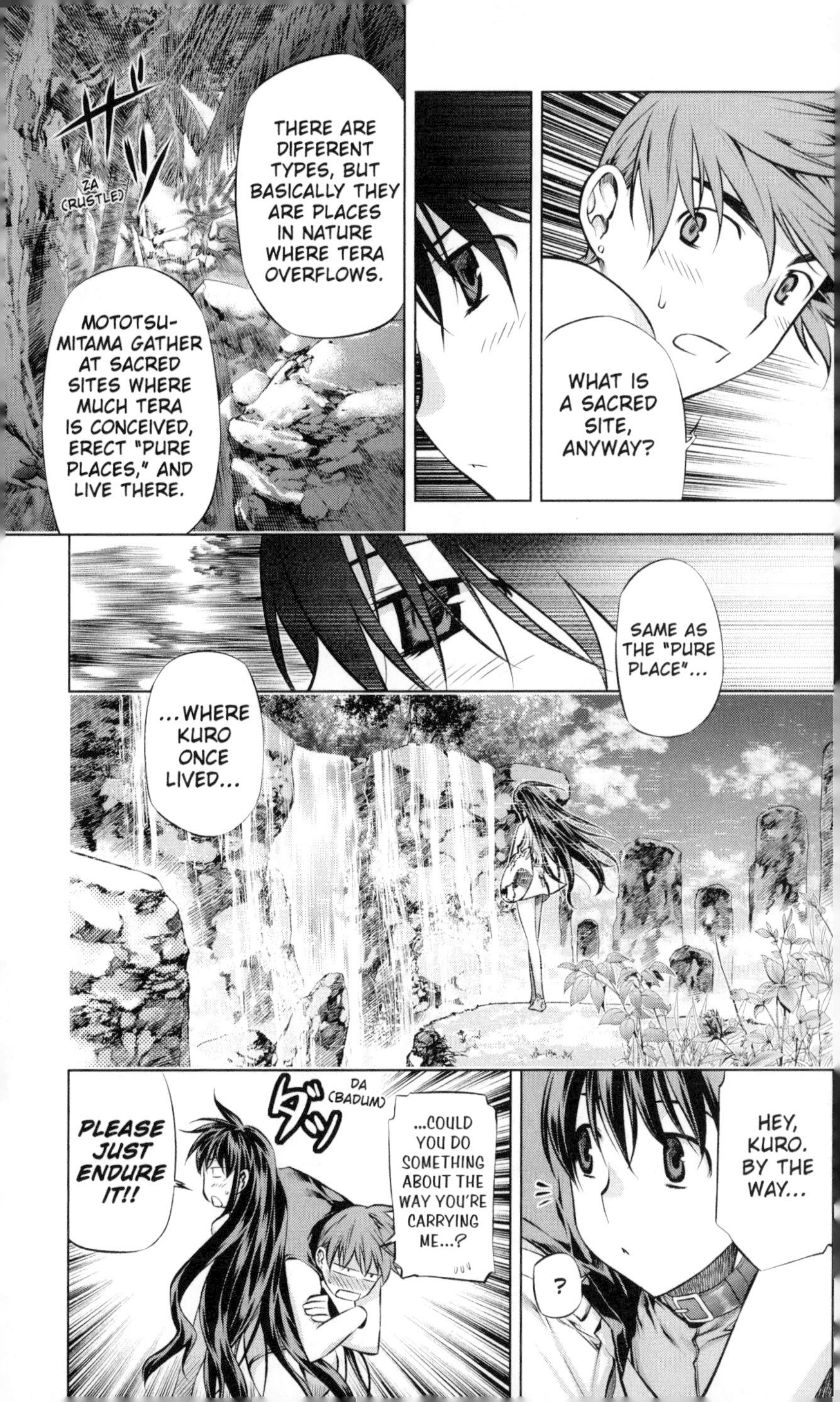

WHAT IS A SACRED SITE, ANYWAY?
THERE ARE DIFFERENT TYPES, BUT BASICALLY THEY ARE PLACES IN NATURE WHERE TERA OVERFLOWS.
ZA (RUSTLE)
MOTOTSU-MITAMA GATHER AT SACRED SITES WHERE MUCH TERA IS CONCEIVED, ERECT "PURE PLACES," AND LIVE THERE.
SAME AS THE "PURE PLACE"...
...WHERE KURO ONCE LIVED...
HEY, KURO. BY THE WAY...
?
...COULD YOU DO SOMETHING ABOUT THE WAY YOU'RE CARRYING ME...?
DA (BADUM)
PLEASE JUST ENDURE IT!!

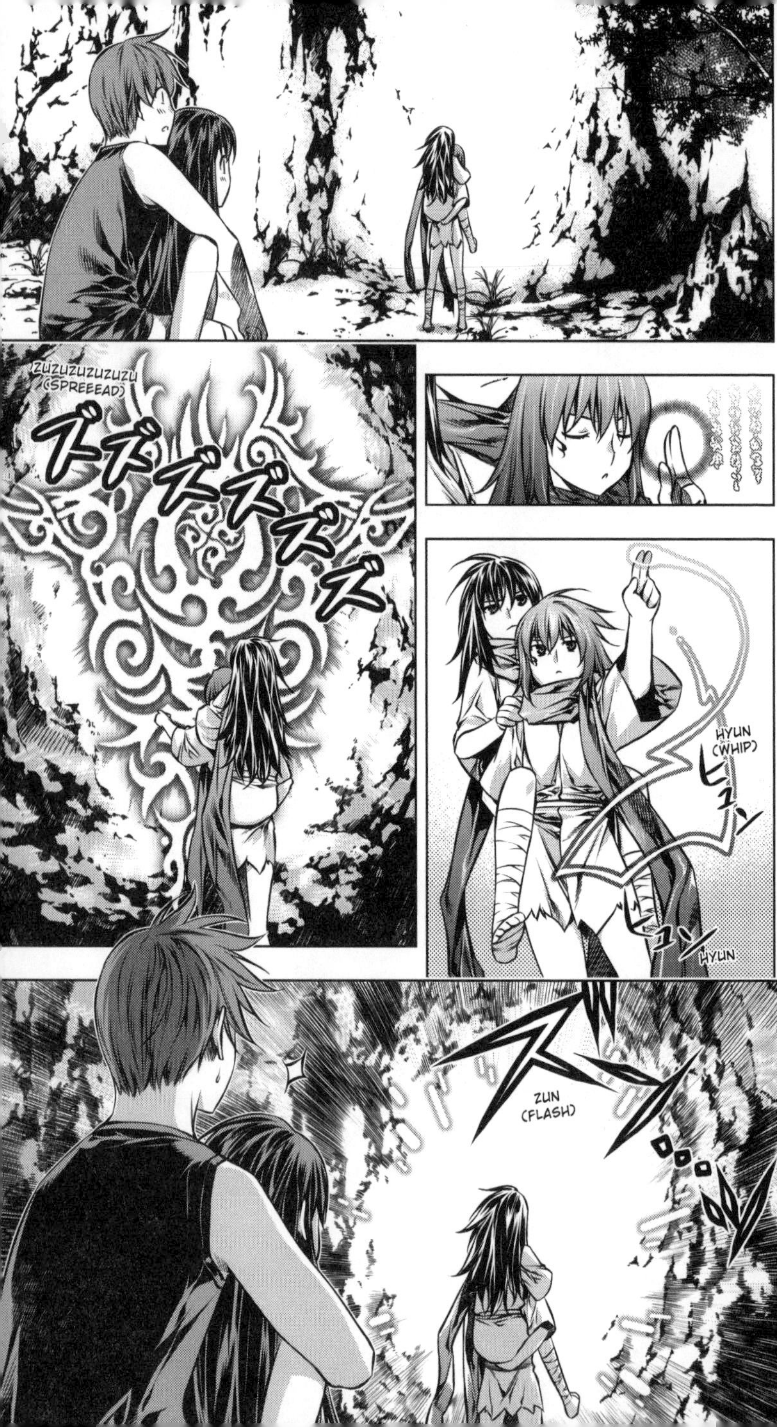
HYUN
(WHIP)
ヒュン
ヒュン
HYUN
ZUZUZUZUZUZU
(SPREEEAD)
ズズズズズズ
ZUN
(FLASH)

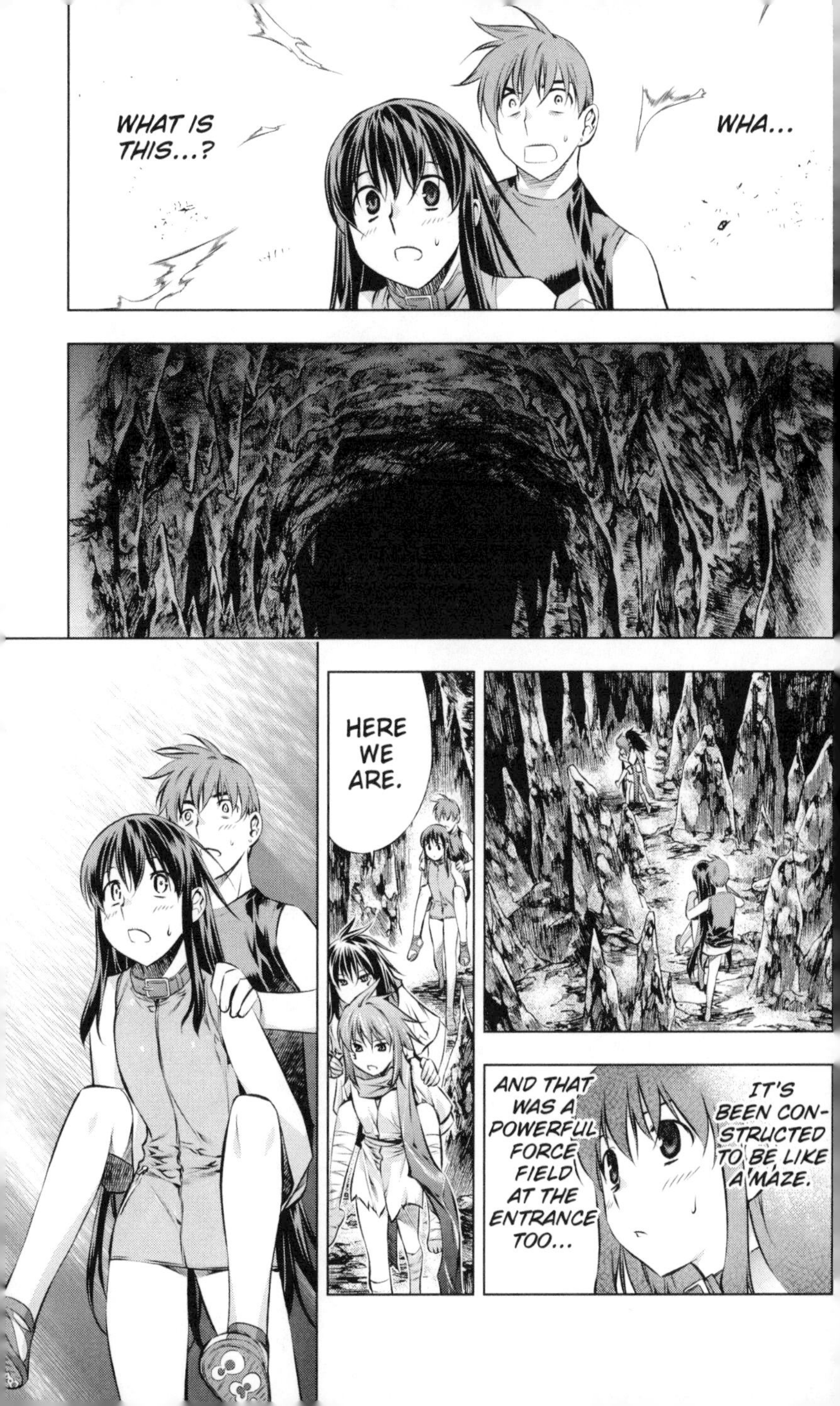
WHA...
WHAT IS THIS...?
IT'S BEEN CONSTRUCTED TO BE LIKE A MAZE.
AND THAT WAS A POWERFUL FORCE FIELD AT THE ENTRANCE TOO...
HERE WE ARE.

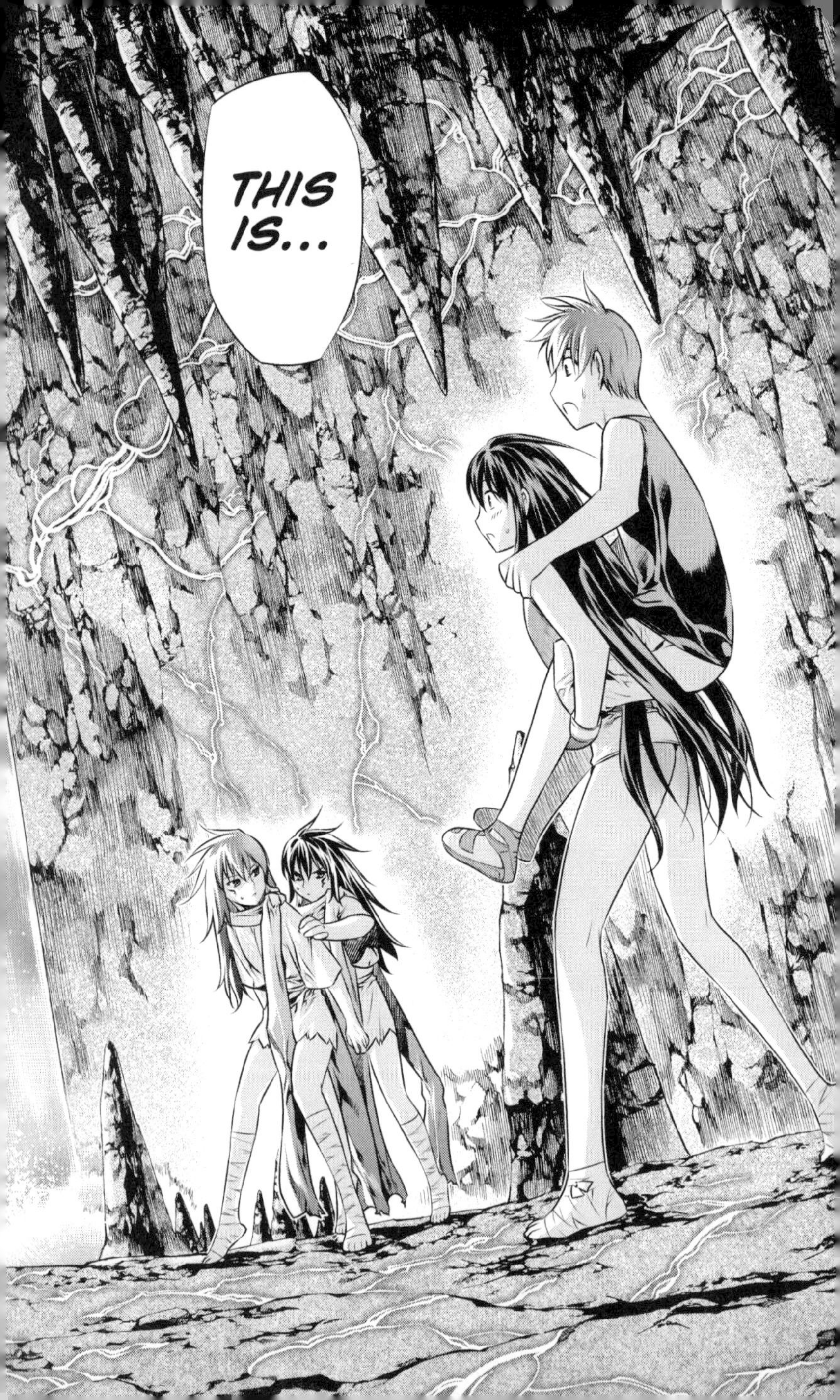
THIS IS...

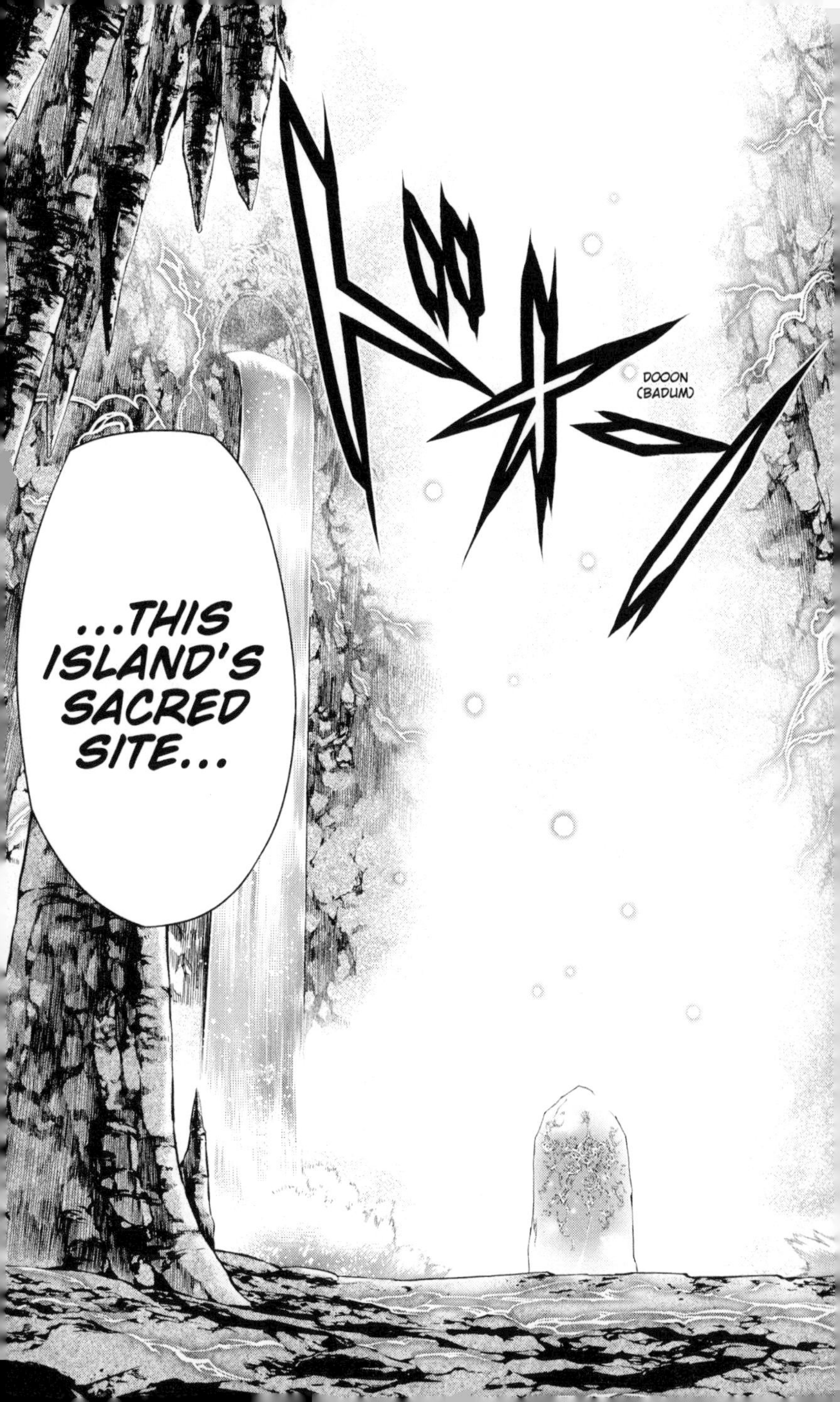
DOOON
(BADUM)
...THIS ISLAND'S SACRED SITE...

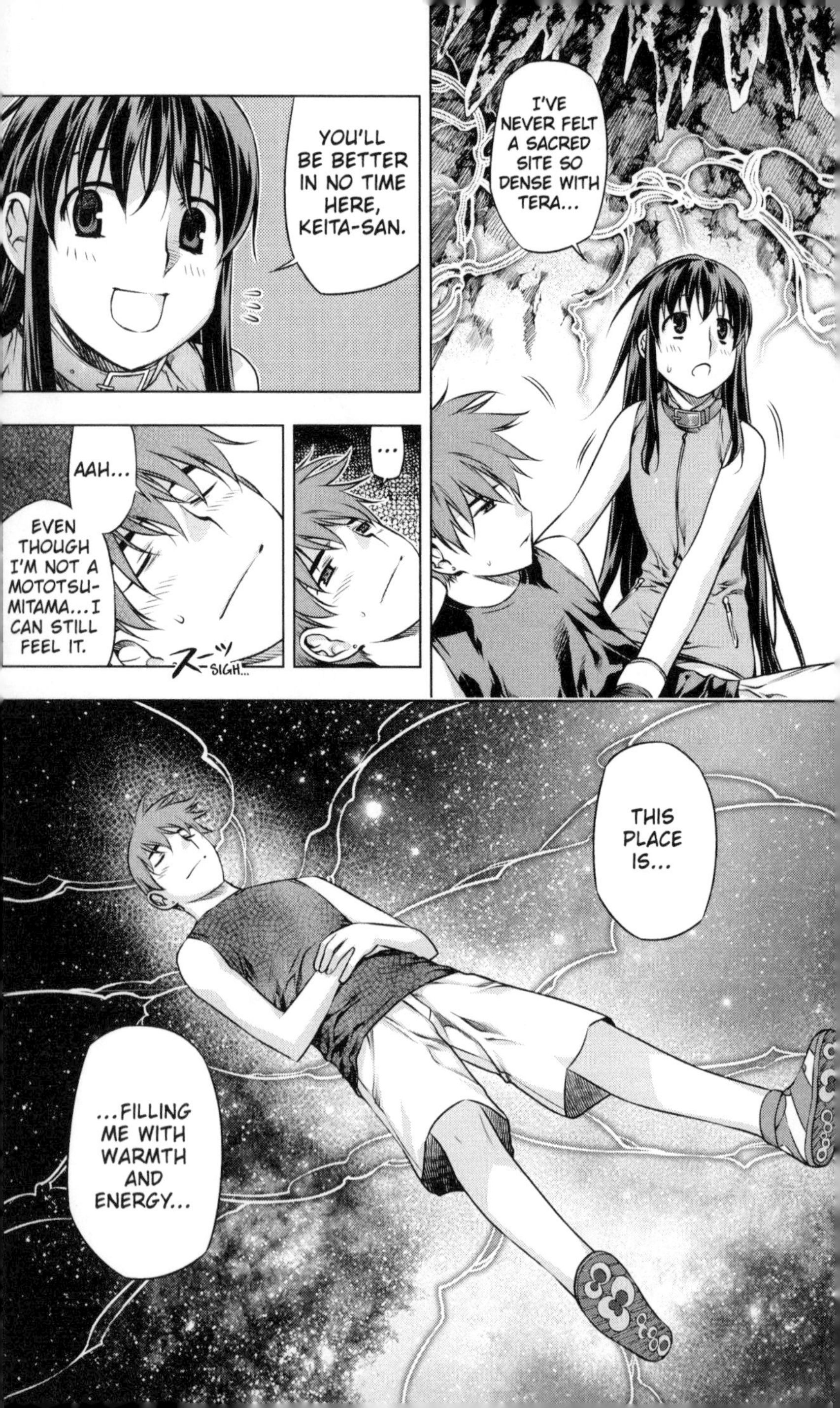

I'VE NEVER FELT A SACRED SITE SO DENSE WITH TERA...
YOU'LL BE BETTER IN NO TIME HERE, KEITA-SAN.
...
AAH...
EVEN THOUGH I'M NOT A MOTOTSU-MITAMA... I CAN STILL FEEL IT.
スーッ
SIGH...
THIS PLACE IS...
...FILLING ME WITH WARMTH AND ENERGY...

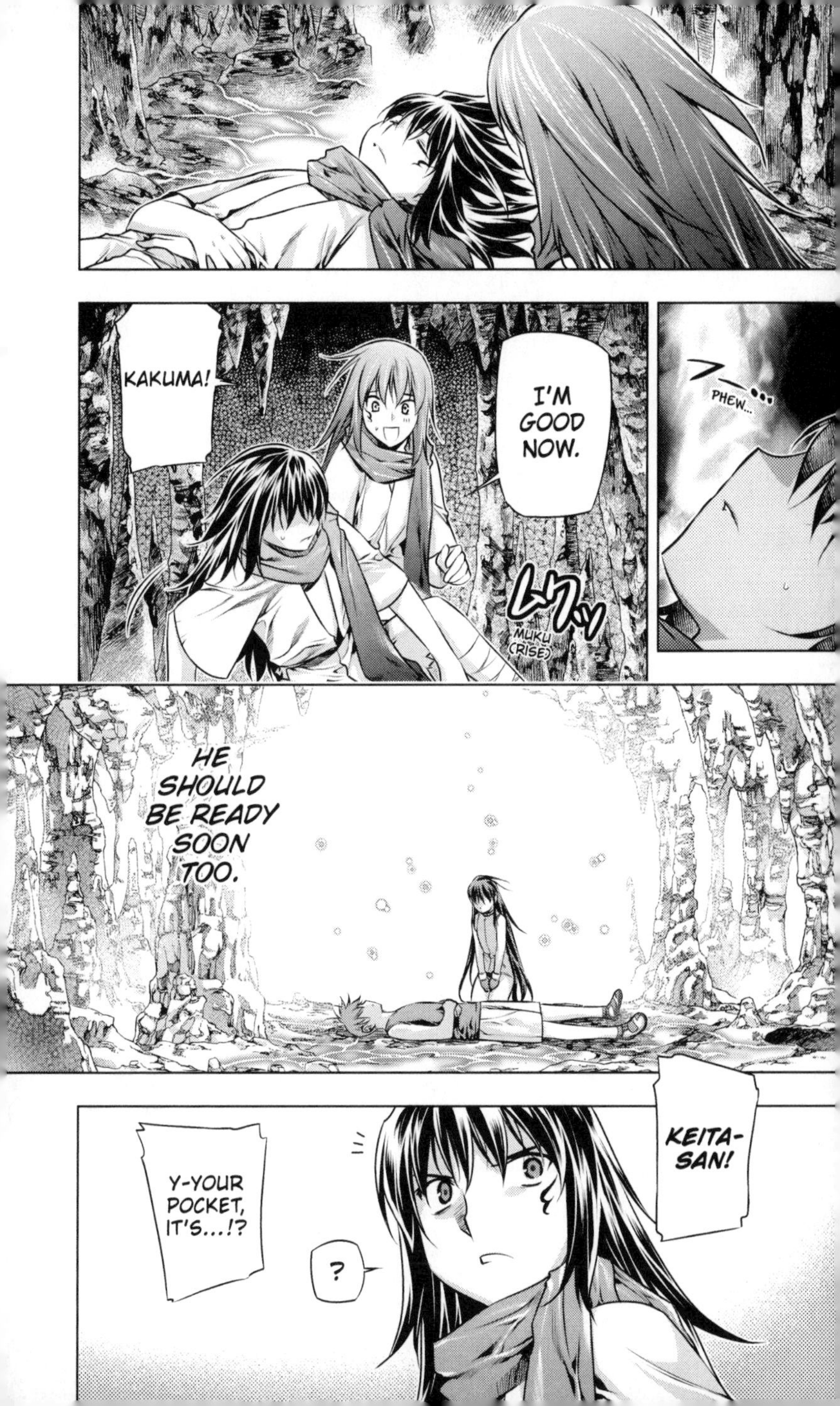
フー…
PHEW...
I'M GOOD NOW.
KAKUMA!
ムクッ
MUKU (RISE)
HE SHOULD BE READY SOON TOO.
KEITA-SAN!
Y-YOUR POCKET, IT'S...!?
?

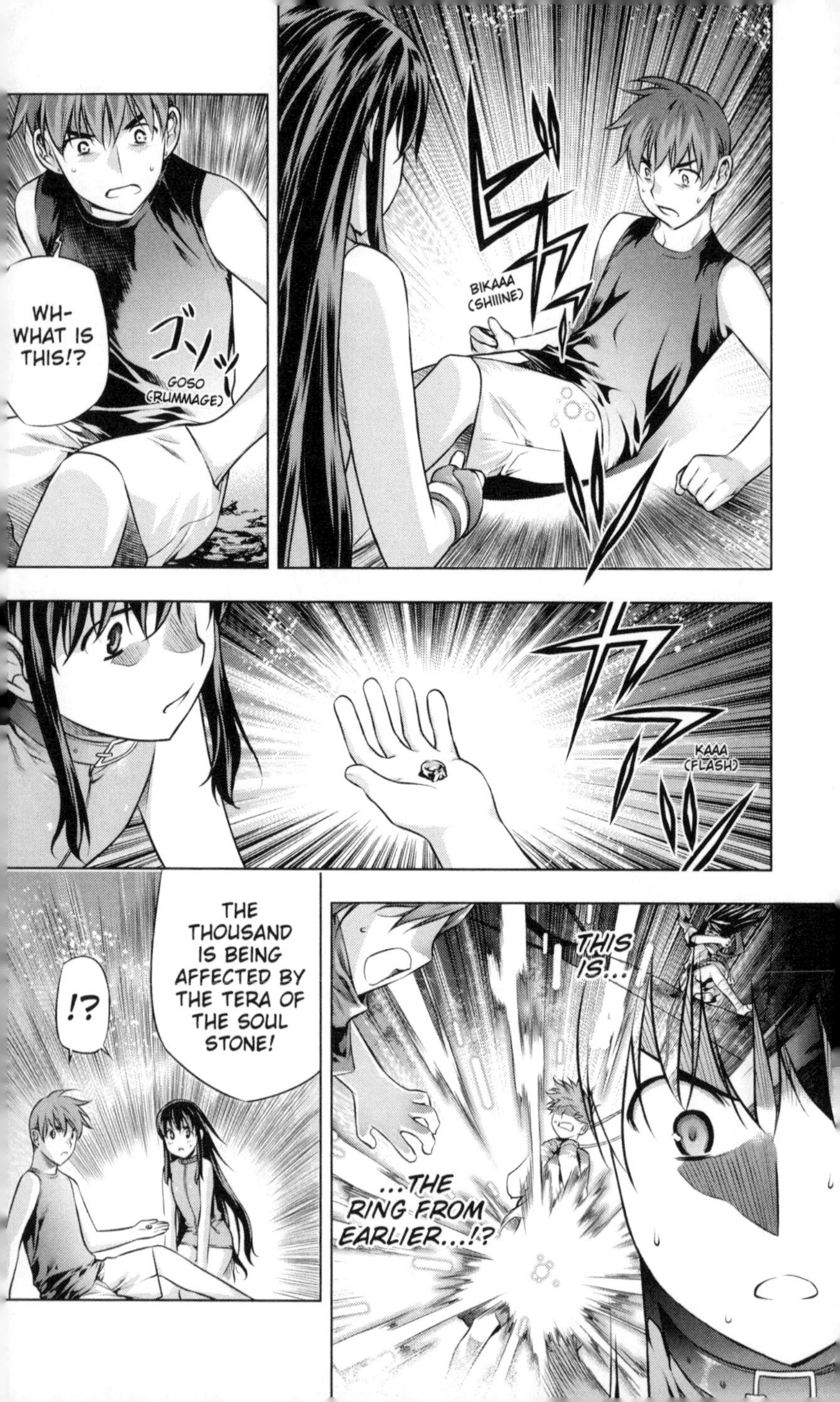
BIKAAA (SHIIINE)
WH- WHAT IS THIS!?
ゴソッ
GOSO (RUMMAGE)
KAAA (FLASH)
THIS IS...
...THE RING FROM EARLIER...!?
THE THOUSAND IS BEING AFFECTED BY THE TERA OF THE SOUL STONE!
!?

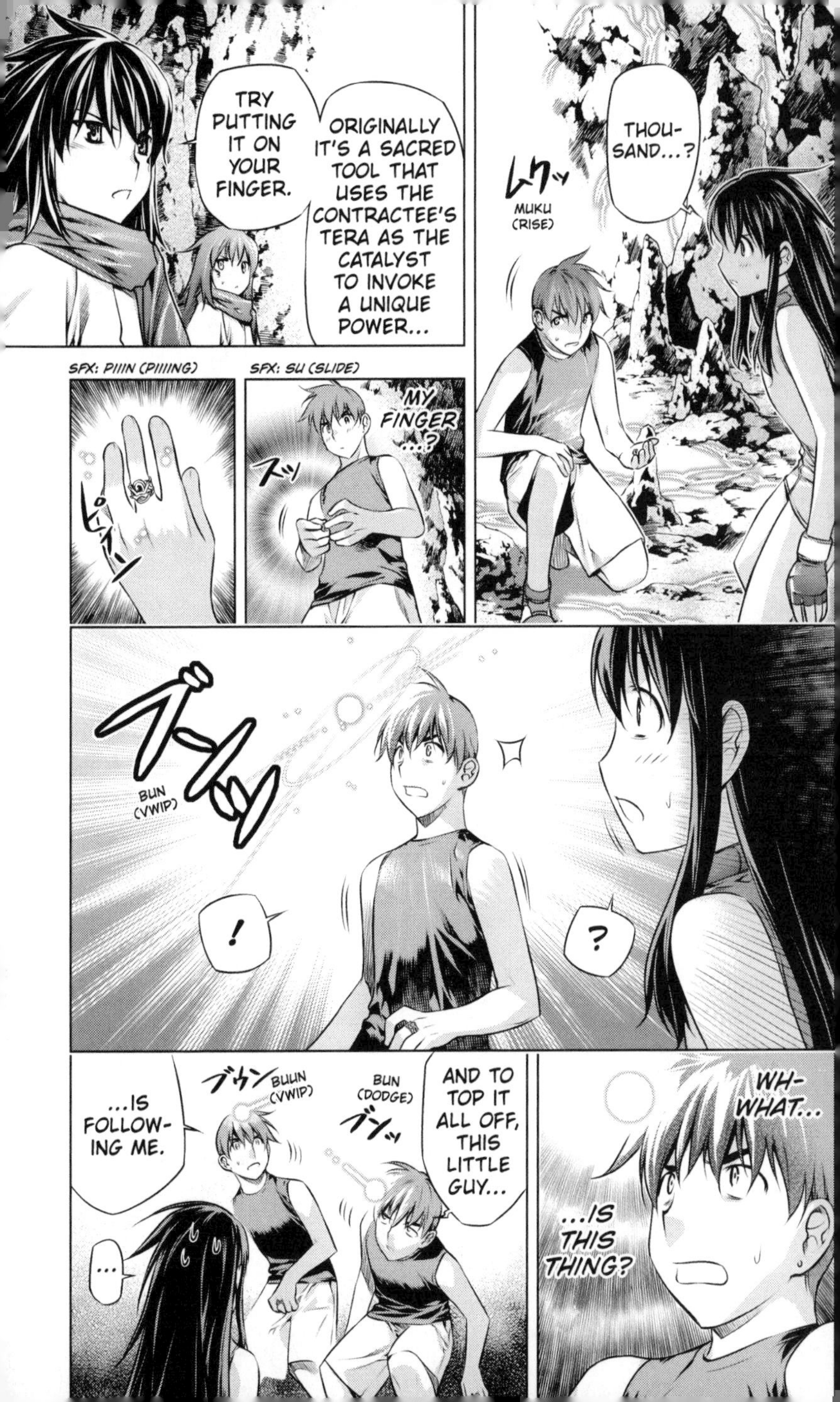
THOU-SAND...?
MUKU (RISE)
ORIGINALLY IT'S A SACRED TOOL THAT USES THE CONTRACTEE'S TERA AS THE CATALYST TO INVOKE A UNIQUE POWER...
TRY PUTTING IT ON YOUR FINGER.
SFX: SU (SLIDE)
MY FINGER...?
SFX: PIIIN (PIIIING)
?
!
BUN (VWIP)
WH-WHAT...
...IS THIS THING?
AND TO TOP IT ALL OFF, THIS LITTLE GUY...
BUN (DODGE)
BUUN (VWIP)
...IS FOLLOWING ME.
...

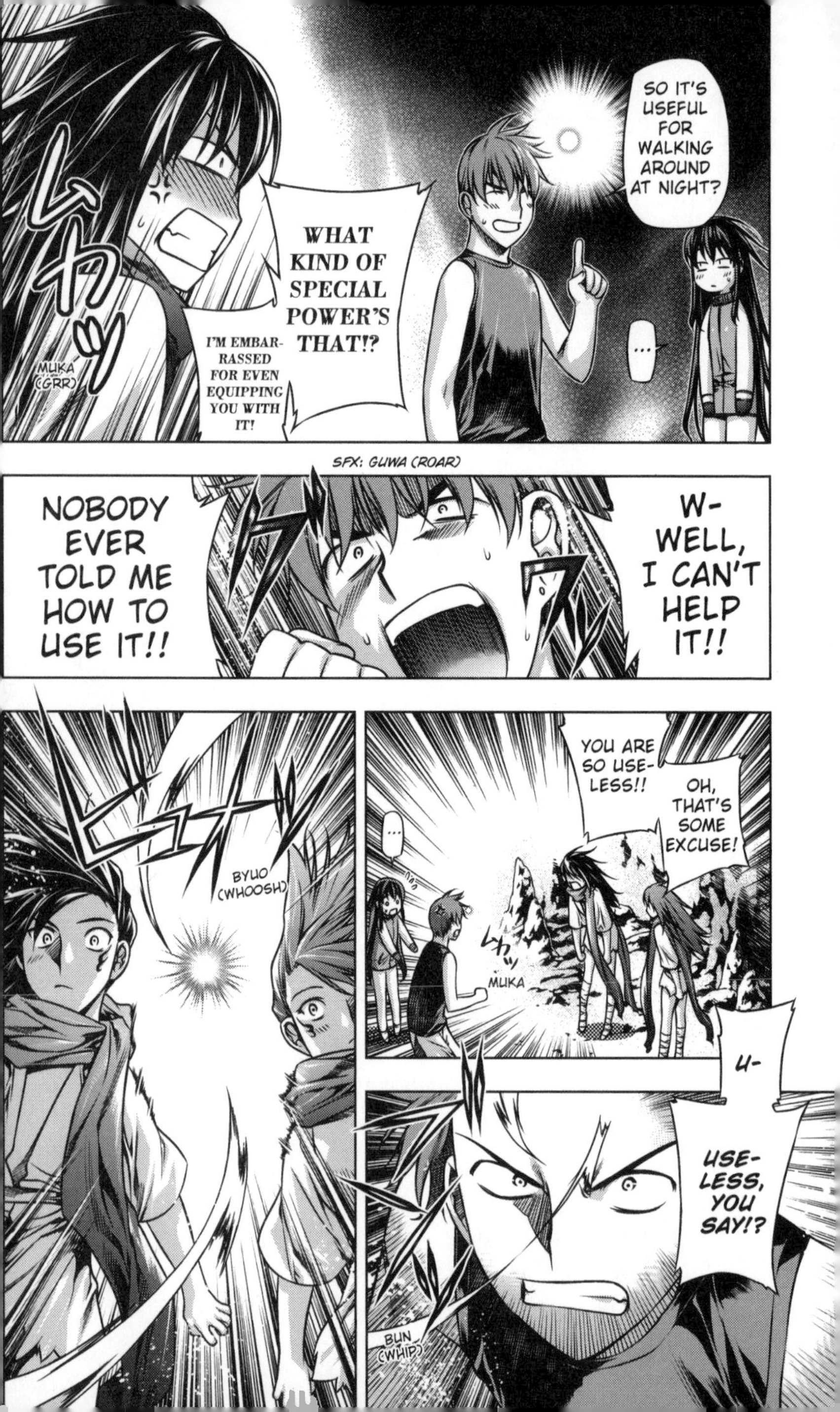

SO IT'S USEFUL FOR WALKING AROUND AT NIGHT?
...
WHAT KIND OF SPECIAL POWER'S THAT!?
I'M EMBARRASSED FOR EVEN EQUIPPING YOU WITH IT!
MUKA (GRR)
SFX: GUWA (ROAR)
W-WELL, I CAN'T HELP IT!!
NOBODY EVER TOLD ME HOW TO USE IT!!
OH, THAT'S SOME EXCUSE!
YOU ARE SO USELESS!!
...
MUKA
U-
USELESS, YOU SAY!?
BUN (WHIP)
BYUO (WHOOSH)

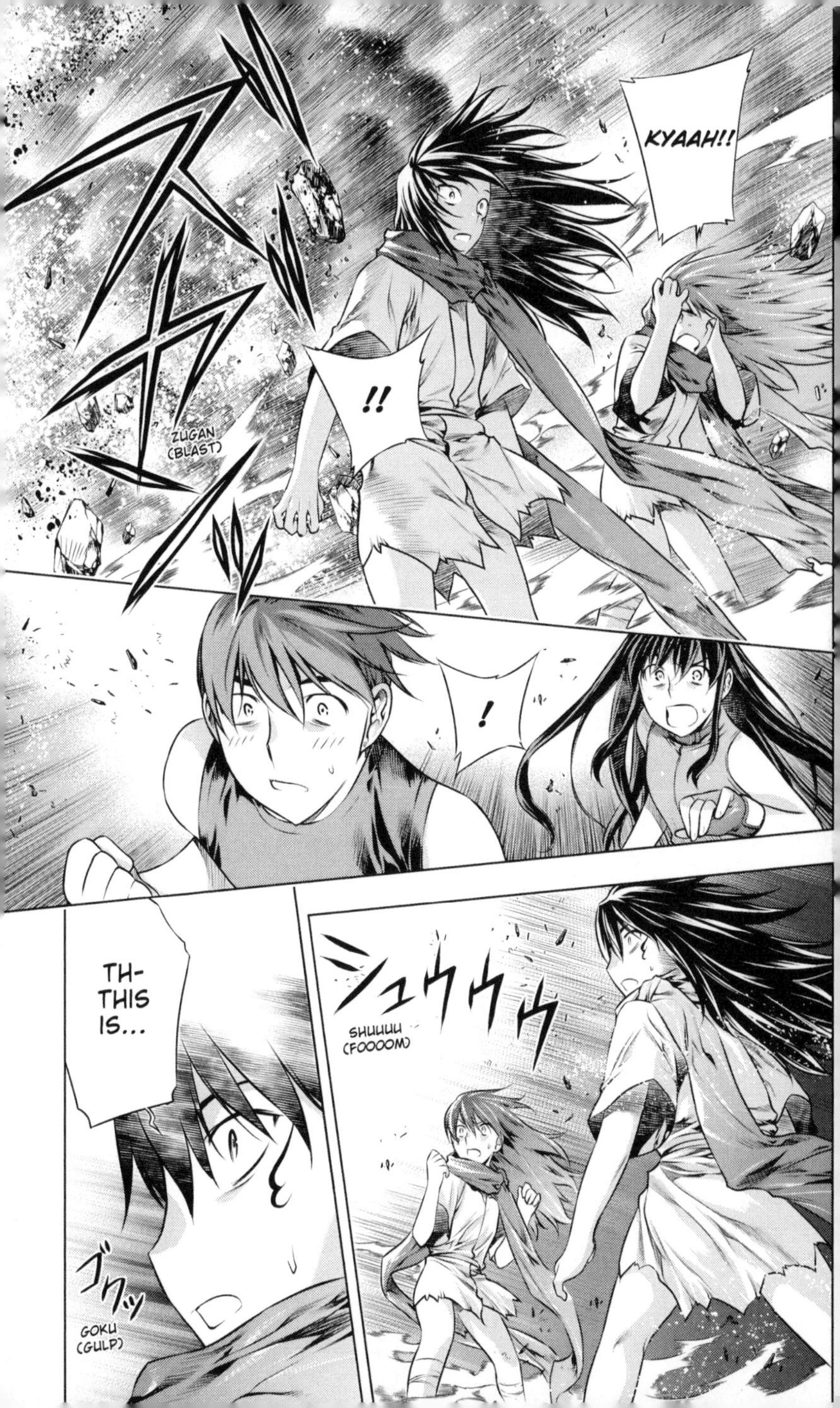
KYAAH!!
!!
ZUGAN (BLAST)
!
シュウウウ
SHUUUU (FOOOOM)
TH- THIS IS...
ゴクッ
GOKU (GULP)

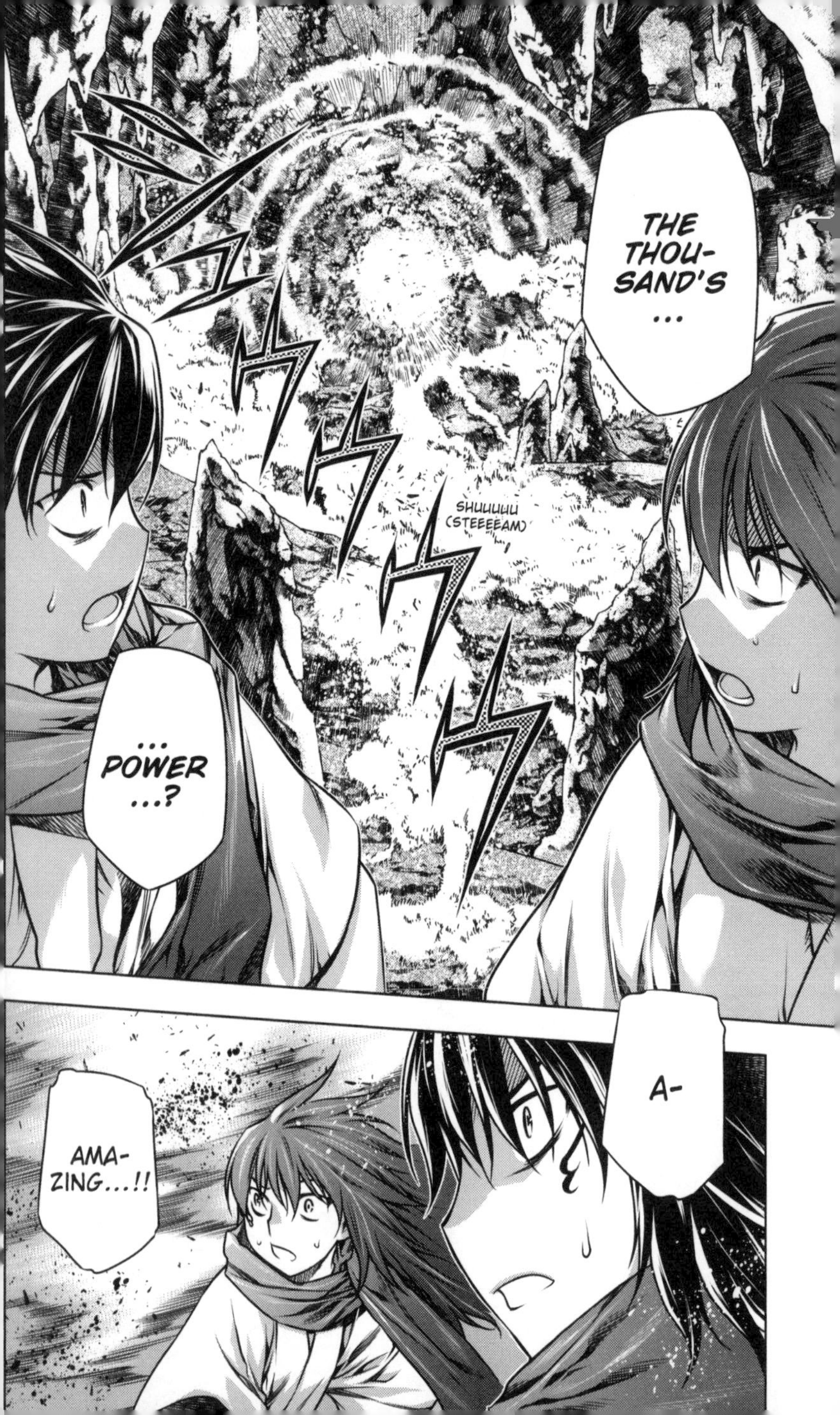
THE THOUSAND'S ...
SHUUUUU (STEEEEAM)
... POWER ...?
A-
AMAZING...!!

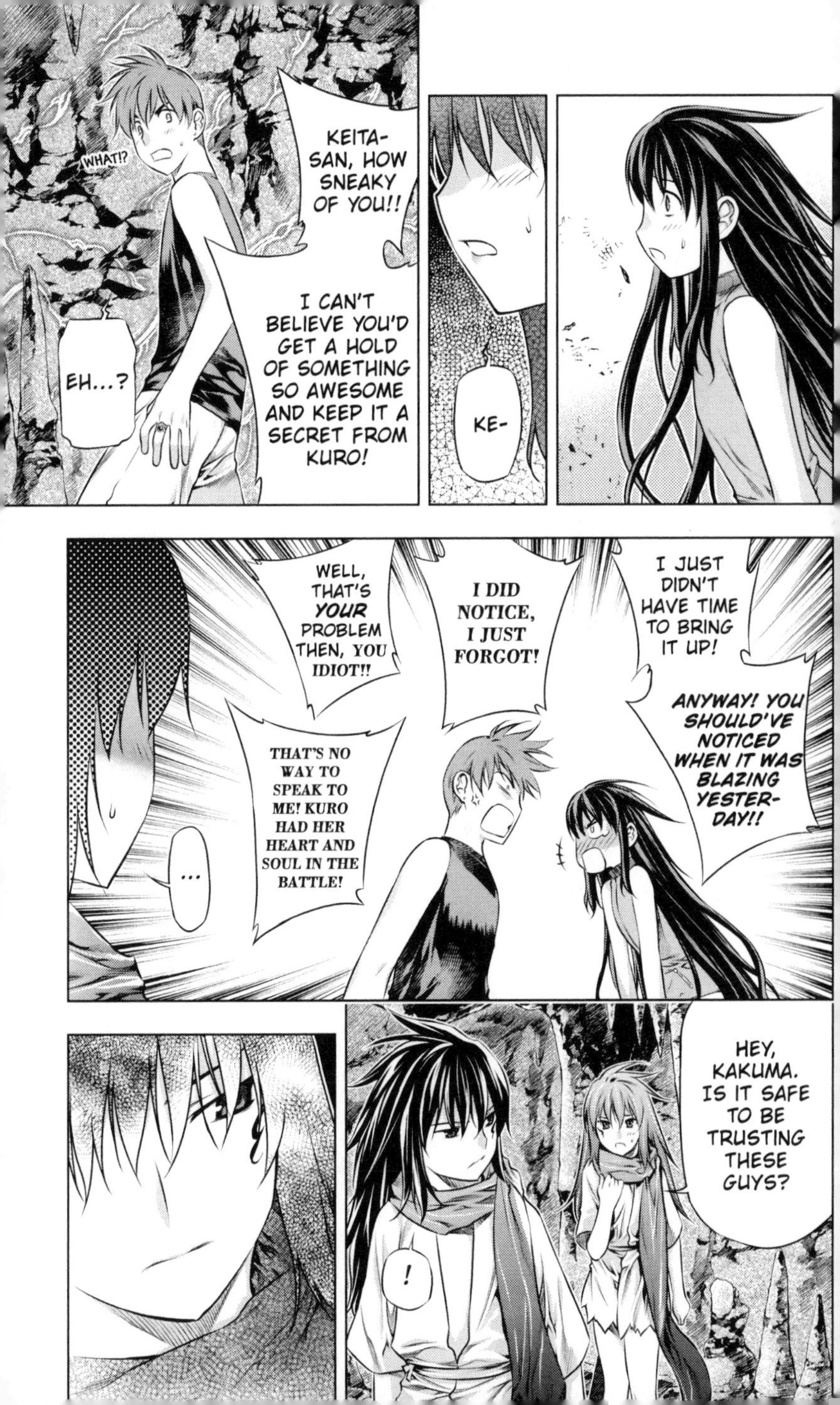
KE-
KEITA-SAN, HOW SNEAKY OF YOU!!
I CAN'T BELIEVE YOU'D GET A HOLD OF SOMETHING SO AWESOME AND KEEP IT A SECRET FROM KURO!
WHAT!?
EH...?
I JUST DIDN'T HAVE TIME TO BRING IT UP!
ANYWAY! YOU SHOULD'VE NOTICED WHEN IT WAS BLAZING YESTERDAY!!
I DID NOTICE, I JUST FORGOT!
WELL, THAT'S *YOUR* PROBLEM THEN, YOU IDIOT!!
THAT'S NO WAY TO SPEAK TO ME! KURO HAD HER HEART AND SOUL IN THE BATTLE!
...
HEY, KAKUMA. IS IT SAFE TO BE TRUSTING THESE GUYS?
!

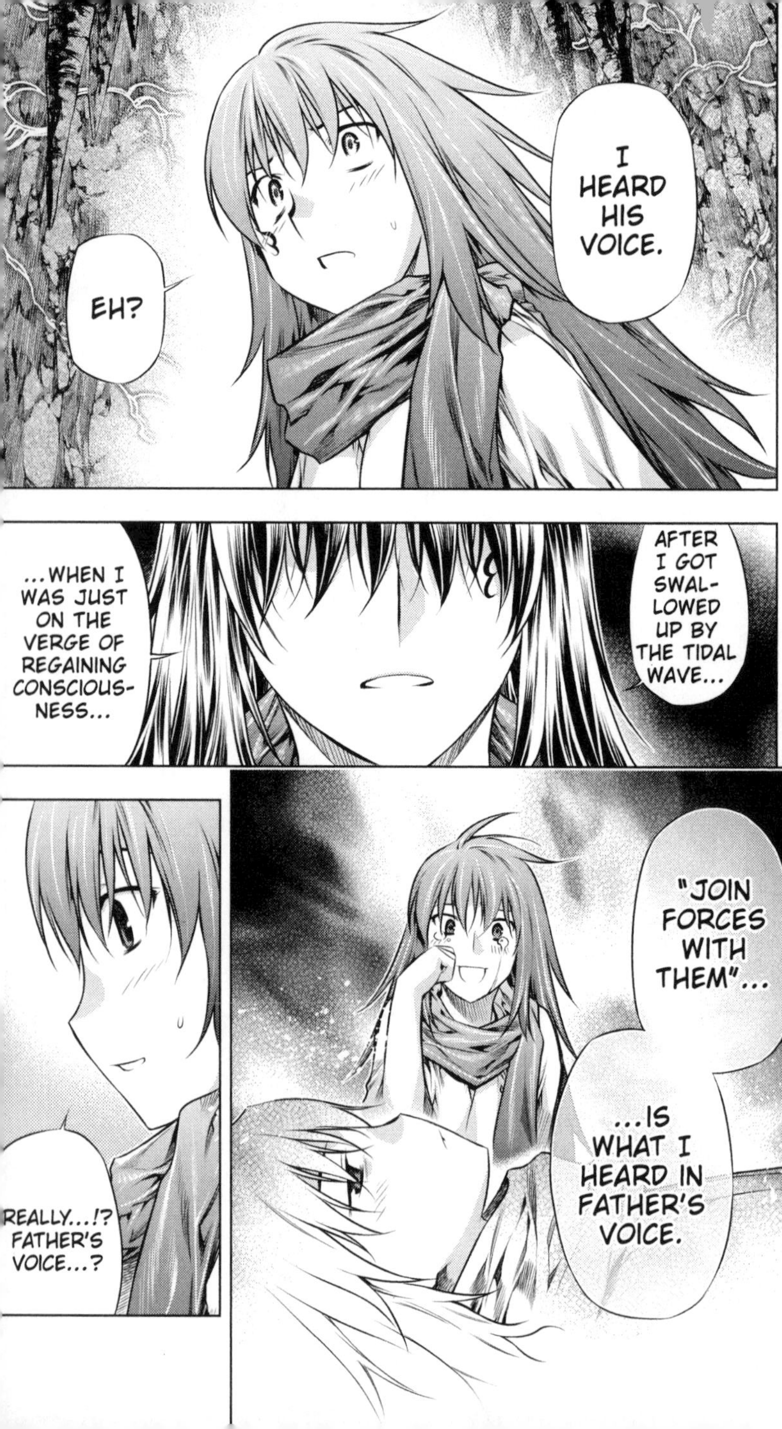
I HEARD HIS VOICE.
EH?
AFTER I GOT SWALLOWED UP BY THE TIDAL WAVE...
...WHEN I WAS JUST ON THE VERGE OF REGAINING CONSCIOUSNESS...
"JOIN FORCES WITH THEM"...
...IS WHAT I HEARD IN FATHER'S VOICE.
REALLY...!? FATHER'S VOICE...?

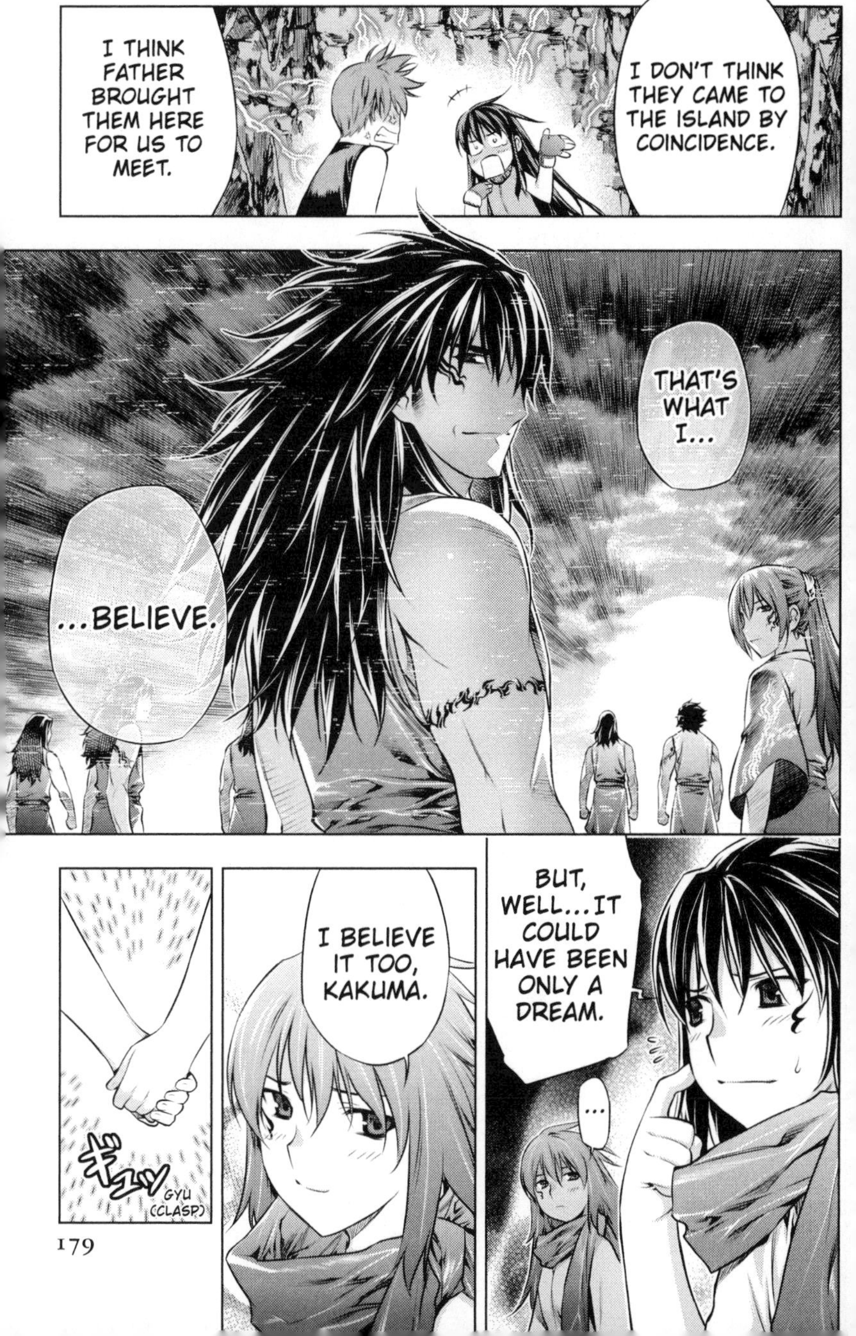
I DON'T THINK THEY CAME TO THE ISLAND BY COINCIDENCE.
I THINK FATHER BROUGHT THEM HERE FOR US TO MEET.
THAT'S WHAT I...
...BELIEVE.
BUT, WELL...IT COULD HAVE BEEN ONLY A DREAM.
...
I BELIEVE IT TOO, KAKUMA.
ギュッ
GYU (CLASP)

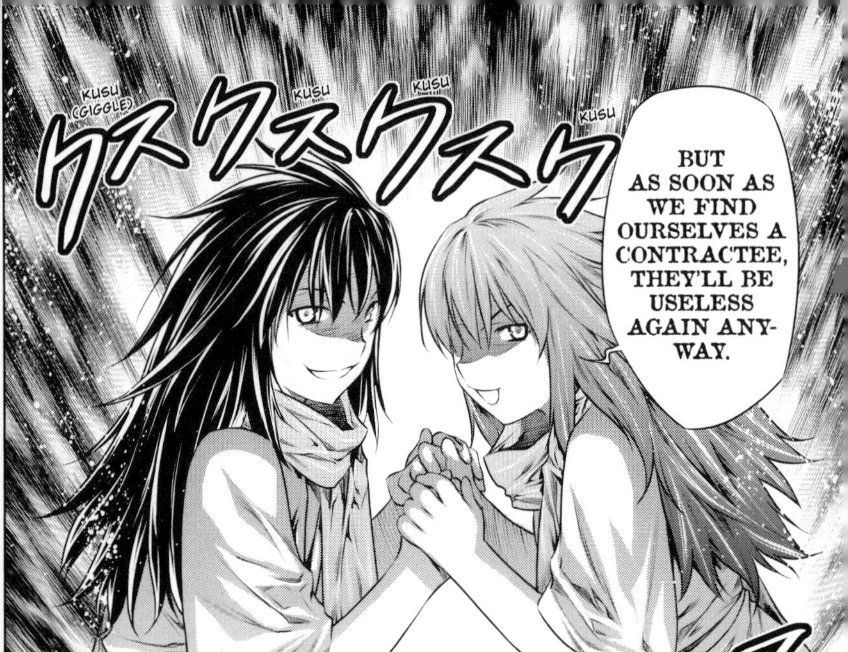
クスクスクスク
KUSU (GIGGLE)
KUSU
KUSU
KUSU
BUT AS SOON AS WE FIND OURSELVES A CONTRACTEE, THEY'LL BE USELESS AGAIN ANY-WAY.
クスクスクス
KUSU
KUSU
KUSU
RIGHT. THEN MAYBE WE CAN TAKE THAT NICE THOUSAND FOR OUR-SELVES, EH?
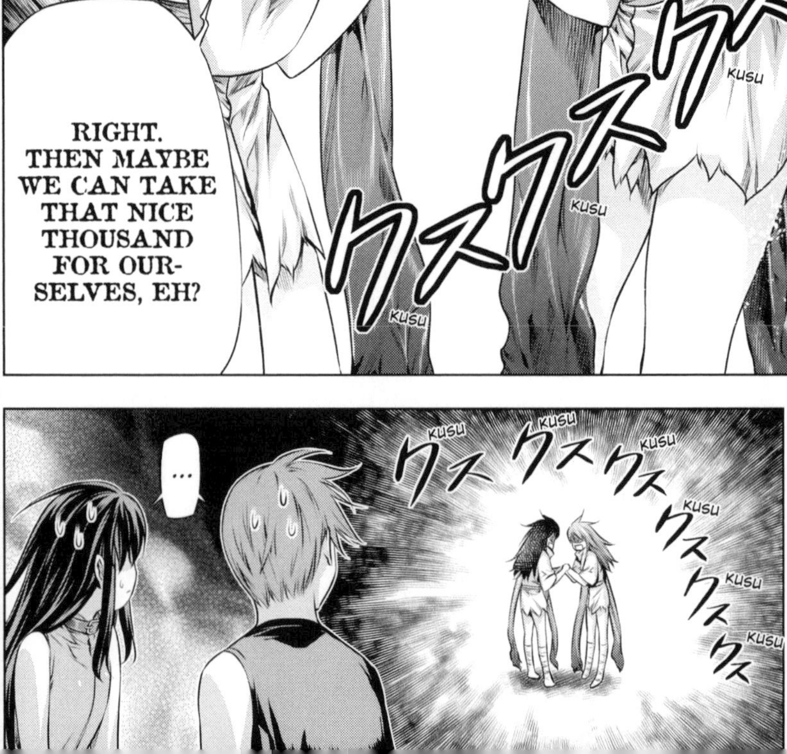
クスクスクスクスクスクス
KUSU
KUSU
KUSU
KUSU
KUSU
KUSU
...

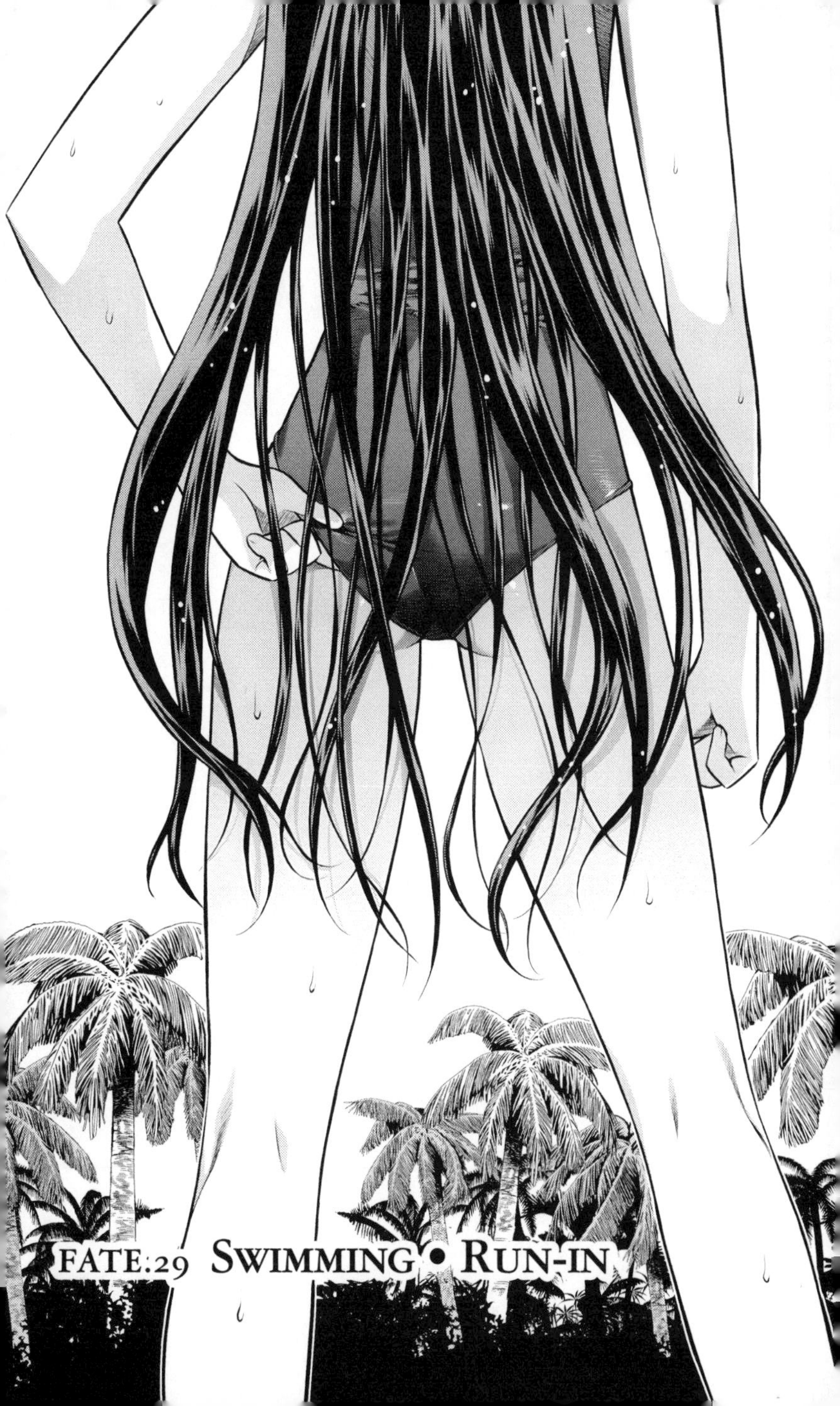
FATE:29 Swimming • Run-in

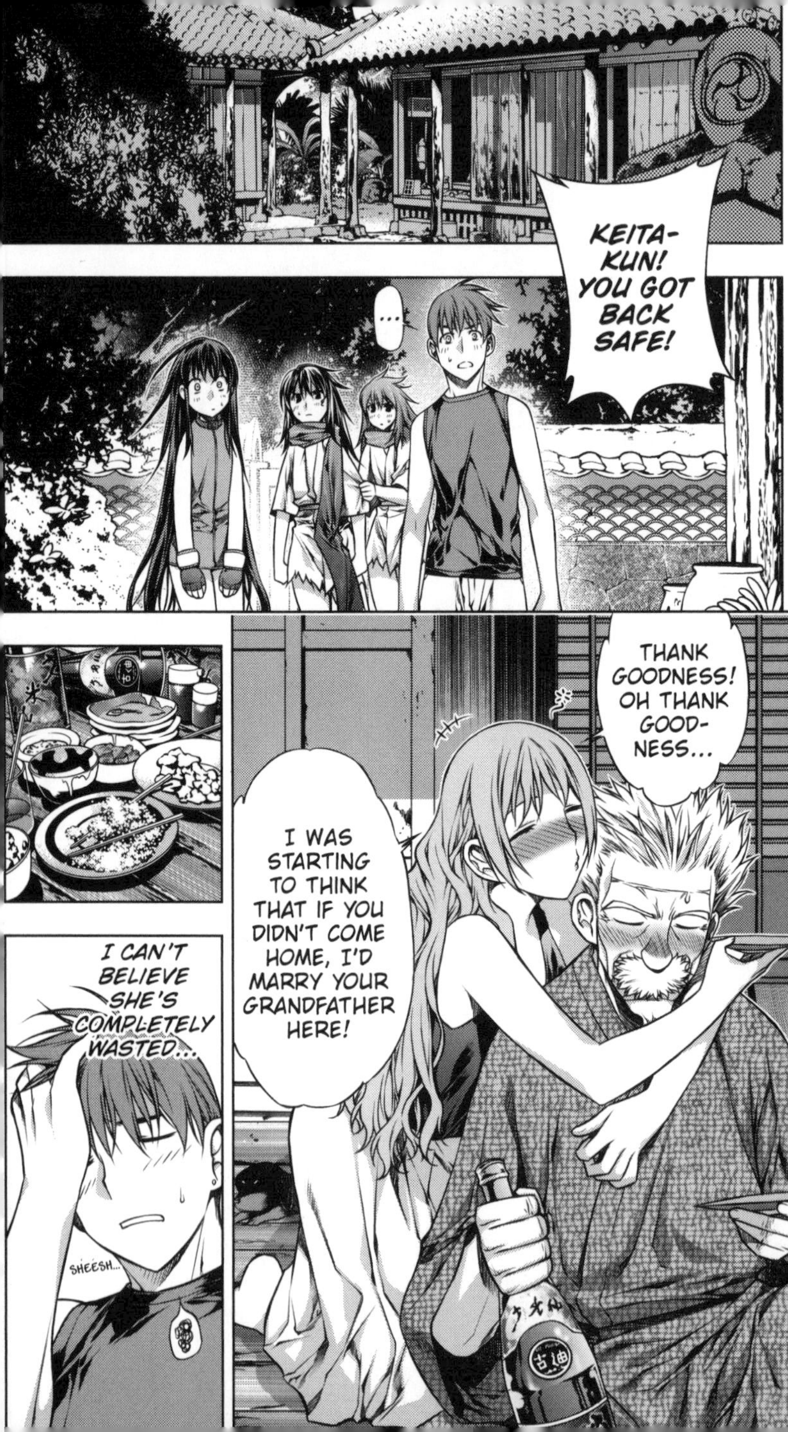
KEITA-KUN! YOU GOT BACK SAFE!
...
THANK GOODNESS! OH THANK GOOD-NESS...
I WAS STARTING TO THINK THAT IF YOU DIDN'T COME HOME, I'D MARRY YOUR GRANDFATHER HERE!
I CAN'T BELIEVE SHE'S COMPLETELY WASTED...
SHEESH...

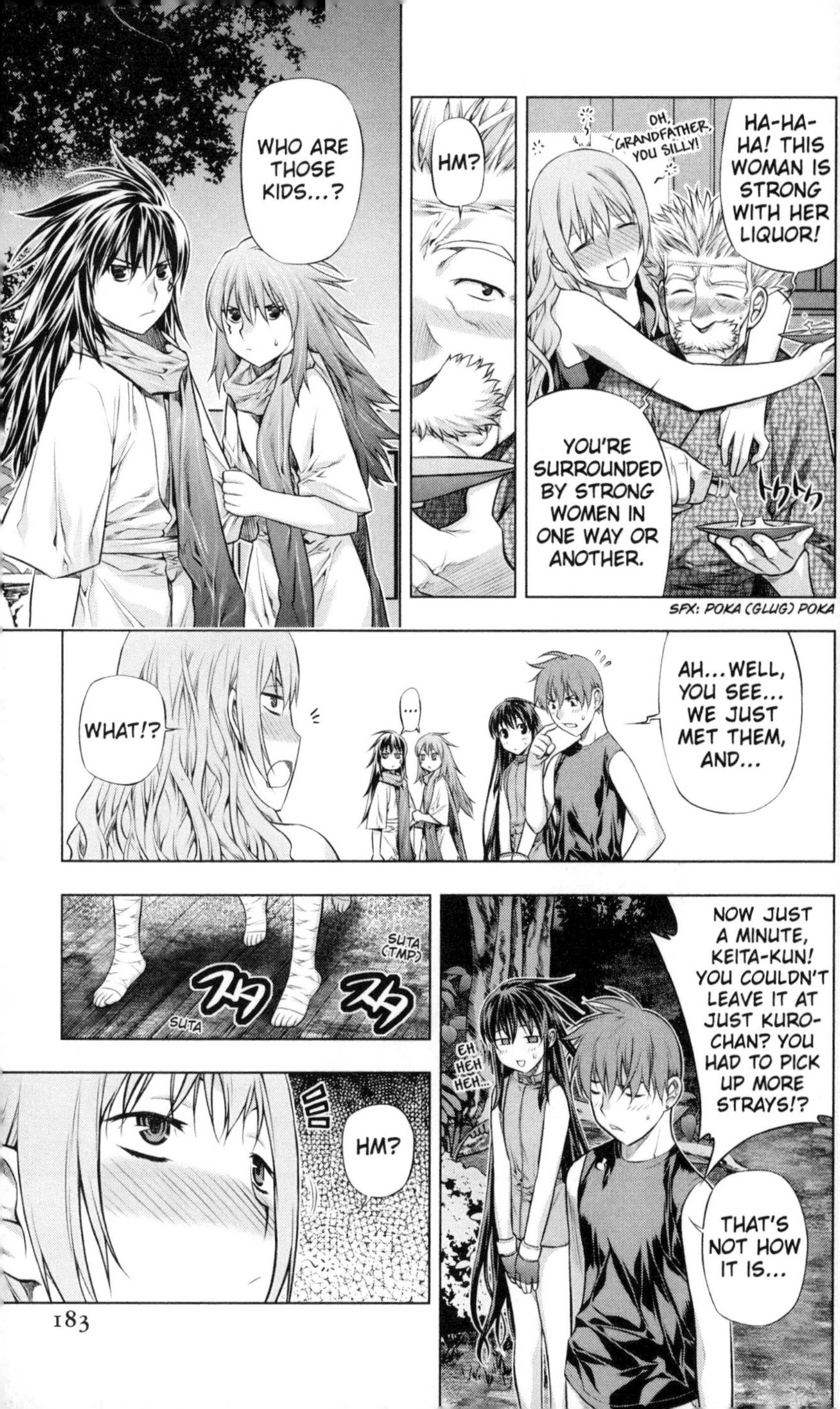

HA-HA-HA! THIS WOMAN IS STRONG WITH HER LIQUOR!
OH, GRANDFATHER, YOU SILLY!
YOU'RE SURROUNDED BY STRONG WOMEN IN ONE WAY OR ANOTHER.
SFX: POKA (GLUG) POKA
HM?
WHO ARE THOSE KIDS...?
AH...WELL, YOU SEE... WE JUST MET THEM, AND...
...
WHAT!?
NOW JUST A MINUTE, KEITA-KUN! YOU COULDN'T LEAVE IT AT JUST KURO-CHAN? YOU HAD TO PICK UP MORE STRAYS!?
EH HEH HEH...
THAT'S NOT HOW IT IS...
SUTA (TMP)
SUTA
HM?

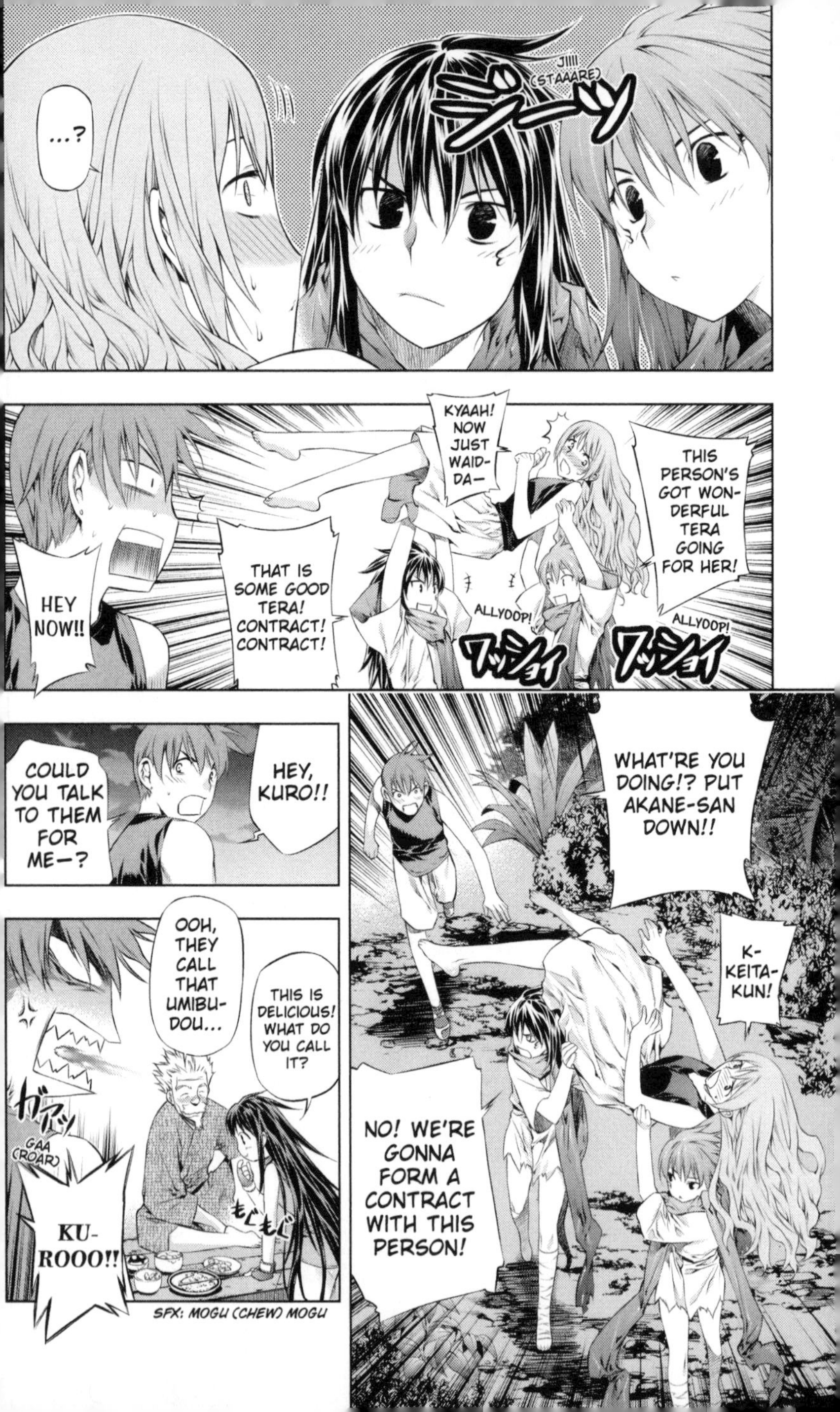
JIIII (STAAARE)
...?
THIS PERSON'S GOT WONDERFUL TERA GOING FOR HER!
KYAAH! NOW JUST WAID-DA—
ALLYOOP!
ALLYOOP!
THAT IS SOME GOOD TERA! CONTRACT! CONTRACT!
HEY NOW!!
WHAT'RE YOU DOING!? PUT AKANE-SAN DOWN!!
K-KEITA-KUN!
NO! WE'RE GONNA FORM A CONTRACT WITH THIS PERSON!
HEY, KURO!!
COULD YOU TALK TO THEM FOR ME—?
THIS IS DELICIOUS! WHAT DO YOU CALL IT?
OOH, THEY CALL THAT UMIBUDOU...
GAA (ROAR)
KU-ROOO!!
SFX: MOGU (CHEW) MOGU

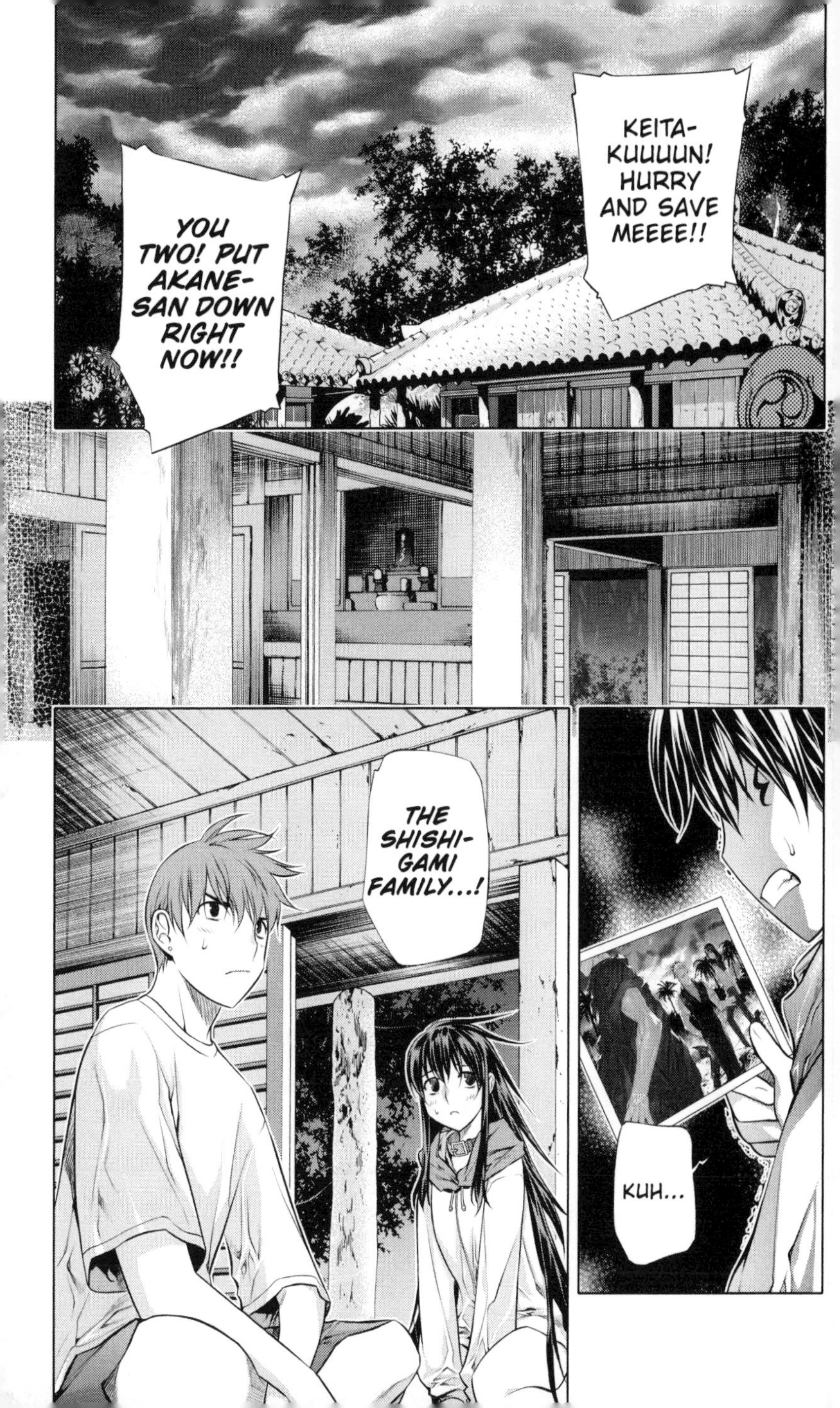
KEITA-KUUUUN! HURRY AND SAVE MEEEE!!
YOU TWO! PUT AKANE-SAN DOWN RIGHT NOW!!
KUH...
THE SHISHI-GAMI FAMILY...!

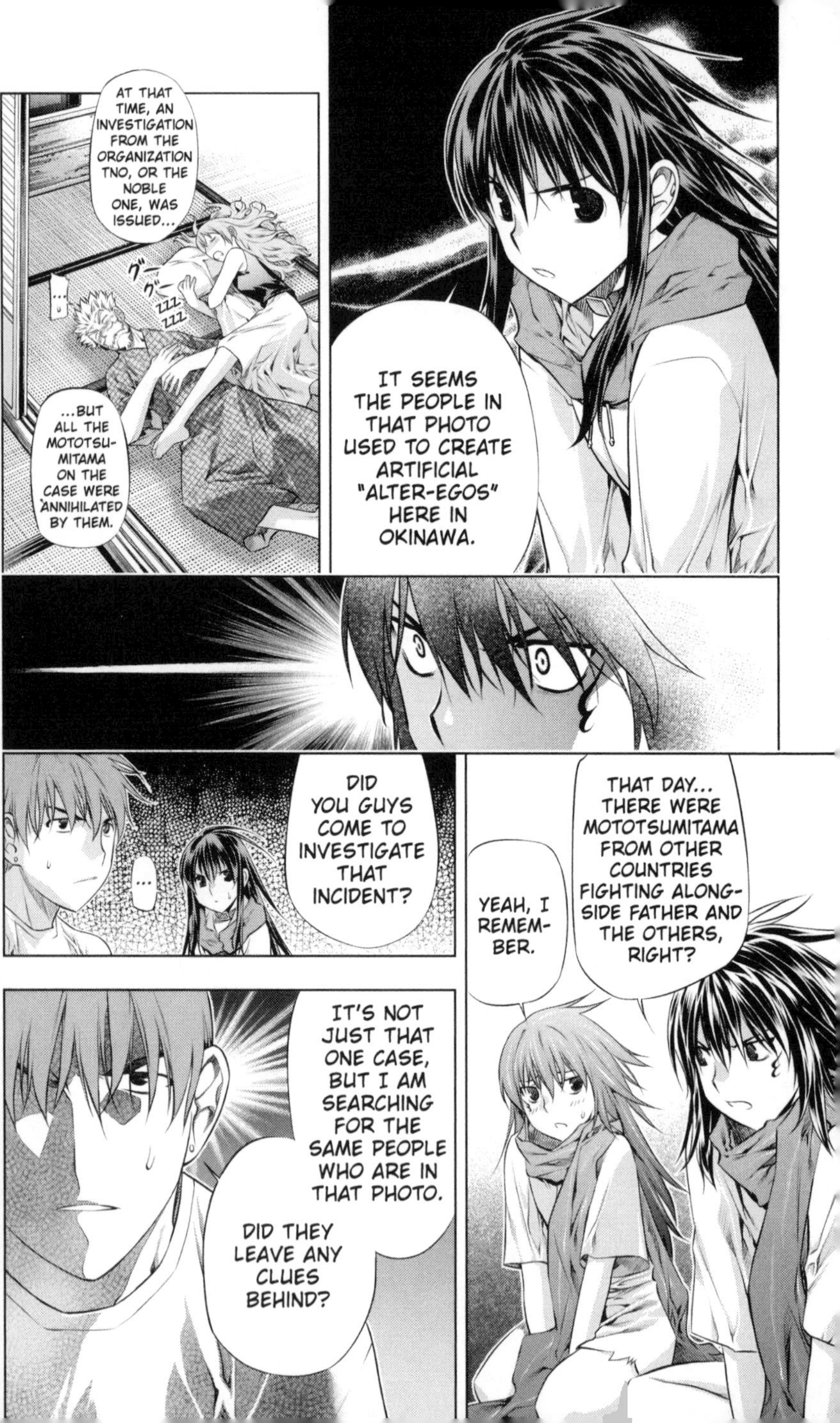
IT SEEMS THE PEOPLE IN THAT PHOTO USED TO CREATE ARTIFICIAL "ALTER-EGOS" HERE IN OKINAWA.
AT THAT TIME, AN INVESTIGATION FROM THE ORGANIZATION TNO, OR THE NOBLE ONE, WAS ISSUED...
グーグー
ZZZ ZZZ
...
...BUT ALL THE MOTOTSU-MITAMA ON THE CASE WERE ANNIHILATED BY THEM.
THAT DAY... THERE WERE MOTOTSUMITAMA FROM OTHER COUNTRIES FIGHTING ALONG-SIDE FATHER AND THE OTHERS, RIGHT?
YEAH, I REMEM-BER.
DID YOU GUYS COME TO INVESTIGATE THAT INCIDENT?
...
IT'S NOT JUST THAT ONE CASE, BUT I AM SEARCHING FOR THE SAME PEOPLE WHO ARE IN THAT PHOTO.
DID THEY LEAVE ANY CLUES BEHIND?

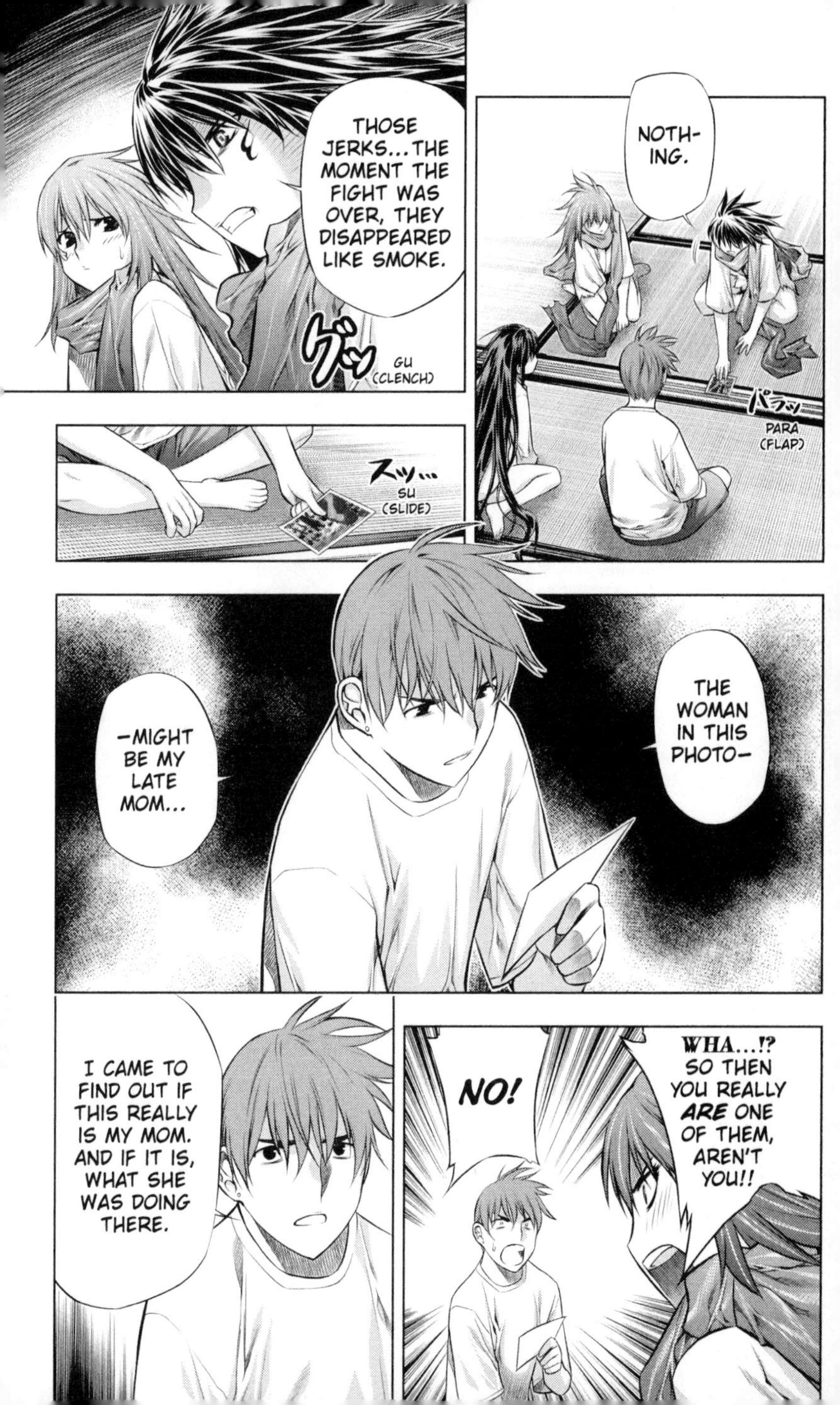
NOTH-ING.
パラッ
PARA (FLAP)
THOSE JERKS...THE MOMENT THE FIGHT WAS OVER, THEY DISAPPEARED LIKE SMOKE.
グッ
GU (CLENCH)
スッ...
SU (SLIDE)
THE WOMAN IN THIS PHOTO—
—MIGHT BE MY LATE MOM...
WHA...!? SO THEN YOU REALLY ARE ONE OF THEM, AREN'T YOU!!
NO!
I CAME TO FIND OUT IF THIS REALLY IS MY MOM. AND IF IT IS, WHAT SHE WAS DOING THERE.

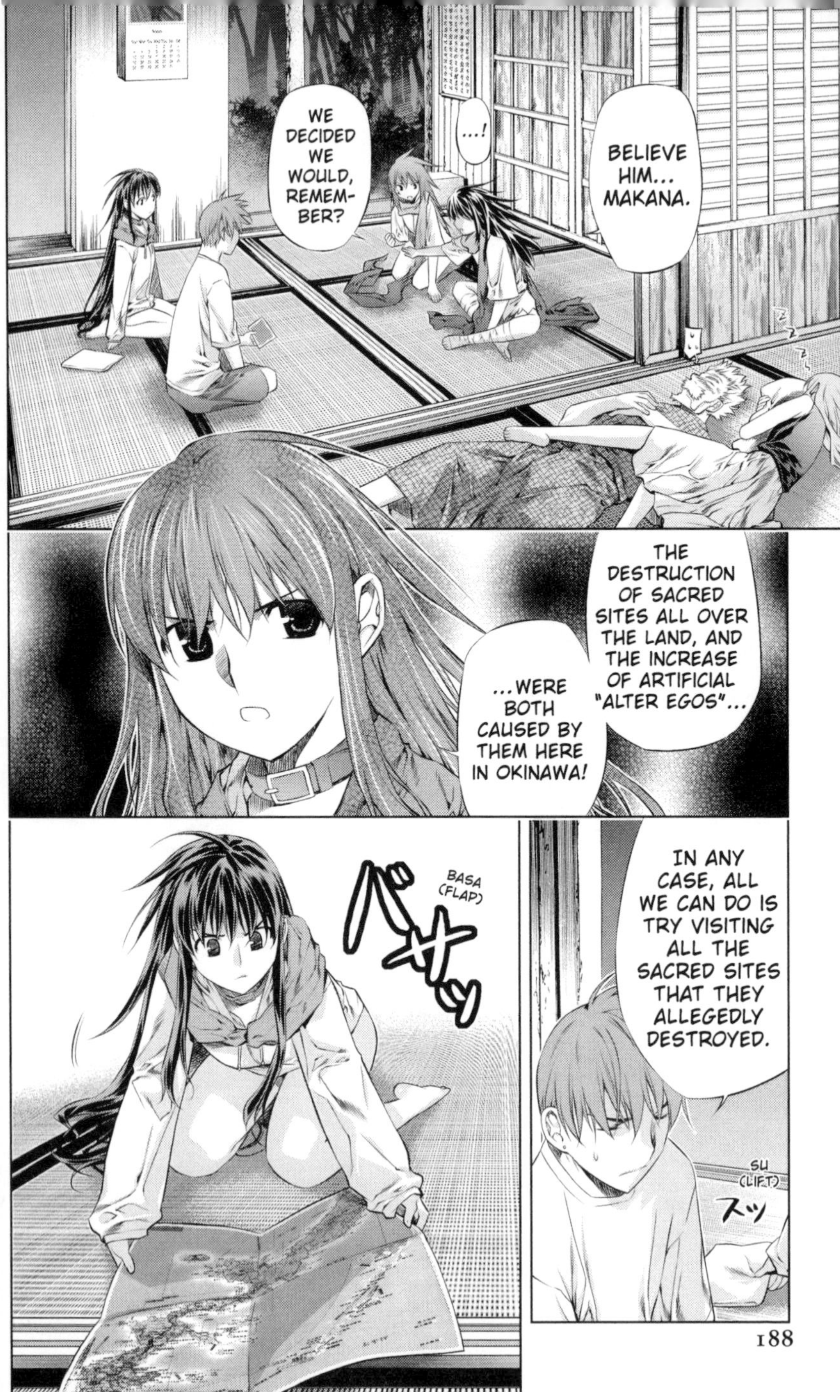
BELIEVE HIM... MAKANA.
...!
WE DECIDED WE WOULD, REMEMBER?
THE DESTRUCTION OF SACRED SITES ALL OVER THE LAND, AND THE INCREASE OF ARTIFICIAL "ALTER EGOS"...
...WERE BOTH CAUSED BY THEM HERE IN OKINAWA!
IN ANY CASE, ALL WE CAN DO IS TRY VISITING ALL THE SACRED SITES THAT THEY ALLEGEDLY DESTROYED.
SU (LIFT)
スッ
BASA (FLAP)
バサッ

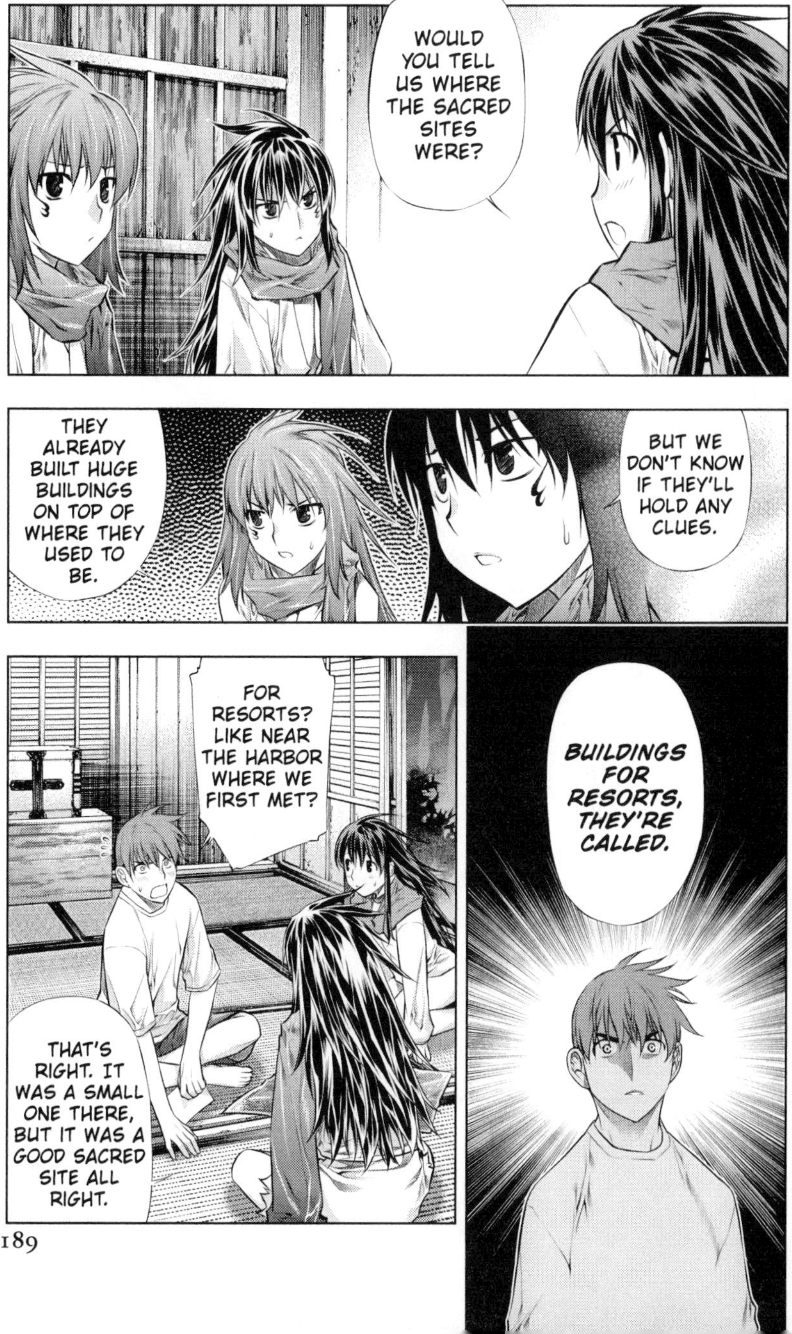
WOULD YOU TELL US WHERE THE SACRED SITES WERE?
BUT WE DON'T KNOW IF THEY'LL HOLD ANY CLUES.
THEY ALREADY BUILT HUGE BUILDINGS ON TOP OF WHERE THEY USED TO BE.
BUILDINGS FOR RESORTS, THEY'RE CALLED.
FOR RESORTS? LIKE NEAR THE HARBOR WHERE WE FIRST MET?
THAT'S RIGHT. IT WAS A SMALL ONE THERE, BUT IT WAS A GOOD SACRED SITE ALL RIGHT.

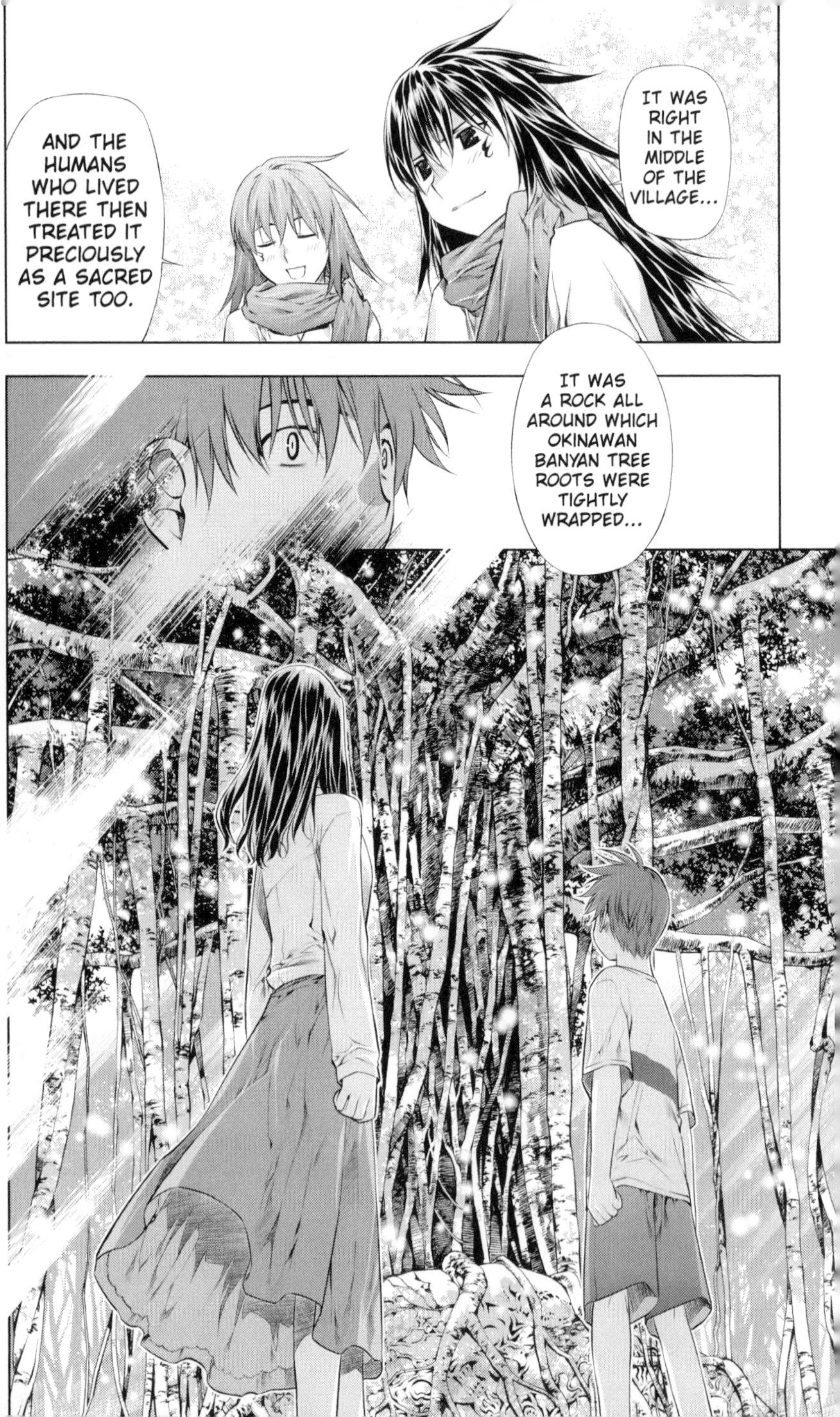
IT WAS RIGHT IN THE MIDDLE OF THE VILLAGE...
AND THE HUMANS WHO LIVED THERE THEN TREATED IT PRECIOUSLY AS A SACRED SITE TOO.
IT WAS A ROCK ALL AROUND WHICH OKINAWAN BANYAN TREE ROOTS WERE TIGHTLY WRAPPED...

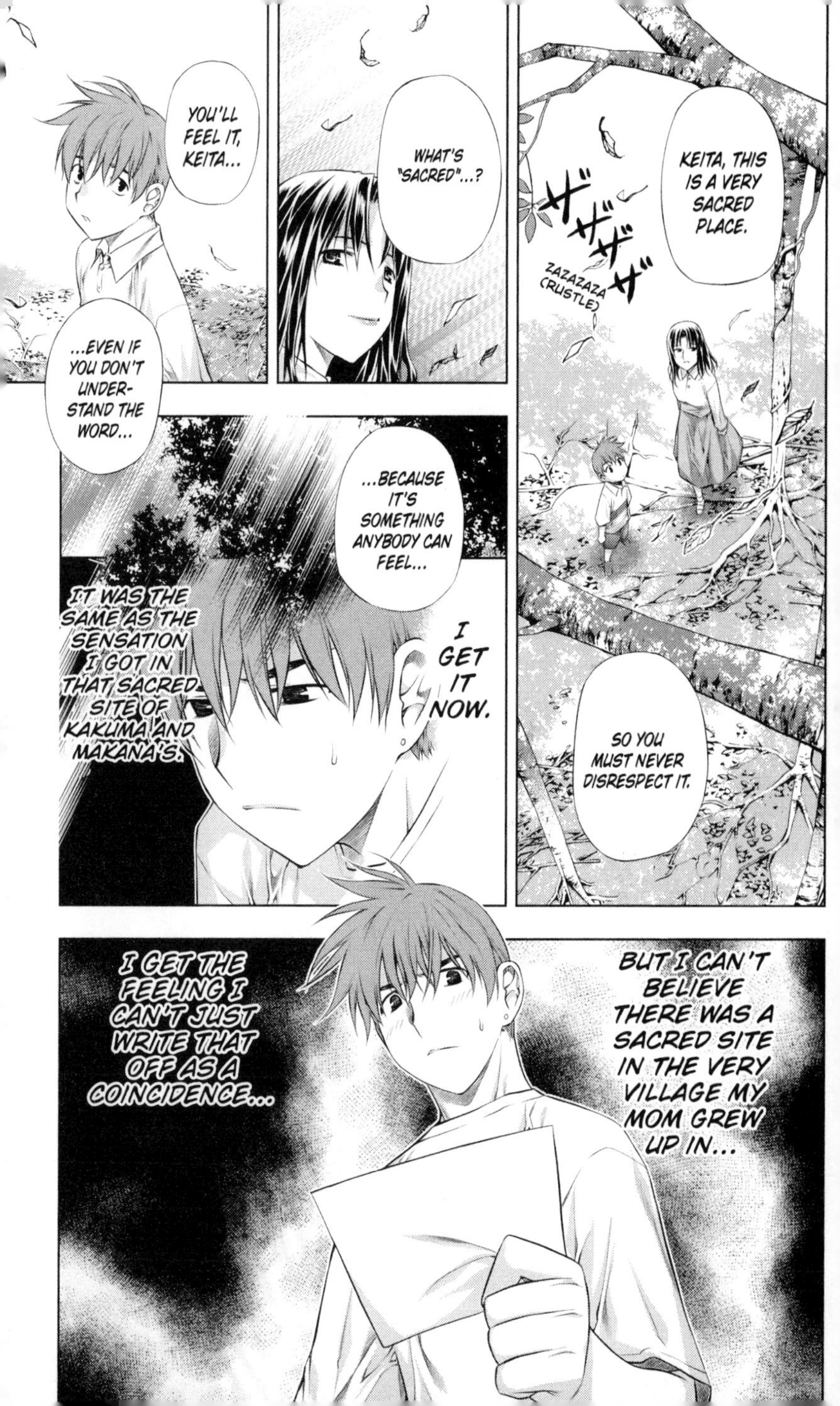
KEITA, THIS IS A VERY SACRED PLACE.
ザザザザ
ZAZAZAZA (RUSTLE)
SO YOU MUST NEVER DISRESPECT IT.
WHAT'S "SACRED"...?
YOU'LL FEEL IT, KEITA...
...EVEN IF YOU DON'T UNDER-STAND THE WORD...
...BECAUSE IT'S SOMETHING ANYBODY CAN FEEL...
I GET IT NOW.
IT WAS THE SAME AS THE SENSATION I GOT IN THAT SACRED SITE OF KAKUMA AND MAKANA'S.
BUT I CAN'T BELIEVE THERE WAS A SACRED SITE IN THE VERY VILLAGE MY MOM GREW UP IN...
I GET THE FEELING I CAN'T JUST WRITE THAT OFF AS A COINCIDENCE...

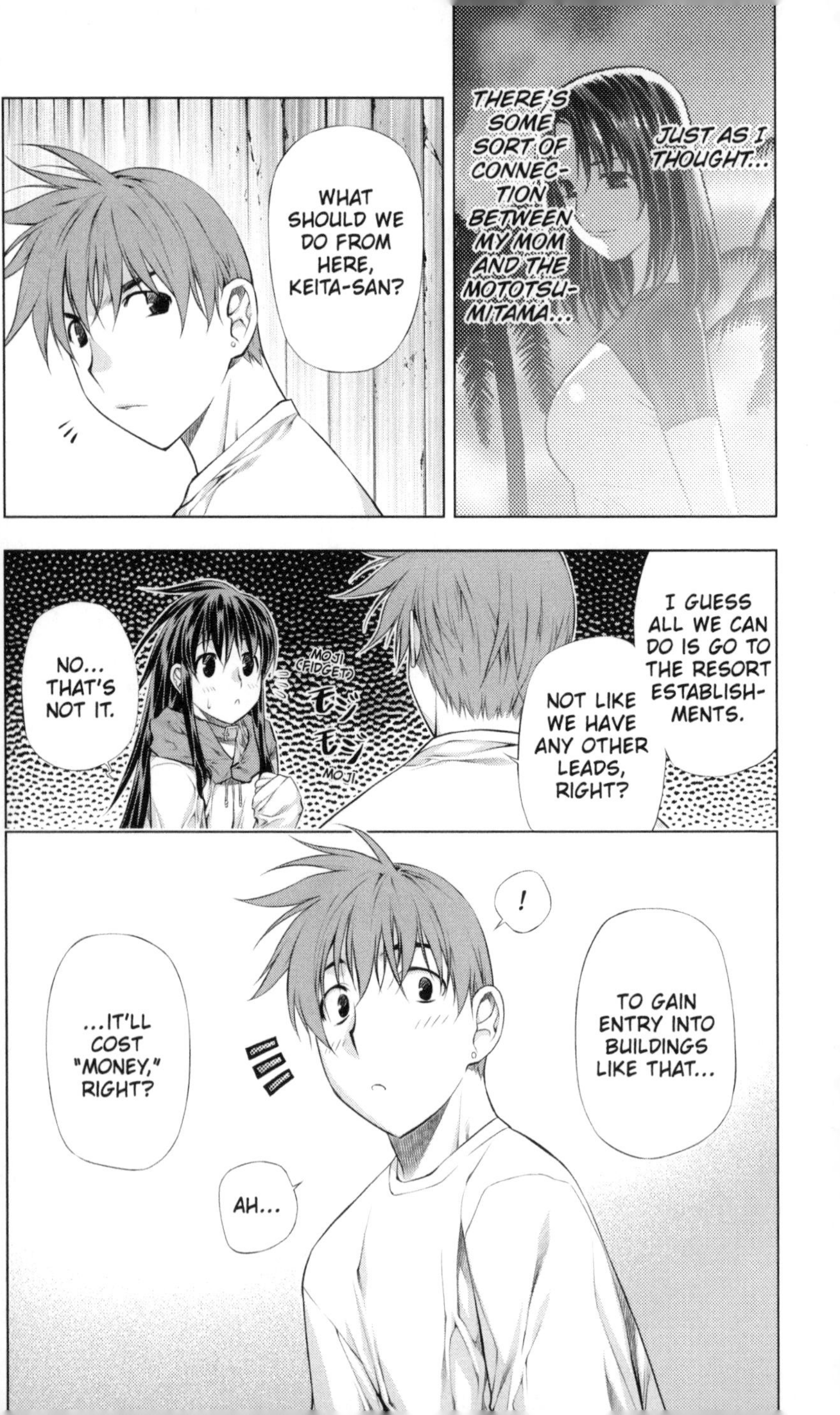
JUST AS I THOUGHT...
THERE'S SOME SORT OF CONNECTION BETWEEN MY MOM AND THE MOTOTSUMITAMA...
WHAT SHOULD WE DO FROM HERE, KEITA-SAN?
I GUESS ALL WE CAN DO IS GO TO THE RESORT ESTABLISHMENTS.
NOT LIKE WE HAVE ANY OTHER LEADS, RIGHT?
MOJI (FIDGET)
モジ
モジ
MOJI
NO... THAT'S NOT IT.
!
TO GAIN ENTRY INTO BUILDINGS LIKE THAT...
...IT'LL COST "MONEY," RIGHT?
AH...

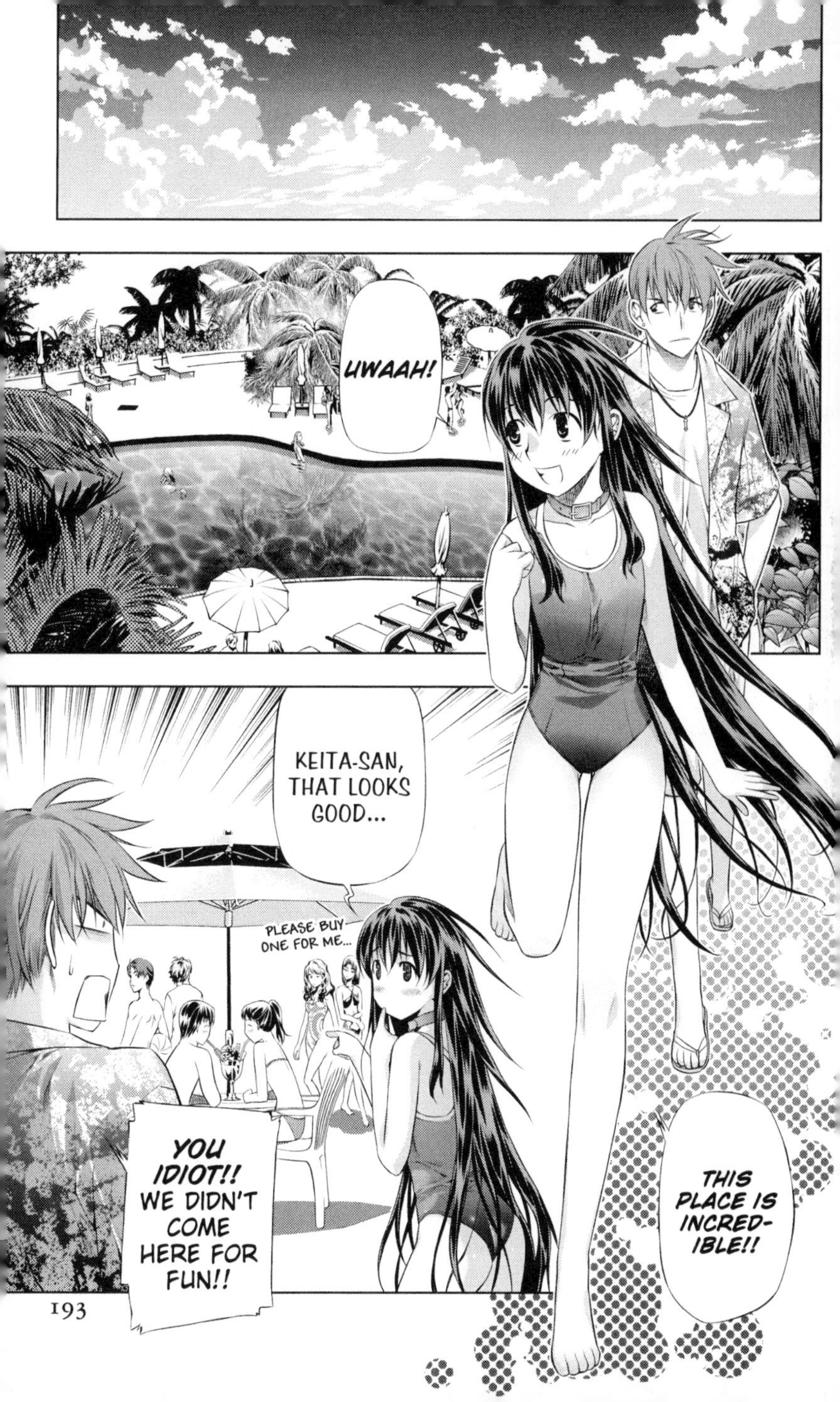
UWAAH!
THIS PLACE IS INCREDIBLE!!
KEITA-SAN, THAT LOOKS GOOD...
PLEASE BUY ONE FOR ME...
YOU IDIOT!! WE DIDN'T COME HERE FOR FUN!!

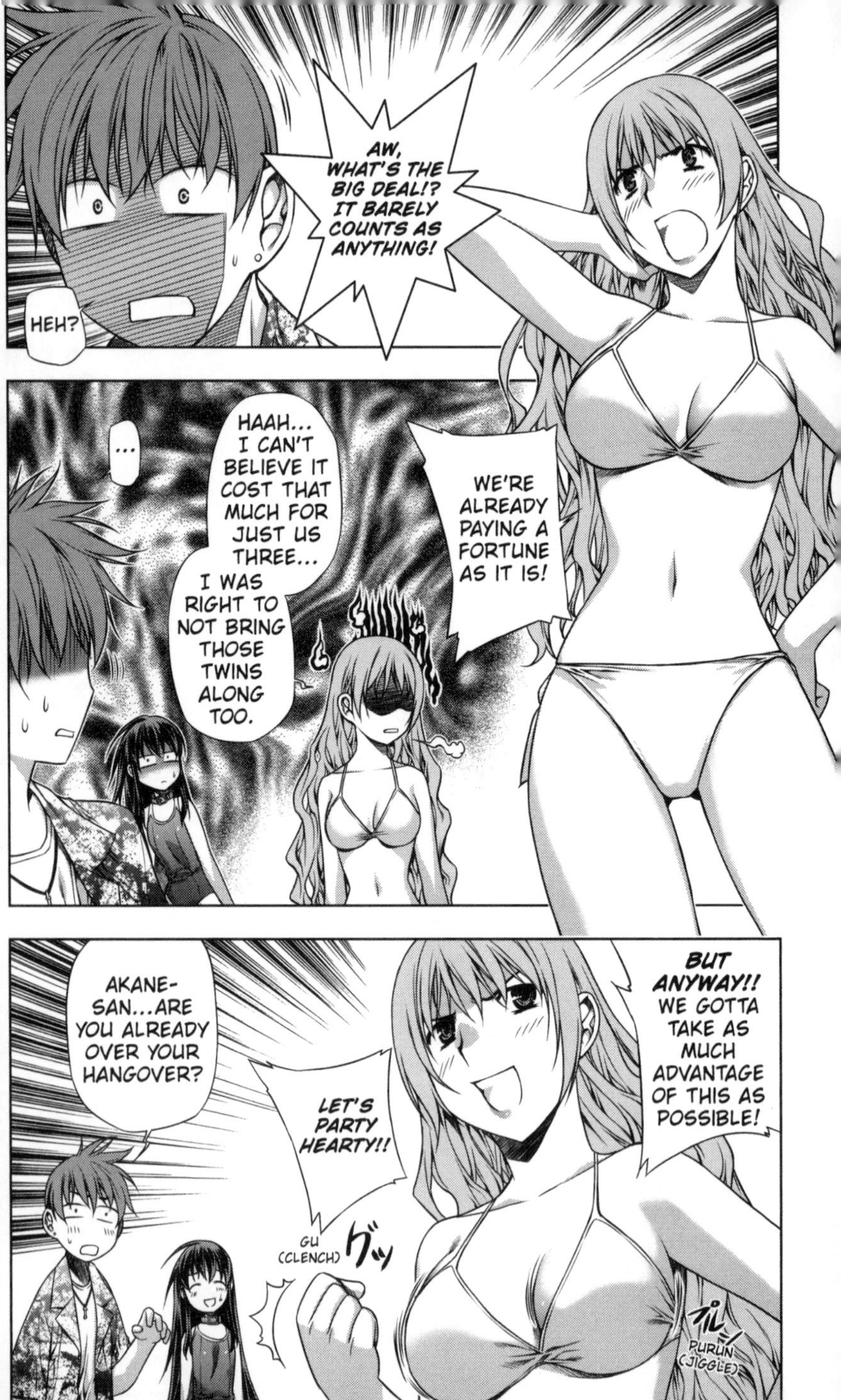
AW, WHAT'S THE BIG DEAL!? IT BARELY COUNTS AS ANYTHING!
HEH?
WE'RE ALREADY PAYING A FORTUNE AS IT IS!
HAAH... I CAN'T BELIEVE IT COST THAT MUCH FOR JUST US THREE...
I WAS RIGHT TO NOT BRING THOSE TWINS ALONG TOO.
...
BUT ANYWAY!! WE GOTTA TAKE AS MUCH ADVANTAGE OF THIS AS POSSIBLE!
PURUN (JIGGLE)
LET'S PARTY HEARTY!!
GU (CLENCH)
AKANE-SAN...ARE YOU ALREADY OVER YOUR HANGOVER?

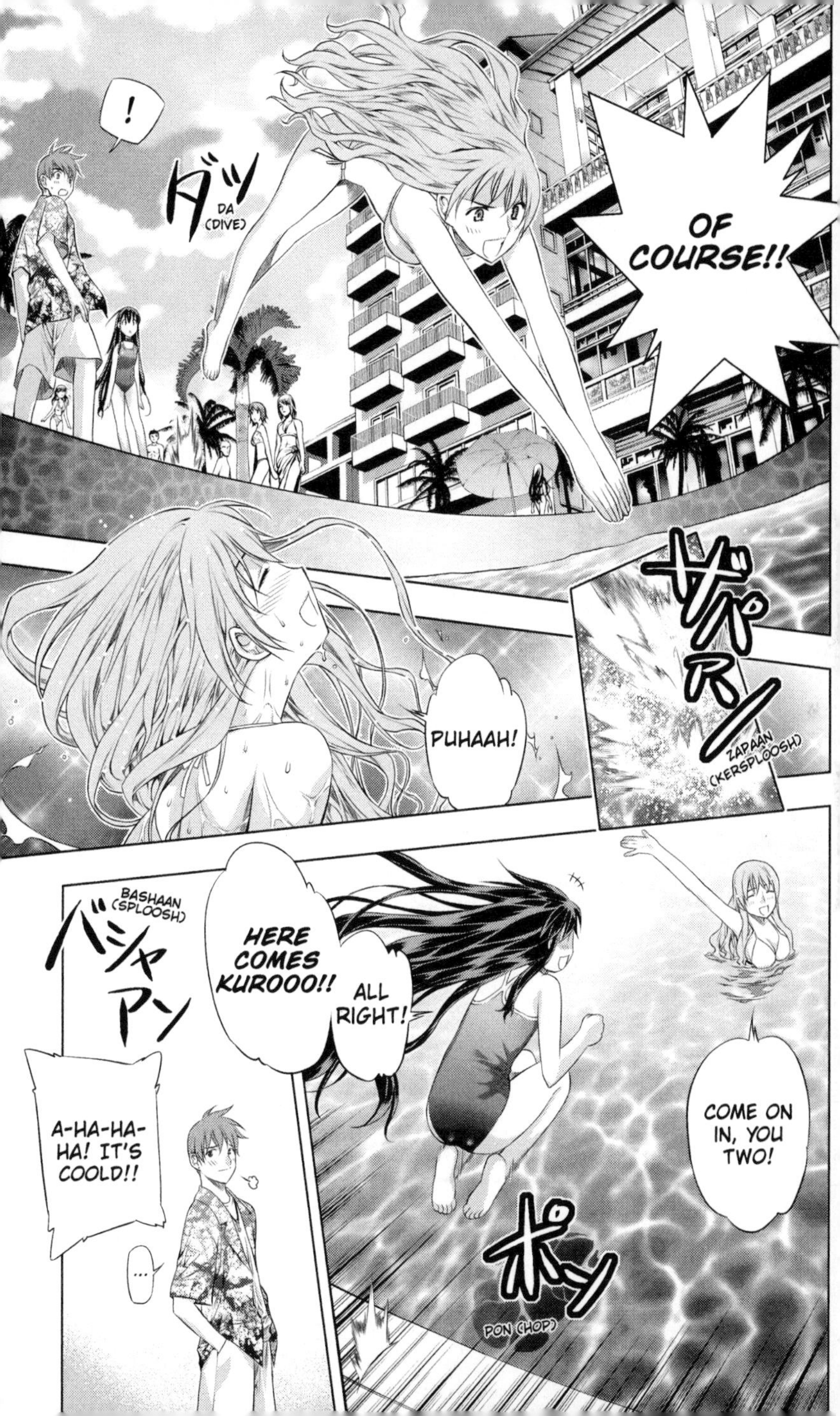
OF COURSE!!
ダッ
DA (DIVE)
!
ザパーン
ZAPAAN (KERSPLOOSH)
PUHAAH!
COME ON IN, YOU TWO!
ALL RIGHT!
HERE COMES KUROOO!!
ポン
PON (HOP)
バシャアン
BASHAAN (SPLOOSH)
A-HA-HA-HA! IT'S COOLD!!
...

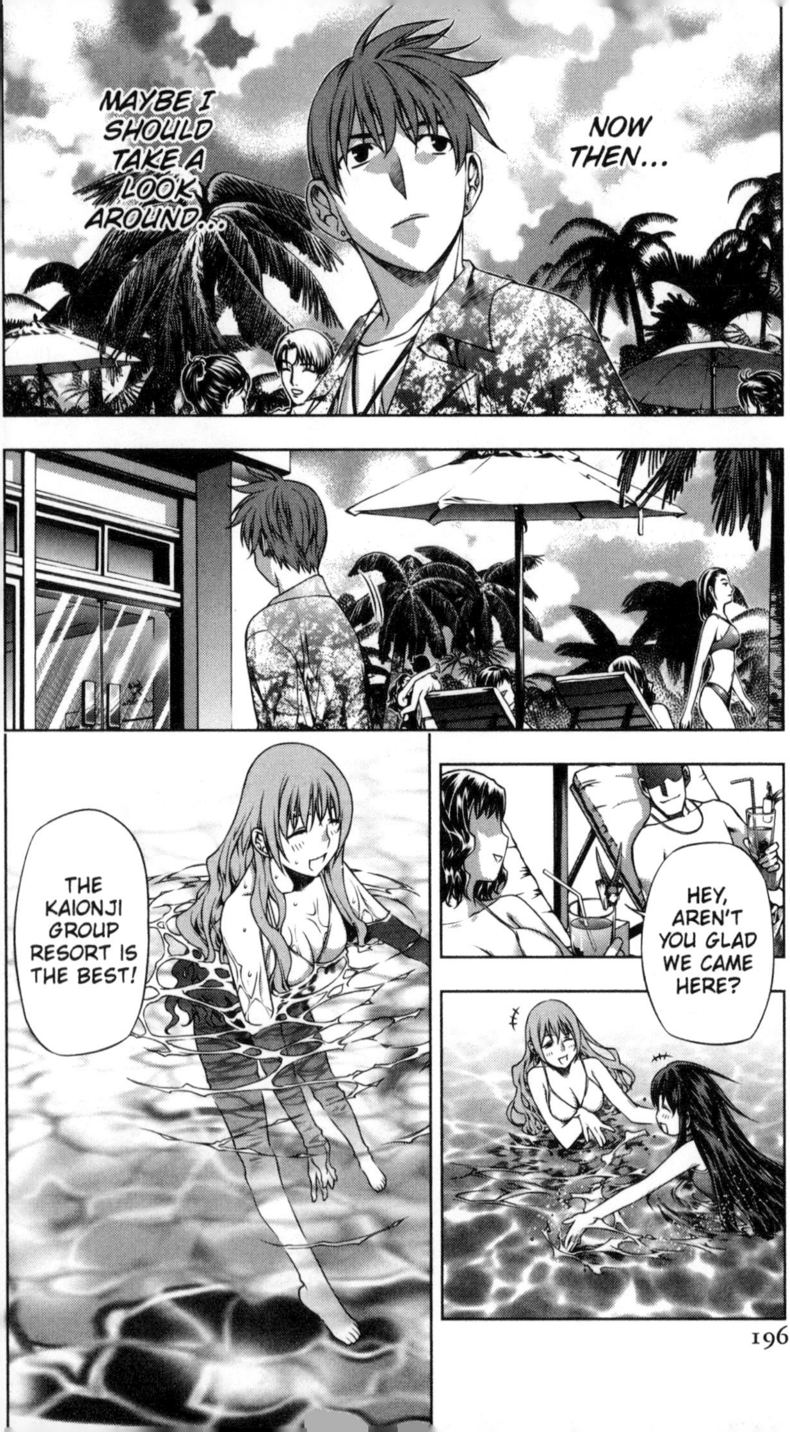
NOW THEN...
MAYBE I SHOULD TAKE A LOOK AROUND...
HEY, AREN'T YOU GLAD WE CAME HERE?
THE KAIONJI GROUP RESORT IS THE BEST!

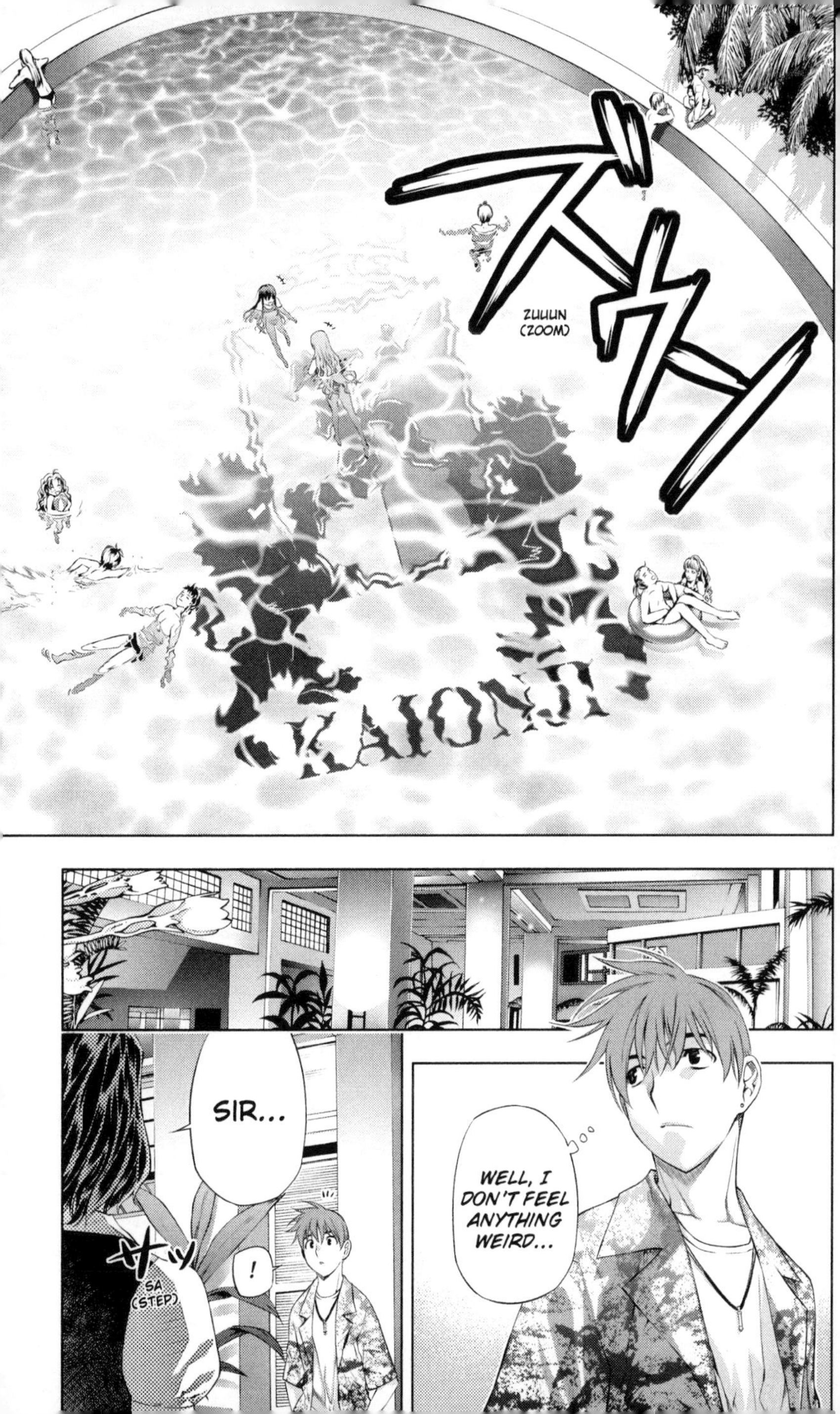
ズウン
ZUUUN (ZOOM)
KAIONJI
WELL, I DON'T FEEL ANYTHING WEIRD...
SIR...
!
サッ
SA (STEP)

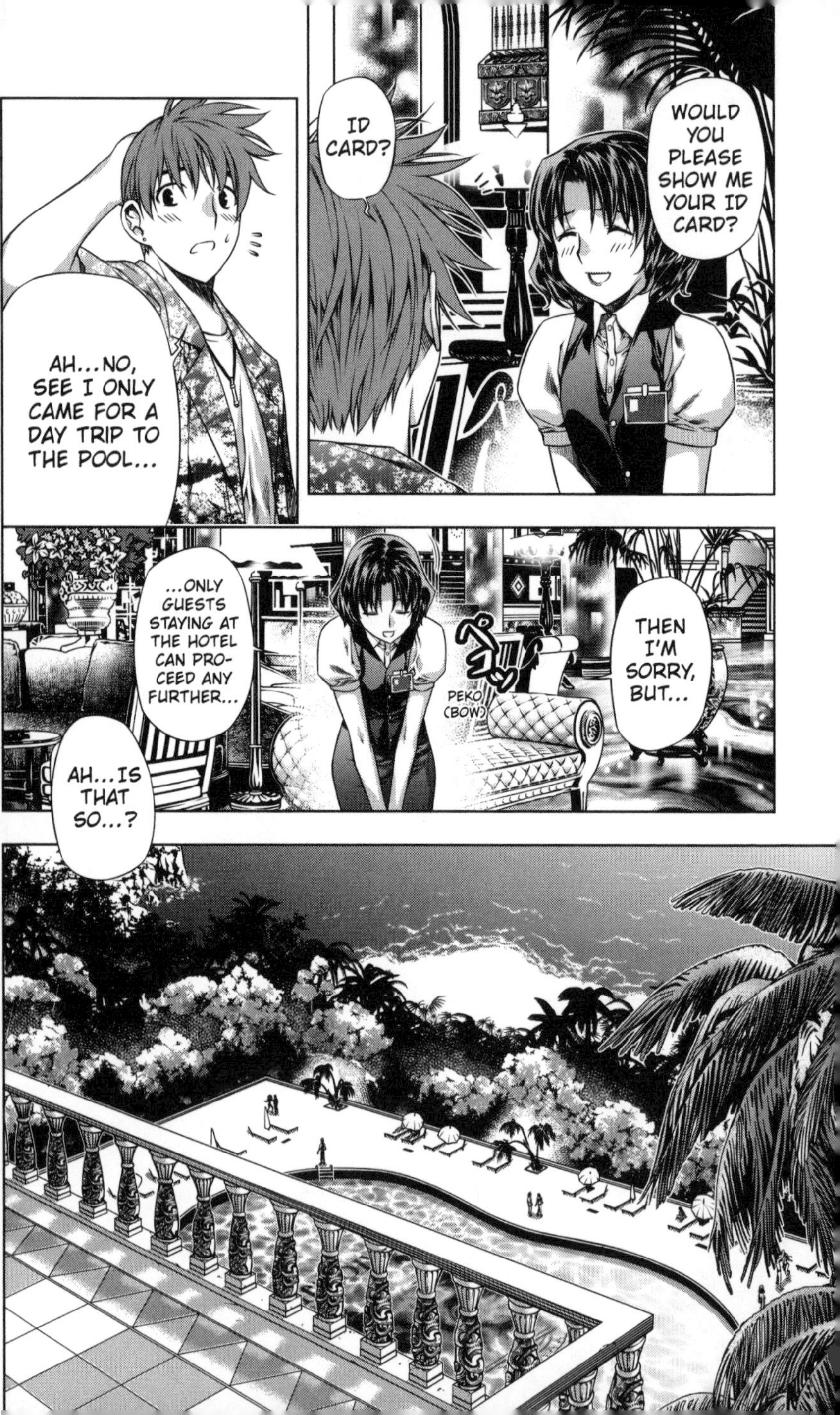
WOULD YOU PLEASE SHOW ME YOUR ID CARD?
ID CARD?
AH...NO, SEE I ONLY CAME FOR A DAY TRIP TO THE POOL...
THEN I'M SORRY, BUT...
PEKO (BOW)
...ONLY GUESTS STAYING AT THE HOTEL CAN PRO-CEED ANY FURTHER...
AH...IS THAT SO...?

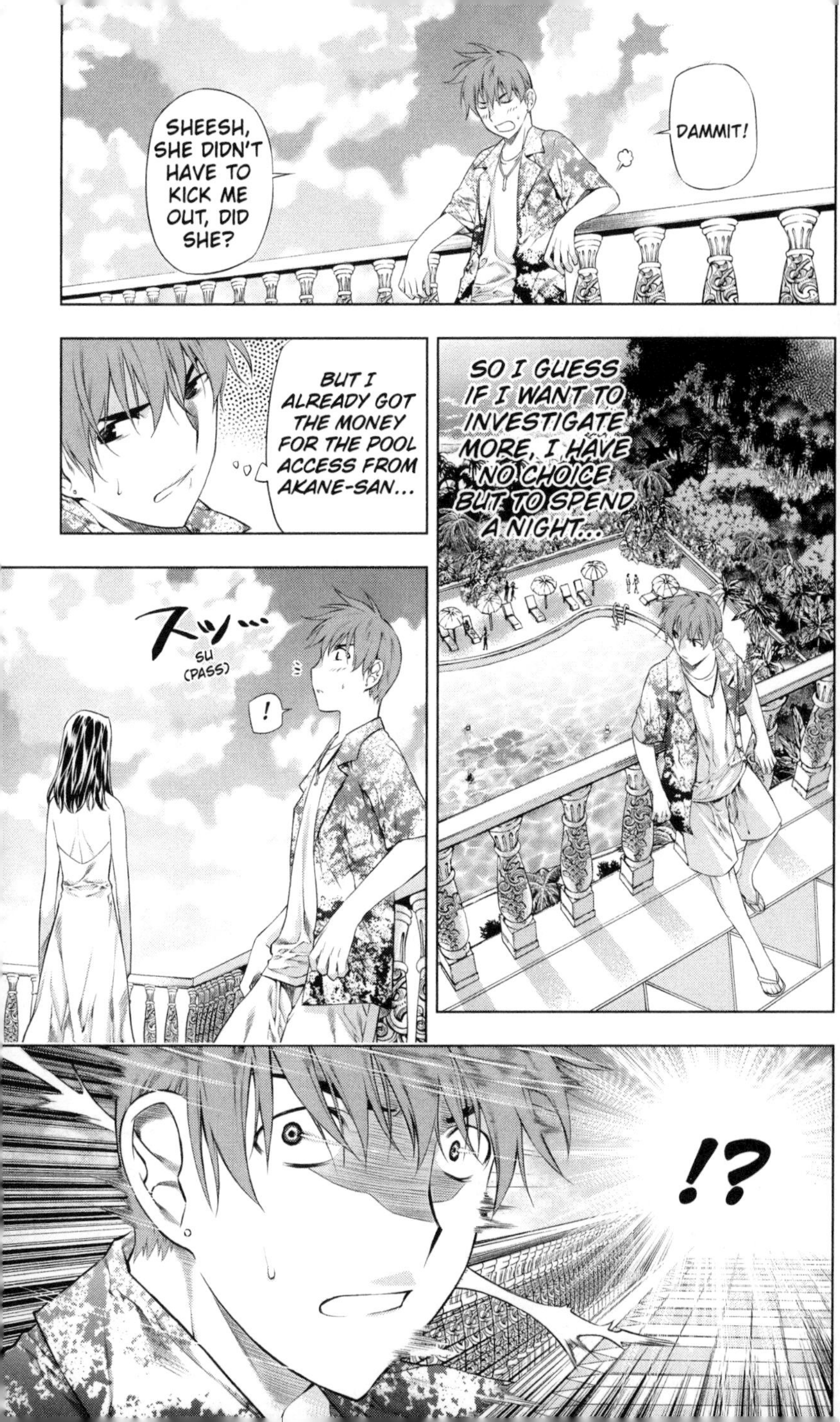
DAMMIT!
SHEESH, SHE DIDN'T HAVE TO KICK ME OUT, DID SHE?
SO I GUESS IF I WANT TO INVESTIGATE MORE, I HAVE NO CHOICE BUT TO SPEND A NIGHT...
BUT I ALREADY GOT THE MONEY FOR THE POOL ACCESS FROM AKANE-SAN...
スッ…
SU (PASS)
!
!?

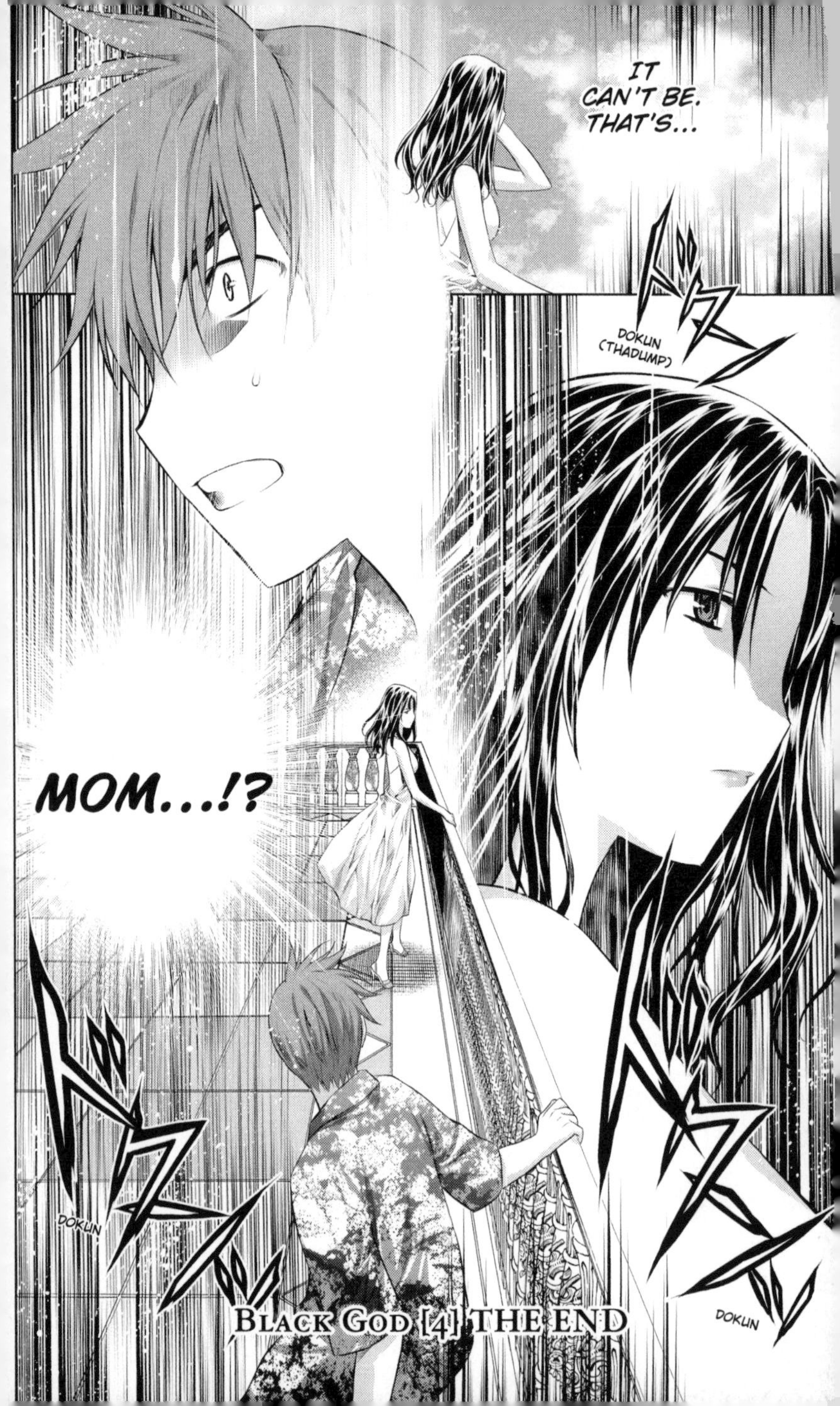
IT CAN'T BE. THAT'S...
DOKUN (THADUMP)
MOM...!?
DOKUN
DOKUN
BLACK GOD [4] THE END

SHINOBU

BLACK GOD
which maintains balance in the world.

Nirai Kanai Arc

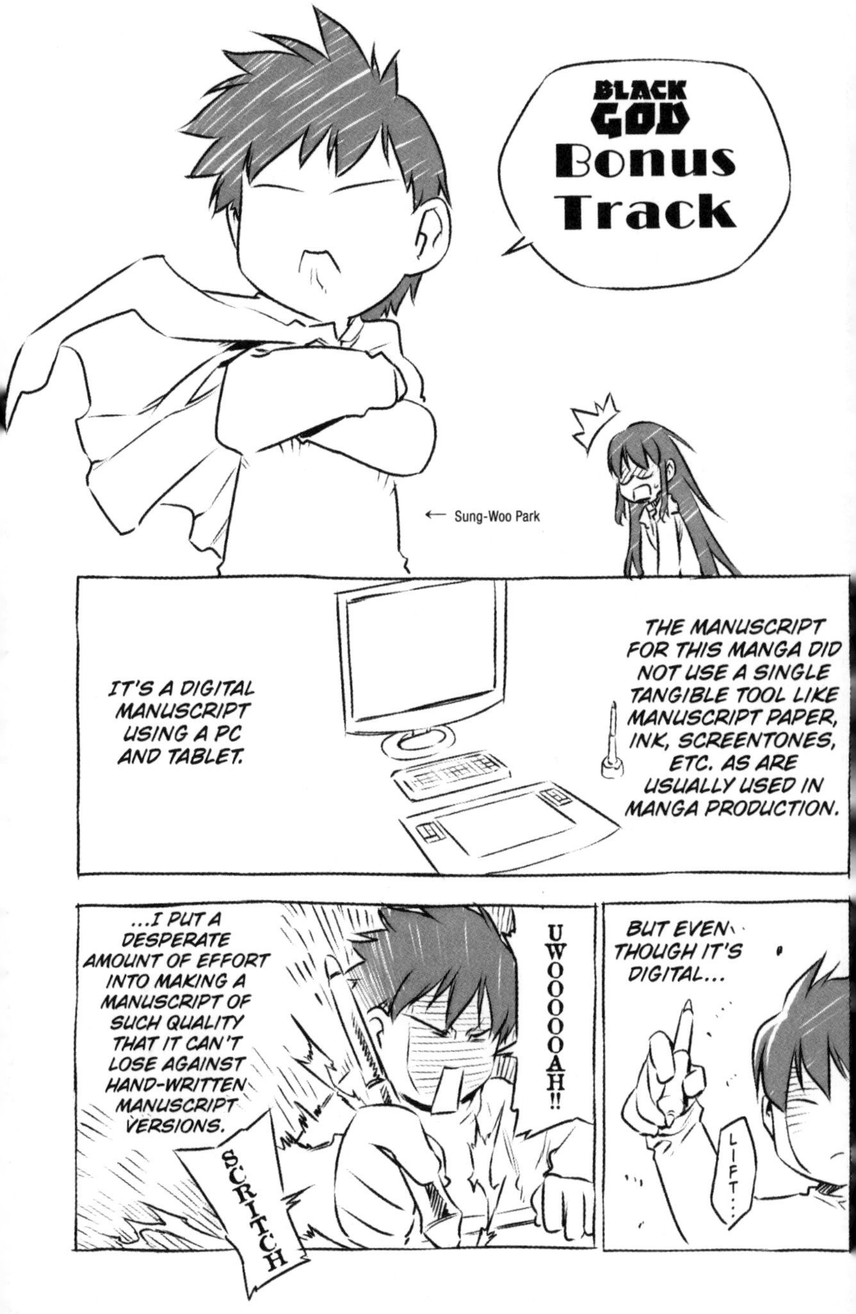

BLACK GOD Bonus Track
← Sung-Woo Park
THE MANUSCRIPT FOR THIS MANGA DID NOT USE A SINGLE TANGIBLE TOOL LIKE MANUSCRIPT PAPER, INK, SCREENTONES, ETC. AS ARE USUALLY USED IN MANGA PRODUCTION.
IT'S A DIGITAL MANUSCRIPT USING A PC AND TABLET.
BUT EVEN THOUGH IT'S DIGITAL...
LIFT...
UWOOOOOOAH!!
...I PUT A DESPERATE AMOUNT OF EFFORT INTO MAKING A MANUSCRIPT OF SUCH QUALITY THAT IT CAN'T LOSE AGAINST HAND-WRITTEN MANUSCRIPT VERSIONS.
SCRITCH

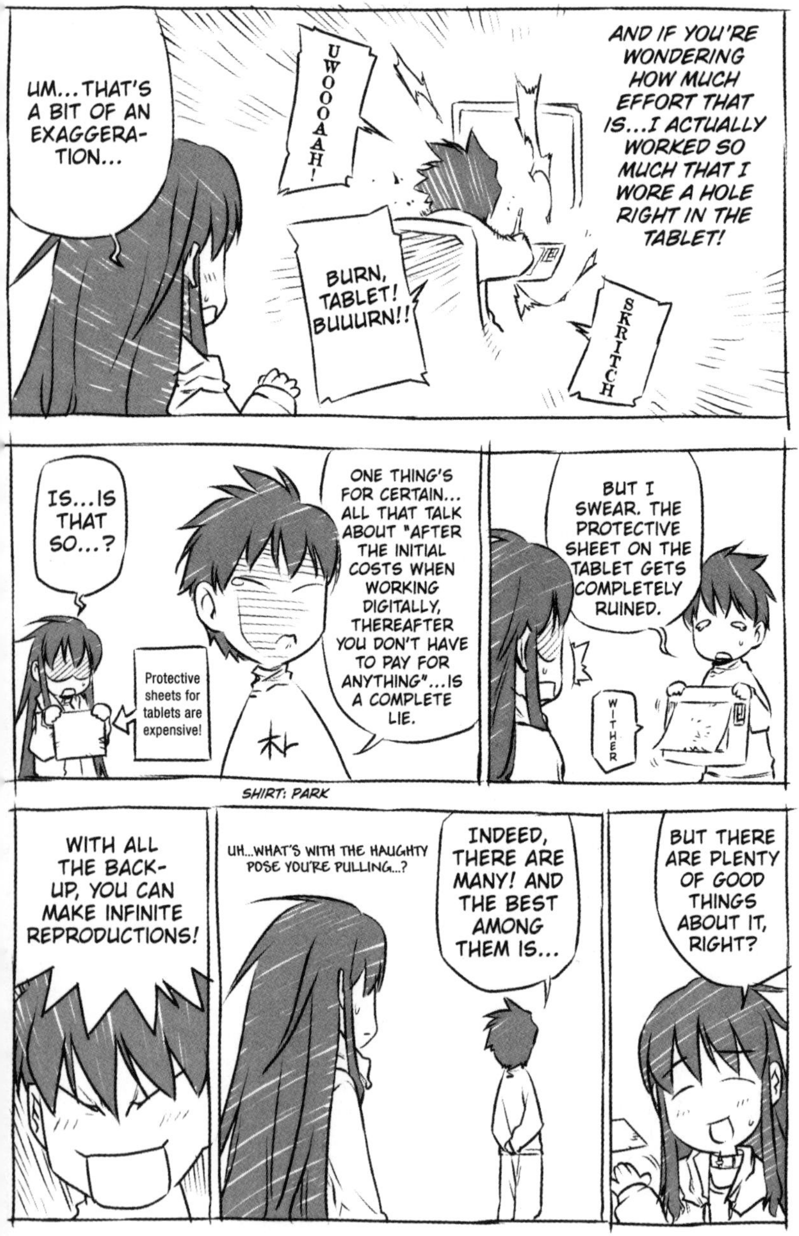
AND IF YOU'RE WONDERING HOW MUCH EFFORT THAT IS...I ACTUALLY WORKED SO MUCH THAT I WORE A HOLE RIGHT IN THE TABLET!
UWOOOOAAH!
BURN, TABLET! BUUURN!!
SKRITCH
UM...THAT'S A BIT OF AN EXAGGERA-TION...
BUT I SWEAR. THE PROTECTIVE SHEET ON THE TABLET GETS COMPLETELY RUINED.
WITHER
ONE THING'S FOR CERTAIN... ALL THAT TALK ABOUT "AFTER THE INITIAL COSTS WHEN WORKING DIGITALLY, THEREAFTER YOU DON'T HAVE TO PAY FOR ANYTHING"...IS A COMPLETE LIE.
IS...IS THAT SO...?
Protective sheets for tablets are expensive!
SHIRT: PARK
BUT THERE ARE PLENTY OF GOOD THINGS ABOUT IT, RIGHT?
INDEED, THERE ARE MANY! AND THE BEST AMONG THEM IS...
UH...WHAT'S WITH THE HAUGHTY POSE YOU'RE PULLING...?
WITH ALL THE BACK-UP, YOU CAN MAKE INFINITE REPRODUCTIONS!

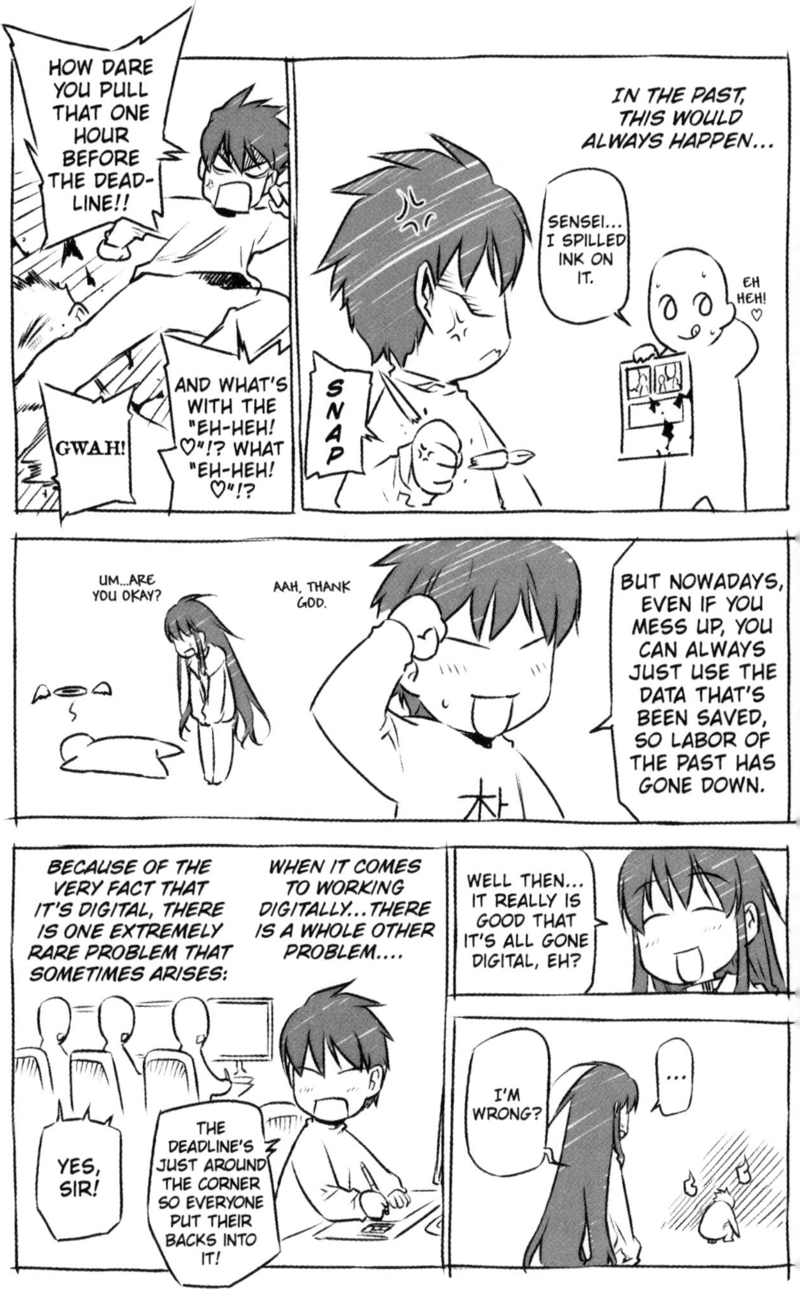
IN THE PAST, THIS WOULD ALWAYS HAPPEN…
SENSEI… I SPILLED INK ON IT.
EH HEH! ♡
SNAP
HOW DARE YOU PULL THAT ONE HOUR BEFORE THE DEAD-LINE!!
AND WHAT'S WITH THE "EH-HEH! ♡"!? WHAT "EH-HEH! ♡"!?
GWAH!
BUT NOWADAYS, EVEN IF YOU MESS UP, YOU CAN ALWAYS JUST USE THE DATA THAT'S BEEN SAVED, SO LABOR OF THE PAST HAS GONE DOWN.
AAH, THANK GOD.
UM...ARE YOU OKAY?
WELL THEN... IT REALLY IS GOOD THAT IT'S ALL GONE DIGITAL, EH?
…
I'M WRONG?
WHEN IT COMES TO WORKING DIGITALLY...THERE IS A WHOLE OTHER PROBLEM....
BECAUSE OF THE VERY FACT THAT IT'S DIGITAL, THERE IS ONE EXTREMELY RARE PROBLEM THAT SOMETIMES ARISES:
THE DEADLINE'S JUST AROUND THE CORNER SO EVERYONE PUT THEIR BACKS INTO IT!
YES, SIR!

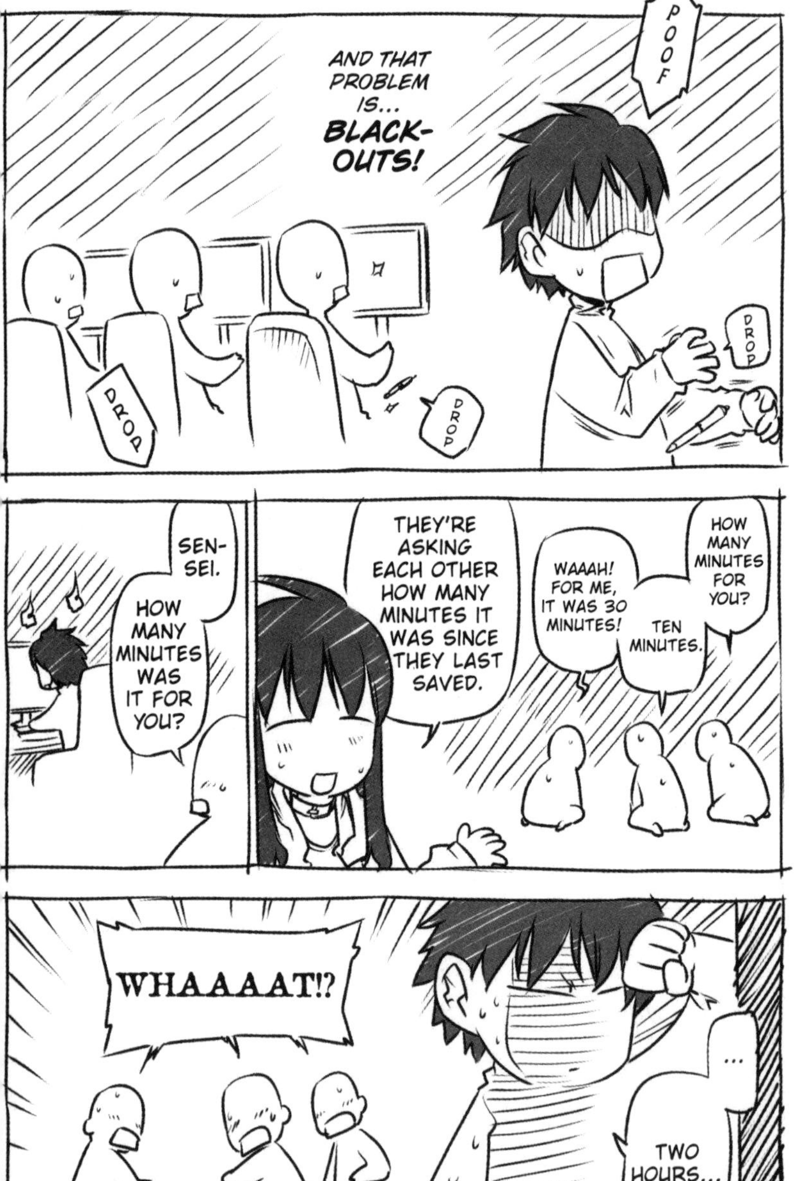

POOF
AND THAT PROBLEM IS... BLACK-OUTS!
DROP
DROP
DROP
HOW MANY MINUTES FOR YOU?
TEN MINUTES.
WAAAH! FOR ME, IT WAS 30 MINUTES!
THEY'RE ASKING EACH OTHER HOW MANY MINUTES IT WAS SINCE THEY LAST SAVED.
SEN-SEI.
HOW MANY MINUTES WAS IT FOR YOU?
...
TWO HOURS...
WHAAAAT!?

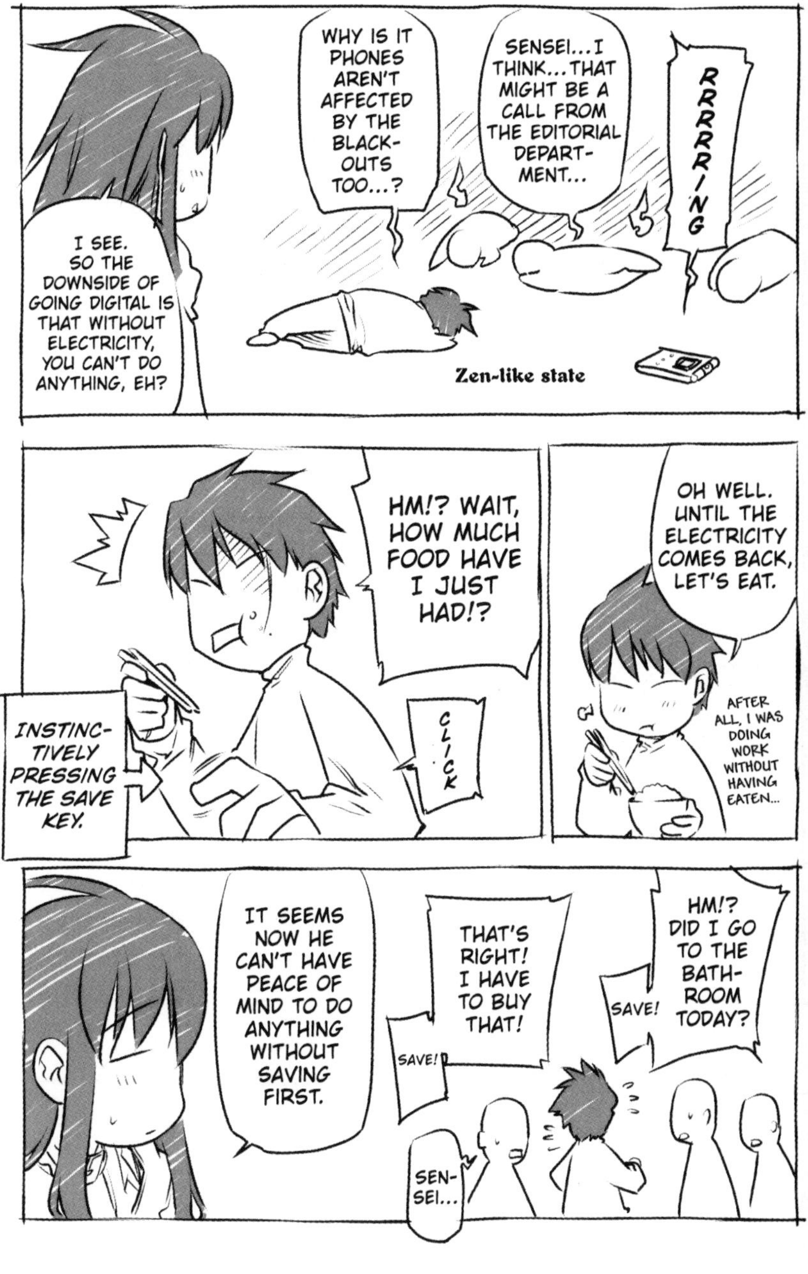
RRRRING
SENSEI...I THINK...THAT MIGHT BE A CALL FROM THE EDITORIAL DEPARTMENT...
WHY IS IT PHONES AREN'T AFFECTED BY THE BLACKOUTS TOO...?
Zen-like state
I SEE. SO THE DOWNSIDE OF GOING DIGITAL IS THAT WITHOUT ELECTRICITY, YOU CAN'T DO ANYTHING, EH?
OH WELL. UNTIL THE ELECTRICITY COMES BACK, LET'S EAT.
AFTER ALL, I WAS DOING WORK WITHOUT HAVING EATEN...
HM!? WAIT, HOW MUCH FOOD HAVE I JUST HAD!?
CLICK
INSTINCTIVELY PRESSING THE SAVE KEY.
HM!? DID I GO TO THE BATHROOM TODAY?
SAVE!
THAT'S RIGHT! I HAVE TO BUY THAT!
SAVE!
IT SEEMS NOW HE CAN'T HAVE PEACE OF MIND TO DO ANYTHING WITHOUT SAVING FIRST.
SENSEI...

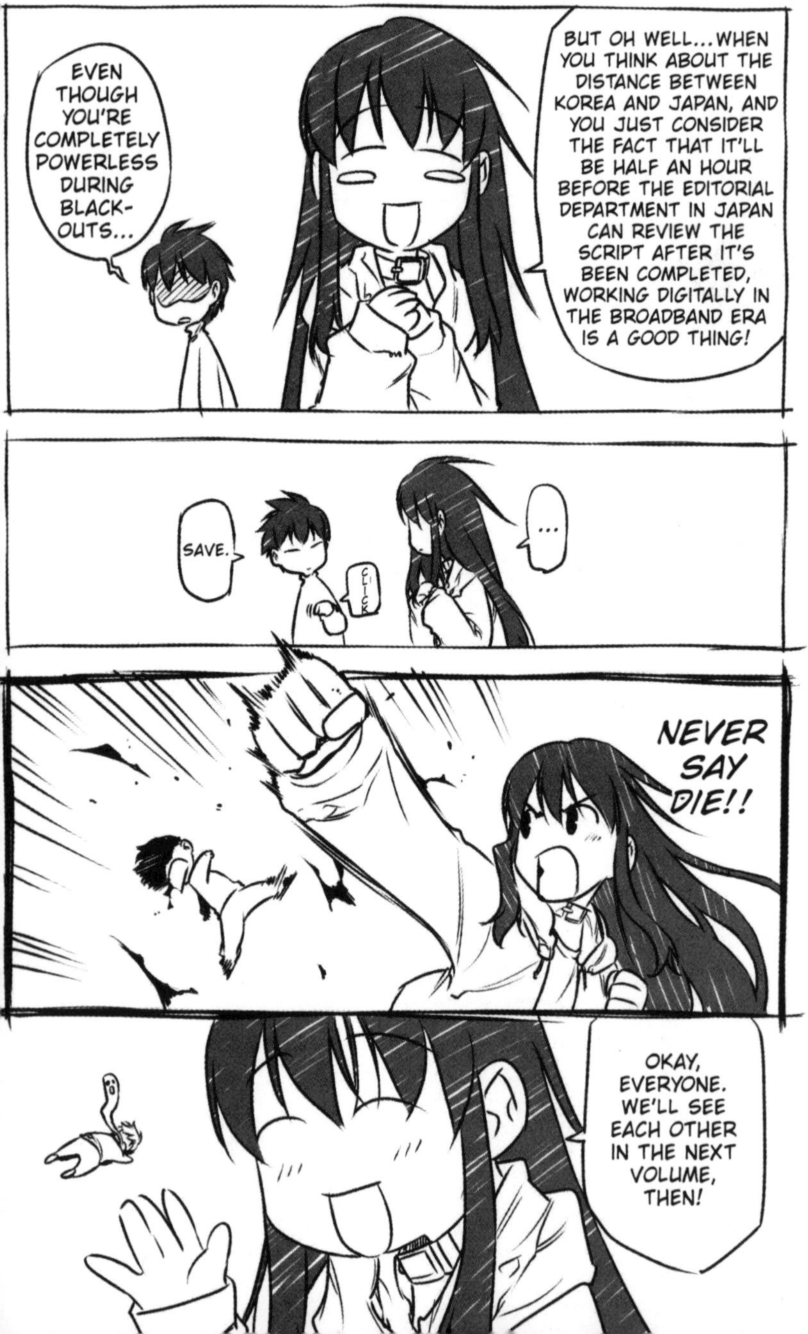
BUT OH WELL...WHEN YOU THINK ABOUT THE DISTANCE BETWEEN KOREA AND JAPAN, AND YOU JUST CONSIDER THE FACT THAT IT'LL BE HALF AN HOUR BEFORE THE EDITORIAL DEPARTMENT IN JAPAN CAN REVIEW THE SCRIPT AFTER IT'S BEEN COMPLETED, WORKING DIGITALLY IN THE BROADBAND ERA IS A GOOD THING!
EVEN THOUGH YOU'RE COMPLETELY POWERLESS DURING BLACK-OUTS...
...
SAVE.
CLICK
NEVER SAY DIE!!
OKAY, EVERYONE. WE'LL SEE EACH OTHER IN THE NEXT VOLUME, THEN!

●Drawing staff（作画スタッフ）

Yun In Suk

Do Young Shin

Shin Yun Hee

Jung Jin Ju

Kim Do Kyoung

──studio zero──

●Manager（マネージャー）

Park Jin Woo

●Project cooperator（企画協力）

Lee Hyun Seok(warmania)

●Translator（翻訳）

Jang Jong Choul（張綜哲）

● Cooperation

Miya Asakawa

Sunrise Inc.

Bandai Visual Inc.

BLACK GOD
4

by Dall-Young Lim and Sung-Woo Park

Translation: Christine Schilling
Lettering: Keiran O'Leary

Yen Press
Hachette Book Group USA
237 Park Avenue, New York, NY 10017

Visit our Web sites at www.HachetteBookGroupUSA.com and www.YenPress.com.

Yen Press is an imprint of Hachette Book Group USA, Inc. The Yen Press name and logo are trademarks of Hachette Book Group USA, Inc.

First Yen Press Edition: October 2008

ISBN-10: 0-7595-2843-8
ISBN-13: 978-0-7595-2843-7

10 9 8 7 6 5 4 3 2 1

BVG

Printed in the United States of America